The Passivhaus Designe

Passivhaus is the fastest-growing energy performance standard in the world, with almost 50,000 buildings realised to date. Applicable to both domestic and non-domestic building types, the strength of Passivhaus lies in the simplicity of the concept. As European and global energy directives move ever closer towards zero (fossil) energy standards, Passivhaus provides a robust 'fabric first' approach from which to make the next step.

The Passivhaus Designer's Manual is the most comprehensive technical guide available to those wishing to design and build Passivhaus and zero energy buildings. As a technical reference for architects, engineers and construction professionals, The Passivhaus Designer's Manual provides:

- state-of-the-art guidance for anyone designing or working on a Passivhaus project;
- in-depth information on building services, including high-performance ventilation systems and ultra-low energy heating and cooling systems;
- holistic design guidance encompassing daylight design, ecological materials, thermal comfort, indoor air quality and economics;
- practical advice on procurement methods, project management and quality assurance;
- renewable energy systems suitable for Passivhaus and zero energy buildings;
- practical case studies from the UK, USA and Germany amongst others;
- detailed worked examples to show you how it's done and what to look out for;
- expert advice from 20 world-renowned Passivhaus designers, architects, building physicists and engineers.

Lavishly illustrated with nearly 200 full colour illustrations, and presented by two highly experienced specialists, this is your one-stop shop for comprehensive practical information on Passivhaus and zero energy buildings.

Christina J. Hopfe is a Senior Lecturer (Associate Professor) in Sustainable Building Design at Loughborough University. She is a Chartered Engineer and a Member of CIBSE. She has a Dipl-Ing in Civil Engineering from TU Darmstadt, Germany and a PhD in Building Performance Simulation from TU/e, the Netherlands.

Robert S. McLeod is an Associate of the Building Research Establishment and a freelance building performance consultant. He is one of the UK's leading Passivhaus designers and experts in low carbon design. He has a PhD in Building Physics from Cardiff University and is a Chartered Engineer and a Member of IMeche.

'There's a mystique around the whole idea of Passivhaus, and there really shouldn't be. As this amazing manual so powerfully reveals, it's a simple, elegant set of design principles, in which lies the promise of a truly sustainable built environment for everyone, anywhere in the world.'

Jonathon Porritt, Founder and Director, Forum for the Future, UK

'Much more than a design guide for Passivhaus, this manual provides an excellent holistic view of good, low energy and sustainable design practice, with contributions from a range of international experts. Principles, theory, and practice are clearly explained without recourse to detailed mathematical analysis, making this guide accessible to a wide range of professionals; an impressive level of detail and scope.'

Michael Holmes, consultant to Arup and principal author of CIBSE Guide A
(Section 5 – Thermal Design), UK

The Passivhaus Designer's Manual

A technical guide to low and zero
energy buildings

Edited by Christina J. Hopfe and Robert S. McLeod

Routledge
Taylor & Francis Group

LONDON AND NEW YORK

First published 2015
by Routledge
2 Park Square, Milton Park, Abingdon, Oxon OX14 4RN

and by Routledge
711 Third Avenue, New York, NY 10017

Routledge is an imprint of the Taylor & Francis Group, an informa business

British Library Cataloguing-in-Publication Data
A catalogue record for this book is available from the British Library

Library of Congress Cataloging in Publication Data
Hopfe, Christina J.
The passivhaus designer's manual : a technical guide to low and zero energy buildings / [compiled by] Christina J. Hopfe and Robert S. McLeod.
pages cm
Includes bibliographical references and index.
1. Ecological houses. 2. Dwellings–Energy conservation. I. McLeod, Robert S. II. Title.
TH4860.H67 2015
720'.472–dc23
2014046349

ISBN: 978-0-415-52269-4 (pbk)
ISBN: 978-1-315-72643-4 (ebk)

Typeset in Univers
by Fakenham Prepress Solutions, Fakenham, Norfolk NR21 8NN
Printed and bound by CPI Group (UK) Ltd, Croydon CR0 4YY

Contents

About this book

Incremental changes to national energy efficiency standards appear to be having no effect on driving down greenhouse gas (GHG) emissions. According to the UK Government Environmental Audit Committee: 'Unless significant measures are put in place to reduce emissions from the housing sector, from their current level of around 40 MtC a year, they could constitute over 55 per cent of the UK's target for carbon emissions in 2050; nearly doubling the current 30 per cent contribution' (House of Commons, 2005).

In order to address these issues across Europe, an Energy Performance in Buildings Directive (EPBD) has been put in place by the European Commission. The EPBD requires all new buildings to be 'nearly zero energy' by the end of 2020 with public sector buildings required to meet this target by the end of 2018. Worldwide, similar developments can be observed; with Japan discussing plans to implement a zero energy building target by 2030 and some US states, such as California, requiring net-zero-energy performance in residential buildings by 2020 and in commercial buildings by 2030 (see European Commission, 2009).

The successful implementation of zero energy building on a global scale will require a radical step change in current design and construction practices. Adopting an integrated design approach based on a well-established methodology, such as the Passivhaus standard, can help to facilitate this transition. Integrated building design requires knowledge and skills drawn from many disciplines, including architecture, building services engineering, building physics, planning, economics, and project management. Such knowledge is often hard won and can involve costly design mistakes for inexperienced practitioners.

This book aims to capture the combined expertise of some of the world's leading Passivhaus and zero energy designers in order to produce an affordable 'state of the art' reference manual aimed at both practitioners and students in the fields of sustainable architecture and engineering. The book is targeted specifically at those wishing to deepen their knowledge in the field of Passivhaus (newbuild) and EnerPHit (refurbishment) as a framework for delivering robust ultra-low and zero energy buildings.

The content is based on 12 chapters, each contributed by a recognised expert (or experts) from across the globe. All of the authors have extensive first-hand experience of the underlying theory as well as the practical design challenges facing the delivery of Passivhaus and Zero Energy performance standards.

List of contributors

Florian Antretter (Dipl-Ing (FH), MEng) Florian Antretter is Group Manager of the working group Hygrothermal Building Analysis at the Fraunhofer Institute for Building Physics, Germany. His main research interest is in energetic and hygric whole performance, and he is responsible for the development of the hygrothermal building simulation software WUFI® Passive and Plus.

Myriam B. C. Aries (MSc, PhD) Myriam is an Assistant Professor in Lighting Technology at the Department of the Built Environment of Eindhoven University of Technology (TU/e), the Netherlands. Her main areas of expertise are the dynamic aspects of daylight, and her research focuses on daylight application, visual comfort, and human lighting demands.

Niall Crosson (BTech, MEngSc, MIEI, CEPHC) Niall is Senior Technical Engineer with Ecological Building Systems and a board member of the Irish Green Building Council. He has particular expertise in the area of airtightness and vapour control, building physics, energy conservation, hygrothermal analysis, and Passivhaus construction. He is an advocate of natural insulation and diffusion open, healthy building.

Marcus Fink (Dipl-Ing (FH)) Marcus Fink is researcher at the Fraunhofer Institute for Building Physics, Germany. His main research interest is user behaviour regarding energetic and hygric building performance. He assures the quality of WUFI® Passive and Plus software and provides user support.

Christina J. Hopfe (Dipl-Ing, MSc, PhD, CEng, MCIBSE, CEPHD) Christina is a Senior Lecturer (Associate Professor) in Sustainable Building Design at Loughborough University, England. In her role at Loughborough, she is also the Programme Director for Low Carbon Building Design and Modelling. She is a Chartered Engineer and a Member of CIBSE. She has a Dipl-Ing (MSc) in Civil Engineering from the Technical University in Darmstadt, Germany and a PhD in Building Performance Simulation from the Eindhoven University of Technology (TU/e) in the Netherlands.

Doreen E. Kalz (Dipl-Ing, MSc, Dr-Ing) Doreen is a Senior Researcher at the Fraunhofer Institute for Solar Energy Systems in Freiburg, Germany, where she is head of the Building Analysis and Energy Concepts group in the Division of Thermal Systems and Buildings. Her research focuses on the development and investigation of low-exergy heating and cooling concepts for non-residential buildings.

Hartwig Künzel (Dr-Ing) Hartwig Künzel heads the Department of Hygrothermics at the Fraunhofer Institute for Building Physics, Germany. He is an internationally renowned expert in hygrothermal building performance. He developed the coupled heat and moisture transfer equations which are the basis of all WUFI® products and he supervises their ongoing development.

Robert S. McLeod (MSc Arch, PhD, CEng, MIMechE, CEPHD) Rob is an Associate of the Building Research Establishment (BRE) and a freelance Building Performance consultant. He is one of the UK's leading Passivhaus designers and experts in low carbon design. His research interests include the influence of microclimates and future climatic change on the performance of ultra-low energy buildings. He has a PhD in Building Physics from Cardiff University, Wales and is a Chartered Engineer and a Member of IMechE.

Marek Miara (Dipl-Ing, MSc, PhD) Marek is a Senior Researcher at the Fraunhofer Institute for Solar Energy Systems in Freiburg, Germany, where he heads the Heat Pumps group and, in particular, leads a large-scale monitoring project on heat pump efficiency. His particular expertise, besides heat pumps, is rational energy use and buildings with low energy consumption.

John Morehead (DipArch, BArchSc, DipAPM, CEPHD) John is the Managing Director of Wain Morehead Architects Ltd. He has over 26 years' experience in a wide variety of architectural and urban design projects for both the public and private sector. He is a member of the Royal Institute of Architects of Ireland and a fully Certified Passivhaus Designer, and he has been a member of the Irish Project Management Institute since 1998. WMA achieved PH certification for their Carrigaline PH project in 2011. John has particular interest in the effects of infrared and local climate on energy and comfort control.

Nick Newman (BArch (Hons), DipArch, RIBA, CEPHD) Nick is the Head of Sustainability at ECD Architects and a Director at Studio Bark. He specialises in post-occupancy evaluation, internal training, design audits and research, alongside low energy refurbishment project work. Nick is a Certified Passivhaus Designer and was included in *Building* magazine's list of Rising Sustainability Stars, 2014.

Matthias Pazold (MEng) Matthias Pazold is researcher at the Fraunhofer Institute for Building Physics, Germany. His main research interest is building air flow modelling and hygric assessment in a whole building context. He develops and implements models for WUFI® Passive and Plus.

Andrew Peel (MSc, Passivhaus Certifier) Andrew is a Director of Peel Passive House Consulting, Beyond Energy Code Consulting, and the Canadian Passive House Institute. He provides low energy building and product consultancy, training, and certification internationally to public and private sector clients.

Ludwig Rongen (Professor Dipl-Ing, Architect and Urban Planner BDA, CEPHD, Passivhaus Certifier) Ludwig Rongen is the head of RoA Rongen Architekten GmbH, Germany. He has completed numerous Passivhaus pilot projects worldwide, including: the first almshouse, the first modular Passive House, the first Passivhaus retrofit with curtain wall, the first EnerPHit-certified non-residential building with internal insulation, and the smallest detached Passivhaus. He has two visiting professorships in China. Ludwig has been involved in various research projects (e.g. Passivhaus for Different Climates: Dubai, Las Vegas, Shanghai, Tokyo, Yekaterinburg), and he has authored specialist books and numerous other publications. He lectures throughout the world about Passivhaus.

Michael Swainson (PhD) Michael is Principal Engineer at the Building Research Establishment (BRE). His work includes research and development, laboratory testing, and on-site investigation of ventilation, heating, and cooling systems used in low energy buildings. He is also known for his extensive research on overheating.

Richard Whidborne (BSc, MRICS) Richard is a Director of e-Griffin Consulting, Chartered Quantity Surveyors, and a member of the Passivhaus Trust. He has been involved in providing cost advice and quantity surveying services for Passivhaus and EnerPHit projects both in the private and public sectors since 2008.

Jan Wienold (Dipl-Ing, Dr-Ing) Jan is a senior scientist at the Interdisciplinary Laboratory of Performance-Integrated Design (LIPID) at EPFL (École Polytechnique Fédérale de Lausanne) in Switzerland. In his research, he focuses on daylight, development of daylight metrics, and visual comfort.

Louise Finnerup Wille (BSc Arch-Eng, MSc Eng, MCIBSE, CEPHD) Louise is a Senior Sustainability Consultant at Hoare Lea where she advises on sustainability and energy strategies for projects on a range of scales, including assessments for heritage buildings and master plan projects. Louise also has experience in dynamic modelling used (among other things) to predict future energy use and potential overheating in buildings.

Darren Woolf (MEng, PhD, CEng, MCIBSE, MAPM) Darren is the Building Physics Principal in Hoare Lea, where he supports, develops, and promotes building physics best practices, R&D, and skills and services across the firm. He also currently holds the position of the Royal Academy of Engineering and is the Chartered Institute of Building Services Engineering Visiting Professor of Building Engineering Physics at Loughborough University, England.

Foreword

In 1982–4, collaborating with architect Steve Conger and energy modeler John Ehlers, I led the conceptual and energy design for my 372 m² passive house, indoor farm, and office, 2,200 m up in the Rocky Mountains near Aspen, Colorado. Temperatures there could then dip as low as –44°C, with up to 39 days of continuous midwinter cloud. With the help of some professionals and a big volunteer crew of amateur builders, we then built it. Not knowing this was impossible made it possible.

Three decades later, the building's 85 m² central jungle has produced 55 passive-solar banana crops, some weighing nearly 40 kg; they harvest themselves by pulling down the tree. But even in 1984, the building saved roughly 99 percent of its space- and water-heating energy, half its water, and about 90 percent of its household electricity, all with a ten-month payback. The superwindows (with center-of-glass insulating value originally k-1.05, now k-0.42 with some as good as k-0.28), superinsulation (k-0.14 walls, k-0.05 roof), and ventilation heat recovery that together eliminated the heating system cost about $1,100 less to build than the heating equipment would have cost to build—not counting the energy savings.

An early visitor was Dr-Ing Wolfgang Feist, who it helped inspire to build the German Passivhaus movement and beyond. Many of our visitors (totaling over 100,000 so far) now come from China. We explain that our building fuses 3,000-year-old North Chinese passive-solar architecture with modern superwindows.

By 2007, the building was turning into a museum of 1983 state of the art, not a living laboratory testing the latest technologies, so we launched a major five-year renovation. It had no business case because so little energy was left to save (the pre-solar household electricity bill was around $5 a month), but we wondered how much better the newer technologies were. So far, the monitoring equipment measuring this by tracking several hundred data streams seems to use more electricity than the lights and appliances we're measuring.

I wish in 1982 we'd had even a tiny fraction of the experience encapsulated in this book. We'd have learned, for example, how to ensure airtightness over decades, avoiding a roughly 14-fold gradual increase in air leakage from original tightness that would have met today's Passivhaus standard if it had existed. (A seven-stage blower-door remediative process did, however, recover about sevenfold, leaving the building only twice as leaky as that standard.) We'd have known whether to superinsulate our masonry building under the slab, not just in a perimeter skirt (at the time, the best experts couldn't agree, so we chose the latter—perhaps wrongly). Our air-to-air heat exchangers would have been much better.

On the other hand, we might still not have anticipated that controlling those heat exchangers with CO_2 (as well as humidity and dew point)—the house wraps around an 85 m² interior jungle with over 100 plant species—made the fans run all night, losing heat and wasting electricity, only to exhaust the CO_2 from plant respiration before the plants could photosynthesize it in the early morning. And we certainly wouldn't have realized that our CO_2 sensors were actually automotive, so sensitive to volatile organics that they'd overrun the main heat exchanger whenever they detected toner volatiles from our xerographic printer/copier. And we might not have anticipated the way the volunteer snakes that controlled the mice (before we discovered ultrasonic mouse-repellants) would live in the photocopier, basking in the warmth of the fuser's standby heater—until we got a cold-fuser copier. Life in a passive house is a lifelong continuing education.

Passive buildings are not all about technology. Their greatest benefits are not in avoided costs and emissions but in quality of life. Why did people meeting around our dining room table stay alert and cheerful all day, then in an ordinary office, become sleepy and irritable in half an hour? Maybe because of the curves, or the natural light, or the clean air, or the healthy thermal design (low air temperature, high radiant temperature, medium humidity), or the alpha-tuned sound of the waterfall, or the lack of noise from the mechanicals we designed out, or the lack of electromagnetic fields, or the sight, smell, oxygen, ions, and (optionally) taste of the plants. But that initial list continues because our house was also an early example of biophilic design, well before the biophilia hypothesis existed. Our colleague Bill Browning, in *The Economics of Biophilia*, lists 14 attributes that our ancestors on the savannah liked to see in the landscape: a vantage point, a biome boundary, water, a place of refuge, etc. By luck and intuition, we checked over half those boxes too. Thus we got a building that creates delight when entered, serenity and health when occupied, and regret when departed.

The state of the art keeps moving; low-hanging fruit grows back faster than you can harvest it. Rocky Mountain Institute is about to break ground for a nearby 1,450 m² office and convening center in Basalt, Colorado that's expected to use just 40 kWh/m²-y for everything—half the site energy intensity of the most efficient US new office building of just four years earlier.

The deep and diverse experience in this book will help you create magical buildings wherever you are. But the deepest lesson I hope you will take away is not the virtue of simplicity, the value of eliminating mechanicals, and the importance of meticulous attention to detail. Rather, it's the secret of integrative design—optimizing the whole building for multiple benefits, not isolated components for single benefits. That's how the arch that holds up the middle of my house has 12 functions but only one cost. It's why the walls have an undulating *re-entrant* shape: ability to admit and control heat and light from each direction, greater torsional strength with less material, ability to slipform the whole building with a single uniform-radius set of movable forms, greater "visual solidity" when you look out the window and see the inside and outside of the 40 cm wall simultaneously, better esthetics, better acoustics, smooth exterior aerodynamics to reduce heat-robbing turbulence and wind noise … eight reasons already! When everything in your building has at least three functions and many have a half-dozen, you're well on the road to integrative design, making very large energy savings cheaper to establish than small ones while making the building ever more pleasant, healthful, beautiful, and economical.

That must be the next book. Meanwhile, use what you learn from this one, share your experience, advance the state of the art, and astonish all those who haven't yet discovered the self-evident way buildings always should have been built!

Amory B. Lovins, Cofounder and Chief Scientist, Rocky Mountain Institute (www.rmi.org), Old Snowmass, Colorado, 16 September 2014

Preface

As the age of abundant cheap energy draws to an end, the consequences of accelerating climatic change and diminishing fossil fuel reserves have prompted a radical rethink about the need for energy efficiency in the built environment. In Europe, emissions from buildings make up a staggering 40 per cent of the total greenhouse gas (GHG) inventory; whilst in the United States, the pattern is similar with the building sector accounting for approximately 48 per cent of GHG emissions, with 36 per cent of this total coming directly from operational energy and an additional 12 per cent of emissions related to the production of construction materials. In almost every economy worldwide, the built environment is an area where massive efficiency gains need to be made.

More than three decades ago, building physicists from Sweden and Germany began to consider this problem, and after substantial research and development, the Passivhaus concept originated in the early 1990s. Over the past decade, interest in the Passivhaus standard has grown steadily across Europe, North America, and further afield. Today, largely through voluntary uptake, it has become the most widely adopted low energy building performance standard in the world. Over 50,000 Passivhaus buildings have been constructed to date, in almost every climatic zone. Documented scientific evidence from dozens of studies has shown that deep savings in energy consumption coupled with high levels of thermal comfort have been achieved by the vast majority of these projects. Such results have prompted a growing number of European cities and regions to mandate the standard as a minimum level of energy performance for all new buildings.

Whilst buildings need to become more resource efficient, there is a concomitant requirement for them to become more resilient. Climatic change implies not simply progressive global warming, but also the increased frequency and severity of extreme weather events, which are already impacting on the way buildings perform and the protection and comfort they provide. As a result, there is an imperative to design buildings that will perform well across their anticipated lifespan under a potentially wide range of climatic conditions and varying usage patterns, without excessive reliance on energy-intensive heating, cooling, and dehumidification systems. It is sobering to note that energy supply and distribution infrastructure is most vulnerable during climatic extremes; in North America, some of the biggest power outages have occurred in the midst of heat wave periods thus rendering grid-connected air conditioning units inoperable.

These compounding challenges pose real questions for the skills, knowledge, and design methodologies of all those working in the built environment today. As design standards and new technologies continually evolve, yesterday's norms and methods need to be constantly revisited and updated.

This book brings together the combined input of over 20 of the world's leading Passivhaus and zero energy designers, architects, engineers, and building physicists. It is intended to provide a technical reference on important topics that often require more detailed explanations than can be found in most introductory handbooks. It is assumed that those reading the book will already be familiar with the fundamental principles of low energy design.

The book begins with an introduction to climate change and the built environment, together with an overview of the Passivhaus standard and its emerging role in the delivery of zero energy buildings. This is followed by an introduction to the Passivhaus concept and the Passive House Planning Package (PHPP) software.

Thermal comfort is one of the most decisive criteria for occupant well-being and can have a major impact on the design of effective building envelopes and systems used to control the indoor environment. Energy use to achieve performance targets is therefore heavily influenced by the choice and application of thermal comfort criteria, and this is addressed in Chapter 2.

The fundamental role of the building envelope including the interrelated roles of insulation, thermal mass, and high-performance windows in Passivhaus design is discussed in Chapter 3.

Daylight is associated with multiple health and well-being benefits. Chapter 4 elaborates on methods for the optimal usage of natural daylight in order to improve well-being whilst minimising artificial lighting, heating, and cooling demand.

The importance of condensation risk analysis and transient heat and moisture assessment is a critical issue in both newbuild and retrofit low energy buildings. Methods for state-of-the-art dynamic energy simulation and transient hygrothermal simulation using the WUFI Passive software are explained in Chapter 5, along with a case study of a building located near to Chicago, USA.

Chapter 6 discusses the importance of reducing hot water distribution losses and the incorporation of solar hot water systems in Passivhaus design, with emphasis on domestic buildings. Heating and cooling of non-residential Passivhaus buildings using passive and low energy environmental energy strategies is addressed in Chapter 7.

In Chapter 8, the process of designing optimal heat recovery ventilation and natural ventilation systems in Passivhaus design is explained. The challenges of avoiding summer overheating and acoustic and hygiene problems are looked into alongside the design, installation, and commissioning of effective MVHR systems.

Chapter 9 explores suitable renewable energy technologies that can be incorporated into the design of Passivhaus buildings in order to facilitate the transition to zero energy domestic and non-domestic buildings. An overview of the most relevant building-level power-generating technologies and their principle characteristics is presented.

Project management and quality assurance are essential aspects in ensuring that good design work is properly implemented in the built form. Chapter 10 describes critical roles in delivering Passivhaus and EnerPHit standards on site, including airtightness and pressure testing in practice, project management, contracts, and site supervision.

How to make informed procurement decisions and why whole life economics is more relevant than capital cost analysis for low energy buildings is elaborated on in Chapter 11.

The book concludes with some 'real world' case studies in Chapter 12, where the different standards for Passivhaus newbuild and refurbishment are discussed. Two case studies highlighting Passivhaus and EnerPHit projects are presented.

This book is the outcome of the collaboration and commitment of many dedicated people (see pp. ix–x). The initial idea came about in 2010 and, although it took longer than anticipated to deliver, we believe it was worth the effort.

We would like to take this opportunity to thank all of the authors for their outstanding contributions, Amory Lovins for his thought-provoking foreword, and the publishers for their faith in the concept. We would also like to thank our families and friends for their patience and support during the time in which this book was written and edited.

Christina J. Hopfe and Robert McLeod, July 2015

Unit conversions – metric/US

Abbreviations

Btu	British thermal unit	Btu at 59°F (US usage)
CFM	cubic foot per minute	
ft	foot	International foot
gallon	US liquid gallon	US gallon, differs from UK gallon
in	inch	
lb	pound	
ton	US ton	
J	Joule	
kWh	kilowatt-hour	
K	Kelvin	
l	litre or liter (US)	
m	metre or meter (US)	

Rules of thumb[1]

					(Tolerance)
1	kWs	≈	1	Btu	5.5%
1	m²	≈	10	ft²	7.1%
1	cm of insulation[2]	≈	R1.5	h.ft².F/Btu	
1	m³	≈	35	ft³	0.9%
10	W/m²	≈	3	Btu/h.ft²	5.4%
15	kWh/m².a	≈	5,000	Btu/ft².a	5.2%

Exact conversion factors

1	in	=	0.0254	m
1	Btu	=	1,054.804	J
1	therm	=	29.3001111	kWh
1	gallon	=	3.785411784	l
Δ1	°F[3]	=	Δ1.8	°C

Definitions

1	ft	=	12	in
1	ton	=	12,000	Btu/h
1	therm	=	100,000	Btu

Derived conversion factors

1	ft	=	0.3048	m
1	Btu	=	0.000293001	kWh
1	CFM	=	1.6990108	m³/h

Notes

1   Adapted from Feist, W., Pfluger, R., Schnieders, J., Kah, O., Kaufmann, B., Krick, B., Bastian, Z. and Ebel, W. 2013. *Passive House Planning Package, version 8 (July 2013): Energy balance and Passive House design tool*. Darmstadt: Passivhaus Institute.

2 To convert an American R-value (h.ft².F/Btu) into a European U-value (W/m².K), take the reciprocal of the R-value, then multiply the result by 5.682. To convert a European U-value to an American R-value, multiply by 0.176, and then form the reciprocal.

3 To convert from °C to °F multiply by 1.8 and then add 32°F. To convert from °F to °C subtract 32°F and then divide by 1.8.

1

Introduction
Climate change and the built environment

ROBERT S. MCLEOD AND CHRISTINA J. HOPFE

1.1 Background – drivers for change

It can have scarcely gone unnoticed that for several decades, eminent scientists have warned that we are polluting the planet at a pace beyond which its natural systems can process. At the same time non-renewable resources are being consumed at a faster rate than at any previous point in history (Kendall, 1992). Fossil fuel emissions and deforestation have been cited as the principal factors which have caused the destabilisation of the earth's carbon cycle resulting in serious and progressive climatic changes. These climatic changes are in turn contributing to the destruction and collapse of a host of natural ecosystems upon which life on earth depends (Stern, 2006; IPCC, 2014).

Despite widespread awareness of these impending issues, global energy demand has continued a steep upwards trend, with consumption nearly doubling in the past three decades (IEA, 2015). Between 1990 and 2008 global energy use rose by 10 per cent per person on average whilst, in the same time period, the world population increased by 27 per cent (IEA, 2015). Although renewable energy capacity has continued to grow, this has had little visible impact on fossil fuel consumption. In October 2012 the International Energy Agency (IEA) noted that the demand for coal accounted for half the increased energy use during the previous decade, with fossil fuel consumption growing faster than all renewable energy sources combined (IEA, 2012).

Increasing demand for energy and diminishing fossil-fuel reserves have led to rising prices. According to the IEA, energy prices are predicted to continue their generally upward spiral in the years ahead (Worldwatch Institute, 2014). In its 2008 Annual Report, the IEA significantly revised its projections of future oil costs due to the changing outlook for demand and increasing production costs. As a result the IEA predicts that crude oil will average $100 (USD) per barrel over the next two decades, rising to more than $200 (USD) per barrel in 2030, in nominal terms. According to Nobuo Tanaka, the IEA's Executive Director, one thing is certain: 'the era of cheap oil is over' (IEA, 2008: 3).

Although the impacts of climate change, resource depletion and biodiversity losses affect the entire planet, the greatest impacts are often felt by the world's poorest inhabitants. In purely economic terms, Stern (2006) calculated that a 2°C rise in global temperature would cost the global economy about 1 per cent of world GDP. More recently the World Bank (2010), in its *World Development Report*, stated that the cost to Africa will be more like 4 per cent of GDP and to India, 5 per cent. Even if environmental costs were distributed equally, developing countries would still bear 80 per cent of the burden, simply because they account for 80 per cent of world population. Due to the localised repercussions of climate change, it appears that these developing nations will have to bear a disproportionately greater share, even though their citizens' carbon footprints are much smaller (Figure 1.1).

Since the time of the first Intergovernmental Panel on Climate Change (IPCC) report in 1990, an enormous body of evidence has been advanced by the international scientific community suggesting that the impacts of climate change are beginning to have catastrophic consequences for the planet. The IPCC 5th Report (2013: 4) confirms that: 'Warming of the climate system is *unequivocal*, as is now evident from observations of increases in global average air and ocean temperatures, widespread melting of snow and ice, and rising global average sea level.'

A 2°C rise in mean surface temperature above pre-industrial levels is widely associated with an unstable tipping point at which positive feedback loops weaken the ability of natural carbon sinks to further absorb CO_2 from the atmosphere and an irreversible 'runaway' process begins (Tirpak *et al.*, 2005; Da Costa, 2007). Evidence suggests that avoiding a 2°C mean surface temperature rise by the end of this century is now highly unlikely. Irrespective of future emissions scenarios, historic emissions of GHGs have already committed the planet to a further average surface temperature increase of at least 0.6°C over the course of this century (IPCC, 2014: 9) in addition to the current 0.7°C degree increase above pre-industrial levels.

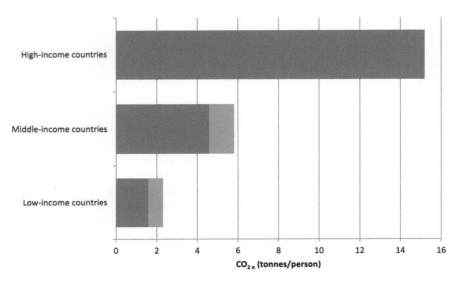

1.1
Average carbon footprint in relation to a country's global income group (2005 data)
Sources: WRI (2008) with land use change emissions from Houghton (2009)

■ Total GHG emissions
■ Emissions from land use change

According to recent reports (IPCC, 2013), the increase in global mean surface temperatures for 2081–2100 relative to 1986–2005 will depend largely upon the level of additional radiative forcing occurring this century. Four distinct Representative Concentration Pathway (RCP) scenarios are considered plausible, depending on the time period at which global emissions peak. RCP predictions are derived from the GHG concentration-driven CMIP5 model and range from 0.3°C to 1.7°C (RCP2.6) up to 2.6°C to 4.8°C (RCP8.5) (see Figure 1.2). Thus a Business As Usual (BAU) trajectory without any additional mitigation (RCP8.5) could see mean global surface temperatures ranging from 3.2°C to 5.4°C above pre-industrial levels by the end of this century (IPCC, 2013).

Faced with the devastating consequences of climate change, high-income countries can no longer justify the continued use of an inequitable share of the atmospheric commons (Meyer, 2000; World Bank, 2010). Many developing countries, whose average per capita emissions are currently less than a third of those of high-income countries, still require massive expansions in energy, transport, urban infrastructure and agricultural production. However, if economic growth is pursued using conventional technologies and carbon intensities, the expansions of developing countries will rapidly accelerate climate change. According to the World Bank (2010: 1), 'the question is not how to make development more resilient to climate change; but rather how to pursue growth and prosperity without causing "dangerous" climate change'.

If clean growth and equitable sharing of the global commons are requisites for a new sustainable global society, then the world's largest, cheapest and cleanest energy resource cannot remain largely untapped. The 'negawatt' is the term Amory Lovins (2011) neologised to describe the unit of energy that is saved via energy efficiency and never enters our national energy inventories. Faced with rising energy prices, increased resource competition and a moral imperative to create a sustainable built environment, energy conservation coupled with the use of freely abundant solar energy should be the first recourse of energy-literate designers.

1.2
Multi-model global average
surface warming
Source: IPCC (2013)
Note: grey band surrounding
black line = multi-model range

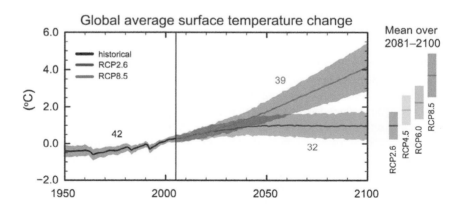

1.2 Climate change and the built environment

Buildings play a substantial role in global energy consumption and greenhouse gas (GHG) emissions (Winter, 2011). In the UK, commercial, residential and industrial buildings use nearly 40 per cent of the energy and produce almost half of the CO_2 emissions at a national scale (CCC, 2010). This situation is reflected across Europe, where according to the Energy Performance in Buildings Directive (EPBD), 'buildings account for 40 per cent of total energy consumption in the Union' (European Commission, 2009). In the US, the situation is largely similar with estimates suggesting that the built environment is responsible for approximately 43 per cent (Brown *et al.*, 2005) of all GHG emissions.

Most concerning, however, is that overall emissions from the built environment are increasing. Between 1971 and 2004, CO_2 emissions, including those arising from electricity consumption in buildings, are estimated to have grown at the rate of 2.5 per cent per year for commercial buildings and at 1.7 per cent per year for residential buildings (Levine *et al.*, 2007).

In the UK, nearly 60 per cent of the energy consumed in the built environment is used for heating and cooling of premises; the rest is consumed by electrical appliances, lighting and other uses (DTI, 2001; Winter, 2011). Consequently many Annex I[1] governments have decided to significantly increase the thermal performance of their building stock as a means of reducing national carbon emissions (WAG, 2004). Despite a continued fall in the proportion of energy used for hot water generation and cooking in UK dwellings since the 1970s, there has been a pronounced rise in the proportion used for lighting and appliances (DECC, 2012a); when coupled with an expanding housing stock (DCLG, 2007), this means that the overall emission situation is worsening. According to the UK Government Environmental Audit Committee:

> Unless significant measures are put in place to reduce emissions from the housing sector, from their current level of around 40 MtC a year, they could constitute over 55% of the UK's target for carbon emissions in 2050; nearly doubling the current 30% contribution.
> (House of Commons Environmental Audit Committee, 2005: 48, item 125)

In order to address these issues across Europe, an Energy Performance in Buildings directive (EPBD) has been put in place by the European Commission. The EPBD requires all new buildings to be 'nearly zero energy' by the end of 2020, with public sector buildings required to meet this target by the end of 2018. The precise definition of a 'nearly zero energy building' has been left open to interpretation in accordance with the national calculation methodologies (NCMs) of individual member states. EPBD policy wording states that, 'the nearly zero or very low amount of energy required should be covered to a very significant extent by energy from renewable sources, including energy from renewable sources produced on-site or nearby' (The European Parliament and the Council of the European Union, 2010: 18).

A number of EU Member States have already put in place strategies and targets for achieving Nearly Zero Energy Buildings (NZEBs). In the Netherlands, for example, there is a voluntary agreement with industry to reduce energy consumption compared to the present building codes by 25 per cent in 2011 and 50 per cent in 2015 (close to Passivhaus standard) and to have energy neutral buildings in 2020. In the UK, the government's stated ambition is to achieve 'zero carbon' homes by 2016 (see Section 1.3.2). In France, all new buildings should be energy positive (i.e. produce energy) by 2020.

Beyond Europe, similar developments can be observed with, for example, Japan currently discussing plans to adopt a zero energy building target by 2030 and some US states such as California requiring net-zero-energy performance in residential buildings by 2020 and in commercial buildings by 2030 (EC, 2009; CEC, 2007). The Chinese government has also decided to set domestic emission reduction goals in the 12th Five Year Plan (2011–15). This is in accord with an ambitious target to reduce the national carbon intensity per unit of GDP (Gross Domestic Product) by 40–45 per cent in 2020 against the intensity of 2005 levels (Leimer, 2014).

In order to be sustainable in the broadest sense, the transition towards zero energy and plus energy buildings must be robust. The Passivhaus standard offers a well-established template for ultra-low energy building that is both economical and resource-efficient, whilst at the same time providing high levels of occupant comfort and resilience to future climatic changes. Whilst some parties have suggested that the Passivhaus standard is a step too far (ZCH, 2009), others are questioning whether in its classic form it goes far enough towards addressing equitable carbon emissions (Vallentin, 2009; McLeod *et al.*, 2012a).

1.3 Passivhaus standard

The Passivhaus concept has evolved from many influences including: pioneering North American passive solar architecture and the superinsulated housing formats developed in Sweden in the 1970s. With the tripling of oil prices and threats of supply insecurity arising during the 1973–4 oil embargo, Sweden revised its SBN1975 Building Code. The newly created Supplement 1 Energihushållning (Energy Conservation) of the Swedish Code sparked a national interest in reducing space heating demand, whilst the tougher fabric and glazing U-values, mandated by the new code, resulted in the commercial development of triple glazing (Adamson, 2011). Around 1977 the physicist William Shurcliff completed the Saskatchewan Conservation House to a standard equivalent to the present day Passivhaus standard.

As far back as 1962, Bo Adamson (at the time, working as an energy consultant) had begun to investigate the economic trade-offs occurring when a better standard of insulation was used to displace the need for a conventional oil-fired central heating system in Swedish housing. Adamson's early work characterises the thought experiments which would later come to be associated with the economic and physical rationale underpinning the Passivhaus standard.

Credit is given to a number of other pioneering contributors including Swiss building researcher Conrad Brunner who began research into low energy buildings in the early 1970s, under the direction of the Swiss architect Peter Steiger. By the mid 1980s, Brunner had developed the concept of using seasonal energy balances as an approach to reducing the heating demand in low energy houses (Feist *et al.*, 2007).

An historic conversation in May 1988 between Bo Adamson, then of Lund University, Sweden, and Wolfgang Feist of the Institut Wohnen und Umwelt (Institute for Housing and Environment), Germany, is reported to have sparked the idea for the subsequent research projects that resulted in the formalisation of the Passivhaus standard.

From the late 1980s until the mid 1990s German researchers Wolfgang Feist, Witta Ebel and Tobias Loga further developed this concept whilst working at the Institut Wohnen und Umwelt. During the design of the first Passivhaus at Kranichstein in 1991 (Figure 1.3), the concept evolved into that of a superinsulated building which could effectively dispense with a conventional heating system (Feist *et al.*, 2013).

1.3
First Passivhaus in Kranichstein close to Darmstadt, Germany

1.3.1 Passivhaus definition

The Passivhaus standard is generally considered to be an ultra-low energy building performance standard, characterised by the following fundamental concepts:

1   superinsulation (Chapter 3);
2   thermal bridge-free construction (Chapter 3);
3   compact form (Chapter 3);
4   airtight building envelope (Chapter 3);
5   optimal use of passive solar gains; e.g. orientation, glazing ratios, daylighting (Chapter 4);
6   mechanical ventilation with heat recovery (MVHR) (Chapter 8).

In addition to optimising the energy efficiency of the building's fabric and services, achieving clearly defined thermal comfort criteria is considered central to the concept (see Chapter 2). The functional definition of a Passivhaus building states that: 'A Passive House is a building in which thermal comfort can be guaranteed solely by heating or cooling of the supply air which is required for sufficient indoor air quality – without using additional recirculated air' (Feist, 2007: 675).

   This functional definition implies that the heat losses from a Passivhaus must be sufficiently low that only a very small amount of supplementary heating or cooling (added to the mechanical ventilation supply air) would suffice to cover the entire peak heating or cooling load.

1.3.2 Passivhaus criteria

Strict design criteria must be met in order to comply with the Passivhaus standard. These criteria are listed in detail in the current version of the Passive House Planning Package (PHPP) (Feist *et al.*, 2013), the technical manual which accompanies the PHPP software. The Passivhaus Institut (PHI) is the German organisation responsible for overseeing the development and certification of this concept worldwide. In most countries, national Passivhaus certification bodies now exist. In some cases these organisations, such as the Passivhaus Institute US (PHIUS), have devolved their own certification criteria that differ from those used elsewhere. In recent years, the classification of Passivhaus buildings has expanded with the advent of the EnerPHit standard for refurbishment projects (see Chapter 12; Figure 1.4) as well as new standards for near zero energy (Passivhaus Plus) and plus energy (Passivhaus Premium) projects. Nonetheless, the principles underpinning the original Passivhaus (Classic) standard (as developed for Central European climates) form the central basis of these new standards.

   Possibly the most important of these requirements states that the maximum specific[2] supply-air heating load should not exceed 10W/m² (in a Central European climate) in order that a comfortable indoor climate can be maintained without recourse to a conventional heating system (Schnieders and Hermelink,

1.4
Mayville community centre
Islington, London – EnerPHit
refurbishment project with
90 per cent energy savings,
completed in 2011

2006). Accordingly, the absolute peak heating load (P_H) of a Passivhaus must be less than or equal to the maximum supply-air heating load ($P_{supply,max}$) in order for the building to be capable of being heated solely by the supply air. In practice, $P_{supply,max}$ is limited by the maximum amount of heat that can be supplied to the incoming fresh air arriving from the heat exchanger without overheating the air or increasing the ventilation flow rate beyond that which is required for good air quality by the occupants. The constraints defining $P_{supply,max}$ are described in equation 1.

$$P_{supply,max} = C_p\,\rho \cdot \dot{\nu}_{system} \cdot (T_{supply,max} - T_{supply,min}) \qquad [1]$$

where:

$P_{supply,max}$ is the maximum supply-air heating load (W),
$C_p\,\rho$ is the volumetric specific heat capacity of air (0.33 Wh/m³.K) at 20°C and atm[3],
$\dot{\nu}_{system}$ is the mean supply-air flow rate through the ventilation system (m³/h),
$T_{supply,max}$ is the maximum off-coil temperature of the air leaving the post-heater (52°C), and
$T_{supply,min}$ is the minimum supply-air temperature in winter, after the MVHR unit (16.5°C).

By dividing the above equation by the Treated Floor Area (TFA), the maximum specific supply-air heating load ($p_{supply,max}$) is given in equation 2.

$$p_{supply,max} = \frac{C_p\,\rho \cdot \dot{\nu}_{system} \cdot (T_{supply,max} - T_{supply,min})}{TFA} \qquad [2]$$

By substituting in typical supply-air flow rates of 30 m³ per person per hour, limiting air temperatures (see Chapter 8) and standard (German) occupant densities, the derivation of the limiting of 10 W/m² can be seen, in equation 3.

$$p_{supply,max} = \frac{0.33\ Wh/m^3K \cdot 30\,m^3/h.person \cdot (52°C - 16.5°C)}{35\,m^2/person} = 10\,W/m^2 \quad [3]$$

where:

$30\,m^3/h.person$ is the recommended residential air flow rate (DIN 1946, Part 6)
$30\,m^2/person$ is a typical residential occupancy density (Germany).

Since $P_{supply,max}$ is limited to *10W/m²* (for certification purposes), it follows that the specific maximum heating load (P_H) must be less than or equal to this figure in order for the building to be certified on the basis of its peak heating load.[4] Despite this theoretical requirement, it is not obligatory to heat or cool a Passivhaus building via the supply air (see Chapter 8).

Typically, a Passivhaus building with a specific heating load that fulfils the above criteria in a Central European climate will have an annual specific heating demand requirement[5] (q_H) not exceeding 15 kWh/m² per annum.[6] For this reason, either $p_H \leq$ *10W/m²* or $q_H \leq$ *15 kWh/m².a* are seen as two of the primary requirements for achieving Passivhaus certification (Feist *et al.*, 2013).

It is for these reasons that the Passivhaus standard originated as an ultra-low energy specification rather than an overall carbon emissions reduction target. With energy efficiency directly incentivised, the resultant carbon emissions depend largely upon the choice of fuel source and heating appliance efficiency.[7] By prioritising energy-efficient design, the Passivhaus standard avoids many of the perverse consequences of low carbon standards which aim to reduce carbon emissions without first substantially addressing demand-side energy reduction and thermal comfort (Figure 1.5).

1.5
Vauban car free Passivhaus housing estate close to Freiburg (left); Energy Plus house in the solar settlement close to Freiburg (right)

Reducing heating loads to such a low level allows high levels of thermal comfort to be achieved by means of a very small heating device, which effectively supplements the 'free' heat gains provided by the sun, the building's occupants and

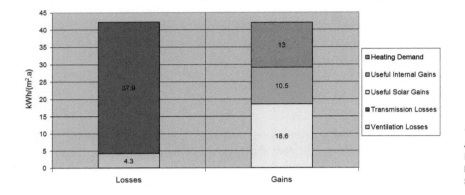

1.6
Annual energy balance: Heat
losses and gains in a typical
European Passivhaus
Source: Feist *et al.* (2005)

appliances (see Figure 1.6 and Figure 12.4). Clearly an ultra-low energy building is not necessarily 'zero carbon' unless the heating, electricity and hot water demand (Chapter 6 and 7) are also met from renewable sources (Chapter 9).

In order to mitigate excessive energy consumption and carbon emissions, PHI has specified a maximum primary energy (PE) demand from all sources of 120 kWh/m² per annum (Feist *et al.*, 2013). This requirement ensures that low energy lighting, appliances and hot water generation systems form part of an integrated approach to Passivhaus design. As a result, the PE consumption from all sources in a Passivhaus building is approximately two to four times lower than the PE consumption levels stipulated by most new building standards across Europe (Schnieders and Hermelink, 2006; McLeod *et al.*, 2012a).

Heat Recovery Ventilation (HRV) is used almost universally in the Passivhaus concept. Whilst HRV can be passive, driven by wind and air pressure differentials alone, predominantly Mechanical Ventilation with Heat Recovery (MVHR) is used to ensure consistently high Indoor Air Quality (IAQ) (Feist *et al.*, 2005; see Chapter 8). Mechanical ventilation necessitates the use of fans powered by electricity; Passivhaus requirements limit the Specific Fan Power (SFP) to 0.45 Wh/m³ (1.62 W/(l/s)) of supply air in order to limit carbon emissions arising from the ventilation system (Feist *et al.*, 2013). Depending on the mean outside air temperature and the overall efficiency of the MVHR unit, the Coefficient of Performance (CoP) (i.e. the ratio of energy saved to energy invested) of a properly installed MVHR unit (in a Central European climate) is likely to be in the order of 6–10. CoPs above 6 can be considered to be very good when compared to the *in situ* efficiencies achieved by most electrically powered heat pumps.

$$CoP_{MVHR} = \frac{C_p \, \rho \cdot \dot{\nu}_{system} \cdot \mu_{MVHR} \cdot \Delta T \cdot t}{SFP \cdot \dot{\nu}_{system} \cdot t} = \frac{C_p \, \rho \cdot \mu_{MVHR} \cdot \Delta T}{SFP} \qquad [4]$$

where:

CoP_{MVHR} refers to the ratio of ventilation heat saved to fan electricity consumed, ΔT refers to the difference between the mean internal air temperature (T_{int}) and the mean external air temperature (T_{ext}) across the period the MVHR is used (i.e. heating season or annually) (K),

t refers to the time period over which the MVHR unit is operating (hours),

μ_{MVHR} refers to the mean installed efficiency of the MVHR system including losses due to ductwork, etc. (%), and

SFP refers to the total Specific Fan Power of the unit in standard operational mode (Wh/m³).

Thus by substituting in some typical flow rates for a notional Passivhaus dwelling with four adult occupants operating a 90 per cent efficient MVHR unit continuously in a central England location (mean external temperature 9°C = 282 K, and mean internal temperature 20°C = 293 K), we can determine the approximate annual CoP of the MVHR system.[8]

$$CoP_{MVHR} = \frac{0.33 \, Wh/m^3K \cdot 0.9 \cdot (293K - 282K)}{0.45 \, Wh/m^3} = 7.26 \qquad [5]$$

The final specific requirement of the Passivhaus standard is that unwanted air leakage through the building fabric is reduced to less than 0.6 ac/h at n_{50}.[9] This level of airtightness ensures that unwanted draughts are avoided and excessive heat does not enter or escape through the building fabric through poor construction detailing (Feist *et al.*, 2013). A number of further technical requirements are stipulated with regard to the limiting thermal transfer (U-values) of building elements and glazing components, and the minimisation of thermal bridging (see Chapter 4).

In summary, the Passivhaus concept is characterised by the use of a highly insulated and airtight thermal envelope. Careful construction detailing is required in order to virtually eliminate the additional two- and three-dimensional thermal

1.7
The US Department of Energy Solar Decathlon TU Darmstadt entry and winner in 2007, currently located at TU Darmstadt/ Germany

bridges commonly occurring at the junctions between thermal elements. This is combined with a highly efficient HRV system which provides continuous ventilation rates in the region of 0.3–0.5 ac/h during the heating season. Dwellings are orientated towards the winter sun (i.e. to the south in the Northern hemisphere) in order to maximise useful solar gains where possible; however this is not seen as a prerequisite of Passivhaus design and the standard has been achieved in a number of urban contexts where optimal solar orientation was not feasible due to site constraints.

Table 1.1 Overview of principal Passivhaus certification criteria

Passivhaus certification criteria (residential) determined according to PHPP	Cool moderate climate, e.g. Central Europe	
Specific Heating Demand (SHD)	≤15	kWh/(m²a)
or Specific Heating Load (SHL)	≤10	W/m²
Specific Cooling Demand (SCD)	≤15	kWh/(m²a) + 0.3 W/(m²aK). DDH
or Specific Cooling Load (SCL)*	≤10	W/m²
and SCD	≤4	kWh/(m²aK) .ϑ_e + 2 · 0.3 W/(m²aK). DDH-75 kWh/(m²a)
Specific total Primary Energy Demand (SPED)**	≤120	kWh/(m²a)
Airtightness n_{50}	≤0.6	h⁻¹ (@50 Pa)
Overheating frequency (percentage of time operative temperature above 25°C)	10%	

Notes: The reference area (m²) refers to the Treated Floor Area (TFA),[10] i.e. the useful living space.

DDH refers to Dry Degree Hours, i.e. the time integral of the difference between the dew point temperature (T_{dp}) and the dehumidification reference temperature of 13°C whenever the T_{dp} is greater than 13°C during the cooling period.

ϑ_e Annual mean external air temperature (°C).

* It should be noted that the cooling and dehumidification criteria are provisional, the current version of PHPP should be consulted for any changes to the above criteria

** This total value includes all of the building's consumer energy including: heating, cooling, hot water, ventilation, pumps, lighting, appliances and cooking

1.4 The role of the Passivhaus standard

1.4.1 Passivhaus in practice: lessons learned from Europe

Between the early 1990s and 2005, some 4,000 certified Passivhaus dwellings are estimated to have been constructed in continental Europe (Feist et al., 2005). To date, it is estimated that around 50,000 Passivhaus buildings have been built worldwide (iPHA, 2014) with approximately 10 per cent of these being fully certified, the majority of which are located in German-speaking countries and Scandinavia (Rosenthal, 2008; iPHA, 2014). Over the past decade, interest in the Passivhaus standard has begun to spread further afield; demonstration projects now exist in diverse climatic regions including almost every European country as well as: Australia, China, Japan, Canada, USA and South America (BRE, 2014), amongst others.

Lessons learned from almost two decades of project monitoring and technological improvements have allowed PHI to take on the more ambitious challenges of applying the Passivhaus standard to more complex situations, including the refurbishment of existing buildings as well as the design of new schools and commercial buildings (see Chapter 12). A number of pan-European research studies have contributed important findings to the development of the standard.

1.4.1.1 CEPHEUS

Research originating from the European Commission-funded Cost Efficient Passive Houses as European Standard (CEPHEUS) project (1999–2001) provides a body of detailed evidence regarding the performance of over 200 Passivhaus dwellings across Europe. The CEPHEUS project set out to establish to what extent the Passivhaus concept could fulfil conditions of social, ecological and economic sustainability (Schnieders, 2003). Some of the project's specific goals included:

- demonstrating the technical feasibility of achieving the Passivhaus energy performance indices in a range of building designs and construction types;
- testing viability in terms of cost-efficient planning and construction in several different countries, and the potential to achieve Passivhaus standards at low additional investment costs;
- studying post-occupancy behaviour and investor/purchaser acceptance under real-world conditions;
- establishing the broad market preconditions for the widespread introduction of cost-efficient Passivhaus construction.

In order to assess these aims, a total of 221 dwelling units were built using a variety of different construction methods, at 14 different CEPHEUS project sites throughout Central Europe and Scandinavia.

Predictably, a number of technical issues emerged as a result of this widespread market test of a relatively new concept; these issues are extensively documented in the final technical report of the CEPHEUS project (Schnieders, 2003). From the perspective of post-occupancy satisfaction, however, the published literature (Schnieders and Hermelink, 2006) indicates generally high levels of acceptance with the year-round indoor climate and the use of MVHR as the principle source of ventilation and heat distribution.

Additional construction and engineering systems investment in order to meet the Passivhaus standard was found to add costs of between 0 per cent and 17 per cent compared to standard construction costs. Averaged across all projects, these extra costs represented an investment premium of 8 per cent of total build cost or 91 Euros/m² (at 2001 prices) (Schnieders, 2003). Included in this additional expenditure was the specification of solar thermal hot water systems. Whilst an increased build cost of 8 per cent is not negligible, it should be recognised that this estimate was based upon a period before volume demand for Passivhaus components could serve to bring market prices down.[11]

It is also important to make 'like for like' value-based comparisons when comparing build costs, and for this reason the inclusion of long-term energy savings are an important whole-life investment consideration. Given the uncertainty regarding long-term energy prices, this issue is difficult to quantify with absolute certainty; however, the recent (and in all probability, continuing) trend is towards steeply rising energy prices (Mobbs, 2005; IEA, 2008; Worldwatch Institute, 2014). Rising energy costs will, generally, reduce the 'payback' period associated with any additional capital needed to build to an ultra-low energy standard (see Chapter 11).

Whilst the CEPHEUS social and economic indicators are generally within an acceptable range, the same cannot be said for the measured energy performance of all projects. Largely due to occupants choosing to operate their dwellings at temperatures well above the 20°C normalisation set point (as used for PH certification), only one of the original CEPHEUS project averages achieved the 15 kWh/m²a Specific Heating Demand (SHD) target in practice. [12] Figure 1.8 illustrates the range of measured heating loads, which have been subsequently normalised to an indoor temperature of 20°C[13] in order to allow for useful comparisons between the measured SHD of individual projects and design predictions (made using the PHPP certification criteria) (Schnieders and Hermelink, 2006).

Figure 1.8 suggests that even after indoor temperatures are normalised, occupant behaviour plays a dominant role in the widely varying energy consumption profiles of identical housing types; this phenomenon is not unique to the Passivhaus concept however. In a historical Swedish study, Lundström (1986) stated that occupant behaviour is the dominant factor in energy consumption and therefore money is better invested in occupant education than energy-efficient housing. Feist counters this claim by pointing out that the same ratio (typically 2:1) of lowest to highest heating consumption is observable in all housing types, and it is therefore the thermal specification that has the greatest effect on the mean energy consumption (Feist et al., 2001). In reality, there is merit to both claims since both occupant behaviour and building energy performance play a role in the final energy consumption. Interestingly, the influence of occupant behaviour and education is clearly shown in the same report, where results of an independent study show that electrical energy consumption figures in a Passivhaus estate were halved as a result of occupant advice (Feist et al., 2001).

What the CEPHEUS results highlight is the common phenomenon of occupants claiming back some of the theoretical energy savings by turning up their thermostats. This behavioural phenomenon (sometimes referred to as 'Jevon's paradox') commonly occurs in low energy dwellings where residents perceive that it is now affordable for them to run their home at a higher heating set point. As a result, the ambitious design predictions in many low energy

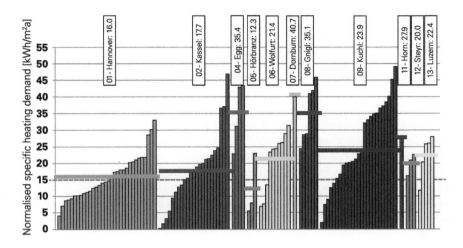

1.8
Measured space heating
consumption of CEPHEUS
dwellings (kWh/m²a)*
Source: Feist *et al.* (2001),
©PHI
Notes: Project means are
indicated as a solid horizontal
bar.
* after measured data
normalisation to $T_i = 20°C$.

developments are rarely achieved in practice. This phenomenon is not the same as a 'performance gap' but is an important issue to reconcile if the energy and carbon savings predicted on paper are to be realised in practice.

According to Schnieders and Hermelink (2006), the reasons for the almost uniform discrepancy between prediction and reality in the CEPHEUS projects can be attributed to the fact that energy consumption for space heating in new buildings is typically higher during the first year after construction (as a result of materials drying out and unfamiliarity with control systems). However a number of project-specific issues regarding airtightness, thermal bridging and control systems are also reflected in these results, and these have been documented in the CEPHEUS final technical report (Feist *et al.*, 2001).

Despite the learning curve that accompanies the development of any new building standard, the primary lesson to be gained from the CEPHEUS project experience is that the Passivhaus standard has repeatedly delivered reductions of over 80 per cent of the equivalent reference newbuild space heating demand (Feist *et al.*, 2001) whilst at the same time providing high levels of thermal comfort and occupant satisfaction (Schnieders, 2003).

1.4.1.2 PassREg

The aim of the EU-funded project Passive House Regions with Renewable Energies (PassREg) is to facilitate the implementation of Nearly Zero Energy Buildings (NZEBs) throughout Europe. This should be accomplished by applying the Passivhaus standard as the foundation and then applying sufficient renewable energy technologies (RETs) to make the building operationally zero energy on an annual basis. Further aims of the PassREg project include: (i) to make Passivhaus solutions more accessible, (ii) to improve training materials, (iii) to boost the market for suitable products and technologies, and (iv) to increase the number of Passivhaus buildings using RET (PassREg, 2013).

The three-year project is based on the experience of early adopters of the Passivhaus concepts in EU regions and aims to pave the way to achieving EU targets as outlined in the Energy Performance in Buildings Directive (EPBD) by 2020. The project was launched in May 2012, following the Passivhaus conference in Hannover, with 14 project partners taking part from ten different countries.

The participants in this project are considered to be 'front runner regions' that already have a large number of successful Passivhaus buildings. One of the aims of the PassREg project is to make the success of these early adopter countries visible to others, including detailed information about the cost-effective strategies they have used to achieve NZEBs.

Outside of the 'front runner regions' a number of 'aspiring regions', such as the Aquitaine region in France, Carmarthenshire Council in Wales, or the Municipality of Cesena in Italy, are also participating in PassREg. These regions have been charged with absorbing the best practice examples from the front runner regions in order to help them to establish their own model for successful implementation of NZEBs using Passivhaus and RET.

Some of the 30 plus beacon projects involved in PassREg are currently undergoing performance monitoring. This is an important quality assurance step in order to investigate the difference between actual built energy consumption and occupant comfort and the projections of the PHPP model.

The transition from using Passivhaus as an ultra-low energy standard to using Passivhaus as a template for NZEBs is predicated upon the successful integration of renewable technologies. The practicalities of this important transition step to creating operationally zero energy buildings are addressed in Chapter 9.

1.4.1.3 EuroPHit

The EuroPHit project started in 2013 and will run until 2016 with project partners from 11 countries. EuroPHit intends to demonstrate the possibilities for step-by-step refurbishment using Passivhaus design principals in line with EU 2020 objectives in terms of refurbished buildings: whereby all refurbished buildings should become NZEBs (Nearly Zero Energy Buildings).

Its main aim is to improve energy efficiency through deep retrofitting measures, which are conducted in stages over a period of years. Thus the eventual target of a NZEB can be achieved in accordance with the replacement cycles of existing components and using phased project budgets; hence 'step-by-step' refurbishment.

Knowledge and experience from previous EnerPHit projects underpins the EuroPHit project approach. The step-by-step retrofit methodology has two main variants: (i) the component step by step and (ii) different façades step by step. Both variants address a similar baseline model; i.e. a non-refurbished building drawn from the current building stock:

1. In (i): additional insulation will be applied (Step 1); new windows will be added, airtightness improved and the ventilation strategy upgraded (Step 2); finally RET and heating systems will be added (Step 3).

2   In (ii): additional insulation on the north elevation only (Step 1); additional insulation on the south elevation (plus windows, airtightness and ventilation) (Step 2); additional insulation on the other elevations and RET and heating system replacement (Step 3).

In reality, depending on the nature of the project and the availability of funding, etc., these two approaches are likely to be applied in a more hybridised manner. The 13 case study buildings that are participating in the EuroPHit project vary from private domestic (single to multifamily residences) to social housing, schools, elderly homes and restaurants, and they are located in eight different European countries.

More information can be found on the project website: http://europhit.eu/

1.4.1.4 Summary

It is important to highlight that although widely replicated throughout Central and Northern Europe, the Passivhaus standard is not the only ultra-low European standard. Minergie P is the Swiss equivalent of the Passivhaus standard; it provides similar thermal performance whilst delivering an even higher standard in terms of net primary energy consumption by tightly restricting electricity consumption (Mennel *et al.*, 2007; Hall, 2012). The emerging Minergie P+ standard achieves a further 25 per cent reduction in total energy demand by incorporating more advanced building services technology (Pfeiffer *et al.*, 2005). Despite such differences in operational energy limits, most of the advanced energy performance standards which now exist throughout Europe and North America share a fundamentally similar concept.

Two prominent factors can be attributed to the success and credibility of the Passivhaus standard: quality assurance and continual improvement. Rather than simply being a design target, the Passivhaus standard requires proof of how the design performance standard has been achieved in the completed project. The final step of this quality assurance process involves an independent third-party audit of the full project documentation (including commissioning tests) carried out by a registered Passivhaus certifier.

Since the Passivhaus concept originally appeared it has been significantly refined and is now being applied to public and commercial buildings as well as to the retrofit upgrading of the existing stock.

1.4.2 Passivhaus and 'zero carbon' lessons from the UK

Attempts to quantify the carbon savings achievable by building zero carbon homes in the UK have arrived at some ambiguous findings. According to a 2007 Energy White Paper, overall carbon reductions from energy efficiency in the residential sector are predicted to be between 4.7 MtC and 7.6 MtC by 2020, relative to a 2006 baseline of 40 MtC (DTI, 2007). When compared to the 1990 baseline, as used by the UK Climate Change Act, this represents a reduction of only 11–18 per cent by 2020 (Boardman, 2007). Even the upper estimate would suggest that energy efficiency measures in the built environment are falling far short of the 40 per cent reduction needed by 2020 in order to maintain the trajectory to an 80 per cent GHG emissions reduction by 2050. According to the White Paper, zero carbon homes will contribute to saving 1.1 MtC to 1.2 MtC of the 2020 total. It is notable moreover that this estimate is based upon the original (2007) definition of a zero carbon home (DTI, 2007) and not the more recently revised definition (Zero Carbon Hub, 2009) which effectively ignores a large portion of the emissions (see Figure 1.9).

The revised 'zero carbon' definition, as set out in the *'Have Your Say'* report (ZCH, 2009) and confirmed in the 2011 Budget (HM Treasury, 2011), implies that a significant reduction in the newbuild housing sector's GHG emissions is achievable whilst ignoring two key sources of emissions. These are: the appliance energy consumption, that may account for up to 50 per cent (DCLG, 2007) of the operational emissions from a dwelling; and the emissions released during the manufacture and construction of the building, which may account for up to 50 per cent of the net 80-year emissions from a low energy or Passivhaus dwelling (McLeod, 2007; Stephan *et al.*, 2012). By using these estimates of the net emissions being truncated in the revised definition, it is possible to visualise the limitations of the current UK 'zero carbon' definition (Figure 1.9).

When the net GHG emissions (including embodied energy) are considered in the context of a 'zero carbon' dwelling, the actual on-site savings (i.e. carbon compliance addressed at the building) diminishes to as little as one-sixth (see orange segment in Figure 1.9) of the total GHG emissions incurred over an 80-year period. Even if the embodied energy component is ignored, the actual emissions reductions addressed at the building accounts for as little as one-quarter of the total operational emissions. Thus, dwellings which just comply with the current UK 'zero carbon' criteria are unlikely to be either zero carbon or NZEBs in real terms. More importantly, however, if the majority of carbon emissions from the future UK building stock remain unregulated then atmospheric GHG emissions will continue to rise.

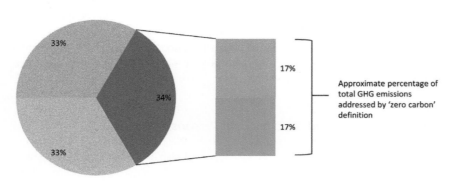

33%

34%

33%

17%

17%

Approximate percentage of total GHG emissions addressed by 'zero carbon' definition

1.9
Indicative ratio of net (operational and embodied) GHG emissions relative to those addressed by the revised UK 'zero carbon' definition
Source: McLeod and Hopfe (2013)

▨ unregulated emissions (incl appliances)
▪ regulated emissions (SAP 2009)
▨ allowable solutions (emissions offset)

▨ embodied emissions
▨ carbon compliance (addressed at building)

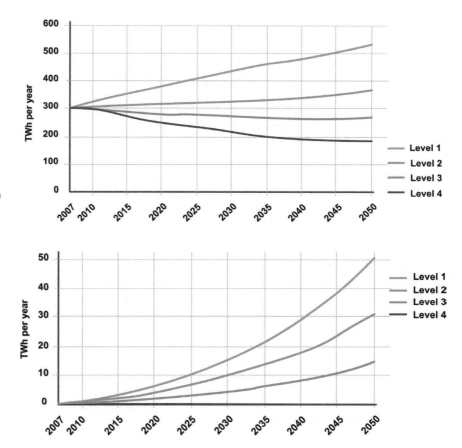

1.10
Trajectories for total domestic
heat demand under four levels
of change in the UK
Source: DECC (2010)

1.11
Trajectories for total domestic
cooling demand under four
levels of change
Source: DECC (2010)

Viewed on a meta scale, modelling by the Department of Energy and Climate Change (DECC) illustrates that the implementation of an advanced energy efficiency standard (such as Level 4; i.e. the Passivhaus standard) is the *only* approach that leads to a long-term reduction in total domestic heating demand.

Given that the scenario modelled as Level 4 (i.e. Passivhaus) requires a contiguous roll-out of extensive refurbishment measures to 96 per cent of the existing stock and an accompanying *drop* in the average heating set point to 16°C, there appears to be no margin to construct new dwellings to a more lax standard (DECC, 2010). When the projected growth in domestic cooling demand is also considered, the importance of adopting a more robust zero carbon definition based on buildings that perform *at or beyond* the Passivhaus standard becomes even more apparent.

The growth in domestic cooling demand forecast to occur by 2050 (Figure 1.11) could place an additional 50 TWh burden (DECC, 2010) on the net climate change impacts from the UK dwelling stock, a fact which appears to have been overlooked by the ZCH energy efficiency proposals. According to the recast EPBD (2010) 'the methodology for calculating energy performance should be based not only on the season in which heating is required, but should cover the annual energy performance of a building. That methodology should take into account existing European standards' (EPCEU, 2010). When total annual energy performance is considered, the DECC modelling shows that *only* the Passivhaus (Level 4) scenario delivers a net overall decrease in heating, cooling and hot water energy demand (DECC, 2010).[14]

These findings are in broad agreement with studies of similar national emissions reductions scenarios in the German built environment (Vallentin, 2009) based upon atmospheric stabilisation in accordance with the Contraction and Convergence (C&C$_{2050}$) model. The C&C mechanism provides a simple and scalable means of implementing GHG emission reduction pathways, based on the principle of an equitable per capita distribution of emission rights (Meyer, 2000). The C&C model involves a transitional phase in order to achieve convergence on equal per capita emissions in a structured manner.

The UK GHG emission reduction profile is similar to Germany's in respect to having similar levels of CO_2 emissions per capita and a planned trajectory for emission reductions of 40 per cent by 2020 and 80 per cent by 2050. According to Vallentin's (2009) trajectory analysis, the total primary energy consumption for domestic heating, ventilation, hot water and appliances should be no greater than $100\,kWh/m^2_{TFA}.yr$ in 2010, and will need to fall progressively to $\leq 60\,kWh/m^2_{TFA}.yr$ by 2050 in order to meet this stabilisation trajectory. Vallentin concluded that: 'By 2015 the Passivhaus standard must be applied to all new buildings, and Passivhaus components must be made mandatory in renovation projects' (2009: 255). This view was endorsed by a European Parliament resolution in an Action Plan for Energy Efficiency which called on the EC to 'propose a binding requirement that all new buildings needing to be heated and/or cooled be constructed to passive house or equivalent non-residential standards from 2011 onwards' (EC, 2008: 6).

Since the emissions trajectories outlined above are only based on addressing the operational emissions from the new building stock, even greater reductions will be needed where net GHG emissions from all sources must be accounted for. When viewed from this wider perspective, it is clear that the Passivhaus standard will need to be progressively enhanced by the integration of Renewable Energy Technologies (RETs) and the use of carbon negative materials if it is to fulfil a pivotal role in defining a 'true zero carbon' approach to sustainable building.

1.5 Passive House Planning Package (PHPP)

The Passive House Planning Package (PHPP) is a building energy calculation tool that is primarily targeted at assisting architects and mechanical engineers in designing Passivhaus buildings. According to the Passivhaus Institute (PHI) the verification of a Passivhaus design must be carried out using the PHPP software (Feist *et al.*, 2013).[15] As a result, this simplified steady state software has become the de facto tool for assessing both the design and compliance predictions of Passivhaus buildings around the world.

1.5.1 Validation and development

Validation of the PHPP model has been carried out using both dynamic thermal simulations, based on the PHI's Dynbil software (Feist, 1998) and empirical data derived from a large number of completed Passivhaus projects (Feist *et al.*, 2001). Dynamic simulation results, predicted by Dynbil, have also been extensively compared to measured data for both dwellings and office buildings (Feist and Loga, 1997; Kaufmann and Feist, 2001; Schnieders and Feist, 2002). PHPP validation studies have generally shown good agreement between measured and predicted results, including those derived from dynamic simulation (Feist *et al.*, 2001). According to PHI, validation testing of PHPP version 8 (released in 2013) based on studies using dynamic simulation demonstrated that, 'the calculation algorithms for the frequency of excess temperatures and demand for cooling and dehumidification produce reliable results' (iPHA, 2013).

At its core, the PHPP thermal model is essentially carrying out a series of monthly steady state energy balance calculations. These calculations are performed broadly in accordance with methods set out in EN ISO 13790:2008 for determining the heating demand according to annual and monthly methods. In addition to this, PHPP contains algorithms to calculate peak heating and cooling loads and assess overheating risks, based on a single zone thermal model. In order to compute these primary outputs, an accurate representation of the building envelope (U-values, areas, windows, shading, etc.) as well as the mechanical design concepts (MVHR system, heat and hot water generation, etc.) is required. The PHPP tool consists of a Microsoft Excel-based workbook and a comprehensive user's manual (Feist *et al.*, 2013). The Excel workbook contains all of the formulas and functions needed to demonstrate compliance with the Passivhaus certification criteria (such as the SHD, SHL, SCD, SCL and SPED; see Table 1.1). Beyond the core certification requirements, a great deal of useful design information (such as domestic hot water distribution losses, appliance electricity usage and internal heat gains) may be determined using the appropriate worksheets. The PHPP workbook contains approximately 35 active worksheets, each of which addresses a different aspect of the design (see Figure 1.12).

The first edition of the PHPP was released in 1998 (PHI, 1998) but was only available in German. Since then the software has been regularly updated, with major updates occurring in 2004 and 2007. In June 2007, additional calculations were introduced in order to determine the sensible cooling demand on a monthly basis (Feist *et al.*, 2007). In Version 8 (2013), additional equations were introduced to account for the radiative heat balance of opaque elements during the heating and cooling seasons. Additional cooling load weather data was also introduced to allow the calculation of peak sensible and latent cooling loads and thereby enable cooling unit sizing. Version 9 is expected to be released mid 2015 and will introduce two new worksheets entitled 'Variants' and 'Comparison'. 'Variants' will enable the user to introduce a number of alternative designs and to compare the results. In 'Comparison', two of these alternatives can be compared with respect to their energy demand and economic viability (iPHA, 2014). This new functionality will allow users to quickly assess cost benefits and comparative energy performance between multiple design options.

1.5.2 PHPP software overview

The 'Verification' worksheet sits at the front of the PHPP workbook and provides a summary of the most important project data, as it is used for Passivhaus certification. In this sheet, the user is required to input project information including: site location, architect's and mechanical engineer's details, year of construction and the number of units, etc. The calculation methods are also selected based on the type of building (residential/non-residential), the utilisation pattern (dwelling/care home/student accommodation/office/school/other), the planned number of occupants, and the certification type (Passive House/EnerPHit [by component]/EnerPHit [by heating demand]). This worksheet also acts as the cover sheet for the 'as built' documentation required as evidence for the Passivhaus Quality Approval Certificate. The 'Verification' worksheet outputs list the key building performance indices normalised in relation to the TFA and highlights whether the certification requirements have been fulfilled; these include:

- Specific Annual Space Heat Demand (kWh/m^2.a);
- Specific Space Heating Load (W/m^2);
- Specific Overall (sensible + latent) Cooling Demand (kWh/m^2.a);
- Specific Cooling Load (W/m^2);
- Frequency of Summer Overheating (hϑ > 25°C) (%);
- Specific Primary Energy Demand (kWh/m^2.a);[16]
- Air Leakage (n$_{50}$ pressurisation) Test Results (h^{-1}).

The verification outputs are automatically calculated based on the data imputed into the various other worksheets provided in the tool. The relationship between the various worksheets in the PHPP workbook is illustrated in Figure 1.12

Although the flowchart illustrating the work sequence for PHPP (Figure 1.12) may appear complicated at first, it can be greatly simplified by grouping it into those worksheets comprising the building fabric inputs and those making up the mechanical systems. Within each of these sections, there are several key worksheets which carry out important verification calculations based upon data which has been collated from a number of other worksheets. Thus for example the 'Monthly heating demand' links information contained in the 'Areas', 'U-values', 'Ventilation', 'Windows' and 'Climate' worksheets in order to determine whether the annual heating demand (q_H) complies with the limiting value using the monthly method.

Some additional spreadsheet tools and inputs derived from reference sources or software are needed to support the PHPP workbook. The 'Ventilation Protocol' worksheet and the 'Ventilation Commissioning' sheet (see Chapter 8), for example, are important adjuncts for the detailed planning and commissioning of the ventilation system. Similarly thermal bridging calculations cannot be carried

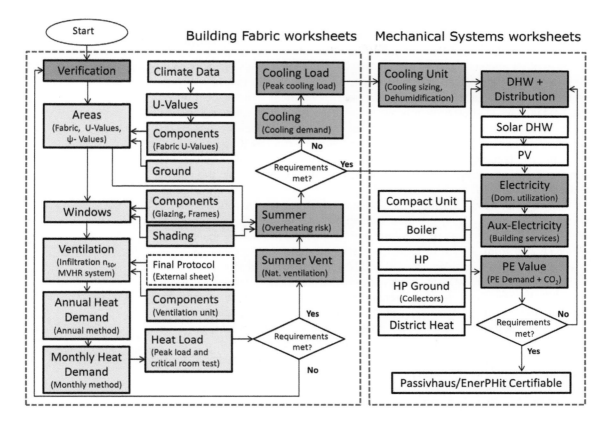

Building Fabric worksheets   Mechanical Systems worksheets

1.12
PHPP (version 8) workflow

out in the PHPP software. Linear thermal bridges must be either calculated for each junction using external software or obtained from reference publications where an established construction detail is being replicated (see Chapter 3). Alternatively thermal bridge inputs may be ignored, on the proviso that it can be demonstrated that 'thermal bridge free' detailing has been used throughout the construction (PHI, 1999). Further details on working with PHPP can be found in Section 10.4.

1.5.3 PHPP limitations

Like all building physics models, the outputs from the PHPP model are predicated upon the use of defined boundary conditions. In the case of PHPP, a steady state model is used which means, for certification purposes, that the internal gains (e.g. residential dwelling, 2.1 W/m²) and operative temperature (20°C) are assumed to remain constant. The key boundary conditions used to determine the monthly heating demand, cooling demand and peak loads therefore depend almost entirely on the external climate file. For this reason, a good understanding of the uncertainty associated with using either a 'near neighbour'[17] or a regional climate file is advised. This is especially relevant when projects are being assessed in a highly localised microclimate (such as an UHI) or for resilience against future climatic scenarios (McLeod *et al.*, 2012b; McLeod *et al.*, 2013).

For monthly energy balancing purposes, the PHPP steady state simplification is often adequate due to the thermal inertia of Passivhaus buildings (see Chapter 5). Limitations can occur, however, when attempting to use PHPP to assess transient situations, for example, when evaluating thermal comfort or overheating risks at short time intervals, when accounting for fluctuating internal and external gains and moisture loads, or during shoulder season periods when both heating and cooling loads may occur on the same day (see Chapter 5).

In more complex situations where multiple thermal zones exist and thermal comfort and overheating risks need to be assessed in greater detail, the use of a dynamic simulation tool is advised. Hygrothermal assessments should also be routinely carried out whenever a project involves substantial refurbishment, particularly when specifying internal insulation, similarly when building in exposed driving rain zones or areas of high humidity. In these cases the designer must either choose from a suite of more sophisticated dynamic hygrothermal tools or assess whether a coupled Heat Air and Moisture (HAM) simulation tool such as WUFI® Passive (see Chapter 5) might provide adequate information within a single platform. Such decisions require considerable experience in order to evaluate the nature of the risk, select the appropriate tool(s), carry out the analysis and interpret the results. Nonetheless these are common everyday tasks for those charged with designing robust low energy buildings.

Further limitations with PHPP have historically included the lack of a 3D visualisation capability. This situation has recently been improved by the development of an interactive plug-in for the Sketch-Up software called Design-PH (PHI, 2014). Those using PHPP without 3D visualisation need to take great care not to omit part of the building envelope area without realising it. A systematic and clearly identified approach to entering envelope areas and physical data is therefore needed. Although there are some error messages generated when incomplete or improbable data is entered into the PHPP model, the process is far from fail-safe. For this reason, even experienced PHPP practitioners tend to have a colleague comprehensively second-check their model inputs before issuing design information.

Integrated design software such as WUFI® Passive (see Chapter 5) has the benefit of 3D visualisation and, in addition, allows more detailed building physics analysis (steady state, dynamic and hygrothermal) to be undertaken, without the need to export geometric and materials data. Similarly, new developments in Building Information Modelling (BIM) have allowed some BIM design tools to export geometric data and materials schedules directly to PHPP without the need to manually re-enter data (Burrell, 2013; Cemesova *et al.*, 2015). Further refinements of BIM extension tools include the possibility for Passivhaus compliance assessments, optimization routines and inter-model comparison assessments to be carried out from a single interface (Cemesova *et al.*, 2015). These types of enhancements point to the future direction of software developments where information can be shared fluidly across platforms. Such an approach will ultimately help to reduce redundant workflows and the contiguous risk of errors and clashes occurring when design collaboration takes place using different model representations of a shared project. Despite these constraints, PHPP provides an affordable, transparent and reliable design tool once such limitations are understood.

Both the *Passive House Planning Package* (Feist *et al.*, 2013) and user guides such as *PHPP Illustrated* (Lewis, 2014) are available to guide novice users with PHPP data inputs.

References

Adamson, B. 2011. *Towards Passive Houses in Cold Climates as in Sweden: Technical Report EBD-R-11/35*. Lund: Lund University, Lund Institute of Technology..

Boardman, B. 2007. *Home Truths: A Low Carbon Strategy to Reduce UK Housing Emissions by 80% by 2050. ECI Research Report 34*. Oxford: University of Oxford.

BRE. 2014. *The Passivhaus Standard*. [Online]. Available at: www.passivhaus.org.uk/standard.jsp?id=122 (accessed August 2014).

Brown, M., Southworth, F. and Stovall, K. 2005. *Towards a Climate-Friendly Built Environment*. Arlington, VA: Pew Center on Global Climate Change. Available at: www.c2es.org/docUploads/Buildings_FINAL.pdf (accessed October 2014).

Burrell, E. 2013. BIM for Passivhaus Design: Delivering Radical Reductions in Energy in Use. *NBS* [Online]. Available at: www.thenbs.com/topics/bim/articles/bimForPassivhausDesign.asp (accessed December 2014).

CEC (California Energy Commission). 2007. *Integrated Energy Policy Report*. [Online]. Available at: www.energy.ca.gov/2007_energypolicy/index.html (accessed July 2014).

Cemesova, A., Hopfe, C. J. and McLeod, R. 2015. PassivBIM: enhancing interoperability between BIM and low energy design. *Automation in Construction*, Volume 57, pp. 17–32.

Committee on Climate Change. 2010. *Fourth Carbon Budget*. London: Committee on Climate Change. Available at: www.theccc.org.uk/reports/fourth-carbon-budget (accessed 5 January 2012).

Da Costa, A. 2007. The Science of Climate Change. *The Ecologist*, 10 (36): 16.

DCLG 2007. *Homes for the Future: More Affordable, More Sustainable*. London: Department for Communities and Local Government. Available at: www.communities.gov.uk/documents/housing/pdf/439986.pdf (accessed 4 January 2011).

DECC (Department of Energy and Climate Change). 2010. *2050 Pathways Analysis*. [Online]. Available at: www.decc.gov.uk (accessed January 15, 2011).

DECC (Department of Energy and Climate Change). 2012a. *Energy Consumption in the UK 2012: Domestic Energy Consumption in the UK since 1970. URN: 12D/291*. [Online]. Available at: www.decc.gov.uk/en/content/cms/statistics/publications/ecuk/ecuk.aspx (accessed December 2013).

DECC (Department of Energy and Climate Change). 2012b. *Standard Assessment Procedure (SAP) SAP 2012 v9.92*. [Online]. Available at: https://www.gov.uk/standard-assessment-procedure (accessed February 2015).

DTI. 2001. *Energy Consumption in the United Kingdom*. London: Energy Publications, Department of Trade and Industry.

DTI. 2007. *Meeting the Energy Challenge: A White Paper on Energy*. [Online]. Available at: www.berr.gov.uk/files/file39579.pdf (accessed 14 January 14 2011).

EC (European Commission). 2008. *European Parliament Resolution of 31 January 2008 on an Action Plan for Energy Efficiency: Realising the Potential (2007/2106(INI))*. [Online]. Available at: www.europarl.europa.eu/sides/getDoc.do?pubRef=-//...2008 (accessed February 2014).

EC (European Commission) 2009. *Low Energy Buildings in Europe: Current State of Play, Definitions and Best Practice*. [Online]. Available at: http://ec.europa.eu/energy/efficiency/doc/buildings/info_note.pdf (accessed November 2011).

EN ISO 13790:2008. *Energy Performance of Buildings – Calculation of Energy Use for Space Heating and Cooling*. s.l. :ISO.

EST (Energy Saving Trust). 2005. *Potential for Microgeneration: Study and Analysis.* London: Energy Saving Trust.

The European Parliament and the Council of the European Union. 2010. Directive 2010/31/EU of the European Parliament and of the Council of 19 May 2010 on the energy performance of buildings. *Official Journal of the European Union,* 53 (L 153): 13–35.

Feist, W. 1998. *Passive Solarenergienutzung im Passivhaus, Arbeitskreis kostengünstige Passivhäuser.* Protocol Volume Number 13, Energiebilanzen mit dem Passivhaus Projektierungs Paket. Darmstadt: Passive House Institute.

Feist, W. and Loga, T. 1997. *Vergleich von Messung und Simulation, Arbeitskreis kostengünstige Passivhäuser.* Protocol Volume Number 5 Energiebilanz und Temperaturverhalten (Energy Balance and Temperature Behaviour) of the Research Group for Cost-efficient Passive Houses (first ed.). Darmstadt: Passive House Institute.

Feist, W., Peper, S. and Gorg, M. 2001. *CEPHEUS Project Information No. 36: Final Technical Report.* Darmstadt: Passive House Institute.

Feist, W., Schnieders, J., Dorer, V. and Haas, A. 2005. Re-inventing air heating: convenient and comfortable within the frame of the Passive House concept. *Energy and Buildings,* 37 (11): 1186–1203.

Feist, W., Pfluger, R., Kaufmann, B., Schnieders, J. and Kah, O. 2007. *Passive House Planning Package 2007: Requirements for Quality Approved Passive Houses. Technical Information PHI-2007/1 (E).* 2nd revised edition. Darmstadt: Passive House Institute.

Feist, W., Pfluger, R., Schnieders, J., Kah, O., Kaufmann, B., Krick, B., Bastian, Z. and Ebel, W. 2013. *Passive House Planning Package, version 8 (2013): Energy balance and Passive House Design Tool.* Darmstadt: Passive House Institute.

Hall, M. 2012. One year Minergie A – Switzerland's big step towards net ZEB. *ZEMCH International Conference,* 20–22 August, Glasgow, UK.

HM Treasury. 2011. *The Plan for Growth.* London: HM Treasury. Available at: hm-treasury.gov.uk. (accessed October 2013).

Houghton, R. A. 2009. *Emissions of Carbon from Land Management.* Background note for the WDR 2010.

House of Commons Environmental Audit Committee. 2005. *Housing: Building a Sustainable Future. First Report of Session 2004–05 Volume I.* London: The Stationery Office.

IEA (International Energy Agency). 2008. *World Energy Outlook 2008.* Paris: International Energy Agency.

IEA (International Energy Agency). 2012. *World Energy Outlook 2012.* Paris: International Energy Agency Available at: www.worldenergyoutlook.org/publications/weo-2012/ (accessed April 2014).

IEA (International Energy Agency). 2015. *Scenarios and Projections.* [Online]. Available at: www.iea. org/publications/scenariosandprojections/ (accessed January 2015).

IPCC. 2013. Summary for policymakers. In Stocker, T. F., Qin, D., Plattner, G.-K., Tignor, M., Allen, S. K., Boschung, J., Nauels, A., Xia, Y., Bex, V. and Midgley, P. M. (eds), *Climate Change 2013: The Physical Science Basis. Contribution of Working Group I contribution to the Intergovernmental Panel on Climate Change (IPCC) Fifth Assessment Report (WGI AR5).* Cambridge and New York: Cambridge University Press, pp. 3–29.

IPCC. 2014. Summary for policymakers. In Field, C. B., Barros, V. R., Dokken, D. J., Mach, K. J., Mastrandrea, M. D., Bilir, T. E., Chatterjee, M., Ebi, K. L., Estrada, Y. O., Genova, R. C., Girma, B., Kissel, E. S., Levy, A. N., MacCracken, S., Mastrandrea, P. R. and White, L.L. (eds), *Climate Change 2014: Impacts, Adaptation, and Vulnerability. Part A: Global and Sectoral Aspects. Contribution of Working Group II to the Fifth Assessment Report of the Intergovernmental Panel on Climate Change.* Cambridge and New York: Cambridge University Press, pp. 1–32.

iPHA. 2013. PHPP 8: Worldwide applicability, added functions, improved user-friendliness and compatibility. *Passipedia – The Passive House Resource.* [Online]. Available at: http:// passipedia.passiv.de/ppediaen/planning/calculating_energy_efficiency/phpp_-_the_passive_ house_planning_package/phpp_8 (accessed April 2014).

iPHA. 2014. *iPHA: The Global Passive House Platform.* [Online]. Available at: www.passivehouse-international.org/index.php?page_id=65 (accessed December 2014).

Kaufmann, B. and Feist, W. 2001. *Vergleich von Messung und Simulation am Beispiel eines*

Passivhauses in Hannover-Kronsberg, CEPHEUS Projektinformation Nr. 21. Hannover: Passivhaus Institute.

Kendall, H. 2011. *World Scientists' Warning to Humanity. (The Heidelberg Appeal) Union of Concerned Scientists, Nov 1992.* [Online]. Available at: www.ucsusa.org/ucs/about/1992-world-scientists-warning-to-humanity.html (accessed February 2011).

Leimer, H.-P. 2014. Low carbon economy in cities of China possibilities to estimate the potential of CO_2-emissions. *Fifth German-Austrian IBPSA Conference: BauSIM 2014*, RWTH Aacen University, 22–24 September.

Levine, M., Urge-Vorsatz, D., Blok, K., Geng, L., Harvey, D., Land, S., Levermore, G., Mongameli Mehlwana, A., Mirasgedis, S., Novikova, A., Rlling, J. and Yoshino, H. 2007. Residential and commercial buildings. In Metz, B., Davidson, O.R., Bosch, P.R., Dave, R. and Meyer, L.A. (eds), *Climate Change 2007: Mitigation, Contribution of Working Group III to the Fourth Assessment Report of the Intergovernmental Panel on Climate Change.* Cambridge and New York: Cambridge University Press, pp. 387–46.

Lewis, S. 2014. *PHPP Illustrated: A Designer's Companion to the Passive House Planning Package.*

Lovins, A. 2011. Energy end-use efficiency (2005). In Burns, C. M. (ed.) *The Essential Amory Lovins,* Oxon: Earthscan, p.132.

Lundström, E. 1986. *Occupant Influence on Energy Consumption in Single Family Dwellings. D5.* Stockholm: Swedish Council of Building Research.

McLeod, R. 2007. *Passivhaus – Local House.* MSc thesis, University of East London.

McLeod, R. and Hopfe, C. 2013. Hygrothermal implications of low and zero energy standards for building envelope performance in the UK. *Journal of Building Performance Simulation*, 6 (5): 1–18, Special Issue: Heat and moisture – issues and applications. DOI: 10.1080/19401493.2012.7628094

McLeod, R., Hopfe, C. and Rezgui, Y. 2012a. An investigation into recent proposals for a revised definition of Zero Carbon homes in the UK. *Energy Policy*, 46 (2012): 25–35.

McLeod, R. S., Hopfe, C. J. and Rezgui, Y. 2012b. A proposed method for generating high resolution current and future climate data for Passivhaus design. *Energy and Buildings*, 55: 481–93.

McLeod, R. S., Hopfe, C. J. and Kwan, A. (2013) An investigation into future performance and overheating risks in Passivhaus dwellings. *Building and Environment*, 70: 189–209.

Mennel, S., Menti, U-P. and Notter, G. 2007. MINERGIE-P® – A building standard of the future. *Proceedings of Clima 2007 WellBeing Indoors*, REHVA World Congress, Helsinki, 10–14 June.

Meyer, A. 2000. *Contraction and Convergence: The Global Solution to Climate Change.* Dartington: Green Books Ltd.

Mobbs, P. 2005. *Energy Beyond Oil.* Leicester: Matador Publishing.

PassREg. 2013. *Newsletter*, 30 June. [Online]. Available at: www.passreg.eu/index.php?page_id=336

Pfeiffer, A., Koschenz, M. and Wokaun, A. 2005. Energy and building technology for the 2000 W society – potential of residential buildings in Switzerland. *Energy and Buildings*, 37 (11): 1158–74 p1169.

PHI. 1998. *Energy Balances with the Passive House Planning Package; Protocol Volume No. 13 of the Research Group for Cost-effective Passive Houses.* Darmstadt: Passive House Institute (only available in German).

PHI. 1999. Schnieders, J. and Feist, W. *Wärmebrückenfreies Konstruieren. CEPHEUS-Projektinformation Nr.6.* Darmstadt: Passive House Institute.

PHI. 2014. *Design PH – the 3D Interface for PHPP.* [Software]. Available at: www.designph.org/ (accessed December 2014).

Rosenthal, E. 2008. Houses with no furnace but plenty of heat. *The New York Times*, 26 December. Available at: www.nytimes.com/2008/12/27/world/europe/27house.html?ref=world&pagewanted=all (accessed 27 December 2008).

Schnieders, J. 2003. CEPHEUS – Measurement results from more than 100 dwelling units in Passive Houses. In *Proceedings of the ECEEE 2003 Summer Study – Time to Turn Down Energy Demand*, Stockholm, ECEEE, pp. 341–51.

Schnieders, J. and Feist, W. 2002. *Passiv-Verwaltungsgebaeude Wagner & Co in Coelbe. Messdatenauswertung mit Hilfe der dynamischen Genaeudesimulation.* Darmstadt: Passivhaus Insitut.

Schnieders, J. and Hermelink, A. (2006) CEPHEUS results: measurements and occupants' satisfaction provide evidence for Passive Houses being an option for sustainable building. *Energy Policy*, 34 (2) 151–71.

Stephan, A., Crawford, R. and de Myttenaereb, K. 2012. Towards a comprehensive life cycle energy analysis framework for residential buildings. *Energy and Buildings*, 55: 592–600. DOI: 10.1016/j.enbuild.2012.09.008

Stern, N. 2006. *The Economics of Climate Change*. Cambridge: Cambridge University Press.

Tirpak, D., Ashton, J., Dadi, Z., Fillho, L. G. M., Metx, B., Parry, M., Schnellnhuber, J., Seng Yap, K., Watson, R. and Wigley, T. 2005. Avoiding dangerous climate change. *International Symposium on the Stabilisation of Green House Gas Emissions*, Hadley Centre Met Office Exeter, UK, 1–3 Feb, p. 5. Available at: www.stabilisation2005.com/Steering_Commitee_Report.pdf

Vallentin, R., 2009. *Energieeffizienter Stadtebau mit Passivhausern- Herleitung belatbarer Klimaschutzstandards im Wohnungsbau*. PhD thesis, Technical University of Munich.

WAG (Welsh Assembly Government). 2004. *Fuel Poverty in Wales, 2004: Evaluating the Impact of Energy Price Rises on Fuel Poverty*. Cardiff: WAG. Available at: http://wales.gov.uk/?lang=en

Winter, S. 2011. *Greenhouse Gas Emissions in Federal Buildings*. [Online] Available at: www.wbcsd.org/resources/greenhousegasemissions.php (accessed June 2011).

World Bank. 2010. *World Development Report 2010: Development and Climate Change*. Washington, DC: World Bank. Available at: https://openknowledge.worldbank.org/handle/10986/4387

Worldwatch Institute, 2014. Energy agency predicts high prices in future. *Worldwatch Institute*, 10 September. [Online]. Available at: www.worldwatch.org/node/5936WRI

World Resources Institute. 2008. *Climate Analysis Indicators Tool (CAIT)*. Washington, DC: WRI.

ZCH (Zero Carbon Hub), 2009. *Defining Zero Carbon Homes: 'Have Your Say' Report*. [Online]. Available at: www.zerocarbonhub.org/sites/default/files/resources/reports/Defining_Zero_Carbon-Have_your_Say_2009.pdf

Notes

1   The United Nations Framework Convention on Climate Change (UNCCC) divides treaty members into three main groups: Annex I governments include industrialised countries that were members of the OECD (Organisation for Economic Co-operation and Development) in 1992, as well as countries with economies in transition (the EIT Parties), including the Russian Federation, the Baltic States, and several Central and Eastern European States. Non-Annex I parties are mostly developing countries.

2   Note that for clarity, lower case 'p' is used to indicate the specific peak load value (i.e. normalised to the Treated Floor Area – TFA) and upper case 'P' is used to indicate the absolute (or total) value. The same applies to other variables such as 'q', which is used for specific heating energy.

3   The standard atmosphere (symbol: atm) is an international reference pressure defined as 101,325 Pa and used as a unit of pressure.

4   In reality the situation is slightly more complex, however, since each PH building will have its own unique $p_{supply,max}$ that may be slightly higher or slightly lower than $10W/m^2$ as a result of its particular design air flow rate, occupant density and limiting air temperatures. For this reason it is technically possible for a given building's p_H to exceed $10W/m^2$ but still be less than its $p_{supply,max}$.

5   The specific annual heat requirement (q_H) refers to the annual useful heat requirement of the building divided by its Treated Floor Area (TFA); for further details see Feist *et al.* (2013).

6   This is an approximate relationship and must always be calculated according to the specific building and context.

7   Thus (as with all buildings) depending on the supplementary heating source used, there is the potential for significant variability in the CO_2 emissions. Assume, for example, the CO_2 intensity of wood pellets is $0.039 kgCO_2/kWh$ vs. $0.519 kgCO_2/kWh$ for electricity (DECC, 2012b: 225); then a factor 13 variation in carbon intensity exists, assuming similar levels of appliance efficiency.

8   In reality, the CoP varies almost constantly as the external air temperature fluctuates and fan speeds adjust to new pressure demands; however, this equation gives a first approximation of the likely efficiency of the system, but does not consider seasonal and in-use performance.

9   n_{50} refers to the reference air change rate due to infiltration and exfiltration at a 50 Pascal pressure differential between the inside and outside of the building in accordance with EN 13829. See BRE Airtightness Primer (2014) for further details.

10 The definition of the Treated Floor Area used by the Passivhaus standard is based on guidelines in the German residential living space ordinance (WoflV) and also the non-residential standard in the German norm DIN 277. Further details can be found in the Passive House Planning Package (Feist *et al.*, 2013).

11 For projections of market volume based cost reductions across a range of micro generation technologies, see EST (2005).

12 The mean reference value for the specific space heating requirement for CEPHEUS projects was approximately 25 kWh/m².

13 This 'normalisation' procedure is pursuant to *EN 832: Thermal Performance of Buildings: Calculation of Energy Use for Heating – Residential Buildings*, European Committee for Standardization, 1998, now superseded by EN ISO 13790:2008.

14 Research (McLeod *et al.*, 2013) has shown that the risks of overheating (and hence potential cooling loads) in warmer future climate scenarios do not preclude overheating risks in Passivhaus dwellings. It is the design optimization (glazing ratios, shading systems, internal loads, etc.) and occupant behaviour of buildings that will largely determine future overheating risks, particularly in Urban Heat Islands (UHIs) and warmer climatic scenarios.

15 Note that some independent national certifying bodies, such as PHIUS, now recognise the use of other tools including WUFI-Passive for design and certification purposes.

16 Primary energy is given as the total primary energy demand for all processes (kWh/m².a) and also for DHW (domestic hot water), heating and auxiliary electricity only (i.e. without lighting and appliances). The primary energy conserved through the use of solar electricity is provided as well; however, this figure does not influence the Primary Energy Requirement target for certification.

17 The term 'near neighbour' refers to the common practice of using a climate file from a location near to the actual building site as a surrogate for the climate which is acting on the building.

2

Thermal and occupant comfort

LOUISE FINNERUP WILLE AND DARREN WOOLF

2.1 Introduction

Thermal comfort is one of the most decisive criteria for occupant well-being in living spaces and can have a major impact on the design of the building envelope and systems used to control the indoor environment. Energy use to achieve thermal comfort targets is therefore heavily influenced by the choice and application of thermal comfort criteria.

Thermal comfort is influenced by a number of subjective perceptions. It is defined in BS EN ISO 7730:2005 (10) as 'that condition of mind which expresses satisfaction with the thermal environment'. The quality of the indoor environment is therefore expressed as the extent to which human requirements are met. Dissatisfaction can be caused by warm or cool discomfort of the body as a whole, as expressed by a thermal comfort index, or by local unwanted cooling or heating of one particular part of the body, for example when sat next to a cold or hot window.

A thermal comfort index is typically derived from a combination of influencing factors:

- occupant parameters: physical activity levels (met) and clothing (clo);
- environmental parameters: air temperature (or dry bulb temperature), mean radiant temperature (related to a measured globe temperature), air velocity and relative air humidity.

The environmental parameters, such as air temperature, may become a primary consideration for sizing of plant, but designing a building envelope and systems that minimise risk of thermal discomfort requires additional considerations. For example, effects due to radiant temperature asymmetry (i.e. large directional variations in surface temperatures), draughts and down draughts from cold glazing, high levels of thermal stratification (i.e. variations in air temperature vertically within the occupied area), and mechanically cooling or warming floors (or ceilings) may all warrant additional considerations (BS EN ISO 7730:2005).

In a Passivhaus, thermal comfort is achieved primarily through the implementation of passive measures, which can be applied not only to the residential sector, but also to commercial, industrial and public buildings.

Because Passivhaus buildings are so cheap to run, they offer affordable comfort. Well-designed Passivhaus buildings provide warm and dry spaces in winter without any surface condensation, and are provided with a constant supply of fresh air without associated draughts or transient drops in temperature.

Overheating is the main concern in terms of thermal comfort in a Passivhaus building. The high levels of thermal inertia and reliance on useful solar gains in winter can lead to a risk of overheating in summer (McLeod et al., 2013; Ridley et al., 2013). A number of strategies can and should be implemented in order to mitigate this situation (e.g. summer bypass on the mechanical ventilation unit, solar shading on windows, careful configuration, orientation and sizing of windows, etc.). However, there is evidence to suggest that the techniques and software used to assess Passivhaus performance does not always accurately predict the risk of overheating. A sophisticated dynamic thermal model may be needed to give a better indication of the indoor thermal environment, and should be considered when assessing the summer situation and climate change-induced risks.

2.2 Basic concepts and terminology

2.2.1 Thermal comfort, discomfort and stress

Thermal comfort is commonly defined as the situation where there is broad satisfaction with the thermal environment – in other words where most people are neither too hot nor too cold. Thermal discomfort is the situation where people start to feel uncomfortable (i.e. they feel too hot or too cold) but are not necessarily made unwell by the conditions and do not suffer medical symptoms due to the discomfort, beyond irritability and tiredness or chills and shivering. Thermal stress (heat stress or cold stress) is defined as the situation where the thermal environment will cause clearly defined potentially harmful medical conditions, such as dehydration or heat exhaustion in hot environments, or frostbite in cold ones. Respiratory problems can occur and there can also be a risk of hypothermia or hyperthermia, where there is a fall or rise in body core temperature which can be harmful and which can potentially prove fatal (CIBSE, 2006b). Such conditions are not uncommon, it is estimated that 31,000 excess winter deaths occurred in England and Wales in 2012/2013 (ONS, 2014).

2.2.2 Surface temperature

An internal surface temperature is often noticed when in direct contact with a building surface through conduction between the surface and the clothing or skin. Internal surface temperatures are a primary driver of heat exchange with the human body through radiant means. Surface temperatures can be measured by a contact thermometer or by using infrared measurement devices (EN ISO 7726:2001).

2.2.3 Air (dry bulb) temperature

This is the temperature registered by a dry thermometer, shielded from radiation, suspended in the air. A typical mercury-in-glass thermometer is not always an accurate measure as sunshine may fall on the bulb or the reading may be affected by a nearby radiant heat or coolth source.

2.2.4 Mean radiant temperature and radiant temperature asymmetry

This is defined as the uniform surface temperature of a radiant black enclosure in which an occupant would exchange the same amount of radiant heat as in an actual (non-uniform) space. It is a function of the respective areas, shapes and surface temperatures of the enclosing surfaces as viewed from a point; i.e. it varies at different points in a room. It is sometimes approximated, under certain conditions, to the average of the surface temperatures at the centre of a room but, in reality, it will also be affected by surface properties (e.g. emissivity) and any solar gains transmitted directly onto the point of interest. In calculations of thermal comfort (overheating for example) it is necessary to include any shortwave radiation that falls on the occupant in the calculation of mean radiant temperature (CIBSE, 2006a: Section 1.3).

The black globe thermometer (sometimes approximated by using a table tennis ball painted black) is frequently used to derive a mean radiant temperature using measured values of globe temperature together with additional measurements of local air temperatures and velocities (EN ISO 7726:2001). In this process, the globe surface serves to effectively 'average' the radiant surface temperatures at the measurement point.

Human comfort is significantly influenced by differences between surface temperatures. A commonly cited example is when a person sits close to a cold window in a heated room. Radiant temperature asymmetry is a measure of the difference in radiant temperatures in two directions from one point. In measurement terms, this quantity is the difference in plane radiant temperature on two opposite sides of a small plane element (EN ISO 7726:2001). Mean radiant temperature can also be calculated from plane radiant temperatures.

2.2.5 Air speed

An air velocity is defined by both its speed and direction and it is not a constant; rather it fluctuates about a mean over time. The air speed (non-directional) describes an air flow rate at a measurement point and can be derived from the average or standard deviation of velocity over an interval of time (EN ISO 7726:2001).

The cooling effect of air movement is well known. If this cooling is not desired, it can give rise to complaints of draught. The temperature of the moving air is not necessarily identical to that of the room air nor that of the incoming ventilation air, but will generally lie between these values. It should also be noted that people are more tolerant of air movement if the direction of the air movement varies. For air speeds greater than 0.15 m/s, the operative temperature should be increased from its 'still air' value to compensate for the cooling effect of air movement (CIBSE, 2006a) as this could otherwise be perceived as a draught.

2.2.6 Operative temperature

Operative temperature (sometimes called dry resultant temperature) combines the dry bulb air temperature and the mean radiant temperature into a single value to express their joint effect. It is a weighted average of the two, the weights depending on the heat transfer coefficients by convection and by radiation at the clothed surface of the occupant. Air speed relates this weighting and a common way operative temperature is expressed is:

$$\theta_c = \frac{\theta_{ai}\sqrt{(10v)} + \theta_r}{1 + \sqrt{(10v)}}$$ [1]

where:

θ_c is the operative temperature (°C),
θ_{ai} is the air temperature (°C),
θ_r is the mean radiant temperature (°C), and
v is the air speed (m/s).

At indoor air speeds less than 0.1 m/s (commonly achieved within well-designed and well-constructed buildings such as Passivhaus developments), this approximates to:

$$\theta_c = \frac{1}{2}\theta_{ai} + \frac{1}{2}\theta_r$$ [2]

2.2.7 Wet (bulb) temperature and relative humidity

Humidity can be expressed as relative or absolute humidity. Absolute humidity influences the evaporative heat loss from a body and therefore the thermal comfort (heat balance). At moderate indoor air conditions and with moderate activity levels, the influence of humidity on thermal comfort is secondary, and therefore a wide range of humidity is acceptable to the human perception of comfort. A maximum indoor air humidity of 12 g/kg is suggested (Feist et al., 2013) as the threshold for determining a dehumidification demand. This corresponds to a relative humidity of approximately 60 per cent at 25°C or 80 per cent at 20°C. This is the point above which mould growth starts to occur on surfaces.

Humidity sources in a residential building typically contribute 2 g of water vapour per m² per hour.

Humid air is made up of a number of gases, including nitrogen, carbon dioxide and oxygen, as well as water vapour, of which it can only hold a certain amount at any given air pressure and temperature. Measurements of air temperature are needed as well as 'wet' temperature to determine the properties of moist air. This relationship is captured in a psychrometric chart that also relates the absolute humidity (moisture content) and relative humidity – see Figure 2.1. Also see CIBSE Guide C – Section 1 (CIBSE, 2007).

At low air speeds the temperature sensed by a wet bulb thermometer is sometimes referred to as a screen temperature and at higher air speeds (>4m/s), as sling temperature. The measurement approach, relying upon the evaporation cooling effect from the bulb, therefore determines the sensed wet bulb temperature value. Care should be taken when correlating the measured wet bulb temperatures to the thermodynamic wet bulb temperature (adiabatic saturation temperature) indicated along the 100 per cent relative humidity curve on the psychrometric chart (EN ISO 7726:2001).

2.3 Setting of traditional thermal comfort targets

As thermal comfort partially describes a person's psychological state of mind, the most common approach to characterising it, forming a thermal comfort model, is to correlate the results of physiological experiments to thermal analysis variables (i.e. the environmental parameters that can be measured). The main

2.1
Example of a Psychrometric chart. As an example, the point shown has a dry bulb temperature of 26°C; a wet bulb temperature of 18°C; relative humidity of 50 per cent; and moisture content of 10 g/kg
Source: adapted from EN ISO 7726:2001

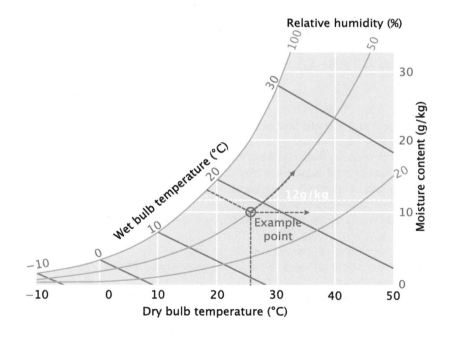

body of this work was carried out by P. Ole Fanger in the 1970s (see Fanger, 1970) with university students as the human subjects providing a vote by expressing their level of comfort under different thermal comfort conditions. This empirical approach has been further developed over subsequent decades and is discussed here as it is traditionally used within studies of the built environment. Alternative methods, such as adaptive comfort, have also been developed and are discussed in the following section.

A common way of setting comfort parameters in a design is to specify both dry bulb and wet bulb targets; for example, 22°C db; 15°C wb.

2.3.1 Thermal heat balance of a human body

The heat balance equation for the human body is the equation describing the rate of heat production to the rate of heat loss. The total metabolic energy produced within the body is the metabolic energy required for the person's activity plus that required for involuntary mechanisms such as shivering. The remaining difference is either stored (which will cause the body's temperature to rise) or dissipated to the environment through the skin surface and respiratory tract. This heat dissipation from the body occurs by several modes of heat exchange: sensible heat flow from the skin and during respiration, latent heat flow from the evaporation of sweat and moisture diffused through the skin, and latent heat released by the evaporation of moisture during respiration. Sensible heat flow from the skin is a mixture of conduction, convection and radiation for a clothed person.

Assuming a body is within an equilibrium (steady) state, the rate of heat production in the body, by metabolism and by performance of external work, equals the heat loss from the body to the environment, by the process of evaporation, respiration, radiation, convection and conduction (Haghighat, 2009). This can be expressed by the equation:

$$M - W = (C + R + E_{sk}) + (C_{res} + E_{res}) \qquad [3]$$

where:

M is the rate of metabolic heat production (W/m^2),
W is the rate of mechanical work accomplished (W/m^2),
$C + R$ is the sensible heat loss from skin (W/m^2),
E_{sk} is the rate of total evaporative heat loss from the skin (W/m^2),
C_{res} is the rate of convective heat loss from respiration (W/m^2), and
E_{res} is the rate of evaporative heat loss from respiration (W/m^2).
The unit m^2 refers to the surface area of the unclothed body.

Thermal discomfort is experienced by an occupant when the body is not in equilibrium for any length of time, or can be experienced if there is an asymmetry in the temperatures of surfaces surrounding the body, either laterally or vertically, or as a result of draughts.

Thermal and occupant comfort

Table 2.1 sets out the main independent quantities involved in the analysis of the thermal balance between the human body and the thermal environment.

Table 2.1 The main independent quantities involved in the analysis of the thermal balance between the human body and the thermal environment

	Air temperature	Mean radiant temperature	Air velocity	Absolute humidity of the air (partial pressure of water vapour)	Insulation of clothing	Evaporative resistance of clothing	Metabolism	External work
Internal heat production							✓	✓
Heat transfer by radiation		✓			✓			
Heat transfer by convection *	✓		✓		✓			
Heat losses through evaporation – Evaporation from the skin			✓	✓		✓		
– Evaporation by respiration				✓			✓	
Convection by respiration	✓						✓	

Source: EN ISO 7726:2001

Note:

* Heat transfer by convection is also influenced by body movements. The resultant air velocity at skin level is called relative air velocity. Heat conduction (surface temperature) only has a limited influence on the total heat balance.

2.3.2 Predicted Mean Vote (PMV)

Due to individual differences, it is impossible to specify a thermal environment that will satisfy everybody. There will always be a percentage of uncomfortable or dissatisfied occupants, as some people naturally feel colder or hotter than the 'norm', or mean. But it is possible to specify environments predicted to be acceptable by a certain percentage of the occupants.

The Predicted Mean Vote (PMV) is an index that predicts the mean value of the votes of a large group of persons on a seven-point thermal sensation scale (see Figure 2.2), based on the heat balance of the human body. Thermal balance, described in the scale as 'neutral', is obtained when the internal heat production in the body is equal to the loss of heat to the environment. In a moderate

Hot: +3 — ●
Warm: +2 — ●
Slightly warm: +1 — ○
Neutral: 0 — ●
Slightly cool: −1 — ●
Cool: −2 — ●
Cold: −3 — ●

environment, the human thermoregulatory system will automatically attempt to modify skin temperature and sweat secretion to maintain heat balance (BS EN ISO 7730:2005).

PMV calculations take into account effective mechanical power, the air temperature, mean radiant temperature, relative air velocity, water vapour partial pressure, convective heat transfer, relative humidity of air and individual parameters such as metabolic rate, insulation from clothing, clothing surface area and clothing surface temperature. For more information, see BS EN ISO 7730:2005. The recommended PMV range for acceptable internal comfort is between −0.5 and +0.5 (ASHRAE, 2013).

2.3.3 Predicted Percentage Dissatisfied (PPD)

The PMV calculation ascertains the mean value of a thermal vote by a large group of people exposed to the same environment. But individual votes are typically scattered around this mean value and it is useful to be able to predict the number of people likely to feel uncomfortably warm or cool.

The Predicted Percentage Dissatisfied (PPD) is another index that establishes a quantitative prediction of the percentage of thermally dissatisfied people (i.e. those feeling too cool or too warm). For the purposes of this International Standard, thermally dissatisfied people are those who will vote hot, warm, cool or cold on the seven-point thermal sensation scale given in Figure 2.2. Figure 2.3 shows the Predicted Percentage Dissatisfied (PPD) as a function of the Predicted Mean Vote (PMV).

It is interesting to note that even where the entire group registers their discomfort level as '0', there will still be 5 per cent of the group who are dissatisfied.

2.3.4 Limitations of traditional approach

Fanger's work was based upon observations from climate chamber experiments in conditions that were kept constant for a number of hours so that a steady state had been reached (CIBSE, 2013). Predictions of conditions for optimal comfort also required information relating to the occupants, such as

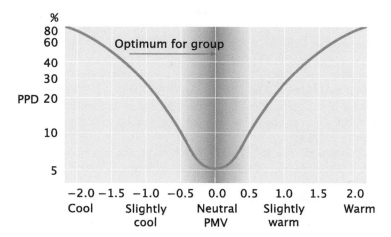

2.3
Predicted Percentage
Dissatisfied (PPD) as a
function of Predicted Mean
Vote (PMV)
Source: adapted from BS EN
ISO 7730:2005

clothing levels and metabolic rates. In addition, all four environmental parameters (air temperature, mean radiant temperature, humidity levels and air speed) need to be measured, calculated or assumed. There are therefore a large number of assumptions or calculations needed which are then applied to a virtual person. There is, however, no allowance made for variation in activity or clothing levels for a large number of occupants. Additional limitations of this 'static' approach are that the chamber approach doesn't allow for cultural, climatic and social context of the targeted environments and their occupants.

This traditional empirical approach does not make any additional allowances for the impact that people may have on their own perceptions of comfort, and how they change these through their own actions. This may be a building control action, such as opening a window or operating a blind, or just a personal action such as removing a jacket. The result of fixing many of the inputs to a comfort index is that the design environment may end up being quite static and inflexible as well as highly serviced. Other challenges in using a traditional approach relate to dealing with mixed-mode buildings (naturally ventilated with comfort cooling available when higher temperatures are experienced) and understanding the operation and targets in each of the different modes. Taking advantage of opportunities for adaptation and applying an alternative approach to the selection of thermal comfort targets is more likely to lead to a positive rating for a particular environment.

2.4 Setting of alternative thermal comfort targets

There are many comfort standards that can be applied to naturally ventilated, mechanically ventilated and mixed-mode buildings. It may be necessary not only to specify an appropriate standard but also to clearly define measurable limits or ranges for each of the environmental parameters for example, making allowance, where possible, for any interactions that might occur. Some international standards that should be considered when developing a strategy for thermal comfort include:

- ISO Standard BS EN ISO 7730:2005 which includes PMV and PPD calculations;
- ANSI/ASHRAE Standard 55 which follows BS EN ISO 7730 for mechanically ventilated buildings but then introduces, for naturally ventilated buildings, an acceptable range of operative temperatures related to the outdoor condition (ASHRAE, 2013);
- CEN Standard BS EN 15251:2007 which is similar in a number of ways to ASHRAE Standard 55 but uses a slightly different definition for the outdoor condition;
- CIBSE TM52 (CIBSE, 2013).

The latter two standards also make allowances for building usage classification – for example, premium office space – but there is an inherent problem that all the standards attempt to be very precise for thermal comfort-related phenomena in a field that is far from precise. Even allowing for the inherent limitations of comfort standards, the adaptive approach to defining thermal comfort is gaining popularity and being added to some of the above standards. This is particularly the case for free-running naturally ventilated buildings and is discussed in further detail below.

2.4.1 Adaptive thermal comfort

Adaptive comfort approaches have been developed over the last 15 years or so and are being applied to more and more building designs (Nicol, 2011). One driver for this has been that traditional approaches, based upon heat balance theory, have been shown to be limited in some applications and that occupants tend to be far more tolerant of variations in indoor conditions than what is predicted using a traditional empirical approach, particularly in naturally ventilated spaces.

The adaptive model is based upon field surveys of people in their normal surroundings (typically office environments) and assumes that the thermal sense is an important element of thermoregulatory behaviour; i.e. people will try to react to discomfort by taking means to restore their comfort. Buildings can therefore start to be viewed not as providers of comfort but rather as providers of the means to achieve their comfort objectives as part of an interactive balancing process.

The adaptive approach to thermal comfort makes no distinction between types of ventilation systems (e.g. mechanical or natural) but only relates the extent to which indoor thermal comfort is adaptive as a function of how closely coupled the indoor environment is to the outdoor one. The adaptability includes both mechanical (e.g. building controls) and non-mechanical (e.g. adjustment of clothing insulation levels) means. It should be noted, however, that one person opening a window could negatively impact on the level of comfort of others.

By having some degree of control over their personal thermal environment, a person is more likely to adjust their expectations leading to a wider comfort temperature range, i.e. an increased tolerance of conditions. This tolerance extends to season and climate; for example, people in warmer climates would be more tolerant of warmer indoor air temperatures and vice versa for cold climates – acclimatisation being a physiological response.

Indoor comfort temperature as a function of outdoor temperature is typically defined in the following form (Halawa and van Hoof, 2012).

$$T_{comf} = A \cdot T_{a,out} + B \qquad\qquad [4]$$

where:

T_{comf} is the comfort temperature (°C),
$T_{a,out}$ is the monthly mean outdoor air temperature (°C) – note a number of formulations of this exist including a running mean value, and
A, B are constants.

Recognition of this acceptance of variable conditions is highlighted within the ASHRAE (American Society of Heating, Refrigerating, and Air-Conditioning Engineers) comfort charts which Figures 2.4 and 2.5 are based on. For example, the mechanical ventilation chart (Figure 2.4) shows that an increase in clothing insulation level (0.5 clo to 1.0 clo) unsurprisingly leads to greater comfort in cooler conditions – the indoor operative temperature. Likewise, for a naturally ventilated building (Figure 2.5), there is a greater acceptance of lower indoor operative temperature when the outdoor air temperature is lower.

2.4
ASHRAE comfort chart for mechanically ventilated buildings
Source: adapted from Halawa and van Hoof (2012)

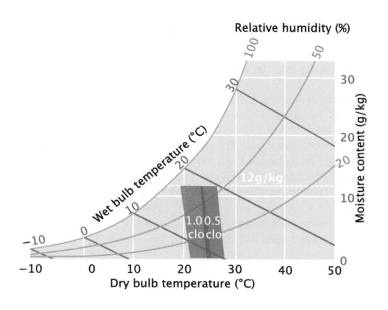

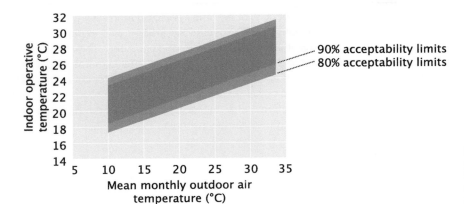

2.5
ASHRAE comfort chart for naturally ventilated buildings
Source: adapted from Halawa and van Hoof (2012)

The risk of overheating is also sometimes defined in relation to multiple criteria. In CIBSE TM52, three criteria are described as follows, where failing two out of three is classed as overheating for a free-running building (CIBSE, 2013):

- Criterion 1: Provides a limit on the number of hours over a period that the indoor operative temperature can exceed an upper defined limit for it;
- Criterion 2: Uses a weighting which allows for the degree to which the targeted range is exceeded;
- Criterion 3: Defines a maximum upper limit not to be exceeded.

Due to the complexities and nuances associated with adaptive comfort models in application, it is advised that the literature cited above together with other related material is reviewed prior to application in order to provide context and guidance in application. Other key publications include CIBSE TM36 (2005) (CIBSE, 2005) and CIBSE AM11 (2015) (CIBSE, 2015).

2.4.2 Limitations of adaptive comfort approaches

While simple in concept, relating an acceptable indoor comfort temperature to the outdoor air temperature has a number of limitations. Some of those limitations relate to the fact that it ignores many of the physical factors captured within the more traditional methods. For example, although some parameters such as clothing level could perhaps be correlated to the outdoor condition, the key environmental parameters of air speed and mean radiant temperature would be much more difficult to correlate against outdoor air temperature (Halawa and van Hoof, 2012).

The field of thermal comfort and how it is applied within comfort standards is being heavily researched and is, therefore, likely to evolve further with time. It is important for the practitioner to be aware of the key options for traditional and alternative methods and how they should be applied to the particular building type in consideration of systems and usage. Impacts on energy use and sustainability are other primary considerations ensuring any comparisons in design performance are comparable; for example, if the adaptive comfort approach leads to a cooler building in winter and warmer in summer.

Thermal comfort research has typically been conducted in very short time steps, often using populations of healthy office workers. It is important to note therefore that the concept of 'thermal comfort' cannot be conflated with ranking the risks of long-term impacts on occupant health (see Chapter 8). There is evidence to suggest that people may report experiencing thermal comfort whilst physiologically displaying signs that suggest they are at risk of long-term health implications (Basu and Samet, 2002a, 2002b).

2.5 Thermal comfort in Passivhaus

Contrary to popular belief, the Passivhaus standard was never intended as a standard solely for reducing energy demand. The functional definition of a Passivhaus states:

> A Passive House is a building, for which thermal comfort ... can be achieved solely by postheating or postcooling of the fresh air mass, which is required to fulfil sufficient indoor air quality conditions ... without a need for additional recirculated air.
>
> (Feist, 2006)

The thermal comfort analysis in a Passivhaus revolves around the same environmental parameters as mentioned in the sections above, and is assessed by looking at four separate measures: radiant temperature asymmetry, temperature stratification, draughts, and risk of overheating (described in more detail below). The first three parameters are mostly important in winter when the thermal comfort revolves around keeping residents feeling sufficiently warm. The overheating parameter is mostly important in summer (for Central and Northern European climates, but for Southern Europe or other warm regions, the overheating parameter will be significant in a greater range of seasons).

In a Passivhaus, thermal comfort is achieved through the use of passive measures listed below which can be applied not only to the residential sector but also to commercial, industrial and public buildings.

- Exemplar levels of insulation with minimal thermal bridges and thermally very high performing windows. This is important to maintain comfortable temperatures at low energy levels and reduce radiant temperature asymmetry.
- Excellent level of airtightness. This is important to reduce cold draughts.
- Good indoor air quality and maintaining comfortable temperatures by use of mechanical ventilation with summer bypass (though openable windows are usually also part of the design in order to maintain a degree of user control over the ventilation strategy). This is important to ensure a good indoor climate without relying on the intake of cold air in winter.
- Optimising the use of heat from passive solar gains and internal heat sources

when needed. This is part of the strategy for keeping comfortable internal temperatures but maintaining a low energy consumption.

- Solar shading externally to windows (fixed; movable, such as venetian blinds; or seasonal, such as deciduous trees). This is important to minimise overheating in summer.

2.5.1 Radiant temperature asymmetry

As described above, human comfort is significantly influenced by differences between surface temperatures. If occupants are exposed to a radiant temperature asymmetry greater than 5 K it can lead to feelings of thermal discomfort (BS EN ISO 7730:2005). The comfort target for radiant temperature asymmetry in a Passivhaus has been set even lower at ≤4 K as part of the strategy to ensure excellent levels of comfort.

The windows in a Passivhaus are the most important element to look at in this respect as this is where the coldest (and warmest) surface temperatures in the building are likely to occur. Only windows with a U-value of $U_W < 0.80$ W/m²K for the glazing and frame combined are likely to lead to a radiant temperature asymmetry below 4 K (valid for Central Europe) without the use of a radiator placed below the window (BS EN ISO 7730:2005). In warmer regions (e.g. Southern Europe) a higher U_W (i.e. a lower thermal resistance) could still see this criterion achieved (Feist, 2007) (see Chapter 3).

This U-value criterion for glazing is currently only fulfilled with triple glazing, although products are developing all the time. New developments in, for example, vacuum glazing could potentially see these U-values achieved with double glazing in the future.

2.5.2 Temperature stratification

Closely linked with perceptions of good thermal comfort is low temperature stratification. Again, windows play an important role. Cold window surface temperatures tend to drive down draughts of air in a room if not counteracted by a radiator located close to and below the surface. Warm air cools down at the cold window and then descends and spreads over the floor. If a human body registers an air temperature difference of more than 2 K between the head and the ankles whilst sitting, this can start to lead to feelings of discomfort (BS EN ISO 7730:2005; Feist, 2007).

This is the reason for the Passivhaus comfort criterion that vertical air temperature difference should be no more than 2 K between ankle height (0.1 m) and the head height of a seated person (1.1 m), measured at a distance of 50 cm from the window.

Passivhaus dwellings achieve this criterion by maintaining the uniformity of internal surface temperatures. Ensuring that air does not cool down at surfaces such as windows and external walls and floors guarantees that occupants will not get a sensation of cold feet or warm head from excessive stratification.

2.5.3 Draughts (US: drafts)

Airtightness is a key requirement of Passivhaus, with a maximum allowable air leakage (infiltration) rate of 0.6 air changes per hour at 50 Pascals. This is a very low permissible air leakage rate; approximately five to ten times lower than typical new-build dwellings in the UK. This requirement is not just set because of energy reductions; it is also a comfort parameter. Localised air leakage and draughts can have a great impact on the occupants' perception of thermal comfort, and can lead to occupants feeling subjectively colder than the mean internal air temperature suggests (BS EN ISO 7730:2005).

Together with the requirement for U-values of windows and low temperature stratification, draughts above 0.15 m/s should not occur in a Passivhaus. This is the speed above which humans would typically begin to notice draughts in buildings at operative temperatures below 22.5°C (Arens *et al.*, 2009).

2.5.4 Overheating

As space heating has historically dominated the CO_2 emissions profile for dwellings in temperate climates, the quest for lowering carbon emissions in dwellings in the UK has focused largely on lowering the heating demand by reducing losses from thermal emissions and making optimum use of passive solar gains. While this strategy generally creates very comfortable homes in the winter situation with relatively low energy uses, the approach may be exacerbating problems with overheating of dwellings.

Overheating of homes over prolonged periods can have serious consequences for the health of occupants, and in extreme cases there can be a risk to life. With average temperatures set to increase, and more extreme hot spells anticipated, overheating of homes is likely to become more commonplace in the future (ZeroCarbonHub, 2010).

Although the increased insulation levels and triple-glazed windows in a Passivhaus reduce the heat transmission through the thermal envelope and help to keep a building cool in summer (as well as warm in winter), the great thermal inertia and reliance on useful solar gains for the winter weather situation means that buildings can be prone to overheat in summer, especially where they have been designed with large south- or west-facing windows. In fact, overheating is the main concern in terms of thermal comfort in a Passivhaus building (McLeod *et al.*, 2013; Ridley *et al.*, 2013).

The Passivhaus Institute (PHI) classifies summer thermal comfort in five different categories as outlined in Table 2.2. This assessment is based on the frequency of overheating beyond the threshold of an operative temperature of 25°C during the occupied period.

2.5.4.1 Mitigating overheating

A number of strategies can and should be implemented in order to mitigate overheating in a Passivhaus, both in the design and operation of the building.

Table 2.2 Assessment of the frequency of overheating calculated in the 'Summer' worksheet

h>25°C	Assessment
>15%	Catastrophic
10–15%	Poor
5–10%	Acceptable
2–5%	Good
0–2%	Excellent

Source: Feist *et al.* (2013)

Solar radiation has a great influence on internal surface temperatures and thereby air temperatures. Direct solar radiation in summer should therefore be limited where possible to protect occupants from the risk of thermal discomfort and overheating.

Careful configuration, orientation and sizing of windows are all important, but external solar shading is also of crucial importance for the thermal comfort in summer, and to some extent in spring and autumn as well. Shading should be considered especially on large windows facing south, east or west.

Shading can be provided from a number of sources such as: surrounding landscape topography, neighbouring buildings, window overhangs, fixed or, preferably, retractable external shading to windows, trees, etc. Deciduous trees can be a good strategy to limit overheating especially for east- and west-facing windows where the sun is low enough to be obstructed by the trees in summer, spring and autumn, and where leaves will fall off the trees in winter to allow maximum solar ingress at the time of year when it is most needed.

It is also recommended to cool a building naturally as long as temperatures outside are lower than inside in summer (e.g. at night), and to bypass the heat recovery on the mechanical ventilation unit during summer months unless active cooling is used (see Chapter 8).

There have already been documented reports of overheating in Passivhaus dwellings in the UK (Bere Architects, 2012; Ridley *et al.*, 2013; McLeod *et al.*, 2013). Anecdotal evidence suggests this may be due to the fact that features installed to reduce overheating are not being employed correctly by occupants (e.g. external blinds not being deployed, windows not being opened at night-time). It is an inherent issue for overheating mitigation strategies that, when relying on occupant behaviour to minimise solar ingress and maximise natural cooling (opening of windows) at appropriate times, the strategies are not always implemented in the way designers have intended. For example, solar shading is often not employed by occupants for visual comfort reasons (feeling of being 'holed up inside'), or windows are not opened at night for security reasons – real or perceived. If relying on openable windows at night as an overheating mitigation strategy, care should be taken by designers to ensure that acoustic and air pollution conditions on the site fall within acceptable limits.

There is also evidence to suggest that the software used to assess Passivhaus performance does not always accurately predict the risk of overheating (Larsen and Jensen, 2011). More sophisticated dynamic thermal modelling analysis would provide a better indication of the indoor thermal environment. This should therefore be considered in the design of a Passivhaus in order to ensure the design enables residents to be comfortable in summer and that designs are future-proofed against projected climatic changes (see Chapter 5).

References

Arens, E., Turner, S., Zhang, H., Paliaga, G. 2009. Moving air for comfort. *ASHRAE Journal*, 51 (5): 18–29. Available at: https://www.ashrae.org/File%20Library/.../arens–052009–feature.pdf (accessed 8 August 2014).

ASHRAE. 2013. *Standard 55: Thermal Environmental Conditions for Human Occupancy*. Atlanta, GA: American Society of Heating, Refrigerating, and Air-Conditioning Engineers (ASHRAE).

Basu, R. and Samet, J. 2002a. Relation between elevated ambient temperature and mortality: a review of the epidemiologic evidence. *Epidemiologic Reviews*, 24 (2): 190–202. Available at: http://dx.doi.org/10.1093/epirev/mxf007

Basu, R. and Samet, J. 2002b. An exposure assessment study of ambient heat exposure in an elderly population in Baltimore, Maryland. *Environmental Health Perspectives*, 110 (12): 1219–24. Available at: http://ehpnet1.niehs.nih.gov/docs/2002/110p1219-24

Bere Architects. 2012. Bere Architects – Larch House: Soft Landings Summer Workshop [Video]. Available at: http://bere.co.uk/films/larch-house-soft-landings-summer-workshop (accessed 13 August 2014).

BS EN ISO 7730:2005. *Ergonomics of the Thermal Environment — Analytical Determination and Interpretation of Thermal Comfort Using Calculation of the PMV and PPD Indices and Local Thermal Comfort Criteria*. s.l.: British Standards (BSi).

BS EN 15251:2007. *Indoor Environmental Input Parameters for Design and Assessment of Energy Performance of Buildings Addressing Indoor Air Quality, Thermal Environment, Lighting and Acoustics*. s.l.: British Standards (BSi).

CIBSE. 2005. *Technical Memorandum (TM) 36: Climate Change and the Indoor Environment: Impacts and Adaptation*. London: The Chartered Institution of Building Services Engineers (CIBSE).

CIBSE. 2006a. *CIBSE Guide A – Environmental Design*. London: The Chartered Institution of Building Services Engineers (CIBSE).

CIBSE. 2006b. *CIBSE Knowledge Series (KS) 6: Comfort*. London: The Chartered Institution of Building Services Engineers (CIBSE).

CIBSE. 2007. *CIBSE Guide C – Reference Data*. London: The Chartered Institution of Building Services Engineers (CIBSE).

CIBSE. 2013. *Technical Memorandum (TM) 52: The Limits of Thermal Comfort: Avoiding Overheating in European Buildings*, London: The Chartered Institution of Building Services Engineers (CIBSE).

CIBSE. 2015. *Applications Manual (AM) 11: Building Performance Modelling*. London: The Chartered Institution of Building Services Engineers (CIBSE).

EN ISO 7726:2001. *Ergonomics of the Thermal Environment – Instruments for Measuring Physical Quantities*. s.l.: British Standards (BSi).

Fanger, P. O. 1970. *Thermal Comfort – Analysis and Applications in Environmental Engineering*. New York: McGraw-Hill.

Feist, W. 2006. *Definition of Passive Houses*. [Online]. Available at: www.passivhaustagung.de/Passive_House_E/passivehouse_definition.html (accessed 5 March 2015).

Feist, W. 2007. *Comfort in the Passive House – Why Better Thermal Insulation Always Leads to Better Comfort*. [Online]. Available at: www.passivhaustagung.de/Passive_House_E/comfort_passive_house.htm (accessed 8 August 2014).

Feist, W., Pfluger, R., Schnieders, J., Kah, O., Kaufmann, B., Krick, B., Bastian, Z. and Ebbel, W. 2013. *Passive House Planning Package (PHPP) Version 8*. [Software]. Darmstadt: Passive House Institute.

Haghighat, F. 2009. Thermal comfort in housing and thermal environments. *Sustainable Built Environment*, 1: 326–47.

Halawa, E. and van Hoof, J. 2012. The adaptive approach to thermal comfort: a critical overview. *Energy and Buildings*, 51: 101–10.

Larsen, T. S. and Jensen, R. L. 2011. Comparison of measured and calculated values for the indoor environment in one of the first Danish Passive Houses. *Proceedings of Building Simulation 2011: 12th Conference of International Building Performance Simulation Association*, Sydney, 14–16 November.

McLeod, R., Hopfe, C. and Kwan, A. 2013. An investigation into future performance and overheating risks in Passivhaus dwellings. *Building and Environment*, 70: 189–209. Available at: http://dx.doi.org/10.1016/j.buildenv.2013.08.024

Nicol, J. F. 2011. Adaptive comfort. *Building Research and Information*, 39 (2): 105–7.

ONS. 2014. *Excess Winter Mortality in England and Wales, 2012/13 (Provisional) and 2011/12 (Final): Statistical Bulletin*. London: Office for National Statistics. Available at: www.ons.gov.uk (accessed 22 August 2014).

Ridley, I., Clarke, A., Bere, J., Altamirano, H., Lewis, S., Durdev, M. and Farr, A. 2013. The monitored performance of the first new London dwelling certified to the Passive House standard. *Energy and Buildings*, 63: 67–78.

ZeroCarbonHub. 2010. *Carbon Compliance for Tomorrow's New Homes: A Review of the Modelling Tool and Assumptions*. Milton Keynes: ZeroCarbonHub.

3

Introduction to building physics
Implications for opaque and transparent building components

NIALL CROSSON, ROBERT S. MCLEOD AND CHRISTINA J. HOPFE

3.1 Introduction

As the human race has evolved, it has become more adept at controlling its living environment. From the Neolithic era, when people first began to live in permanent constructions, to modern times the building envelope has been transformed from primarily providing shelter to also preventing heat loss, providing ventilation, and controlling humidity and comfort, while at the same time being aesthetically pleasing. Today the modern building envelope controls the passage of heat, air, moisture, light, sound and even pollutants.

Historically, humans adapted their buildings to cope with macro- and micro-climatic conditions depending on the local environment using vernacular forms and local building materials. The compact forms of ancient buildings such as Newgrange in Ireland were even designed to receive solar gains during the winter solstice, the shortest days of the year. Every winter during the solstice, the entrance passage of this Neolithic building is illuminated by the sun's rays. Man's understanding of construction and the close relationship and dependence on the

3.1
An external view of Newgrange, Ireland built about 3200 BC during the Neolithic period (left) compared with a Passivhaus located at the Technical University in Darmstadt (right) Sources: BoyneValleyTours.com (left) and C. Hopfe (right)

environment was deeply understood even as far back as 6000 BC, evidence shows that the sole opening in Chinese village houses typically faces south (Perlin, 2013).

In the modern era, thanks to advances in heating and cooling technologies (and until recently, an abundant amount of cheap fossil fuels), buildings could be designed and inhabited in areas which were once uninhabitable simply by mechanically conditioning the living environment.

As fossil fuel resources diminish, and with the discernible link between carbon emissions and climate change, it is essential that the foundation of any low energy building design is built on an energy-efficient fabric using, and where possible, materials with minimal environmental impact.

In contrast to our agrarian past, people in the developed world now spend up to 90 per cent of their lives living and working in buildings (Mitchell, 2014). It is clear that the internal environment within buildings has a direct impact on human comfort, health and general well-being. While renewable energy is to be championed, this form of energy will not provide optimal thermal comfort if the building envelope is not designed to complement local climatic conditions.

High levels of thermal insulation, the elimination of thermal bridges and significantly improved levels of airtightness are becoming the norm in modern forms of construction, and are a prerequisite for low energy buildings and Passivhaus construction. Whilst this approach is designed to reduce unwanted heat losses and gains, it will also significantly alter the building envelope's relationship with the external environment. Without forethought and an understanding of the mechanisms by which various environmental processes and materials interact, significant problems such as condensation and overheating can occur. Long-term condensation build-up, for example, can lead to structural degradation as well as negative impacts on indoor air quality. In the development of low energy building fabrics it is critical that structural integrity and occupant health are not compromised.

This chapter provides an introduction to the opaque and glazed building envelope, and looks at the underlying principles as well as some of the construction types and materials commonly found in Passivhaus buildings, including requirements for glazing in different climatic zones.

3.2 Building envelope – opaque

3.2.1 Building form

The shape, size and orientation of a building can all have a significant impact on its useful energy requirements. The compactness ratio (SA/V ratio; SA: surface area of building envelope, V: volume of the building) has a pronounced influence on the heating and cooling demand, independently of the thermal transmittance value (U-value) of the building fabric.

Thus buildings can have identical U-values, air change rates, window areas and orientations yet feature very different heating and cooling demands simply because of their SA/V ratio. Very small buildings (such as detached bungalows) have an inherently high surface area to volume ratio compared to larger buildings.

This can be demonstrated mathematically by considering the SA/V equation for a cube (equation 1).

$$S/AV_{cube} = \frac{6x^2}{x^3} = \frac{6}{x}$$ [1]

where:

S/AV_{cube} is the surface area to volume ratio of a perfect cube (regular hexahedron), and
x is the length of one side of the cube (m).
Thus it can be seen that the larger the dimension (x), the smaller the SA/V ratio.

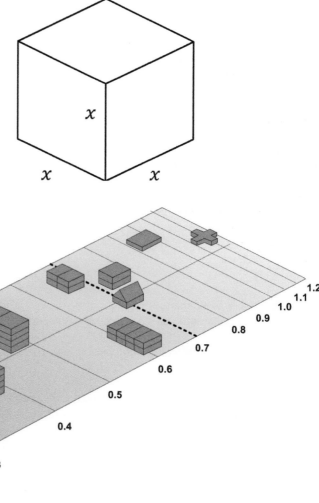

3.2
Surface area to volume ratio
of a compact cube form

3.3
SA/V ratios of different
building types. A cost-effective
SA/V for small domestic
building should generally be
less than 0.7 m²/m³
Source: adapted from PHD

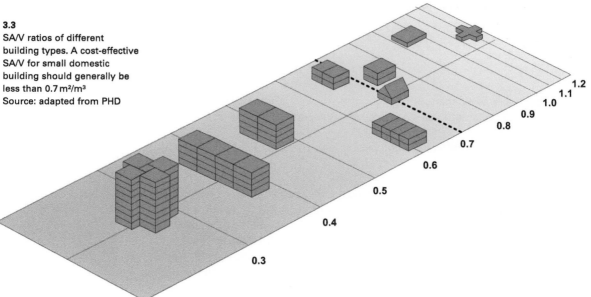

A similar indicator of compactness is the 'form factor', which describes the Surface Area to Treated Floor Area ratio (SA/TFA). This ratio can be helpful when comparing the compactness of different building variants which have the same TFA.

An SA/V ratio of $0.7\,m^{-1}$ (or a form factor of 3) is considered to be approaching the upper limit beyond which small domestic dwellings (in a Central European climate) may become uneconomic (or incur additional costs) in order to comply with the Passivhaus standard. Conversely as buildings become bigger, there is increased tolerance to relax the compactness ratio without substantially reducing thermal performance (Figure 3.3).

3.2.2 Airtight envelopes

Uncontrolled air leakage into and out of a structure occurs due to small holes and cracks in the building fabric as well as through poorly sealed windows and doors. Air leakage is driven by pressure differentials occurring between the inside and the outside of a building as a result of temperature differences, air currents and wind pressure. The consequences of air leakage include an increased demand for space heating and cooling, reduced comfort, draughts, and moisture convection.

For Passivhaus certification the airtightness target is expressed as n_{50}, which is defined as the number of air changes occurring each hour in the building at a reference pressure differential of +/– 50 Pascals (i.e. when tested both above and below the outside air pressure). Since the result is calculated using the building's net internal air volume (m^3) rather than its envelope area (m^2), the units are expressed as ac/h or h^{-1} (equation 2).

$$n_{50} = \frac{v_{50}}{V_{n50}}$$

[2]

where

n_{50} is the number of air changes per hour at a pressure differential of 50 Pa (h^{-1}),
v_{50} is the mean volumetric air flow rate at a pressure differential of +/– 50 Pa (m^3/h),
V_{n50} is the net air volume within the building (as defined by BS EN 13829:2001 and PHI)[1] (m^3).

In order to comply with the Passivhaus standard, the final air pressure test carried out at completion of the building must demonstrate $n_{50} \leq 0.6\ h^{-1}$ @ 50 Pa.[2] This level of air leakage is approximately five times less (McLeod et al., 2014) than the maximum currently allowed by the UK Building regulations (HM Government, 2013).

To achieve such stringent targets it is essential to specify a single continuous airtight barrier using appropriate materials. In practice the airtight barrier is usually also a vapour control layer (VCL), and is positioned on the warm side of the construction assembly in order to prevent both warm air and moisture vapour from entering the insulation and structural layers. An additional

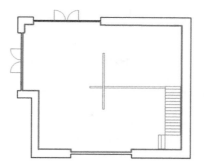

3.4
Floor plan showing position of
airtight barrier (red) and wind
barrier (blue)

wind barrier layer (WBL) is often used on the outside of framed constructions; this barrier is diffusion open but wind resistant and is designed to stop unwanted cold external air from entering the construction. These two barriers serve different functions and should be clearly marked (using different colours) on all construction drawings (as shown in Figure 3.4).

An airtight barrier must be impermeable or virtually impermeable (i.e. not allow air to pass through at 50 Pascals). Typical air barrier materials include:

- vapour control layer (VCL) membranes (used in timber-frame construction);
- cast concrete (but not unparged concrete blocks);
- orientated strand board[3] (used for closed panel systems and in timber-frame);
- plaster or parging coat (applied directly to a masonry substrate, but not plasterboard).

Whichever system is chosen for the airtight barrier, it is essential that its integrity is maintained both during and after construction (see Chapter 10, Section 10.8). Specialist airtight tapes are needed to seal between junctions such as where windows and doors connect to the wall assembly, or at joints where panels or surfaces meet. Penetrations such as wiring and plumbing require special consideration and proprietary grommets and seals will be required to ensure a robust airtight seal is achieved. Further details on achieving an effective Passivhaus airtightness strategy and pressure testing protocol can be found in McLeod *et al.* (2014) and in PHI (1999).

3.2.3 Thermal properties

3.2.3.1 Thermal conductivity

Outside of a perfect vacuum, all materials conduct heat. Thermal conductivity or lambda value (λ) is the term used to describe the rate at which heat (in watts) passes through a length of material at a given temperature difference (W/m.K).

The thermal conductivity of materials is temperature dependent and also varies according to moisture content and density. Variations in the conductivity of most materials can also occur due to the inhomogeneous nature of materials at the microscopic or cellular level. In the case of plant-based products, such as timber, the thermal conductivity is also directionally dependent and can be significantly higher when heat is flowing in the direction of the grain, as compared to across the grain (McLeod and Hopfe, 2013).

When deciding which lambda value is the 'correct' value to use, it is important to consider the *in situ* context; that is, the lambda value that the material will have when it is installed and has reached its equilibrium moisture content. ISO 10456:2007 is the international standard that provides methods for determining both declared and design thermal values for homogeneous building materials, together with procedures for converting values obtained under one set of conditions to those valid for another set of conditions. These procedures have been validated for the ambient design temperature range affecting most buildings (–30°C to +60°C).

Controlled tests are used to determine the declared lambda values of products manufactured for use in the built environment. The introduction of new harmonised European product standards EN 13162 to EN 13171 (amongst others) is intended to establish a level European playing field for all commercially manufactured insulation materials. This has led to the adoption of what is known as the λ90/90 assessment method for insulation materials, whereby the 0.9 fractile of the distribution represents the compliance criterion for the product group. In other words, the declared product λ-value represents the 90th percentile confidence level being achieved by 90 per cent of production output (Figure 3.5) (BBA, 2012). Use of the performance benchmark λ-value derived from a manufacturer's λ90/90 assessment is therefore more conservative than using the mean test value (0.5 fractile) and has become the accepted method used for generating the thermal values used in PHPP modelling.

In some situations, further adjustment of the declared (λ90/90) value may

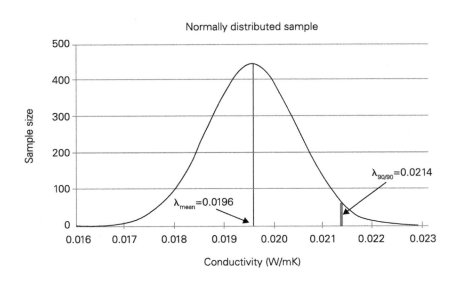

Normally distributed sample

$\lambda_{mean}=0.0196$

$\lambda_{90/90}=0.0214$

Conductivity (W/mK)

3.5
Example showing the λ90/90 assessment method
Source: adapted from BBA (2012)

be needed to obtain a realistic *in situ* design value, and this should be carried out in accordance with ISO 10456:2007 and/or through consultation with the Passivhaus certifying body.

When natural (non-manufactured) insulation products such as straw bale are used, caution must be exercised in relation to the design lambda value. Sutton *et al.* (2011) recorded variations in straw bale density from $100 \, \text{kg/m}^3$ to $130 \, \text{kg/m}^3$ and thermal conductivity varying in the range of 0.05W/mK to 0.065W/mK. Furthermore, organic materials such as straw, cork, etc. are often strongly hygroscopic and therefore have non-linear vapour permeability and conductivity characteristics.

3.2.3.2 Thermal transmittance

Thermal transmittance (also known as U-value) describes the rate of transfer of heat (in watts) through one square metre of a structure for every one degree of temperature difference across the structure (W/m²K). Thermal resistance (R) is the inverse of the U-value, and well-insulated elements with a high thermal resistance will have a correspondingly low thermal transmittance. Losses due to thermal convection, thermal conduction and to some extent thermal radiation are taken into account in the U-value. In homogenous building elements, the U-value can be calculated quite simply as the reciprocal of the sum of the individual layer resistances, including the resistance of the surface air layers on either side of the element (where exposed to room or ambient air).

$$U = \frac{1}{R_{total}}$$ [3]

where:

$$R_{total} = R_{si} + \frac{d_1}{\lambda_1} + \frac{d_2}{\lambda_2} + \frac{d_3}{\lambda_3} \dots \frac{d_n}{\lambda_n} + R_{se}$$

R_{si} is the surface resistance of the internal air layer, and
R_{se} is the surface resistance of the external air layer.
Surface thermal resistance values R_{si} and R_{se} can be found in EN ISO 6946:2007. A summary of commonly used values is shown in Table 13.1.[4]

Table 3.1 Directionally dependent surface thermal resistances (see EN ISO 6946:2007)

	Direction of Heat Flow		
	Upward	Horizontal	Downward
R_{si} (m²K/W) interior surface	0.10	0.13	0.17
R_{se} (m²K/W) exterior ambient air	0.04	0.04	0.04
R_{se} (m²K/W) below ground	0.0	0.0	0.0

Where well-ventilated cavities or voids exist in the outer layer of an exterior wall or construction assembly, the adjacent air space and cladding material is not included in the U-value calculation (Feist *et al.*, 2013, EN ISO 6946:2007). 'Well-ventilated' implies that there are openings in the external cladding of 1,500 mm² (or more) per metre length for vertical air layers; and openings of 1,500 mm² per m² (or more) for horizontal air layers, which would allow external air to enter the cavity. In such cases, the thermal resistance of the external surface (R_{se} inside the cavity) is considered to be the same as the internal surface resistance (R_{si}). Where vents or openings exist in the external cladding which are smaller in area than those defined above, the cavity is considered to be 'partly ventilated' and may be assigned a thermal resistance according to EN ISO 6946:2007, and included in the U-value.

U-values essentially describe one-dimensional heat flow; however, most construction assemblies contain some repeated thermal bridging and hence an element of two-dimensional heat flow. In some cases it is possible to manually calculate U-values for more complex construction build-ups where some or all of the layers are repeatedly bridged. The procedure for doing so is known as the 'combined method' and is described in EN ISO 6946:2007. Provided that the thermal conductivity of the bridging material is not more than five times greater than the layer being bridged, such methods retain sufficient accuracy. The PHPP software contains a 'U-value calculator' which utilises the combined method and is sufficiently accurate for most standard construction assemblies. For more complex situations, involving highly conductive materials which result in two-dimensional and possibly three-dimensional repeated thermal bridges occurring, detailed numerical modelling procedures involving finite element software may be needed to determine a representative U-value.

Once the U-values of each element of the construction have been determined, it is possible to calculate the one-dimensional transmission heat load (P_T) through each element according to equation 4.

$$P_{Tj} = A_j \cdot U_j \cdot (T_i - T_e)_j \qquad [4]$$

where:

P_{Tj} is the one-dimensional transmission heat load, through the jth element (W),
U_j is the thermal transmittance of the jth element,
A_j is the external area[5] of the jth element, and
$T_i - T_e$ is the difference between the internal and the external boundary temperatures (K) during a given peak load design period.

When the transmission losses are not to the outside air but are to the ground or a partially heated (buffer) zone, a temperature correction factor must be applied to equation 4 to account for the reduced rate of losses relative to the external air temperature. The reduction factor (f_t) depends on the relative difference between the mean temperature of the ground (or other boundary) and the external air; the boundary temperature for the ground is, therefore, climate dependent and is calculated specifically for each location in the PHPP software.

In general, colder climates have temperature correction factors for ground heat losses nearer to unity (e.g. Trondheim, Norway, $f_t = 0.78$ which implies a 22 per cent reduction in heat losses to the ground relative to the ambient air) whilst warmer climates have lower temperature correction factors (e.g. Madrid, $f_t = 0.53$ which implies a 47 per cent reduction in heat losses to the ground relative to the ambient air).

The term heating degree hours (G_t) is used to describe the length of time (h or Kh) and degree (K) of heating required in a given climatic location (kKh). In simple terms, the heating degree hours are the difference between the external ambient air temperature and an internal base reference temperature (K), above which auxiliary heating is assumed not to be needed, multiplied by the length of the heating season (h or Kh). Commonly, an internal base temperature of 16°C (Figure 3.6) is chosen as the cut-off point above which heating would not be required due to the availability of internal and passive gains. Further explanation of the derivation of G_t in PHPP is provided in Chapter 5.

In PHPP, G_t is derived for each climate region based on monthly ambient air temperatures provided in the 'Climate data' worksheet.[6]

Once (G_t) and (f_t) are known, the annual one-dimensional transmission heat loss (Q_{T1D}) through any element can be calculated according to equation 5.

$$Q_{Tj,annual} = A_j \cdot U_j \cdot f_{tj} \cdot G_t \qquad [5]$$

where:

Q_{Tj} is the annual one-dimensional transmission heat loss through the jth element (kWh/m².a), and
G_t is the climate-dependent heating degree hours (kKh).

To calculate the total annual transmission heat losses (Q_T) through the entire building fabric, the additional two-dimensional (and potentially three-dimensional) thermal bridges occurring at geometric junctions and penetrations in the building fabric must be added to equation 5.

3.6
Heating degree hours (G_t) calculation based on an internal base temperature of 16°C as the cut-off point above which heating would not be required due to the availability of internal and passive gains

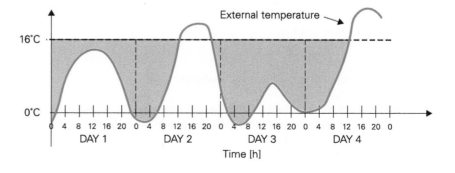

3.2.3.3 Thermal bridging

A thermal bridge is a part of the building envelope where the heat flow, normally perpendicular to the surface, is clearly changed as a result of increased or decreased heat flow density. Changes in heat flow density commonly occur as a result of complex geometries or the insertion of structural or fastening materials with high thermal conductivity. In these locations, the rate of specific heat loss (H) is raised, and will exceed the value that results out of the simple product of the thermal transmission coefficient multiplied by the surface area ($U \times A$). The additional two-dimensional and possibly three-dimensional heat flow occurring in this region is defined as the thermal bridge effect.

Thermal bridges are potentially one of the main sources of unquantified thermal losses in low energy buildings. Unaddressed they can contribute to as much as 50 percent of the total transmission heat exchange in a Passivhaus construction (Schnieders, 2009). Therefore, thermal bridges have to be carefully assessed when the architect or designer is detailing the thermal envelope. One of the main principles of Passivhaus design is to achieve a 'thermal bridge-free' construction (Feist *et al.*, 2013). In practical terms this means that whenever a linear thermal transmittance coefficient, or psi-value (Ψ), exceeds 0.01W/mK, the additional specific heat losses must be considered.[7] Similarly where a three-dimensional thermal transmittance coefficient,[8] or chi-value (χ) exceeds 0.01W/K, the additional heat losses must be considered.

When assessing the thermal bridging impacts resulting from a particular building design, it is helpful to distinguish between geometric thermal bridges and construction thermal bridges (Hopfe and Hall, 2012).

There are a number of useful reference sources which provide predetermined psi-values suitable for Passivhaus constructions such as the Passivhaus Bauteilkatalog (Pokorny *et al.*, 2009). Considerable calculation time (and design expense) can be saved where such details are precisely replicated in a project. Whenever non-standard details are used or the thermal transmittance values of flanking details differ from those used in a reference source, a unique psi-value must be calculated.

Numerical modelling software packages are required to undertake both two-dimensional (Ψ-value) calculations and three-dimensional (χ-value) calculations. In most cases, two-dimensional models are both quicker to create and sufficiently accurate for the vast majority of junction details required for Passivhaus design. However, three-dimensional models are required, for example, when point bridges occur or as a result of two (or more) pronounced linear thermal bridges meeting.

CALCULATING LINEAR AND POINT THERMAL TRANSMITTANCE

The linear thermal transmittance (Ψ-value) of a junction is derived by calculating the total two-dimensional heat flow through the junction detail and then subtracting the one-dimensional heat flow components occurring through the planar building elements that flank the junction. The Ψ-value therefore represents the additional two-dimensional heat flow resulting from the junction, which has not been accounted for in the one-dimensional U-value calculation (equation 6).

$$\Psi = L^{2D} - \sum_{j=1}^{nj} U_j \cdot l_j \qquad [6]$$

where:

Ψ is the linear thermal transmittance (W/mK),
L^{2D} is the total heat flow through the two-dimensional numerical model (W/mK),
U_j is the U-value of the flanking element (W/m²K), and
l_j is the modelled length of the flanking element (m).

The method for calculating internal and external psi-values is virtually identical. Since the total heat flow through the two-dimensional model (L^{2D}) is constant and the U-values of the flanking elements (U_j) are the same irrespective of whether internal or external psi-values are being calculated, the only difference is that the length of the internal (l_i) and external (l_e) flanking elements will differ due to the thickness of the junction (Figure 3.7). Externally calculated psi-values are therefore

3.7
Flux view of intermediate floor thermal bridge showing internal and external flanking lengths

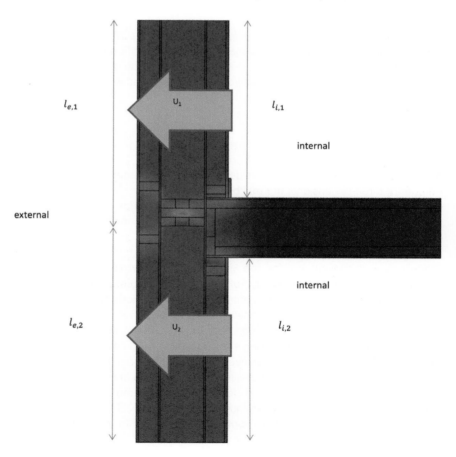

typically lower[9] than internally calculated psi-values simply because $l_e > l_i$ and this explains why it is possible to achieve negative psi-values with some Passivhaus construction details. A negative psi-value does not imply that heat is flowing in the opposite direction, but simply indicates that the total heat flow (L^{2D}) through the two-dimensional junction is less than the *relative* one-dimensional heat flows that would occur through an equivalent external area of planar flanking elements.

The treatment of three-dimensional thermal bridges follows a similar procedure as for linear thermal bridges, whereby the χ-value can be seen, in equation 7, as the residual three-dimensional heat flow (W/K) occurring after the one- and two-dimensional flanking heat flows are subtracted from the total three-dimensional heat flow (L^{3D}).

$$\chi = L^{3D} - \sum_{j=1}^{n} U_j \cdot A_j - \sum_{i=1}^{n} \Psi_i \cdot l_i \qquad [7]$$

where:

χ is the three-dimensional (or point) thermal transmittance (W/K), and
L^{3D} is the total heat flow through the three-dimensional numerical model divided by the temperature difference between the internal and external boundaries (W/K).

The additional specific heat loss which is attributed to the sum of all three-dimensional thermal bridges may be added directly to the total specific heat loss coefficient (H_T) or alternatively it may be treated as an adjustment to the elemental U-value of the element in which the point bridging occurs, as described in equation 8.

$$\Delta U_{TB,m} = \sum_{k=1}^{n} \chi_k / A_m \qquad [8]$$

where:

$\Delta U_{TB,m}$ is the adjustment to the U-value of a thermal element m as a result of k number of three-dimensional thermal bridges (W/m²K),
χ_k is the chi-value of the kth three-dimensional thermal bridge (W/K), and
A_m is the total area of the mth thermal element in which the three-dimensional bridging occurs (m²).

Guidelines and conventions for the preparation of thermal bridging models, including the use of appropriate cut-off planes, are discussed in Section 5 of EN ISO 10211:2007. This standard defines accepted methods for the calculation of two-dimensional and three-dimensional heat flow. When using the EN ISO standard in relation to a Passivhaus construction, care must be taken to define the correct junction line between flanking elements, which should be consistent with the external balance boundary areas used in the PHPP model. Since the U-values required for PHPP are external psi-values, a conversion may be necessary if internal psi-values are also required (for example, to demonstrate compliance with a national calculation methodology, such as the UK SAP procedure). The PHPP 'Areas' worksheet provides a useful conversion tool for converting internal psi-values to external values.

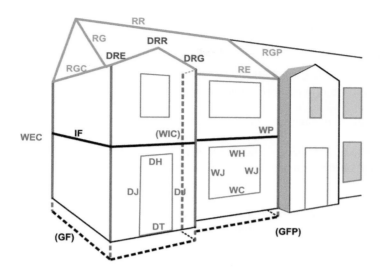

WIC: wall internal corner
WEC: wall external corner
WP: wall to party wall
RGC: roof gable ceiling (verge)
RG: roof gable
RE: roof eaves
RGP: roof to party wall
RR: roof ridge
DRE: dormer roof eaves
DRG: dormer roof gable
DRR: dormer roof ridge
WH/DH: window/door to wall at head
WJ/DJ: window/door to wall at jamb
WC: window to wall at cill
DT: door threshold
IF: intermediate floor to wall
GF: ground floor to wall
GFP: ground floor to party wall

3.8
Wire-frame catalogue of thermal bridges in an end terrace house

DOCUMENTING THERMAL BRIDGES AT THE EARLY DESIGN STAGE

During the early stages of a Passivhaus project, the final construction details are unlikely to have been resolved; however, it is useful to identify all of the potential thermal bridges (Figure 3.8) and record their approximate lengths at this stage. In this way, an allowance for the worst thermal bridges can be made in the PHPP model at the early design stage. 'Rule of thumb' default values can be entered as placeholder Ψ-values in PHPP for the windows, doors and ground floor perimeter connections until more accurate values can be determined. Experience suggests that $\Psi_{inst.} \approx 0.05$ W/mK for window installation and $\Psi_{GF} \approx 0.04$ W/mK for perimeters are appropriate default values[10] for typical residential Passivhaus constructions. At this stage, it is reasonable to assume that the remaining junctions can be designed to be 'thermally bridge free'.[11]

3.2.3.4 Internal surface temperature factor (f_{Rsi})

The internal surface temperatures of the building envelope play an important role in determining whether surface condensation and mould growth will occur. With knowledge of the internal surface temperature, internal air temperature and relative humidity, it is possible to predict whether the dew point temperature will be reached and condensation will form. Mould will typically grow on substrates where the surface relative humidity is at or above 80 per cent (Hens, 1990).

In the absence of relative humidity readings, knowledge of the internal surface temperature and the internal and external design air temperatures is sufficient to calculate the internal surface temperature factor (f_{Rsi}) which is used as a risk indicator for surface condensation and mould growth. The f_{Rsi} is effectively a ratio of the internal surface temperature to external air temperature (equation 9).

$$f_{Rsi} = \frac{T_{si} - T_e}{T_i - T_e}$$

[9]

where:

f_{Rsi} is the internal surface temperature factor [–], according to BS EN 13788:2012,[12]
T_{si} is the internal surface temperature (derived from numerical modelling or by manual calculation),
T_e is the ambient external design temperature (representative of the building's location),[13] and
T_i is the internal operative temperature (20°C is a commonly used Passivhaus default, but this should reflect the actual building zone's typical operative temperature).

High f_{Rsi}-values indicate that a building is well insulated and that there is a large difference between the external air temperatures and internal surface temperatures during the cold period design conditions. In order to limit the risk of surface condensation and mould growth, f_{Rsi} should be greater than or equal to a critical value f_{CRsi}, where the critical value corresponds to the type of building and its usage pattern (hence likely relative humidity), see Table 3.2.

Spot temperatures and/or minimum internal surface temperature readings are typically available from most thermal bridge modelling software; alternatively they may be interpolated from temperature contours, under appropriate boundary conditions.

In the absence of a detailed numerical model, the internal surface temperature for a planar surface may be approximated from equation 10.

$$T_{si} = T_i - U \cdot R_{si} \cdot (T_i - T_e)$$

[10]

where:

T_{si} is the internal surface temperature,
R_{si} is the internal surface resistance (according to EN ISO 6946:2007)[14] specific to the direction of heat flow ($m^2 K/W$) – however, where T_{si} is being derived for the purpose of mould or structural risk assessment, R_{si} values defined in BS EN 13788:2012 section 4.4 should be used – and U is the U-value of the component being assessed.

Table 3.2 Critical surface temperature factors according to building type

Type of building	Critical surface temperature factor (f_{CRsi})
Passivhaus (residential and schools)	0.70
UK Part L (residential and schools)	0.75
Swimming pools (including residential with pool)	0.90

Note that f_{CRsi} values are also climate dependent, see Table 3.6.

3.2.3.5 Thermal mass and thermal diffusivity principles

Construction types can broadly be categorised as lightweight, medium weight or heavyweight constructions, according to the level of available thermal mass. Each of these construction types have a number of advantages and disadvantages and the final choice may be dictated by a number of factors including the geographic location of the building, microclimatic factors, building occupancy levels, building regulations and planning constraints. Heavyweight constructions tend to inherently have a high thermal mass, though materials with a high thermal mass may be built into lightweight constructions. Thermal mass or thermal inertia are terms which are commonly used to describe the ability of building materials to store heat.

In simple terms, the thermal storage capacity of a material is quantified as the product of the density (R) of a material and its specific heat capacity (C_p). This is known as the volumetric specific heat capacity ($C_p\rho$) (equation 11).

$$C_p\rho = C_p \cdot \rho \qquad [11]$$

where:

$C_p\rho$ is the volumetric specific heat capacity, (J/m^3.K or kWh/m^3.K).
C_p is the specific heat capacity (J/kg.K).

Volumetric specific heat capacity therefore describes how much heat or energy (kWh) a cubic meter of material (m^3) can store for a one degree rise in temperature (K). The term 'active' or 'effective' thermal mass refers to thermal mass which is located inside the insulation layer of a building and is directly coupled to the inside air (i.e. not thermally disconnected by insulation, floor coverings and service cavities).

The 'specific thermal capacity'[15] (or specific capacity) describes the active thermal mass per unit floor area (kWh/m^2.K) and this is the reference value used for thermal mass in PHPP. A range of default thermal capacity values are provided in PHPP for different construction types. The specific thermal capacity (Wh/m^2K) (referred to as C_{spec} in PHPP) can be calculated by summing the product of each material's volumetric specific heat capacity (Wh/m^3.K), and its volume (m^3) and then dividing the sum of the products by the total internal floor area (m^2).[16]

Thermal diffusivity (α) is a closely related property to thermal mass and describes the rate at which heat is transferred through the cross-sectional depth of a material. Thermal diffusivity (m^2/s) is calculated by dividing the thermal conductivity of a material (W/mK) by the volumetric specific heat capacity (at a constant pressure) (equation 12). As such, it describes the ability of a material to conduct thermal energy relative to its ability to store thermal energy. Thus materials with high thermal storage capacity and low conductivity will have low rates of thermal diffusion.

$$\alpha = \frac{k}{C_p \cdot \rho} \qquad [12]$$

where:

α is the thermal diffusivity (m²/s),
k is thermal conductivity (W/m.K),
C_p is specific heat capacity (J/kg.K), and
ρ is density (kg/m³).

Single insulating element

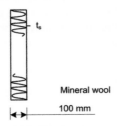

Changes in internal surface
temperatures (t_s)

Influence of external heat gain
(ignoring ventilation and internal gains)

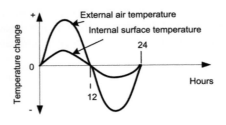

Single dense element

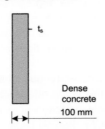

Changes in internal surface
temperatures (t_s)

Influence of external heat gain
(ignoring ventilation and internal gains)

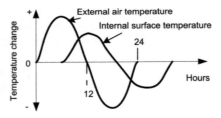

Composite element

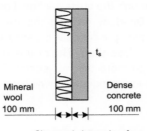

Changes in internal surface
temperatures (t_s)

Influence of external heat gain
(ignoring ventilation and internal gains)

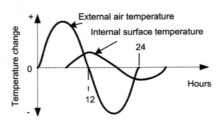

3.9
Changes in internal surface
temperature resulting
from heat transfer through
insulating, dense and
composite elements
Source: adapted from BRE
Digest

The Decrement delay (ω) is the heat transmission delay time (hours) resulting from the thermal diffusivity of a particular construction element, see Figure 3.10. *The Decrement factor* (Df) is the ratio by which the amplitude of the external temperature sine wave is dampened as a result of the materials' specific thermal capacity (equation 13).

$$Df = T_{i,amp}/T_{e,amp}$$ [13]

where:

$T_{e,amp}$ is the amplitude of the external temp sine wave (K)
$T_{i,amp}$ is the amplitude of the internal temp sine wave (K)

It should be noted that both the decrement delay and decrement factor relate to the theoretical properties of a specific material or construction assembly, and do not account for the effects of additional variables such as solar gain and ventilation air changes that will influence the behaviour of a real building. Thus the actual lag time and dampening occurring between peak internal and external temperatures inside a room or building can only be accurately calculated using dynamic simulation methods which account for all of the compounding factors.

3.10
Decrement delay (ω) and decrement factor (Df) for materials with high and low thermal mass

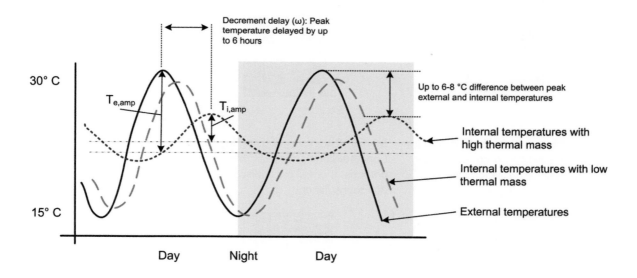

3.2.3.6 Thermal mass in practice

Adding thermal mass within the insulated building envelope helps to dampen the extremes of daily internal temperature cycles, thus making the average internal temperature more stable throughout a diurnal cycle and the building typically more comfortable to inhabit. Figure 3.11 provides examples of some forms of lightweight (low thermal mass) constructions and heavyweight (high thermal mass) constructions commonly used in Passivhaus design.

Thermal mass is particularly important for comfort in temperate and warmer climates which receive marked swings in the diurnal temperature range as a result of relatively high solar loads. Such climates are common in the southern states of USA, Southern Europe, Africa and much of Southern Asia and Australasia, where summer temperatures are high and there is a large difference between average daily maximum and minimum temperatures. Thermal mass also plays an important role in buildings with high internal gains, where night purging of excess gains is possible.

Lightweight, using timber I-joists

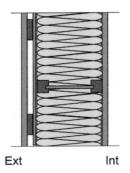

Ext   Int

Medium-weight, using Cross Laminated Timber (CLT) plate

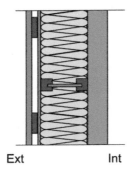

Ext   Int

Medium/heavyweight using External Thermal Insulation Composite System (ETICS)/Exterior Insulation and Finishing System (EIFS)

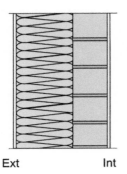

Ext   Int

Medium/heavyweight using Insulated Concrete Formwork (ICF) (note potential thermal mass disconnection due to insulation)

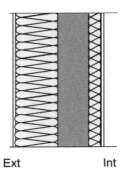

Ext   Int

3.11
Selection of common Passivhaus wall construction types

3.12
A mock solid-stud timber frame wall assembly displaying a cross section of the materials (left) used to construct the Larch House, Wales (right) (light–medium weight construction)

3.13
A mock wall (left) displaying a cross section of the materials used to construct the Denby Dale Passivhaus (right) (heavyweight construction)
Source: ©Green Building Store

Thermal mass is less important, but still beneficial, in locations with more temperate summer climates.

It must be emphasised that thermal mass does not provide free cooling or heating energy, and any reduction in heating loads must be attributed to an improved utilisation factor for solar and internal gains. In cold continental climates during the heating season, Passivhaus buildings make very high utilisation or solar and internal gains (i.e. almost all gains are useful), and therefore further improvement via thermal mass will be marginal. In situations where solar access is poor and intermittent heating regimes are used, thermal mass could even increase winter heating requirements. Materials which store heat typically also absorb moisture vapour and the additional phase change energy associated with releasing absorbed moisture can add to the latent heating load and to summer dehumidification loads.

When determining how much thermal mass is appropriate, consideration must be given to the building's location and occupancy profile as well as its ability to release unwanted stored heat during the summer months (see Chapter 8, Section 18) since any excess heat that is stored during the warmer periods may exacerbate overheating unless it can be fully purged during a 24-hour diurnal cycle.

3.2.4 The environmental impact of the building fabric

When designing and constructing low energy/low carbon buildings, the environmental impact of the building envelope should not be underestimated. This is particularly pertinent when one considers that overall the life cycle of buildings accounts for 40 per cent of total global energy (Dixit et al., 2010). In Europe, construction accounts for a staggering 4.8 tonnes of raw mineral extraction per person per year (Bribian et al., 2008).

Embodied energy and embodied carbon are key components in the delivery of truly sustainable buildings. Embodied energy (EE) (MJ/kg or kWh/t) is commonly defined as the total primary energy required to produce a material (Boyle et al., 2004). Embodied carbon dioxide often referred to as embodied carbon (EC) ($kgCO_{2\,eq}$/kg) represents the total global warming potential (GWP) of all the Green House Gas (GHG) emissions in the manufacture of a product (McInerney and Tucker, 2012).

While Passivhaus design principles lead to a building requiring minimal energy input for space heating and cooling, the embodied energy of the building envelope can vary drastically (according to the construction method) and may have a significant impact on the environmental footprint of the building. As buildings become more energy efficient, the proportional contribution of the building envelope to the total life cycle carbon emissions becomes more substantial. This was clearly illustrated in a recent study of a 222 m^2 low energy dwelling (SHD 42 kWh/m^2/a) where the EE accounted for 30 per cent of the total primary energy requirement over 50 years and fabric related GHG emissions accounted for 41 per cent of the total GWP (Bribian et al., 2009).

A number of detailed life cycle assessment studies have now been carried out specifically in relation to Passivhaus and ultra-low energy buildings (Stephan et al., 2013; Lemanis, 2009; McLeod, 2007). The results of such studies show conclusively that the embodied energy (using traditional construction methods) can typically be on a par with (or even greater than) the operational energy over an evaluation period of 80–100 years. This is an alarming finding, particularly since the majority of the embodied emissions occur during the manufacturing and production stages – well before the building is even occupied.

The environmental impact of various building materials can be clearly shown by comparing two common building materials, timber and cement: 1 kg of responsibly sourced dried timber can sequester in excess of 1.8 kg of $CO_{2\,eq}$/kg (Berge, 2009) whereas, 1 kg of cement generates about 1 kg of CO_2 (Fischer-Kowalski et al., 2011). In fact it is estimated that cement accounts for between about 5 per cent (Kruse, 2004) and 10 per cent (Faludi, 2004) of total global anthropogenic CO_2 emissions. With global cement consumption reportedly increasing by approximately 5 per cent per annum (Davidovits, 2004), there is an urgent need to find low carbon cement alternatives and to move towards carbon sequestering construction methods, wherever possible.

Table 3.3 provides a summary of the embodied energy and global warming potential (GWP) of a range of common building materials. The University of Bath in the UK produced a resource called the 'Inventory of Carbon and Energy' (ICE) for hundreds of building materials based on their 'cradle to gate' energy inputs including manufacture and the energy impacts for transport (Hammond and Jones, 2011). Despite the apparently comprehensive nature of such reference sources (and their subsequent incorporation in a number of embodied energy calculator tools), there is evidence to suggest that such inventories should be used with caution (Dixit *et al.*, 2010). It is not uncommon for Life Cycle Assessment (LCA) inventories to be collated from disparate data sources, incorporating data originating in different geographic locations and across widely varying time frames. A number of LCA inventories and carbon calculators have shown widely divergent results (Dixit *et al.*, 2010), notably in relation to the net CO_2 emission reductions associated with timber-framed and biomaterial constructions (Peurportier and Putzeys, 2005; McLeod, 2007). This variation between sources exists partly as a result of varying primary material sources and processes (Perez-Garcia *et al.*, 2005), and partly as a result of differing LCA assessment methodologies (Peurportier and Putzeys, 2005; Dixit *et al.*, 2010). This situation highlights the necessity of undertaking geographically normalised context-specific LCA studies, using transparent boundary conditions and pathway assumptions. McLeod (2007) suggests that the use of incomplete ('cradle to gate') LCA assessment procedures, as used in a number of early European LCA methodologies, may be substantially underestimating the true CO_2 mitigation potential of buildings constructed predominantly from timber and other biomaterials.

Until relatively recently, natural insulation products struggled to be accepted by the conventional construction industry due to perceptions that they could not compete in the areas of performance and cost. When correctly installed, all insulation materials are beneficial to the environment because they save energy and reduce operational emissions. However, natural fibre insulants (such as wood fibre, cellulose, hemp and straw) have the added benefit that the trees or plants from which they were sourced sequester CO_2, making a further contribution to reducing the embodied energy and global warming potential of the building fabric (Murphy and Norton, 2008) (Figure 3.14).

When the wider array of environmental benefits are considered (e.g. embodied carbon, acoustic attenuation, heat storage, vapour and thermal diffusivity, and waste disposal, etc.), it is clear that natural materials often outperform man-made insulation products in terms of their overall integrated design performance and whole life cost.

Table 3.3 Raw density, primary energy content (PEC) and global warming potential (GWP) of common building materials

Material	Raw density(ρ) kg/m³	PEC (Non-renewable) NR MJ/kg	GWP kg CO_{2eq}/kg
Battens/joists (planed kiln-dried spruce)	500	3.86	−1.436
Building paper	0.10	15.10	−0.975
Cellulose insulation	35	7.03	−0.907
Cement screed	2,000	0.88	0.102
Chipboard	690	13.35	−1.296
Concrete	2,300	0.69	0.103–0.180
EPS rigid expanded polystyrene foam	18	98.50	3.350
Flax insulation (without fibres)	30	34.0	0.121
Foamed glass insulation	105	15.70	0.943
Gypsum plasterboard	850	4.34	0.203
Honeycomb bricks	800	2.49	0.176
Lean concrete mix	2,000	0.44	0.060–0.077
Lime cement mortar	1,800	1.79	0.168
MDF panel	780	11.90	−1.040
Open diffusion membrane	0.08	77.00	2.020
OSB	660	9.32	−1.168
PE vapour barrier	0.20	93.40	2.550
Perlite insulation	85	9.35	0.493
Polymer bitumen	4.30	50.00	0.987
Steel reinforcement to concrete	7,800	22.70	0.935
Rock wool MW-PT insulation*	130	23.30	1.640
Roof tiles (clay)	1,800	4.56	0.200
Sheep wool	30	14.70	0.045
Silicate plaster	1,800	12.10	0.485
Wood fibre panels	270	13.70	−0.183
XPS (CO_2 foamed) insulation	38	102.00	3.440

Source: adapted from Pokorny et al. (2009)

Note: *English: mineral wool slab

3.14
Volumetric embodied CO_2
emissions and storage
comparison of four different
insulation materials
Source: McLeod (2007),
re-graphed from RTS data in
Reid *et al.* (2004)

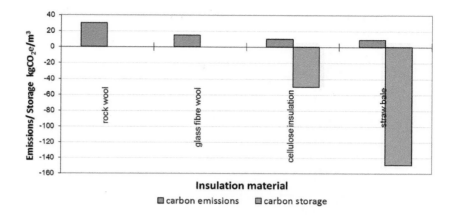

Table 3.4 Material properties of a number of natural insulation materials

	Semi-rigid woodfibre	Hemp	Sheep wool	Cellulose	Cork
Thermal conductivity (W/mK)	0.038	0.038	0.038	0.037	0.040
Density (Kg/m³)	45	38	23	25–50	150
Diffusion resistance factor (μ)	1	1	1	1	10
Specific heat capacity J/(kg.K)	2,100	2,300	1,800	2,100	1,880

3.3 Passivhaus windows

Windows have been described as the radiators of a Passivhaus (Feist, 1998). The advent of advanced glazing systems has made it possible for passive solar gains to offset a large percentage of the heating demand even during the winter months in a Central European climate. The three modes of heat transfer (conduction, convection and radiation) play a significant role in the performance of a window and their interaction is shown schematically in Figure 3.15. Heat flows from warmer to cooler bodies, thus convection and conduction flows are predominantly from the interior to the exterior for much of the year in Central and Northern Europe. Conversely whenever the external surface temperature is greater than the internal surface temperature, the direction of these heat flows will change. The conduction and convection components of energy transfer through a glazing system are accounted for in terms of the U-value of the combined window or fenestration assembly (U_w).

Radiation flows in accordance to the laws governing black and grey bodies,[17] which state that the rate of heat transfer per unit time (W) is proportional to the fourth power of the absolute temperature of the body (K) multiplied by its area (m²), according to the Stefan–Boltzmann equation (equation 14).

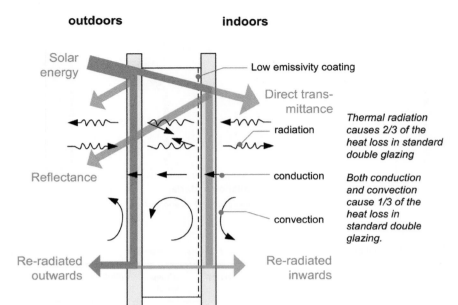

outdoors　　**indoors**

Solar energy

Low emissivity coating

Direct trans-mittance

Thermal radiation causes 2/3 of the heat loss in standard double glazing

radiation

Reflectance

conduction

Both conduction and convection cause 1/3 of the heat loss in standard double glazing.

convection

Re-radiated outwards

Re-radiated inwards

3.15
Conduction, convection and radiation heat transfer through a double-glazed low emissivity coated window

$$j^\star = \epsilon \cdot \sigma \cdot T^4 \qquad\qquad [14]$$

where:

$j^\star$ is the radiant energy flux (W/m²),
ϵ is the emissivity of the emitting body (-),
σ is the Stefan–Boltzmann constant (5.67×10^{-8}) W/m²K⁴, and
T is the absolute temperature of the emitting body (K).
To calculate the total power (P) radiated from an object to radiant energy flux $j^\star$ is multiplied by the object's surface area (A).

Therefore irrespective of the outside air temperature, heat can be transferred through glazed components by direct or indirect solar radiation. The proportion of useful heat gain transmitted through a glazed component by radiation is described in terms of the solar heat gain coefficient (SHGC) or g-value of the glazing. Typical g-values for single-, double- and triple-glazing systems can be found in Table 3.5.

In the context of buildings, radiative transfer can be conveniently divided into two subcategories: shortwave[18] (<2.5 μm) and longwave[19] (> 8 < 14 μm) (Figure 3.16). The radiative transfer properties of most building materials vary significantly according to wavelength. Standard glass, for example, is virtually transparent to shortwave radiation but almost opaque to longwave radiation. For this reason, shortwave radiation is the dominant component of the total radiative transfer through glazed elements.

Shortwave radiation is emitted directly by the sun and either reaches the glazing directly (hence direct radiation) or is scattered en route by cloud cover

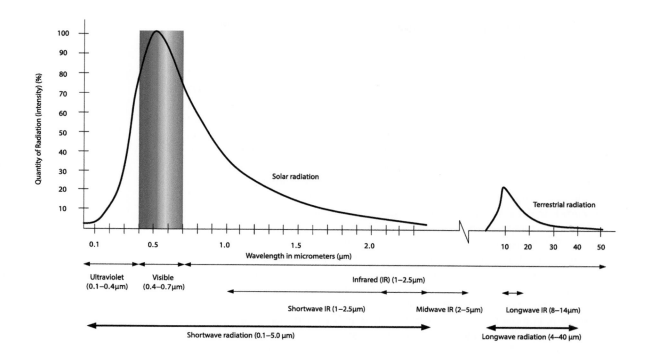

3.16

The electromagnetic spectrum: heat transfer by emission and absorption of radiation occurs in a part of the ultraviolet, and throughout the entire visible and infrared spectrum

and atmospheric particles (referred to as diffuse radiation). Shortwave radiation may also be reflected back from the ground onto a glazed surface depending on the surface reflectivity (albedo) of the ground cover in front of the window. The Global Irradiation incident on a surface is the sum of the direct (or beam), diffuse and ground (reflected) components.

Longwave radiation is often described as re-radiation or outgoing radiation leaving a building's external surface and radiating towards the sky and other objects. This is because the longwave component of the incoming solar radiation is almost negligible in comparison with the longwave radiation emitted by terrestrial sources.

Although the absolute temperature of the surface of the sun is approximately 5,800 K, it is the effective sky temperature (an approximation of the radiative surface temperature of the upper atmosphere) which governs the rate of longwave heat transfer between the sky and terrestrial building components.

The effective sky temperature is not constant but depends on the clearness of the sky (i.e. cloud cover) and it varies in a sinusoidal manner across the year (being warmest during the summer months). On clear nights even during the summer months (in Central and Northern Europe), the effective sky temperature can be colder than external building surface temperatures, and during these periods, longwave radiation will flow outwards towards space. As a result, the external surface temperatures of glazed and opaque components with an unobstructed 'sky view' can fall well below ambient air temperatures on clear nights.

3.3.1 Requirements for PH windows

Passivhaus windows are often referred to as 'warm windows' (German: *Warmfenster*). In the low energy concept of the Passivhaus, the windows are of great importance in order to ensure thermal comfort (see Chapter 2). Windows with a higher thermal transmittance (U-value) will result in increased heat transfer; this can be felt as a cold surface when touching the glass in the winter period and, conversely, as a warm surface in summer. Not only the glass itself, but also the frames of poor-quality windows will suffer from higher rates of heat transfer to and from the outside. Designers should be aware that even a very good Passivhaus window (U_w-value < 0.8 W/m²K) has approximately five to ten times less thermal resistance than a Passivhaus wall (with typical U-values of 0.08 W/m²K to 0.15 W/m²K). Windows must therefore be used wisely.

Radiant temperature asymmetry plays an important role in occupant comfort. For humans it is uncomfortable if objects simultaneously radiate different temperatures towards our body. The window is important in this respect as this is where the coldest and also some of the warmest radiant surface temperatures in the building may occur (see Chapter 2).

In comparison to standard double-glazed windows, the Passivhaus requirement, in most of continental Europe (Figure 3.20 and Table 3.6), for triple-glazed inert gas-filled windows reduces the glazed area heat losses by more than 50 per cent (CIBSE, 2006). The following aspects are important in order to achieve this level of thermal performance:

- triple glazing using inert gas fill and optimal glass cavity width;
- thermally broken frame (insulated frame);
- warm edge spacer;
- low emissivity glass coatings;

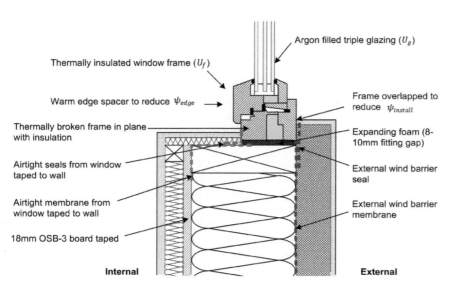

Thermally insulated window frame (U_f)

Warm edge spacer to reduce ψ_{edge} →

Thermally broken frame in plane with insulation

Airtight seals from window taped to wall

Airtight membrane from window taped to wall

18mm OSB-3 board taped

Argon filled triple glazing (U_g)

Frame overlapped to reduce $\psi_{install}$

Expanding foam (8-10mm fitting gap)

External wind barrier seal

External wind barrier membrane

Internal　　　　　　　　　　　　　　　　**External**

3.17
Features of a correctly installed Passivhaus window with U-values ≤ 0.85 W/(m²K), guaranteeing high thermal comfort and energy savings

Table 3.5 Comparison of single, double and triple glazing with respect to spacer, U-value, internal surface temperature and *g*-value (adapted from PHI)

Type of glazing	Single glazing	Air-filled double glazing	Double glazing with gas-filled spaces and selective coating	Triple glazing with two gas-filled spaces and two selective coatings
Spacer	none	Stainless steel	Warm edge spacer	Warm edge spacer
U_w value in [W/m²K]	5.60	2.80	1.20	0.65
Internal surface temperature* [°C]	−1.8	9.1	15.3	17.5
g value [–]	0.92	0.80	0.62	0.48

* Note: the above internal surface temperatures are based on an external design temperature of −10°C.

- multiple airtight seals;
- effective gearing system (airtight seals);
- optimised installation of the glazed unit into the building envelope.

The thermal transmittance of a Passivhaus window (for Central European locations, see Table 3.5) is limited to a maximum U_w-value of 0.8W/(m²K) or, when installed, $U_{w(inst)}$ of 0.85 W/(m²K). This criterion provides protection against the inside surface temperature of the window falling below 17°C, even when it is −10°C outside. Passivhaus compliant windows are required in newbuild Passivhaus buildings and also when retrofitting to the EnerPHit standard (see Chapter 12). In warmer climates, it may be possible to achieve the Passivhaus standard using good-quality double-glazed windows (see Table 3.5); however, this needs to be determined in conjunction with the certifying body.

3.3.1.1 Glazing technology evolution

The evolution of glazing technology has led to improvements from single glazing through to sophisticated triple and even quadruple glazing systems. Only the Passivhaus-compatible glazing systems (shown in Tables 3.5 and 3.6) have an appropriate winter heat loss/heat gain ratio whilst achieving acceptable internal radiant surface temperatures.

3.3.1.2 Total product U_w-value

The combined U_w-value of a window, glazed door or glazed unit takes into account the thermal transmittance of the glazing and frame and the linear thermal bridging occurring at the glazing edge (spacer) and must be accounted for in accordance with the relevant ISO/EN standards.

- The U-value of the glazing (U_g) is determined in accordance with calculation procedures set out in EN 673. Technically this is referred to as the centre of pane U-value.
- The U-value of the frame (U_f) and two-dimensional linear thermal bridging, psi-value (Ψ), of the spacer are determined using numerical modelling procedures in accordance with EN ISO 10077-2:2012.
- The combined (whole window) U_w-value is an area-weighted average of the frame and the glazing components as well as the linear thermal bridge at the spacer between the glass and the frame (as described in equation 15). For normative reference, windows are given their rated U_w-value in relation to a standard window size and opening type. The British Fenestration Rating Council's (BFRC) standard window size is 1.23 m wide × 1.48 m high and assesses a window unit comprising of a fixed pane adjacent to an opening casement.[20]
- The U_w-value of windows which are smaller or larger than this standard reference size will therefore vary as a function of the glazing area (A_g) to frame area (A_f) ratio.[21]
- For curtain walling systems the thermal transmittance is calculated according to ISO 12631:2012.

Once a window is installed in a wall or roof component, the installed U-value of the total fenestration assembly ($U_{w,inst}$) is a result of the thermal transfer coefficient of the glazing assembly itself (U_w) and the average installed linear thermal bridge (Ψ_{inst}) occurring at the junction between the outer edge of the frame and the wall (or roof). All of the factors contributing to the two-dimensional heat losses need to be considered, according to equation 15.

$$U_{w(inst)} = \frac{A_g \cdot U_g + A_f \cdot U_f + l_g \cdot \psi_g \, (+ \, l_{inst} \cdot \psi_{inst.})}{A_g + A_f}$$

[15]

where:

U_w refers to the whole window U-value,

$U_{w(inst)}$ refers to the installed window U-value when the additional term (+ l_{inst} · $\psi_{inst.}$) is included,

ψ_g describes the additional two-dimensional heat flow or linear thermal bridge (W/(mK) occurring between the glazing edge and the frame, this is calculated according to EN ISO 10077-2:2012.

$\psi_{inst.}$ is not a material-specific parameter but depends on the way the window is installed at the junction with the wall. Installed psi-values are calculated using numerical modelling software in accordance with general procedures described in EN ISO 10211:2007 and BR 497:2007 (or equivalent national standards). Since the head, cill and jam psi-values can all be different (depending on the specific window installation and profile), $\psi_{inst.}$ is taken to be the average value.

The importance of good window installation cannot be overstated; with careful attention to detail, it is possible to almost completely eliminate the thermal bridge caused by the installation. This is significant as the total length around the perimeter of each window is typically very long and the sum of all of these bridges can otherwise have a substantial impact on the Specific Heating Demand (SHD).

3.3.1.3 Solar energy transmittance of glass (g-value) and annual solar transmission coefficient (S)

By reducing thermal losses as described above and allowing useful direct and diffuse sunlight into the building, a positive energy balance can be achieved, even in winter in Central European latitudes provided that the windows are suitably orientated and don't suffer from over-shading.

Since the g-value (EN 410:2011) indicates the percentage of the incident

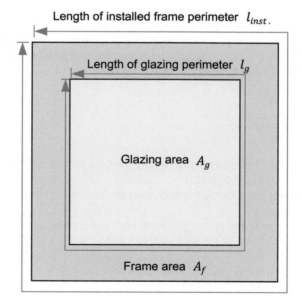

Length of installed frame perimeter $l_{inst.}$

Length of glazing perimeter l_g

Glazing area A_g

Frame area A_f

3.18
Sketch of a window showing the relevant measurements of the glazing area (A_g), the window frame (A_f), and the corresponding lengths used for the glazing edge (Ψ_g) and installed thermal bridges ($\Psi_{inst.}$)

3.19
The external frame and drip of a newly installed Passivhaus window; note the overlapping external insulation and compressive tape seal to reduce the installed thermal bridge

solar energy that will travel through the glazing and into the building, and the U_g-value indicates the rate at which heat will be lost, a rule-of-thumb equation can be used to determine whether the glazing properties of the window are sufficient to achieve a positive energy balance. By using an annual solar transmission coefficient (S) which is derived for each climatic location, the appropriate U_g-value and g-value required to achieve a positive energy balance in winter can be estimated according to equation 16.

$$U_g - S \cdot g < 0 \qquad\qquad [16]$$

where:

U_g is the U-value of the glass (typically less than 0.8 W/m²K for Passivhaus triple glazing), according to EN 673:2011
g is the solar heat gain coefficient according to EN 410:2011 (typically g = 0.5 to 0.65 for triple glazing),
S is the solar factor (W/m²K), = 1.6 W/m²K for Central Europe;[22]

where:

$S = (c \cdot l)/(G_t \cdot 24\ h/d)$,

c is a correction factor (for frame percentage, dirt, orientation),
I is the mean incident radiation (location specific), and
G_t is the heating degree days (kKd) – see Section 2 in Chapter 5.

If this condition is fulfilled, more useful solar energy can be gained during the heating period than the window actually loses as heat to the outside.[23]

It is this positive energy balance that turns the window into a source for energy retrieval, provided the main glazing areas are orientated to face between southeast and southwest (in the Northern hemisphere) and there is not too much shading occurring during the heating season. When assessing a site layout from a master planning perspective, a useful rule of thumb is to ensure that all south-facing windows are able to receive direct solar gains between the hours of 10 am and 2 pm during the winter solstice period (see Chapter 4).

3.3.1.4 Total thermal bridge loss coefficient ($\Psi_{opaq.}$)

For the Passivhaus standard, energy efficiency classes are defined for the glazing and the whole window unit, which are based partly on the total thermal bridge loss coefficient of the opaque components ($\Psi_{opaq.}$). The opaque thermal bridge loss coefficient includes the frame U-value and area, and the Ψ_g-value and length (equation 17). The average values of these variables are used in the calculation of the total thermal bridge loss coefficient.

$$\psi_{opaq.} = \psi_g + \frac{U_f \cdot A_f}{l_g} \qquad [17]$$

where $\psi_{opaq.}$ refers to the total two-dimensional heat flow through the opaque elements of the frame (W/mK).

3.3.2 Determination of window rating criteria

The suitability of a Passivhaus building component for a given climatic zone is determined by assessing $U_{w,inst.}$, U_w and U_g and then determining the corresponding minimum internal surface temperature (T_{si}) and surface temperature factor (f_{Rsi}) at the glass edge, which is the coldest part of the window unit. Boundary conditions, acceptable certification criteria and efficiency classes for glazing in different climatic regions across the world are shown in Table 3.6 and Figure 3.20.

3.3.2.1 Gearing systems and airtightness of window and door systems

The openable casements of windows and doors can only be made airtight if they have good gearing systems and rubber seals to prevent air leakage. These matters are frequently overlooked when procuring windows; however, windows and door seals are highly vulnerable to air leakage and typically deteriorate over

Table 3.6 Boundary conditions, acceptable certification criteria and efficiency classes for glazing

Region No.	Name	Boundary condition for hygiene criterion		Hygiene criterion		Ambient temperature for comfort criterion [°C]	Maximum heat transmission coefficient					Solar-factor	Glazing efficiency classes For each class, U_{eq}* must be less than		
		Ambient external design temperature T_e	Relative humidity internal RH_i	Internal surface temperature T_{si}	Surface temperature factor f_{Rsi}		Orientation (tilt) angle	[°]	$U_{w,installed}$	U_w	U_g	S	A	B	C
1	Arctic	−34	0.40	9	0.80	−50	vertical	90	0.45	0.40	0.35	0.70	−0.10	−0.05	0.00
							inclined	45	0.50	0.50	0.50				
							horizontal	0	0.60	0.60	0.60				
2	Cold	−16	0.45	11	0.75	−28	vertical	90	0.65	0.60	0.55	1.00	−0.15	−0.07	0.00
							inclined	45	0.70	0.70	0.70				
							horizontal	0	0.80	0.80	0.80				
3	Cool-temperate	−5	0.50	13	0.70	−16	vertical	90	0.85	0.80	0.75	1.60	−0.35	−0.20	0.00
							inclined	45	1.00	1.00	1.00				
							horizontal	0	1.10	1.10	1.10				
4	Warm-temperate	5	0.55	14	0.60	−3	vertical	90	1.30	1.25	1.20	3.20	−1.20	−0.90	−0.60
							inclined	45	1.50	1.50	1.50				
							horizontal	0	1.70	1.70	1.70				
5	Warm	10	0.70	16	0.55	11	vertical	90	2.90	2.85	2.80	6.40	−3.00	−2.50	−2.00
							inclined	45	3.30	3.30	3.30				
							horizontal	0	3.80	3.80	3.80				
6	Hot	not relevant		not defined		not relevant			1.60	1.55	1.50	not defined			
7	Very hot, often humid	not relevant		not defined		not relevant			1.30	1.25	1.20	not defined			

Source: PHI (2012)

Note: * $U_{eq} = U_w - S \cdot g \cdot F_W$ (with F_W = glass surface divided by window surface)

Introduction to building physics

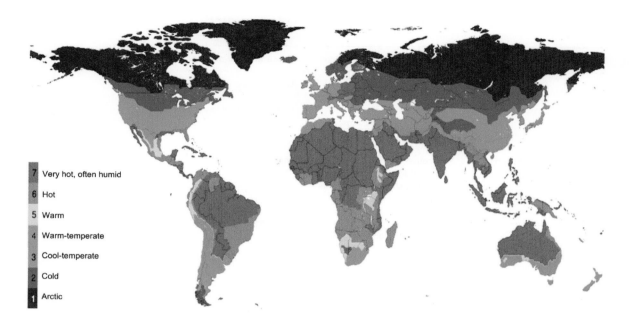

3.20
The classification of regions with equivalent requirements for certified glazing and transparent components
Source: PHI (2012)

3.21
Eurogroove system

time. Achieving the n_{50} air pressure test requirement during commissioning is one thing but maintaining it over time requires high-quality components that are intelligently designed.

A 'Eurogroove' is the name given to a specific type of gearing system located in the rebate or groove in the window sash profile in which multi-point locking mechanisms or espagnolettes (or 'spags') are fitted. There are different types of Eurogroove mechanisms available in a variety of opening styles including conventional casement and European-style 'tilt and turn' and 'lift and slide' systems. The general advantage of Eurogroove systems is that when a window is closed, the last movement drops the sash into place and evenly compresses the gasket before locking it in place. The Eurogroove system enables a window sash to be pulled tight onto its seals by virtue of the 'spags' which engage the locking points on each side of a window. With conventional windows that have fixed hinges on one side, it can be harder to maintain the airtightness along the hinge edge of the seal since there is often no possibility to marginally adjust the hinges once they are in place (Figure 3.21).

3.3.2.2 Airtightness sealing and rating of window and door systems

The rubber seals (or gaskets) situated between the openable casement and the outer frame of the windows and doors play a very important role in the overall airtight strategy of a Passivhaus. Even when new, most seals will contain at least one joint at the point where they have been cut to length during manufacture. Over time, seals deteriorate due to repeated compression and weathering. Since windows and doors are in frequent use, reliance on a single airtight seal is

Table 3.7 Recommended glazing specifications for Passivhaus in applicable cities and subregions

Region No.	Name	Applicable cities/ subregions	Recommended glazing
1	Arctic	Tromso, Novosibirsk	Vacuum low-e
2	Cold	Quebec, Reykjavik, Oslo, Stockholm, Warsaw, Moscow, Yinchuan	Quadruple-glazed low-e
3	Cool-temperate	Vancouver, Seattle, Ottawa, New York, London, Paris, Vienna, Rome, Budapest, Istanbul, Beijing, Seoul, Tokyo, Christchurch, Tehran	Triple-glazed low-e
4	Warm-temperate	San Francisco, Los Angeles, Lisbon, Porto, Toulouse, Marseilles, Sardinia, Melbourne, Wellington, Buenos Aires, Cape Town	Double-glazed low-e
5	Warm	Johannesburg, Hawaii, Mexico City, Quito	Double-glazed
6	Hot	Havana, Salvador, Rio de Janeiro, Florianopolis, North Vietnam, Burma	Double-glazed anti-sun
7	Very hot, often humid	Southern California, Houston, New Orleans, Sahara, Central Africa, Saudi Arabia, India, Indonesia, Philippines	Triple-glazed anti-sun

therefore unadvisable. Most Passivhaus windows will use two or more seals to help mitigate this problem.[24]

Windows and doors are tested for air leakage in accordance with the test methods described in EN 1026:2000. This test calculates the effective air leakage of a fully assembled window or door in the closed position, at a given range of (internal–external) pressure differentials. Although not explicitly referred to in the Passivhaus glazing criteria documentation (PHI, 2012), it has been previously recommended that the total air leakage (based on joint length air permeability) for Passivhaus windows and doors should not exceed 2.25 m³/h.m @ 100 Pa (PEP, 2007). This level of EN 1026:2000 test result would correspond to compliance with EN 12207:2000 at Class 3 or above. Class 4 is currently the highest airtightness category described by EN 12207:2000 and requires a joint length permeability of ≤0.75 m³/h.m @ 100 Pa. There are now many products available that meet this standard and it is recommended that all window and door components procured for Passivhaus and zero energy projects meet or exceed[25] Class 4 of EN 12207:2000. This recommendation is particularly pertinent to small buildings projects and projects located on exposed sites.

Introduction to building physics

3.4 Summary

Throughout history, mankind has adapted to the environment by constructing buildings which respond to their microclimatic surroundings, primarily using materials sourced within the immediate region. Passivhaus is an evolved response to this concept, aiming to optimise the energy freely available from the sun and internal heat gains during the winter months and, at the same time, protect against overheating in summer.

A Passivhaus can be built using a wide variety of construction types, each with their individual merits. In warmer climates, it is generally advantageous to integrate a construction with high thermal mass combined with an effective passive cooling strategy. In cooler climates, lightweight constructions which feature a rapid response to heat can also be beneficial. With forethought, rigorous design assessment and the selection of suitable construction materials, both forms of construction can be utilised in either very warm or cool climates.

Delivering a Passivhaus requires an in-depth understanding of how to deliver an airtight, thermal bridge-free construction. Many of these skills can only be mastered through hands-on training and practical experience. To avoid slippage between design-based predictions and as-built performance, it is essential that high levels of workmanship, site planning and coordination of key stages of the build process are maintained (see Chapter 10).

At the Passivhaus level, the energy required for space heating and cooling is reduced to extremely low levels, and the contribution of embodied energy from the building fabric begins to play a dominant role. In order to address increasingly constrained carbon emission targets, it is desirable to use materials which are sourced from a renewable resource and which contain as little embodied energy as possible with minimal impact on the environment.

It is essential that designers prioritise the well-being and health and thermal comfort of occupants (Chapter 2 and Chapter 4). Energy conservation is a high priority but it should not be to the detriment of optimal health, indoor air quality, and good daylight design.

References

BBA (British Board of Agrément). 2012. *Lambda 90/90,.BBA Policy Sheet No 40/10.* Watford: BBA. Available at: www.bbacerts.co.uk/download/document-types/literature/BBAdatasheet_040i6.pdf

Beedel, C., Phillips, R. and Hodgson, G. 2007. *PEP: Promotion of European Passive Houses. Final Report WP 3.4 PassivHaus Certification.* Watford: BRE. Available at: http://erg.ucd.ie/pep/pdf/Final%20Report_WP3.4_PassivHaus_Certification.pdf

Berge, B. 2009. *The Ecology of Building Materials.* Oxford: Elsevier.

Boyle, G., Everett, B. and Ramage, J. 2004. *Energy Systems and Sustainability Power for a Sustainable Future.* Oxford: Oxford University Press.

BR 497:2007 *Conventions for Calculating Linear Thermal Transmittance and Temperature Factors.* Watford: BRE.

BRE. 2012. *Certified Passivhaus Designer Training.* Training course material (B6 Passive House windows). Watford: BRE.

Bribian, I. Z., Capilla, A. V. and Uson, A. A. 2008. Life cycle assessment of building materials:

comparative analysis of energy and environmental impacts and evaluation of the eco-efficiency improvement potential. *Building and Environment*, 40 (5), 837–48.

Bribian, I. Z., Uson, A. A. and Scarpellini, S. 2009. Life cycle assessment in buildings: state of the art and simplified LCA methodology as a complement for building certification. *Buildings and Environment*, 44 (12), 2510–20.

BS EN 1026:2000. *Windows and Doors. Air Permeability. Test Method.* s.l.: British Standards (BSi).

BS EN 12207:2000. *Windows and Doors. Air Permeability. Classification.* s.l.: British Standards (BSi).

BS EN 13829:2001. *Thermal Performance of Buildings: Determination of Air Permeability of Buildings – Fan Pressurization Method.* s.l.: British Standards (BSi).

BS EN 13788:2012. *Hygrothermal Performance of Building Components and Building Elements – Internal Surface Temperature to Avoid Critical Surface Humidity and Interstitial Condensation – Calculation Methods.* s.l.: British Standards (BSi).

CIBSE. 2006. *CIBSE Guide A – Environmental Design.* London: The Chartered Institution of Building Services Engineers (CIBSE).

CSTC. 2012. *Classes de performance d'étanchéité à l'air des menuiseries extérieures.* [Online] (only in French). Available at: www.cstc.be/homepage/index.cfm?cat=publications&sub=bbri-contact&pag=Contact33&art=510 (accessed 2 February 2015).

Davidovits, J. 2004. Up to 80% reduction of CO_2 greenhouse gas emissions during cement manufacture. *Geopolymer Institute.* [Online]. Available at: www.geopolymer.org/library

DIN EN 13947:2006. *Thermal Performance of Curtain Walling – Calculation of Thermal Transmittance*; German version. Berlin: Beuth Verlag GmbH.

DIN EN 410:2011-04. *Glass in Building – Determination of Luminous and Solar Characteristics of Glazing*; German version. Berlin: Beuth Verlag GmbH.

DIN 4108-2:2013. *Thermal Protection and Energy Economy in Buildings- Part 2: Minimum Requirements to Thermal Insulation.* Berlin: Beuth Verlag GmbH.

Dixit, M. K., Fernández-Solís, J. L., Lavy, S. and Culp, C. H. 2010. Identification of parameters for embodied energy measurement: a literature review. *Energy and Buildings*, 42 (8), 1238–74.

EN ISO 10077-1:2006. *Thermal Performance of Windows, Doors and Shutters – Calculation of Thermal Transmittance – Part 1: General.* Geneva: ISO.

EN ISO 6946:2007. *Building Components and Building Elements – Thermal Resistance and Thermal Transmittance – Calculation Method.* Geneva: ISO.

EN ISO 10211:2007. *Thermal Bridges in Building Construction – Heat Flows and Surface Temperatures – Detailed Calculations.* Geneva: ISO.

EN ISO 10077-2:2012. *Thermal Performance of Windows, Doors and Shutters – Calculation of Thermal Transmittance – Part 2: Numerical Method for Frames.* Geneva: ISO.

Faludi, J., 2004. Concrete: A burning issue. *World Changing*, 18 November. [Online]. Available at: www.worldchanging.com/

Feist, W., Pfluger, R., Schnieders, J., Kah, O, Kaufmann, B., Krick, B., Bastian, Z. and Ebel, W. 2013. *Passive House Planning Package, Version 8 (2013): Energy Balance and Passive House Design Tool.* Darmstadt: Passivhaus Institute.

Feist, W. 1998. Passive Solarenergienutzung im Passivhaus, Arbeitskreis kostengünstige Passivhäuser. Protocol Volume Number 13, Energiebilanzen mit dem Passivhaus Projektierungs PaketPassivhaus Institut, Darmstadt (December 1998).

Fischer-Kowalski, M., Swilling, M., von Weizsäcker, E., Ren, Y., Moriguchi, Y., Crane, W., Krausmann, F., Eisenmenger, N., Giljum, S., Hennicke, P., Romero Lankao, P., Siriban Manalang, A. and Sewerin, S. 2011. *Decoupling Natural Resource Use and Environmental Impacts from Economic Growth: A Report of the Working Group on Decoupling to The International Resource Panel.* Paris: UNEP.

Hammond, G. and Jones, C. 2011. *Inventory of Carbon & Energy (ICE): Version 2.0.* [Database]. Bath: University of Bath. Available at: www.circularecology.com/ice-database.html (accessed 10 December 2014).

Hens, H. 1990. *Guidelines & Practice. Vol. 2.* s.l.:International Energy Agency. Available at: www.ecbcs.org/docs/annex_14_guidelines_and_practice.pdf

HM Government. 2013. *The Building Regulations Approved Document Part L. Conservation of Fuel and Power.* London: Department for Communities and Local Government.

Hopfe, C. J. and Hall, M. R. 2012 Fabric insulation, thermal bridging and acoustics in modern earth buildings. In Hall, M. R., Lindsay, R. and Krayenhoff, M. (eds) *Modern Earth Buildings: Materials, Engineering, Constructions and Applications*. Cambridge: Woodhead Publishing, pp. 41–71.

ISO 10456:2007. *Building Materials and Products – Hygrothermal Properties –Tabulated Design Values and Procedures for Determining Declared and Design Thermal Values*. Geneva: ISO. Available at: www.iso.org/iso/catalogue_detail.htm?csnumber=40966

ISO 12631:2012. *Thermal Performance of Curtain Walling – Calculation of Thermal Transmittance*. Geneva: ISO.

Kruse, C. 2004. *IIGCC Briefing Note Climate Change and the Construction Sector*. [Online]. Available at: http://libro.sostenibilidad.icai.upcomillas.es/referencias/3.%20Vivienda%20 y%20lugar%20de%20trabajo/Construccion/Climate%20change%20and%20the%20 construction%20sector.pdf

Langmans, J., Klein, R. and Roels, S. 2010. Air permeability requirements for air barrier materials in passive houses. *5th International Symposium on Building and Ductwork Airtightness*, Copenhagen/Lyngby, Denmark, October 21–22.

Lemanis, J. 2009. *Refurbish or Demolish: Redevelopment of English Secondary Schools*. MSc thesis, Oxford Brookes University

McInerney, M. and Tucker, S. 2012. Renewable versus non-renewable building fabric: a comparative study in the effect of material choice on the embodied energy and global warming potential of low energy dwellings available. In *Proceedings of Advances in Computing and Technology*, School of Architecture Computing and Engineering, University of East London, UK, 19 January.

McLeod, R. 2007. *Passivhaus – Local House*. MSc thesis, University of East London.

McLeod, R. S. and Hopfe, C. J. 2013. Hygrothermal implications of low and zero energy standards for building envelope performance in the UK. *Journal of Building Performance Simulation*, 6 (5): 1–18.

McLeod, R., Jaggs, M., Cheeseman, B., Tilford, A. and Mead, K. 2014. *Passivhaus Primer: Airtightness Guide*. Watford: Passivhaus. Available at: www.passivhaus.org.uk/page.jsp?id=110 (accessed 2 February 2015).

Mitchell, B. 2014. OHSI 22nd Annual Conference III Health Prevention 20th and 21st February 2013. *Airmid Health Group*. [Online]. Available at: www.airmidhealthgroup.com/component/content/ article/14/574-ohsi-22nd-annual-conference-ill-health-prevention-20th-and-21st-february-2013. html (accessed 8 November 2014).

Murphy, R. J. and Norton, A. 2008. *Life Cycle Assessments of Natural Fibre Insulation Materials*. York: NNFCC.

Peper, S., Bangert, A. and Bastian, Z. 2014. *Integrating Wood Beams into a Passive House: Technical paper*. Darmstadt: Passivhaus Institute.

Perez-Garcia, J., Lippke, J., Briggs, D., Wilson, J. B., Bowyer, B. and Meil, J. 2005. The environmental performance of renewable building materials in the context of residential construction. *Wood and Fibre Science*, 37, Corrim special issue: 3–17.

Perlin, J. 2013. *Let it shine: the 6000-year story of Solar Energy*.

Peurportier, B. and Putzeys, K. 2005. *Inter-comparison and Benchmarking of LCA based Assessment and Design Tools. PRESCO Working Package 2 Final report*. [Online]. Available at: www.etn-presco.net/generalinfo/index.html (accessed July 2014).

PHI. 1999. *Luftdichte Projektierung von Passivhäusern – Eine Planungshilfe. Fachinformation PHI-1999/6*. Darmstadt: Passivhaus Institute.

PHI. 2012. *Certification Criteria for Certified Passive House Certified Passive House Glazings and Transparent Components*. [Online]. Available at: http://passiv.de/ downloads/03_certification_criteria_transparent_components_en.pdf

Pokorny, W., Zelger, T. and Torghele, K. 2009. *Passivhaus-Bauteilkatalog/Details for Passive Houses: Okologisch Bewertete Konstruktionen/A Catalogue of Ecologically Rated Constructions* (in German). Vienna and New York: Springer.

Reid, H., Huq, S., Inkinen, A., MacGregor, J., Macqueen, D., Mayers, J., Murray, L. and Tipper, R. 2004. *Using Wood Products to Mitigate Climate Change: A Review of Evidence and Key Issues for Sustainable Development*. London: International Institute for Environment and Development and Edinburgh: The Edinburgh Centre for Carbon Management.

Schnieders, J. 2009. *Passive Houses in South West Europe: A Quantitative Investigation of Some Passive and Active Space Conditioning Techniques for Highly Energy Efficient Dwellings in the South West European Region*. 2nd corrected edition. Darmstadt: Passivhaus Institut.

Stephan, A., Crawford, R. and de Myttenaere, K. 2013. A comprehensive assessment of the life cycle energy demand of passive houses. *Applied Energy*, 112 (2013): 23–34. Available at: www.sciencedirect.com/science/article/pii/S0306261913004996

Sutton, A., Black, D. and Walker, P. 2011. *Straw Bale: An Introduction to Low-Impact Building Materials*. Watford: BRE. Available at: www.bre.co.uk/filelibrary/pdf/projects/low_impact_materials/IP15_11.pdf

Notes

1 Further guidance can be found on the iPHA website and in the BRE Passivhaus Airtightness Guide (McLeod *et al.*, 2014), available at www.passivhaus.org.uk.

2 Note that for projects being tested for compliance with the EnerPHit standard (refurbishment), a slightly higher air leakage of $n_{50} \leq 1.0\,h^{-1}$ @ 50 Pa is permitted.

3 Note that caution is needed when procuring OSB boards for use as an airtight layer since manufacturers do not currently test or guarantee boards for airtightness. See McLeod *et al.* (2014), Peper *et al.* (2014) and Langmans *et al.* (2010). A number of proprietary boards which are airtight do exist, but they will generally incur a cost premium.

4 It should be noted that R_{si} and R_{se} are in turn comprised of convective and radiative surface coefficients and will, therefore, vary in accordance with local mean air speeds and surface emissivity values.

5 Note that the convention for determining heat loss areas in PHPP is to use the external balance boundary area, which corresponds to the external boundary for which the U-value was calculated (and not necessarily the external physical boundary). This approach tends to slightly overestimate the one-dimensional heat losses relative to the use of internal dimensions.

6 To derive heating degree hours from monthly climatic data in PHPP, months where $T_e < 6°C$ count as one (i.e the entire month is included), months where $T_e > 16°C$ count as zero (i.e. the entire month is excluded). For months where $6°C < T_e < 16°C$, a fitted quadratic expression is used to interpolate the fraction of heating degree hours in that month as a function of the monthly average. Further adjustments are also made to account for radiation and convection gains which modify the external boundary (sol-air) temperature during this period.

7 For linear thermal transmittance values ≤0.01 W/mK it is at the discretion of the Passivhaus designer to include them in the overall PHPP transmission heat losses. Where U-values are known to be negative it is advantageous to include them in the overall transmission heat losses.

8 Also referred to as a 'point' thermal bridge.

9 With the exception of inverted corners.

10 Where $\Psi_{inst.}$ is the average value of the installed thermal bridge between the window head, jams and sill, $\Psi_{WH,WJ,WC}$ and the wall and Ψ_{GF} is the perimeter thermal bridge at the ground floor.

11 Unless non-standard Passivhaus construction details are being used.

12 Note that methods of calculating the temperature factor in complex constructions are provided in EN ISO 10211:2007.

13 See BS EN 13788:2012 Section 4.2. Note that for the calculation of surface mould or structural risk, one in ten years mean monthly temperature should be used.

14 Note that in some contexts it is appropriate to use higher internal surface resistances than are shown in Table 3.1. This has the effect of reducing the calculated surface temperature; Annex A of EN ISO 6946:2007 and DIN 4108-2:2013 should be consulted for further information. For the purpose of calculating mould risk on opaque surfaces, an internal R_{si} of 0.25 m²K/W should be used; see BS EN 13788:2012 Section 4.4.

15 Specific active thermal mass is sometimes confused with 'surface heat capacity', where the product of the volumetric specific heat capacity (kWh/m³.K) and the volume of material (m³) is divided by the surface area.

16 C_{spec} is approximately equal to 60+ n (heavy) *24 Wh/m²K; where n (heavy) signifies the number of massive enclosing wall surfaces; typical values are lightweight: 60 Wh/m²K; medium weight: 132 Wh/m²K; and heavyweight: 204 Wh/m²K.

17 Black bodies are 'ideal' bodies that have an emissivity (ϵ) of 1; i.e. they absorb all incoming radiation. Grey bodies describe 'real world' materials which have an emissivity (ϵ) < 1.

18 Predominantly in the visible 0.4–0.7 µm and near infrared 0.8–1.7 µm range.

19 Predominantly around 10 µm.

20 EN 10077-1:2006) provides further details regarding the characteristic dimensions of windows and doors; DIN EN 13947:2006 provides the characteristic dimensions used for curtain wall glazing systems.

21 Smaller Passivhaus windows typically have a higher U_w-value than larger windows, even when using identical frame and glazing components. This is because the frame area to glazing area (A_f/A_g) ratio is greater on a smaller window and the U_f-value is typically higher than the U_g-value.

22 See Table 3.6, for S factors for other global climatic regions.

23 More detailed analysis of the energy balance can be carried out on a window-by-window basis, either by replicating equation 16 using data derived for each window (accounting for individual shading and orientation) or by opening the hidden cells in the 'Windows' worksheet to access this information.

24 Conversely, it should be noted that the use of a large number of seals can reduce the compression achieved on each individual seal; hence increasing the number of seals does not equate to a linear improvement in airtightness.

25 Due to the large distribution of air leakage rates between products currently complying with the Class 4 category, two further classes (5 and 6) have been proposed as future additions to the BS EN 12207:2000 system (CSTC, 2012). However, these have not yet been implemented at the time of writing.

4

Lighting and daylighting for visual comfort and energy efficiency

MYRIAM B. C. ARIES AND JAN WIENOLD

4.1 Introduction

Light influences the daily rhythm and well-being of humans in a physiological, psychological and biological way. Light doesn't only enable humans to see; beside the visual rods and cones the human eye also contains (recently discovered) non-visual photoreceptors (Berson *et al.*, 2002). Supported by light perception, the human biological clock system tells the human body when to regulate multiple body functions such as body temperature, sleep patterns, cognitive performance, mood, well-being, and the release and production of hormones. Compared to the sensitivity of the visual system (Vλ), the maximum effect of the non-visual system (Cλ) is shifted towards the shortwave radiation and has its peak in the blue part of the spectrum.

Daylight has been associated with multiple health advantages (Aries *et al.*, 2013) and the use of natural light has become an important strategy to improve energy efficiency by minimizing lighting, heating, and cooling (IEA Task 21, 2000). The focus of the first Passivhaus was initially on insulation and airtightness. However, a number of wider aspects are important for accomplishing Passivhaus buildings, of which the key factors (Heier and Österbring, 2012) that are related to *lighting* and *daylighting* are:

1 to utilize the energy of the sun for heating during the winter;
2 to place appropriate windows in different orientations for good daylight levels;
3 to shade the sun during summer to avoid overheating, and at other times to avoid glare;
4 (indirectly) to improve insulation in the building envelope, including windows.

4.2 Principles of daylight design

Daylighting is the design of daylight openings and surrounding surfaces in order to control the admission of daylight into a building (Leslie, 2003). Good daylighting can create pleasant dynamic environments that simultaneously reduce the energy consumption of electric lighting, heating, and cooling. However, improper daylighting creates problems in terms of glare, overheating, and waste of energy. Buildings that are designed using passive strategies take advantage of nature (sun, wind, and water) to achieve comfort and energy savings. Passive solar design involves arranging the form, fabric and systems of a building (Littlefair, 1998). Site layout is a key factor affecting the viability of a passive solar building, particularly where new developments may restrict solar gain to existing buildings nearby (Littlefair, 1998, 2001). Since these buildings can also limit the possibilities for other new buildings, an initial site study should assess the limitations and possibilities.

Daylight can enter a room directly or indirectly. An indirect method is to use reflected daylight to illuminate a room (Tregenza and Wilson, 2011). Plants and bushes are often the best means for creating a diffuse outdoor field, even though trees should generally not be higher than the building itself. Light-coloured and potentially deciduous foliage is preferred. Ground materials like pavement, grass, or dirt, and surrounding buildings all reflect daylight. However, it is difficult or impossible to influence the materialization of surrounding buildings, and often modern, highly reflective building materials are more discomforting than beneficial. Where possible it is best to reflect direct daylight upwards to the ceiling via the ground, roof, or a balcony (Figure 4.1), and to avoid bright surfaces near the horizontal line of view (Tregenza and Wilson, 2011).

4.1
Direct daylight reflected indoors via the ground, walls, and roof
Source: Passivhaus Witven
© Architect: Thomas Kemme Architecten; Photography Ruud Peijnenburg

The direct use of daylight for lighting of a room depends on the fundamental **form** and the (main) orientation of a building (Tregenza and Wilson, 2011). The building design can be used to guide light to enter a room (or prevent it from entering). Optimum lighting of a room involves more than making the necessary illuminance calculations. It also requires attention for creating a **view**, avoiding *glare* and other *sources of visual discomfort* (see Sections 4.3 and 4.4.), and balancing *electric lighting* (see Section 4.5).

Daylight openings characterize energy use and visual comfort patterns in buildings. Choosing their areas and proportions is part of fundamental early design-stage decisions, which are complicated to change later. Therefore, window dimensions must result from a careful process and be part of an integral design process, considering multiple aspects at the same time (Ghisi and Tinker, 2005; Ochoa *et al.*, 2012).

Everywhere in the world the sun is lower in the sky in winter than in summer, and everywhere the sun rises in the east and sets in the west. These two facts suggest placing most of the main daylight openings on a south or north *orientation*. East and west orientations result in the highest overall energy consumption in relation to heating, cooling, lighting, and ventilation, the science behind which is detailed in Ochoa *et al.* (2012).

In studies of office buildings, the least energy use is observed at *window-to-wall ratios* (WWR) of about 30 per cent for north, while at 20 per cent WWR for south, east, and west orientations (Ochoa *et al.*, 2012). The simulations in the study of Ochoa *et al.* (2012) were done for a one-person office room, and they are consistent with the results of Persson *et al.* (2006). Persson *et al.'s* (2006) study showed that the size of energy-efficient windows in a Passivhaus is highly relevant to the cooling demand in the summer (optimum for a south opening of circa 20 per cent WWR). McLeod *et al.* (2013) also concluded that optimization based on smaller south-facing glazing areas (circa 25 per cent) yielded lower risks of overheating compared to traditional approaches.

Conversely, solutions with least total energy consumption often have low visual performance. One of the solutions to overcome this is to combine more openings in one room. This should preferably be in different walls and potentially include a roof opening. For the top floor of deep plan buildings, skylights, roof monitors, clerestory windows, and translucent roofs can be used to light areas beyond the perimeter zone (Leslie, 2003). In case only one daylight opening is possible, recommended WWR for daylight openings that optimize basic visual comfort are respectively for each orientation: north 70 per cent, south 60 per cent, and east/west 60 per cent (Ochoa *et al.*, 2012). Clearly a balance must be reached between optimal visual comfort and year-round energy efficiency and thermal comfort.

Beyond the WWR, the actual *geometry* of the daylight opening must also be considered. Wide windows placed high in the wall are more efficient for lighting and the penetration of solar energy than low vertical windows. However since a good-quality view (both in seated and in standing position) is important (e.g. Aries *et al.*, 2010; Hellinga and Hordijk, 2014; Xue *et al.*, 2014), an opening from floor to ceiling offers all three aspects that are important for a good view quality: a layer of sky, a layer of city or landscape (horizon), and a layer of ground (Markus, 1967) (see Figure 4.2).

In Ochoa *et al.*'s (2012) study, the building location was assumed to be unobstructed, and in that case, a typical vertical sky component is approximately 40 per cent. The vertical sky component describes the ratio of the sky light illuminance on a vertical plane relative to the illuminance on unobstructed horizontal ground (Littlefair, 1998). If the vertical sky component on a glazed façade is greater than 27 per cent, then it is generally considered that sufficient sky light reaches the vertical daylight opening.

4.2
Good view quality containing a layer of sky, a layer of landscape (horizon), and a layer of ground

Using daylight openings in the roof can increase potential solar heat gains and also conduction losses, since an insulated roof surface is nearly always replaced with glazing which is less insulating (Leslie, 2003). However, daylight openings in the roof provide an effective means to light a horizontal plane and often require only half of the opening area relative to a wall opening. Nevertheless, opening areas that are too small compared to the room dimensions can result in the appearance of dark walls leading to visually unpleasant spaces.

A light-coloured *finishing* of ceiling and walls facilitates the reflection of incoming light and distributes it more evenly throughout the space. Large surfaces must in no case be finished in a specular (i.e. highly reflective mirrored) material. Application of light-coloured materials not only reflects incoming light, it also reduces potentially large contrasts; for example, between the window frame and the sky (see Figure 4.2). Dramatic contrasts can also be reduced by contouring areas around the daylight openings in order to diffuse the daylight gradually.

The insulating qualities of *glazing* have improved tremendously over the last decades and triple glazing is now widely available (see Chapter 3). Due to the inert gas-filled gap, triple-glazed windows are even more energy efficient than modern double glazing. Passive buildings require glazed U-values lower than 0.8 $W/m^2 \cdot K$. High-performance double-glazed windows (with argon gas) can achieve U-values of 1.1 $W/m^2 \cdot K$ or lower, while some triple-glazed windows (with argon gas) can achieve U-values as low as 0.6 $W/m^2 \cdot K$. However, as a general rule, better thermal insulation means a lower *light transmittance*. High-performance triple glazing has a light transmittance of circa 72 per cent while double glazing has a light transmittance of circa 79 per cent. This potential daylight contribution loss of 7 per cent can be compensated by choosing the right WWR and window geometry. While choosing the proper glazing, attention has to be paid to the application of heat-reflective foils on the outer layer of the glass. These foils are very useful in preventing unwanted gains or losses, but since they limit or reduce the admittance of certain wavelengths of solar radiation, they can influence the occupant's perception of the outside world. This can also be true for fritted glass (widely used for colouring and patterning architectural glazing) if applied in the field of view.

In winter, it is desirable to collect solar gains; however, in summer a large daylight opening often yields too much solar energy resulting in a thermally and visually uncomfortable environment. Proper *solar shading and luminance screening* has to be present for daylight openings on the south, east, and west orientations. In practice this means that the best shading systems permit a variable shading that responds to current climatic conditions (e.g. solar altitude), and are adjustable to weather and personal choices. (See also Section 4.4.)

From a lighting point of view, *building and task organization* has to be arranged in order to make it possible to execute most tasks within areas with good daylight. Generally this daylight zone extends approximately five meters from the façade. In case a room is deeper than five meters, the application of an atrium to enable daylight to enter from the other side should be considered. Daylight can also be used to light and guide people in a certain direction. This is useful in staircases and corridors (Figure 4.3).

The frequency and timing of room use should determine its orientation towards the sun. The *north* orientation gets the least daylight/sunlight (and thereby the least solar gain/most heat loss), but the quality of the light is pretty much stable. Due to the limited amount of direct sunlight, rooms with a northerly orientation can be best used as 'short stay' rooms (i.e. utility rooms, storage locations, the entry, or art-workshop rooms). The *east* orientation gets the morning sun (including potential for warming up). This orientation is suitable to serve as a good place for a breakfast room, a kitchen (see Figure 4.4), and bedrooms. This is particularly true for early risers, although bedrooms with an east orientation are also cooler in the afternoon and therefore more comfortable during warm summers. The *south* orientation receives the most and longest duration of sunlight (Northern Hemisphere), and is therefore suitable for the placement of a living room (long-stay room) and for a home office/workspace. The *west* gets afternoon and evening light which is therefore fitting for a dining location. However, this orientation often needs shading to prevent overheating and excessive glare, particularly during the summer. A bedroom for late risers can be appropriately located on the west orientation as well.

In larger residential and non-domestic buildings, the flexibility of determining room location by orientation may be more limited; however, the same design principles apply. Where possible, rooms with high internal gains, such as server rooms, commercial kitchens, and plant rooms, should be located in the north.

4.4
Kitchen on the east orientation of the house with dining table in broad daylight
Source: © Architect: Thomas Kemme Architecten; Photography Ruud Peijnenburg

4.3 Daylight metrics

Several daylight *metrics* have been developed in order to evaluate the daylight performance of a building. Daylight in general is a very broad topic, ranging from daylight availability, colour, glare, contrast, view to the exterior, and non-visual effects. For each project or building, the goals for 'good daylighting' might be different; therefore, it is difficult to summarize 'daylight performance' into one single number or metric. Nevertheless, the daylight performance can be grouped into three main categories: daylight availability, visual comfort, and well-being.

1 *Daylight availability:* Availability corresponds to the amount of daylight arriving in a space in a certain climate and influencing both visual and non-visual effects.
2 *Visual comfort:* Several criteria belong to the field of visual comfort. The most important ones are: glare, contrast ratios in the field of view, legibility of displays, view to the exterior, and colour and colour rendering of the light.
3 *Well-being:* Daylight is known to have a positive influence on the perceived room appearance and well-being.

4.3.1 Daylight availability metrics

Several metrics describe the amount of daylight arriving in space. The *Daylight Factor* (DF) is one of the oldest metrics for this and is defined as the ratio between external and interior horizontal illuminance under a fully overcast sky, expressed as a percentage (Moon and Spencer, 1942). The DF is easy to determine – either with simulations, calculations, or measurements. On the other hand, the DF has important disadvantages. It does not take into account the real sky and weather conditions; it does not take into account the orientation of the windows/daylight openings; and last but not least, the values are difficult to understand for planners since it does not say anything about the frequency of illuminance levels in a space throughout the year. For side-lit spaces, a daylight factor greater than 2 per cent in the main usage area indicates a good daylight potential.

The *Daylight Autonomy* (DA) is a climate-based metric and describes the fraction of the occupied time during a year when a certain threshold illuminance at a certain point (usually at the workplace) is exceeded and no electric lighting is needed (Reinhart *et al.*, 2006). Typically, a threshold of 300 lux is used, since at lower illuminance levels the probability that the lighting is switched on rises. The DA metric, expressed as a percentage, should be applied whilst including the usage of shading devices. In the main usage areas, the DA should be between 60 and 75 per cent (of the usage period) to be considered to have good daylight availability.

The *spatial Daylight Autonomy* (sDA) is an extension of the daylight autonomy and is expressed as a percentage. It describes the percentage of floor area exceeding a certain illuminance threshold (e.g. 300 lux) for a given time fraction of the year within usage times (e.g. 50 per cent of the time between 8 am and 6 pm). As for the DA, it is based on climatic data and considers the usage of shading devices.

The *Useful Daylight Illuminance* (UDI) is also a climate-based metric and bins the occurring illuminance values into three categories (Mardaljevic and Nabil, 2006). The useful illuminance category is defined as a range between a certain lower level (typically 100 lux) and a certain upper illuminance level (typically 2,000 lux). The other two ranges (outside the useful band) indicate if there is a lack of daylight or too much. For example, a room has a UDI for 60 per cent of the time, too little daylight (<100 lux) for 24 per cent of the time, and too much daylight (>2,000 lux) for 15 per cent of the time. The upper category can be questioned because the horizontal illuminance is neither an indication of glare nor of overheating – which are the main reasons for introducing an upper range. User assessments also show that people often prefer higher illuminance levels. Besides this shortcoming, the metric, when applied with annual data on a calculation grid, gives a good indication about the daylight performance of a space.

4.3.2 Visual comfort metrics

4.3.2.1 Glare

Glare is a negative sensation, caused by bright areas with sufficiently greater luminance than that which the eyes are adapted to, causing annoyance, discomfort, or loss of visual performance. Generally, glare can be divided into three main categories:

1 *Reflections or veiling glare:* this means reflections on computer screens or other task materials, which reduce the contrast and the readability. Existing metrics for veiling reflections are under investigation and currently not commonly agreed on. Therefore these metrics are currently not implemented in any design tool. As rough estimation and for LCD displays with anti-reflective screens (as is state of the art in the year 2013), reflections are mostly avoided when the illuminance in the monitor plane is lower than 1,500 lux (Vandahl *et al.*, 2012).

2 *Disability glare:* this type of glare impairs the vision, but not necessarily causing discomfort (Vos, 2003). Usually in the context of buildings, disability glare plays a minor role. It can be quantified in principal by the equations from Stiles-Holladay (Vos, 2003), with or without an age correction factor. The applicability for daylight situations is unclear, and currently it is not implemented in any design tool.

3 *Discomfort glare:* with this type of glare, people report discomfort but the vision is not necessarily impaired (Vos, 2003). Two metrics to describe discomfort glare from daylight are currently used – the *Daylight Glare Index (DGI)* and the *Daylight Glare Probability (DGP)*. The DGI describes the glare intensity on a scale, whereas the DGP describes the probability that a person is disturbed by daylight glare (Hopkinson, 1972). The latter metric was developed under daylight conditions and has been shown in several experiments to correspond better with users' perceptions of daylight glare than the DGI (Wienold and Christoffersen, 2006). To avoid discomfort glare for office-like spaces, the DGP for the main viewing direction should not exceed a value of 0.45 for 95 per cent of the occupied time. A value less than 0.35 indicates very good glare protection. A value between 0.35 and 0.45 increases the risk of discomfort glare – especially for glare-sensitive people. Glare sensitivity increases with age. In addition to this, the variance of glare perception between different individuals is large. Lower DGP values indicate a higher probability of acceptance.

4.3.2.2 Contrast ratios in the field of view

While the discomfort glare metrics DGI and DGP describe the glare sensation from a glare source, visually uncomfortable situations also occur when high *contrast ratios* exist between the task luminance, immediate surroundings, and the peripheral surroundings. The Illuminating Engineering Society of North America (IES) recommends contrast ratios 1:3:10 (task : immediate surrounding : peripheral surrounding) (DiLaura *et al.*, 2014). However for daylit environments, this ratio might be too strict.

4.3.2.3 Sunlight exposure

Whereas at workplaces, *direct sunlight* might cause problems with glare or excessive contrast, for dwellings, it is usually a desirable quality to have access to. It is often considered an important selling point by real estate managers. The German standard DIN 5034-1:2011 demands at least one hour of possible sunlight in one of the occupied rooms of a dwelling on 17 January and four hours at the equinox. These values might be adapted when applied to locations at higher latitudes.

4.3.2.4 View to the exterior

As mentioned previously, the possibility to have a *view* to the exterior is one of the most important aspects in determining whether people rate a space attractive or not (Shin *et al.*, 2012). Also, it is known to be the major secondary criterion for people when adjusting shading systems to prevent glare, reflections, or overheating. According to the German standard DIN 5034-1:2011, the following criteria should be fulfilled to provide a reasonable view to the exterior:

- The sum of all widths of the windows should be 55 per cent of the total width of the façade.
- The glazed area should be at least 10 per cent of the floor area and 30 per cent of the façade area.
- For rooms with a depth less than 5 m, the minimum glazing area should be 1.25 m²; for rooms with a larger depth it should be at least 1.5 m².
- The lowest point of the glazing should not be higher than 0.95 m above floor level.
- The highest point of the glazing should be at least 2.2 m above floor level.

4.3.2.5 Colour and colour rendering of the light

Inside rooms, the perception of natural colours and accurate colour rendering is desired and, therefore, the shift in the colour of the incoming daylight should be kept as low as possible. Modern glazing usually has coatings to reduce the energy losses of the incoming radiation (solar control glazing), which may change the colour of the daylight. Shading systems may also change the colour of the light. A metric to describe the quality of colour rendering is the *colour rendering index (Ra)*. It describes the colour rendering in comparison to a reference light source (i.e. the reference daylight spectrum). The higher the value, the more natural colours appear. For glazing, the Ra should be higher than 90 to keep a good colour rendering inside rooms.

4.3.3 Perceived space appearance

The dynamic nature of daylight, both direct and diffuse, seems to create an instinctive connection between the occupant and the surrounding environment. Spatial contrast and (day)light variability are fundamental to the *perceived appearance* of the built environment. Also the directionality of the light plays an important role in how a room is perceived. A totally homogeneous and diffuse light distribution is known to generate uninteresting spaces without shades. Some of the first metrics to evaluate this subjective perception of daylight are: the Annual Spatial Contrast and Annual Luminance Variability (Andersen *et al.*, 2013); and the Directional-to-Diffuse ratio (Inanici, 2007). However, these metrics are still under development and have to be validated.

4.4 Shading systems for glare control

The glazed parts of buildings not only offer views and access to daylight; they can also cause unwanted solar gains and glare. In order to reduce these disadvantages, *shading systems* can be used. Many systems are able to protect against solar gains and glare at the same time, especially those which are mounted outside the building envelope. For protection against solar gains, externally mounted systems are the most effective. For glare control, the mounting position is less important. These systems should be able to protect against potential glare from the sun, the sky, and externally reflecting surfaces. At workplaces, or places that are used to work at computer screens, the shading devices should be able to protect from direct sun penetration.

Louvers, blinds, awnings, and shutters, etc. can all be suitable to minimize glare; however, when operated, the devices should be able to maintain access to daylight and views. The material properties of the shading device should be chosen carefully so it will not become an additional source of glare (i.e. avoidance of glossy surfaces in the field of view towards the sun). Movable and retractable devices can be individually adjusted according to personal needs. Such systems are preferable since they offer the possibility to adapt to the weather situation and therefore maximize daylight usage. Fixed systems will also reduce daylight in overcast situations and may lead to higher energy consumption for the electric lighting. If fixed shading devices are used, additional movable shading devices could be necessary where occupants are sensitive towards glare from the sky, or to protect people from sun admittance at low incidence angles.

Venetian blinds and screens are the most common and also the most effective systems to reduce glare. Both can be individually adjusted. Venetian blinds can still offer views during average and high sun positions through use of horizontal or slightly tilted louvers. Also, they serve to redirect the daylight into deeper parts of the rooms. For screens, the choice of the fabric is important. While some fabrics still offer some view through the material, they cannot then block the sun completely – which may still cause glare. For screens to offer a very good glare protection, the viewing contact to the sun should be blocked by the fabric. This means that the direct transmission would be 0 (i.e. no natural sunlight would enter).

A complete overview of shading systems can be found in IEA Task 21 (2000).

4.5 Electric lighting

Recommendations for the design of Passivhaus buildings all refer to the application of low-energy lighting (and high-efficiency electrical appliances) in order to minimize the energy use. There are currently two main kinds of low-energy lighting technologies to choose from for indoor lighting: Compact Fluorescent Lamps (CFLs) and Light Emitting Diodes (LEDs). Incandescent bulbs and halogen lights are also frequently used in homes, but are not considered energy efficient. A *CFL* is a fluorescent lamp or tube designed to replace an incandescent lamp since a CFL uses approximately five times less energy than an equivalent incandescent. *LEDs* are a lighting technology that can also be used to replace incandescent light bulbs because LEDs use as little as 25 per cent of the electricity required by an incandescent. Both lighting technologies have a high luminous efficacy, with a relatively low heat loss. The light quality (i.e. colour rendering) of CFLs and LEDs is, however, not (yet) comparable with incandescent light bulbs.

Lighting accounts for approximately 8 per cent of a typical UK household's energy bill. In a Passivhaus, the total energy consumption is supposed to be drastically lowered compared to a standard (new) house. However, the electrical power for lighting often stays approximately the same, hence making up a relatively large part of the total energy consumption (see Figure 4.5).

In the average home on a regular weekday, two peaks occur in the lighting demand, corresponding with morning and evening activities (Stokes *et al.*, 2004). The use of electric lighting in the domestic sector depends mainly on the level of

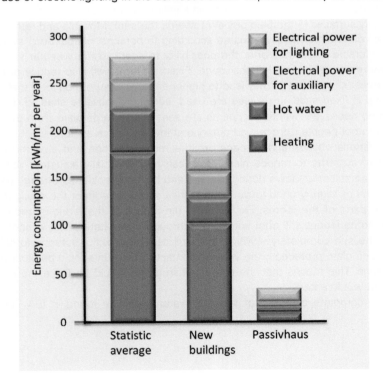

4.5
Typical energy use for residential buildings in a heating-dominated climate (example: Canadian residential buildings in kWh/m² per year) Source: after Light House Sustainable Building Centre and Wimmers (2009)

natural light coming in from outdoors, coupled with the activity of the household residents (Richardson *et al.*, 2009). *Human perception of the natural light level* within a building is a key factor determining the use of electric lighting. In cases where the window is very bright and the rest of the room appears dark, one is very likely to turn on an electric light source to counterbalance the contrast. Conversely, where a person has started a task in full daylight and the outdoor light level dims, the human eyes adapt gradually to the decreased light level. At the moment the light level is too low for the task, the person will turn on electric lighting.

The number of people who are at home and awake is the other key factor for domestic lighting use – so-called *active occupancy* (Richardson *et al.*, 2009). This is of course also dependent on the size of the home. People within a particular dwelling will often *share* lighting by virtue of being in the same room, and this effect is larger for a small home than for a house with multiple rooms. On average, the bedroom is the room that contains the most household lights. However, the lights in the living room and kitchen are used (and shared) for the greatest number of hours (see Figure 4.6). One reason bedrooms have the highest number of lights is simply that the average home in the US has 2.6 bedrooms (US Department of Energy, 2004).

Energy-saving control innovations and solutions can help to reduce the household's energy bill. An *occupancy sensor* turns lights on automatically when somebody enters the room and an *absence sensor* turns lights off when there is no movement detected for a certain period of time. An absence sensor is

4.6
Amount of lights (yellow) and hours used (red) by room (percent of total)
Source: after US Department of Energy (2004)

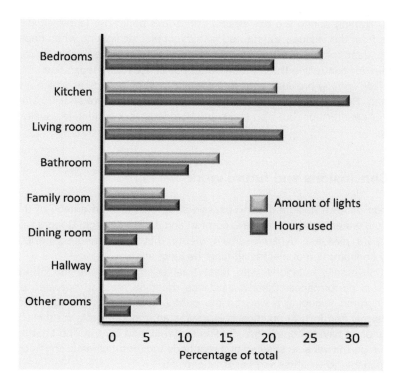

suitable for rooms where lights are often inadvertently left on (e.g. children's rooms). Electric lights can be controlled via daylight sensors according to the availability of natural daylight. For office applications, the reduction of electric lighting depends on the daylight illuminance level, the illuminance set point, the fraction of zone controlled, and the type of lighting control. It is still unclear whether the investment in a domestic lighting control system is recouped in energy savings, especially in the case of homes that are optimized for daylight use and given the fact that the average home, on a typical weekday, has only two peak moments of lighting demand. Installing dimmers is one of the easiest energy-saving improvements one can make. There are dimmers for incandescent and halogen lamps and also dimmable CFLs and LEDs. Nevertheless, a permanently dimmed lamp can indicate that a lamp with a lower wattage is sufficient enough for its task. Wireless switches, dimmers, and controls (that can be simply stuck to a surface) are suitable for Passivhaus buildings because they help to avoid cable runs and penetrations that may cause air leakage or reduced insulation space.

Lighting can be direct, indirect, or a combination of both. For general lighting purposes, luminaires of different types are installed or luminaires are used that emit light both up to the ceiling and down to the workspace. Direct lighting provides light toward a specific task or area and often creates sharp shadows and highlights. Indirect lighting provides illumination to surrounding areas and often prevents excessive brightness and contrast. Lighting techniques may be used to help light an area or highlight a specific object, whilst the *general lighting* provides the overall lighting in a space. Daylight can offer part of the general lighting during the day around the room's perimeter (approximately five meters from the façade), substituted with direct electric lighting when necessary. In large, deep rooms, the best electric lighting systems have double (or multiple) switches for controlling the front and the back of the room separately.

Task lighting provides light to a specific area or surface at which a task is occurring. Residential spaces use this technique to illuminate specific areas like desks or countertops, but also stairs and corridors. Task lighting is usually direct lighting.

4.6 Conclusions and future work

Buildings that are designed using passive strategies take advantage of the sun, wind, and water in order to achieve comfort and energy savings. Good daylighting can create pleasant dynamic environments that simultaneously reduce the energy consumption of electric lighting, heating, and cooling.

Conversely, solutions with least total energy consumption often have low visual performance. Clearly a balance must be reached between optimal visual comfort including a view to the outdoors, year-round energy efficiency, and thermal comfort. In practice, this means an important role for the size and orientation of daylight openings, shading systems, and control. The best shading systems permit variable shading that responds to current climatic conditions and are adjustable to weather and personal choices.

For assessment of visual performance and visual comfort of a building, several metrics are available. However, not all of these are easy to use for designers and planners; and in particular, the metrics with regard to veiling reflections and perceived space appearance are currently not commonly agreed upon. Besides, some of the metrics are still under development and have to be validated, and most metrics are currently not implemented in any Passivhaus design tool.

Energy-saving control innovations and solutions can help to reduce the household's energy bill. Wireless switches, dimmers, and controls are suitable for Passivhaus buildings because they help to avoid cable runs and penetrations that may cause air leakage or reduced insulation space. Future research may focus on further development of sensors and controls in agreement with human technology interaction.

References

Andersen, M., Guillemin, A., Amundadottir, M. and Rockcastle, S. 2013. Beyond illumination: an interactive simulation framework for non-visual and perceptual aspects of daylighting performance. *Proceedings of the 13th International Building Performance Simulation Association (IBPSA) Conference*, Chambéry, France, 26–30 August, pp. 2749–56.

Aries, M. B. C., Veitch, J. A. and Newsham, G. R. 2010. Windows, view, and office characteristics predict physical and psychological discomfort. *Journal of Environmental Psychology*, 30 (4): 533–41.

Aries, M. B. C., Aarts, M. P. J. and van Hoof, J. 2013. Daylight and health: a review of the evidence and consequences for the built environment. *Lighting Research and Technology*. [Online]. doi: 10.1177/1477153513509258

Berson, D. M., Dunn, F. A. and Takao, M. 2002. Phototransduction by Retinal Ganglion Cells That Set the Circadian Clock. *Science*, 295 (5557): 1070–3.

DiLaura, D., Houser, K., Mistrick, R. and Steffy, G. 2014. *IES Lighting Handbook*. 10th edition. New York: IES.

DIN 5034-1:2011. *Daylight in interiors – Part 1: General requirements (Tageslicht in Innenräumen – Teil 1: Allgemeine Anforderungen)*. Berlin: Beuth Verlag GmbH. Available at: www.beuth.de/en/standard/din-5034-1/141642928 (accessed 17 August 2014).

Ghisi, E. and Tinker, J. A. 2005. An ideal window area concept for energy efficient integration of daylight and artificial light in buildings. *Building and Environment*, 40(1): 51–61.

Heier, M. and Österbring, M. 2012. *Daylight and Thermal Comfort in a Residential Passive House – A Simulations Study Based on Environmental Classification Systems*. Thesis (*Master of Science*), Chalmers University of Technology, Goteborg, Sweden.

Hellinga, H. and Hordijk, T. 2014. The D&V analysis method: a method for the analysis of daylight access and view quality. *Building and Environment*, 79: 101–14.

Hopkinson, R. G. 1972. Glare from daylighting in buildings. *Applied Ergonomics*, 3 (4): 206–15.

IEA. 2000. *Daylight in Buildings: A Sourcebook on Daylighting, Systems and Components. IEA SHC Task 21 Report*. Berkeley, CA: Lawrence Berkeley National Laboratory.

Inanici, M. 2007. Computational approach for determining the directionality of light: directional-to-diffuse ratio. *Proceedings of the 10th International Building Performance Simulation Association (IBPSA) Conference*, Beijing, China, September 3–6, pp. 1182–8.

Leslie, R. P. 2003. Capturing the daylight dividend in buildings: why and how? *Building and Environment*, 38 (2): 381–5.

Light House Sustainable Building Centre, and Wimmers, G. 2009. *Passive Design Toolkit for Homes*. [Online]. Available from http://vancouver.ca/files/cov/passive-home-design.pdf (accessed 13 August 2014).

Littlefair, P. 1998. Passive solar urban design: ensuring the penetration of solar energy into the city. *Renewable and Sustainable Energy Reviews*, 2 (3): 303–26.

Littlefair, P. 2001. Daylight, sunlight and solar gain in the urban environment. *Solar Energy*, 70 (3): 177–85.

McLeod, R., Hopfe, C. and Kwan, A. 2013. An investigation into future performance and overheating risks in Passivhaus dwellings. *Building and Environment*, 70: 189–209.

Mardaljevic, J. and Nabil, A. 2006. The useful daylight illuminance paradigm: a replacement for daylight factors. *Energy and Buildings*, 38 (7): 905–13.

Markus, T. A. 1967. The function of windows – a reappraisal. *Building Science*, 2 (2): 97–121.

Moon, P. and Spencer, D. 1942. Illumination for a non-uniform sky. *Illuminating Engineering*, 37 (10): 797–826.

Ochoa, C. E., Aries, M. B. C., van Loenen, E. J. and Hensen, J. L. M. 2012. Considerations on design optimization criteria for windows providing low energy consumption and high visual comfort. *Applied Energy*, 95: 238–45.

Persson, M. L., Roos, A. and Wall, M. 2006. Influence of window size on the energy balance of low energy houses. *Energy and Buildings*, 38 (3): 181–8.

Reinhart, C., Mardaljevic, J. and Rogers, Z. 2006. Dynamic Daylight Performance Metrics for Sustainable Building Design. *Leukos*, 3 (1): 7–31.

Richardson, I., Thomson, M., Infield, D. and Delahunty, A. 2009. Domestic lighting: a high-resolution energy demand model. *Energy and Buildings*, 41 (7): 781–9.

Shin, J. Y., Yun, G. Y. and Kim, J. T. 2012. View types and luminance effects on discomfort glare assessment from windows. *Energy and Buildings*, 46: 139–145.

Stokes, M., Rylatt, M. and Lomas, K. 2004. A simple model of domestic lighting demand. *Energy and Buildings*, 36 (2): 103–16.

Tregenza, P. and Wilson, M. 2011. *Daylighting: Architecture and Lighting Design*. Abingdon: Routledge.

US Department of Energy. 2004. *Energy Information Administration, Residential Energy Consumption Survey, Mean Annual Electricity Consumption for Lighting by Family Income by Number of Household Members (1993)*. [Online]. Available at: www.eia.doe.gov/emeu/lighting/ (accessed 26 October 2012).

Vandahl, C., Schmits, P. and Schierz, C. 2012. *Evaluation zur Störung der Anzeigen von LCD-Bildschirmen durch die Beleuchtung*. Final Project Report of the TU-Ilmenau, Ilmenau, Germany. [Online] in German. Available at: https://www.tu-ilmenau.de/en/lichttechnik/ publikationen/publikationen-2012/

Vos, J. J. 2003. Reflections on glare. *Lighting Research and Technology*, 35 (2): 163–75.

Wienold, J. and Christoffersen, J. 2006. Evaluation methods and development of a new glare prediction model for daylight environments with the use of CCD cameras. *Energy and Buildings*, 38 (7): 743–57.

Xue, P., Mak, C. M. and Cheung, H. D. 2014. The effects of daylighting and human behavior on luminous comfort in residential buildings: a questionnaire survey. *Building and Environment*, 81: 51–9.

5

Hygrothermal simulation (transient heat and moisture assessment)

FLORIAN ANTRETTER, MATTHIAS PAZOLD, MARCUS FINK
AND HARTWIG KÜNZEL

5.1 Introduction

The Passivhaus Planning Package (PHPP) uses a steady state energy modelling method (see Chapter 1). This approach is based on a monthly calculation principle, which takes into account heat gains and heat losses at fixed indoor conditions and during a month of constant external boundary conditions.

In contrast, dynamic simulation (usually hourly or sub-hourly time steps) calculates the energy balance based on the current boundary conditions and the former time steps. Transient hygrothermal simulation tools take the dynamic interaction of heat and moisture transfer into account. As a result, they are able to provide detailed and context-specific information not only regarding dynamic building energy performance and comfort conditions but also regarding moisture movement through the building envelope.

This chapter will introduce state-of-the-art software (called WUFI® Passive) that combines both approaches, a steady state and a dynamic model, into one simulation tool. It furthermore allows for hygrothermal component simulation. This means that the majority of the workflow for Passivhaus and EnerPHit planning can be achieved via a single interface. This starts with a monthly balance method for energy design, detailing the building in dynamic building simulation in order to optimize the transient building performance. This is combined with a hygrothermal component simulation to identify the most critical components to ensure damage-free constructions whereby all updated information is mirrored in the balance-based method for certification. This reduces the time for designing the building, improves the quality and resilience of the design and last but not least eliminates errors due to the transfer of information from one design tool to another.

5.2 Implementation of the monthly based method in WUFI® Passive

The underlying method for Passivhaus design is an accurate energy balancing of the thermal losses or gains through the envelope with the internal gains or losses of that building. In the heating case in a cold climate, the losses need to be almost equal to the internal gains, and only a small difference can be made up for by an auxiliary heating system. Similarly, the balancing is performed for the cooling case; except that in this case, all internal gains are added to the thermal peak cooling load and they are not helpful to offset it.

The monthly balance-based method depends strongly on the overall heat transfer coefficients, temperature difference and considered time period. It is in accordance with EN ISO 13790:2008, in particular, the simplified approach. The heat transfer coefficient (U-value), the reciprocal of the thermal resistance, is an important input value for opaque components. It is calculated from the thermal conductivity and layer thickness of the building envelope materials. The monthly heat losses across the building envelope are calculated by determining the heat transfer coefficients, corresponding areas of the components and the appropriate boundary temperature differences according to component location. The external boundary condition of exterior walls can be: the ambient air temperature, the ground temperature (in case of a basement wall) or a decreased derivative of the ambient air temperature (in cases of attached spaces that are exterior to the thermal envelope, such as garages). With the temperature difference and a considered time period, the heating degree hours are calculated following Feist *et al.* (2007) (equation 1). The calculated heating degree hours are multiplied by a factor depending on month and outdoor temperature: 1 for October to March – see Chapter 3; a factor derived from outdoor temperature for April, May, August, September and October; and 0 for June and July. This procedure is only valid for the Northern Hemisphere and requires a monthly translation procedure in order to correctly convert climates in the Southern Hemisphere. In PHPP (version 8.5 onwards) converted climate data is now available for Southern Hemisphere locations.

Monthly heating degree hours consider the hour count of a month. The period under consideration for the annual demand depends on the monthly difference between the heat losses and the heat gains. If this difference is greater than 0.1 kWh, the month will be considered in the calculation of the total annual heating demand. This means that the length of the heating period could vary between buildings in the same location. Ventilation heat losses are calculated considering the effective air change rate, building volume, effective heat recovery efficiency and annual heating degree hours as well.

$$G_t = (\vartheta_i - \vartheta_e) \cdot t/1000 \qquad [1]$$

where:

G_t is the heating degree hours,

ϑ_i is the interior temperature (always fixed at 20°C),
ϑ_e is the exterior temperature (°C), and
t is the period under review (h).

Climate data for the steady state method contains information on the solar radiation for north, east, south, west and horizontal directions. Each component is associated with a cardinal or horizontal direction. For transparent components, the solar heat gain is calculated, considering SHGC transmittance, shading reduction factors due to obstructions, overhangs and window reveals. The solar heat gain of opaque components is computed considering the exterior absorptivity and emissivity. The required heating demand, over a specified time period, is calculated by equation 2 following Feist *et al.* (2007) and in accordance with EN ISO 13790:2008.

$$Q_H = (Q_{T,H} + Q_{V,H}) - (Q_{S,H} + Q_{I,H}) \cdot \eta_H \qquad [2]$$

where:

Q_H is the heating demand,
$Q_{T,H}$ is the transmission heat loss,
$Q_{V,H}$ is the ventilation heat loss,
$Q_{S,H}$ is the solar heat gain,
$Q_{I,H}$ is the internal heat gain, and
η_H is the heat gain utilization factor.

The monthly utilization factors (equation 3) indicate how much of the available heat gains can be used to counteract the heating demand during the heating period. They are calculated from the heat gain and loss ratio and a so-called time constant (a_H) which depends on the internal heat capacity and the total heat loss coefficient of the building.

$$\eta_H = \frac{1 - \gamma_H{}^{a_H}}{1 - \gamma_H{}^{(a_H + 1)}} \qquad [3]$$

with:

γ_H is the heat gain and loss ratio for heating demand ($\gamma_H = \dfrac{Q_T + Q_V}{Q_S + Q_I}$) (–), and
a_H is the time constant for heating demand (h).

For the time constant equation 4, a continuously heated building (more than 12 hours per day) is considered and the coefficients $a_0 = 1$ and $\tau_0 = 16$ are used.

$$a_H = a_0 + \frac{C/H_{L,H}}{\tau_0} \qquad [4]$$

where:

C is the internal building heat capacity (Wh/K) (i.e. volume · density · specific heat capacity) (i.e. $\frac{1}{g} \sum_{i=1}^{j} A_i \cdot U_i$),

$H_{L,H}$ is the total heat loss coefficient of the building for heating demand (W/K), and a_0, τ_0 are the defined coefficients.

The monthly losses are calculated using monthly heating degree hours and the annual losses using annual heating degree hours. The total heating demand, including the transmission heat losses (equation 5) for all components and thermal bridges and the ventilation heat loss (equation 6) is decreased by the total heat gain comprised of the solar (equation 7) and internal heat gain, multiplied by a utilization factor. Monthly heating degree hours are determined by multiplying the hour count of the month with a temperature difference. The difference between the interior set point and the ambient air temperature is used for components adjacent to the ambient air. The ground heating degree hours are calculated using the interior set point difference to the ground temperature. If the difference between monthly heat loss and monthly heat gain is greater than 0.1 kWh then the heating degree hours of that month are considered to contribute to the annual heating degree hours. To make projects comparable independent of their size, the total heat demand is then divided by the treated floor area (TFA) to make it specific to the treated floor area of the building.

$$Q_T = \sum_j (A_j \cdot U_j \cdot f_{T,j} \cdot G_{t,j}) + \sum_k (L_k \cdot \psi_k \cdot f_{T,k} \cdot G_{t,k}) \qquad [5]$$

where:

Q_T is the transmission heat loss,
A_j is the component area (m²),
U_j is the thermal transmittance (W/m² · K),
$f_{T,j}$ is the reduction factor for decreased temperature difference (–),
$G_{t,j}$ is the heating degree hours (kK · h),
L_k is the thermal bridge length (m), and
ψ_k is the linear thermal transmittance (W/m · K).

$$Q_V = V_V \cdot [n_{V,Sys} \cdot (1 - \eta_{SHX}) \cdot (1 - \eta_{HR}) + n_{V,Res}] \cdot C_p \rho_{,air} \cdot G_{t,e} + V_V \cdot [n_{V,Sys} \cdot \eta_{SHX} \cdot (1 - \eta_{HR})] \cdot C_p \rho_{,air} \cdot G_{t,g} \qquad [6]$$

where:

Q_V is the ventilation heat loss,
$G_{t,e}$ is the heating degree hours against ambient air (kK · h),
$G_{t,g}$ is the heating degree hours against ground (kK · h),
V_V is the effective ventilation air volume (m³),
$n_{V,Sys}$ is the mean system air change rate 1/h,
$n_{V,Res}$ is the mean natural air change rate 1/h,
η_{HR} is the effective ventilation heat recovery efficiency (–),

η_{SHX} is the effective recovery efficiency soil heat exchanger (–), and
$C_p \rho_{air}$ is the volumetric specific heat capacity of air (0.33 Wh/m³.K).

$$Q_s = \sum_\theta (r_\theta \cdot g_\theta \cdot A_{w,\theta} \cdot J_\theta)$$ [7]

where:

θ is the associated direction (north, east, south, west, horizontal) (–),
r_θ is the radiation reduction factor (averaged per orientation) (–),
g_θ is the g-value (used in Europe, averaged per orientation) (–),
$A_{w,\theta}$ is the window rough opening area (averaged per orientation) (m²), and
J_θ is the global heat gains from windows (summarized per orientation) (KWh/m²).
Note:

$$Q_I = t_{heat} \cdot q_i \cdot A_{TFA}$$ [8]

where:

Q_I is the heat energy from internal gains (kWh/a), and
t_{heat} is the length of heating season in kilohours.
q_i is the specific power (W/m²) resulting from the sum of the internal heat gains and losses.[1]

One of the Passivhaus certification criteria is the total annual primary energy demand. To calculate the primary energy demand of a building, the electrical and non-electrical demand of the mechanical system, including auxiliary energy, plug loads, appliances and lighting, are summed up. The heating demand of the domestic hot water production and distribution is taken into account, and where solar hot water generation is used, it is reduced by an estimated solar utilization fraction. It is assumed that the energy use by any device or service is not necessarily continuous. The uses are therefore reduced by different utilization factors stemming from predetermined utilization patterns, or a certain frequency is assumed for each usage. If such energy use takes place within the thermal envelope, it is added to the internal heat gains. Heat gains from occupants are already included in the heat gains. By summing these gains, an annual specific internal heat gain is estimated. The total is then multiplied by the treated floor area and hours of the month resulting in the total monthly internal heat gains.

The cooling demand is calculated using a very similar algorithm to the heating demand. One difference is that the heat gains are not weighted by the utilization factor as the heat losses are. Here the utilization factor indicates the extent to which heat losses are useful, as shown in equation 9. Another difference is the calculation of the heating degree hours. The interior temperature is set to the overheating limit temperature or summer interior temperature (slightly higher). Furthermore, the month of July is divided into 1-, 4- and 12-day peaks with increased ambient temperatures, and the rest of July results mostly in negative heating degree hours (i.e. heat gains across the building envelope).

The time constant for the cooling demand depends on the heat gains computed with the total heat loss coefficient of the components.

$$Q_C = (Q_{S,C} + Q_{I,C}) - (Q_{T,C} + Q_{V,C}) \cdot \eta_C \qquad [9]$$

where:

Q_C is the cooling demand,
$Q_{T,C}$ is the transmission heat losses,
$Q_{V,C}$ is the ventilation heat losses,
$Q_{S,C}$ is the solar heat gains,
$Q_{I,C}$ is the internal heat gains, and
η_C is the heat loss utilization factor;

and

$$\eta_C = \frac{1 - \gamma_C{}^{a_c}}{1 - \gamma_C{}^{a_c+1}} \qquad [10]$$

where:

γ_C is the heat loss and gain ratio for cooling demand ($\gamma_C = \dfrac{Q_s + Q_1}{Q_T + Q_V}$) (–), and
a_c is the time constant for cooling demand (h).

A frequency of overheating is calculated for the entire year by determining the length of the time period when the maximum allowed summer temperature is exceeded. If this frequency is too high (see Chapter 2) then additional shading measures are necessary to decrease summer overheating. Natural ventilation strategies can be employed to increase ventilation losses if the climate permits. If shading measures or natural ventilation strategies alone are not sufficient to decrease overheating then active cooling will become necessary.

For sizing of the mechanical system, peak heating and cooling loads are determined during the worst-case scenario climate conditions for winter and summer. The values used are different from ASHRAE's worst-case design temperatures. Here the worst-case periods are determined using 24-hour or longer averages to account for the delayed response time of well-insulated buildings to short-term extreme temperature swings. The conditions are provided as part of the climate data set. It contains two weather conditions to determine the peak heat load (one very cold day and one with very low solar radiation but with milder temperatures) and currently one weather condition to determine the peak cooling load. The transmission heat losses across the building envelope are calculated for these peak design conditions similarly to the annual demand calculations. Peak ventilation heat losses and the solar and internal peak heat gains are calculated similarly, and a utilization factor is not required.

5.3 Dynamic hygrothermal whole building simulation

The dynamic hygrothermal simulation combines single building components such as walls, floors and roofs to be modeled as a whole building. Coupled heat and moisture transport is simulated for each opaque component composed of different layers of materials such as wood, insulation, membranes or even air layers. This model was developed by Künzel (1994). It considers capillary action, diffusion and vapor ab- and desorption. The conductive heat and enthalpy flow by vapor diffusion with phase changes strongly depends on the moisture field. The vapor flow is simultaneously governed by the temperature and moisture field due to the exponential changes in the saturation vapor pressure with temperature. Resulting differential equations are discretized by means of an implicit finite volume method. The component model was validated by comparing its simulation results with measured data from extensive field experiments (Künzel, 1994). The temperature and moisture field within the component is simulated as a result of the model. The differential equation for heat and enthalpy flow is equation 11 and the one for liquid and vapor flow in a component is equation 12.

$$\frac{\partial H}{\partial \vartheta} \cdot \frac{\partial \vartheta}{\partial t} = \frac{\partial}{\partial x}\left(\lambda \frac{\partial \vartheta}{\partial x}\right) + h_V \frac{\partial}{\partial x}\left(\frac{\delta}{\mu} \cdot \frac{\partial(\varphi p_{sat})}{\partial x}\right) \qquad [11]$$

$$\rho_w \frac{\partial u}{\partial \varphi} \cdot \frac{\partial \varphi}{\partial t} = \frac{\partial}{\partial x}\left(\rho_w D\varphi \frac{\partial u}{\partial \varphi} \cdot \frac{\partial \varphi}{\partial t}\right) + \frac{\partial}{\partial x}\left(\frac{\delta}{\mu} \cdot \frac{\partial(\varphi p_{sat})}{\partial x}\right) \qquad [12]$$

where:

$D\varphi$ is the liquid conduction coefficient (m²/s),
H is the enthalpy of the moist building material (J/m³),
h_V is the evaporation enthalpy of the water (J/kg),
p_{sat} is the water vapor saturation pressure (Pa),
u is the water content (m³/m³),
ϑ is the temperature (°C),
λ is the thermal conductivity of the moist building material (W/m·K),
μ is the water vapor diffusion resistance factor of a dry building material (–),
ρ_w is the density of water (kg/m³),
φ is the relative humidity (–), and
t is the time (s).

Coupling all the envelope components leads to the multi-zone building model. A zone constitutes one or more rooms with the same indoor climate. The zone boundaries are the components. There is also an outdoor zone. If there are two zones attached to each other then the respective indoor climates of the neighboring zones become the exterior boundary conditions of the other. The outdoor climate is specified by location in the climate files, assuming that the building itself does not influence the microclimate. However, the indoor climate is influenced by the simulation results of the components – the component simulation is in turn influenced by the indoor climate. By considering this coupled interaction, the indoor climate can be simulated. With every time step, the change in the zonal air temperature and humidity values are generated by solving the heat- and moisture balance equations 13 and 14 (Künzel *et al.*, 2005). Besides the heat and moisture flow across the building envelope, the internal heat and moisture sources and sinks are taken into account. They are caused by people, lighting, mechanical equipment, infiltration and solar radiation. Such sources or sinks can occur not only in the zones of the building itself but also in the building envelope component with a direct influence on the heat- and moisture field of that component. Additionally transparent components, like windows, can be modeled more accurately in this way. The solar transmission that passes through a transparent component is calculated taking into account the sun elevation and azimuth angle and the orientation and inclination of the component. The solar heat gain that results from direct radiation is dependent on the sun's incidence angle. Therefore the solar heat gain coefficient is a varying input for different incidence angles. The solar heat gain – due to diffuse radiation – is calculated using the hemispherical solar heat gain coefficient. Solar heat gain contributions that pass through the transparent components are apportioned out directly to the indoor air and to the inner surfaces of opaque components according to a defined percentage (user defined, or estimated according to surface area). In addition to the shortwave solar radiation, the longwave balance is also considered for the opaque building components. Therefore not only the solar heat gains but also the longwave radiation balance can be calculated.

Equation for change in zonal air temperature:

$$\rho \cdot C_p \cdot V \cdot \frac{d\vartheta_i}{dt} = \sum_j A_j \cdot \alpha_j (\vartheta_j - \vartheta_i) + \dot{Q}_{Sol} + \dot{Q}_{IHG} + n \cdot V \cdot \rho \cdot C_p \cdot (\vartheta_a - \vartheta_i) + \dot{Q}_{VAC} \qquad [13]$$

where:

ρ is the air density (kg/m^3),
α_j is the heat transfer coefficient (W/$m^2 K$),
ϑ_a is the ambient air temperature (°C),
ϑ_j is the component indoor surface temperatures (°C),
ϑ_i is the indoor air temperature (°C),
t is the time (s),
A_j is the component areas (m²),
C_p is the specific heat capacity of air (J/kg·K),
n is the air change rate (h^{-1}),
$\dot{Q}_{Sol}$ is the shortwave solar irradiance, direct to indoor air (W),
$\dot{Q}_{IHG}$ is the internal heat sources due to people, lighting, equipment (W),
$\dot{Q}_{VAC}$ is the heat flow due to mechanical ventilation (W), and
V is the zone volume (m³).

Equation for change in zonal indoor air absolute humidity:

$$V \cdot \frac{dc_i}{dt} = \sum_j A_j \cdot \dot{g}_{wj} + n \cdot V(c_a - c_i) + \dot{W}_{IMS} + \dot{W}_{VAC} \qquad [14]$$

where:

c_a is the absolute humidity of ambient air (kg/m³),

c_i is the absolute humidity of indoor air (kg/m³),

$\dot{g}_{wj}$ is the moisture flow from indoor surface to indoor air (kg/s·m²),

$\dot{W}_{IMS}$ is the internal moisture source (kg/h), and

$\dot{W}_{VAC}$ is the moisture flow due to mechanical ventilation (kg/h).

The zone model was validated via cross-validation with other tools, experiments and standards including ASHRAE 140 (2007). The validation of both the energetic and the hygric parts of the zone model is described in Antretter *et al.* (2011). Currently, the ideal mechanical system has the capacity to supply all the heating, cooling, humidification, dehumidification and mechanical ventilation loads. As long as the system's capacity is sufficient, the indoor temperature and humidity can be maintained between defined design conditions, and thus the hourly theoretical demand can be calculated. If the capacity is not sufficient, then the temperature or moisture will either rise above or fall below the specified design conditions. If there is no ideal mechanical equipment defined, a 'free floating' indoor climate is simulated.

Every time step depends strongly on the previous steps because of the water content and thermal energy storage within the envelope and the air in the zones. A time step is thus characterized by the previous dynamic variables. New boundary conditions are created with each time step due to varying input data, primarily the outdoor climate. Using these initialization values, the coupled heat and moisture transport is calculated and consequently the zone heat and moisture balance equations are created. Should these balances not be within an expected defined accuracy range then the indoor temperature and relative humidity are iteratively adapted.

5.4 Combining steady state with transient heat and moisture models in WUFI® Passive

Both models, the monthly Passivhaus calculation and the dynamic whole building simulation, rely on user inputs and assumptions. Some inputs are predefined, such as specific building materials, their dimensions, location and orientation. Some have to be estimated by measurements or experience.

The predefined input is fundamentally the same for both models, though significantly more detailed for the dynamic simulation, partially because of the additional consideration of moisture. For example, the moisture storage function provides the information regarding the water content depending on the relative humidity of a material. However, the building geometry, room and component dimensions, widths and heights, roof inclination, etc. are the same. Fenestration parameters – like solar heat gain coefficients, frame geometries, shading reduction factors – and many other boundary conditions – such as the design indoor temperature, the overheating limit temperature and the natural air change rate – may be the same as well.

There are more differences in respect of the climate data. For the monthly method, only monthly mean values for temperatures and solar radiation are necessary. For the dynamic hourly simulation, hourly input data for the outdoor climate must be provided. For the more detailed radiation calculation, hourly diffuse and direct global solar radiation data is required. Additionally, information is needed on wind velocity and the quantity of rainfall to calculate the driving rain on the external surfaces. Aside from predefined input data, some results of the steady state method can be used for the dynamic simulation; for example, the mechanical ventilation volume flow rates for summer and winter ventilation, the simplified effective heat recovery efficiency and the space heating and cooling capacities of the mechanical equipment. Internal heat sources due to people, lighting, household and mechanical equipment are the same, but also have to be supplemented with moisture characteristics. For the monthly method, it is possible to calculate these sources using a utilization factor depending on the average usage. This is a good first assumption for the dynamic hourly simulation, but it might be more realistic to create specific time schedules.

Basically, the main difference between both models is the level of detail. A much more detailed simulation needs more computational time. The monthly method is fast and an ordinary PC can compute all results within less than a second. The dynamic results may need some minutes up to some hours, depending on the complexity of the building model. Within the dynamic simulation, it is not just the indoor air temperature that is simulated. The temperatures of the surfaces of a room are computed (e.g. to calculate the operative temperature), as is the humidity. Assessments of comfort conditions become possible once those values have been generated. The predicted mean vote (PMV) or the predicted percentage dissatisfied (PPD) are calculated hourly (see Chapter 2). Even when generally accepted boundary conditions are exceeded, one can assess how long they will be exceeded for.

The combination of both models, using many of the same initial inputs, results in numerous positive synergistic effects. On one hand, it is possible to obtain very fast results using only the monthly method, including heating, cooling, electricity and primary energy demand; and on the other, with some additional calculation time, it is possible to get detailed information on risk of mold growth and damage to components as well as detailed information on interior comfort conditions.

To simulate a building, different inputs for the desired results are necessary (as shown in Figure 5.1). Typically, a user starts with the Passivhaus calculation. The first thing to do is to input the building geometry including structure, materials, location and all of the essential Passivhaus verification data. A useful function allows the import of a 3-D building model from Sketch-Up (other commercial drawing programs can typically save files as a Sketch-Up file which can then be imported as well). Another approach is to use the integrated building wizard to create simple building geometries. It is important to designate inner and outer sides of each component correctly to ensure that boundary conditions get assigned accurately. Direct input using component lists and databases is also possible; however, the model cannot be visualized in 3-D if this option is used. Once the geometry is set, thermal bridges and windows can be defined. The

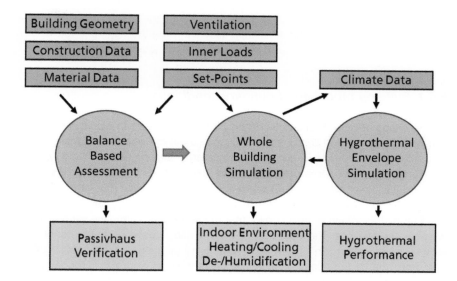

5.1
Inputs, interactions between different parts of the simulation engine, and outputs

next step is to define the usage of the building (residential or non-residential) as the input for internal loads is different for each type. Last but not least, the user has to define the mechanical equipment. Therefore different systems for heating, domestic hot water production and ventilation can be defined, as well as their distribution. The software gives feedback at all times during the entry process to inform the user about any missing inputs. Once all inputs are complete, the heating demand and all other Passivhaus verification results are calculated instantly.

For dynamic hygrothermal simulation, a user can switch to the 'WUFI Plus' mode, where some input screens will change to the dynamic input data. Some boundary conditions will not be applied automatically because more detailed information may be required (like the indoor set point temperature, which can be defined via time schedules), but there is an option to select them with just one click. If a user requires building materials or assemblies provided within the database, no additional information is needed. Only some additional parameters, such as indoor moisture loads, should be defined. The software will verify all inputs for completeness and prompt the user for missing information before the simulation begins. During the simulation, a user can monitor the heat and moisture profiles of each component or the hourly heating demand. At the end of the simulation, detailed reports and graphs can be output to illustrate the results.

An example in the following section illustrates the workflow and analysis of outputs.

5.5 Application example

The WUFI® Passive design and certification tool[2] is used in this chapter to reassess an existing certified Passivhaus. The results for the steady state method match the results of the PHPP software previously used to certify the

Passivhaus. It can be seen that the combination of the steady state methodology with a dynamic building simulation allows a more thorough analysis of the thermal and hygric performance of the building and its components.

5.5.1 Building model and boundary conditions

A Passivhaus designed for the Northern Central climate of the United States is used as a case study to demonstrate how to use the tool and to demonstrate the range of possible results. The building is located in Urbana, Illinois. Cold winters and relatively warm summers have to be taken into account while designing an energy-efficient building in this location. The built-in WUFI® weather file for Chicago, Illinois was used for the dynamic simulation. But it is also possible to use Energy Plus Weather files (.epw), test reference years (.try) and various other weather file formats. The hourly temperature and relative humidity conditions as well as the mean, minimum and maximum conditions of the cold weather year from the WUFI® weather database are shown in Figure 5.2. Those conditions were the basis for the dynamic simulation whilst the monthly method uses monthly conditions as described above. Figure 5.3 shows the monthly values for temperature and relative humidity in the steady state model.

5.2
Hourly weather data in Chicago, Illinois representing the weather file used
Note: The outputs from WUFI Passive use the comma instead of the decimal point locator (in accordance with German conventions).

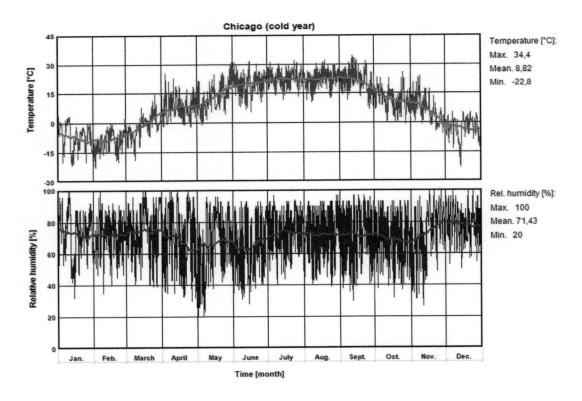

Temperature [°C]:
Max. 34,4
Mean. 8,82
Min. -22,8

Rel. humidity [%]:
Max. 100
Mean. 71,43
Min. 20

Hygrothermal simulation

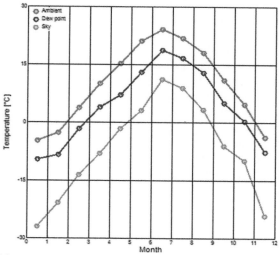

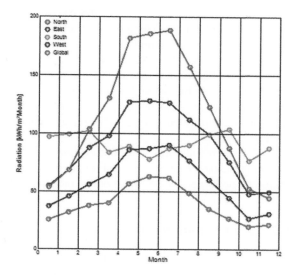

5.3
Monthly mean weather data
used for the steady state
assessment

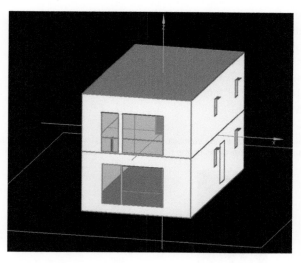

5.4
3-D building representation in
WUFI® Passive

The case study building is a two-story building with a relatively open floor plan. First and second floors are connected by an open staircase. The dwelling has three bedrooms and two bathrooms and a TFA of approximately 1,000 square feet (approx. 93 m²). The wall construction type is a lightweight frame insulated with high-density blown-in fiberglass, and with cellulose blown into the vented attic. The foundation is a fully insulated raft slab foundation system, with finished concrete floors which are insulated with expanded polystyrene (EPS). The envelope is thermal bridge free other than the installation thermal bridges from windows and doors and bridges due to services penetrations. A 3-D building model representation from the software is shown in Figure 5.4.

The standard boundary conditions for Passivhaus verification are used for the balance method.

The dynamic simulation uses the same assumptions for ventilation (0.05 air changes per hour [ac/h] for infiltration and a mechanical ventilation with 83 per cent heat recovery providing 0.32 air changes per hour), set points (temperature between 73°F and 77°F or 22.8°C and 25°C) and internal loads (4.2 kWh/d).

The verification assessment is suitable for comparison purposes. To get more detailed information on the building performance under transient boundary conditions, it is possible to apply schedules for daily profiles on different days (e.g. weekday vs. weekend) or differing occupancy periods (e.g. work day vs. holiday).

During this analysis, the building geometry is kept exactly the same; i.e. the same building model is used throughout. Also all component information is shared by both models (i.e. the monthly balance and the dynamic assessment).

5.5.2 Steady state results

In the steady state mode, monthly balances are used to compute the heating and cooling energy demand. To do this, the heat flux for each component is calculated. This allows an energy balance to be graphed identifying the highest contributors to heating and cooling loads and their improvement potential respectively. Figure 5.5 shows the contribution of different components, ventilation, internal heat gains, solar gains and heating or cooling to the overall energy balance.

All the information is available in both graphical and numerical presentations. Figure 5.6 shows a breakdown of the numerical results contributing to the heating and cooling energy balance.

5.5
Steady state results for the winter and summer energy balance (negative values for blue bars represent effective heat gains; e.g. the thermal bridges on the left)

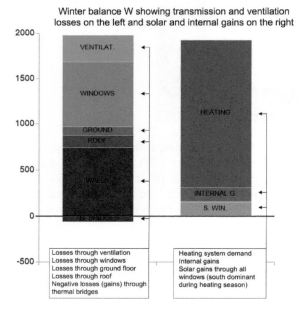

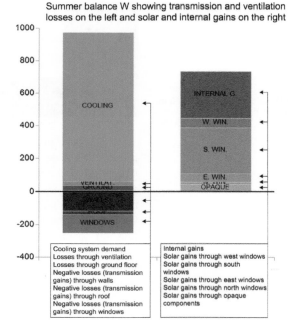

ANNUAL HEAT DEMAND		
Transmission Losses :	**3646,5**	kWh/a
Ventilation Losses:	**418,3**	kWh/a
Total Heat Losses:	**4064,8**	kWh/a
Solar Heat Gains:	**2156,9**	kWh/a
Internal Heat Gains:	**994,9**	kWh/a
Total Heat Gains:	**3151,8**	kWh/a
Utilization Factor:	**89,1**	%
Useful Heat Gains:	**2808,4**	kWh/a
Annual Heat Demand:	**1256,4**	kWh/a
Specific Annual Heat Demand:	**13,5**	kWh/m²a

ANNUAL COOLING DEMAND		
Solar Heat Gains:	**2355,7**	kWh/a
Internal Heat Gains:	**1290,5**	kWh/a
Total Heat Gains:	**3646,2**	kWh/a
Transmission Losses :	**2970,2**	kWh/a
Ventilation Losses:	**1986,9**	kWh/a
Total Heat Losses:	**4957**	kWh/a
Utilization Factor:	**62,3**	%
Useful Heat Losses:	**3088,7**	kWh/a
Cooling Demand - sensible:	**557,5**	kWh/a
Cooling Demand - latent:	**40,7**	kWh/a
Annual Cooling Demand:	**598,2**	kWh/a
Specific Annual Cooling Demand:	**6,4**	kWh/m²a

5.6
Numerical results for the annual heating and cooling demand contributions

5.5.3 Dynamic results

A dynamic building simulation enables the user to assess the overall energy performance of a building and get a more detailed look at the transient interactions between the building envelope and interior space. The integrated model also takes into account the coupled heat and moisture transport into the envelope components. Hence, the hygrothermal component performance can also be assessed.

Some example results from the dynamic simulation are shown in the following. The energy performance can be assessed in greater detail by looking at the hourly values. Thermal comfort values in the building can be computed according to common standards such as ASHRAE 55 (2010). Possible moisture-related problems can also be identified by analyzing the time-dependent temperature and moisture distributions in each component layer.

5.5.3.1 Energy demand

During the design phase of a building, it is often helpful to divide up the different contributions to the overall energy balance of the building. Figure 5.7 shows the monthly sum of all different heat fluxes in the case study building. In this example it can be seen that in the heating period, the ventilation losses are small compared to the losses through opaque elements and to the large losses through windows. The solar gains are high all year round; this leads to potential overheating (or a high cooling demand) in the summer period when gains through opaque wall assemblies and internal gains are added to the balance. By iterative analysis, it is shown that an initial improvement for both heating and cooling demand can be achieved by using better windows, whereby a lower overall U-value reduces the losses in winter and a lower solar heat gain coefficient combined with better shading reduces the gains in summer.

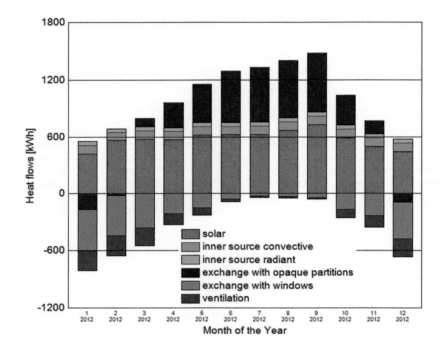

5.7
Monthly sums for all heat flows in the dynamic simulation

Use of the dynamic model yields other important insights. A closer look at the hourly values in Figure 5.8 reveals some other shortcomings with the current design. During the shoulder seasons, for example, the daily internal temperature swing reaches both the heating and the cooling set point temperatures. The graphs illustrate clearly that on some sequential days, both heating and cooling are required on the same day. One design option would be to add some additional thermal inertia to store the excess gains and release this energy later on. These effects can only be diagnosed and assessed with a dynamic simulation, since a monthly balance gives no information about problems occurring at an hourly time step.

5.5.3.2 Indoor environment

Indoor environment, especially thermal comfort, can be assessed with different standards such as the North American standard ASHRAE 55 (2010) or the international standard EN ISO 15251:2007-08 (see Chapter 2). Both approaches allow the assessment of the overall thermal comfort and localized thermal discomfort. The overall thermal comfort is in general assessed by the predicted mean vote (PMV) according to Fanger (1982) (see Chapter 2). Figure 5.9 shows the calculated PMV and the predicted percentage dissatisfied (PPD) for the example building with the standard assumptions of a 0.1 m/s air speed, a clothing insulation value of 0.9 clo and a metabolic rate of 1 met. It shows that the conditions are fluctuating between the two temperature set points causing slightly

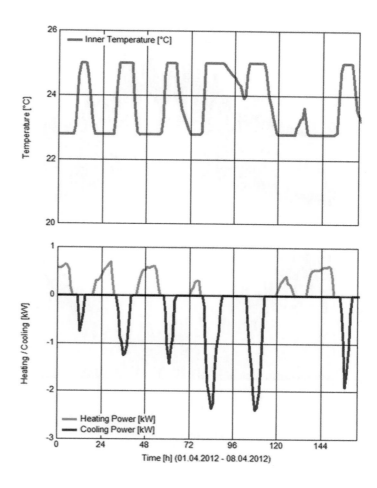

5.8
Hourly internal temperatures
and corresponding heating/
cooling loads for the first
week in April 2012

cool conditions in winter with a PMV close to –1 for the assumed clothing level. During summer, the mean vote suggests that it is slightly warm but overall the conditions are within an acceptable range, registering between –0.5 and +0.5 for the majority of the time.

5.5.3.3 Hygrothermal component assessment

The hygrothermal component assessment is used to assess the risk of moisture damage occurring in individual building components. The assessment usually contains two parts. First, the total water content and the water content of individual layers is assessed. In simple terms, the total water content should not continuously increase over time and its annual fluctuations should remain within certain limits. Figure 5.10 shows the total water content of the south-facing exterior wall. Regular annual fluctuations are visible over a four-year period and the total water content is not increasing over time.

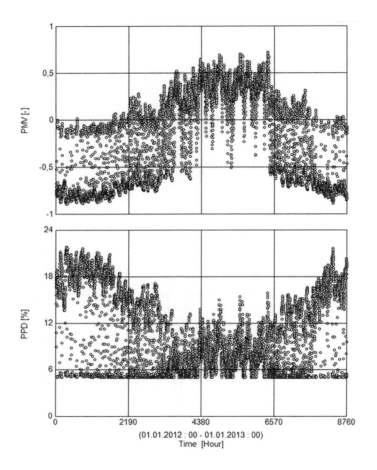

5.9
Scatter plots of the calculated PMV and PPD values for the example building

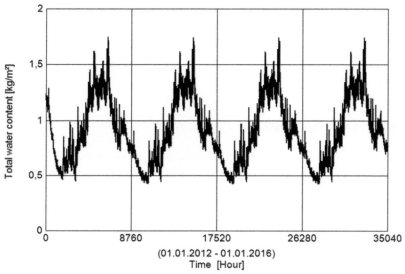

5.10
Analysis of the total water content of the south-facing exterior wall over a four-year period

Hygrothermal simulation

Furthermore, the water content of individual layers should remain below a certain limit. For example, it would be useful to analyze the mass percentage of the fiberboard sheathing to make sure that there is no long-term risk of wood rot. The drying capacity with respect to built-in moisture can also be assessed. This is helpful where, for example, wet materials are involved in the construction process or where the risk of accidental wetting (e.g. driving rain) may occur before the building is watertight.

Second, the hygrothermal conditions for critical locations can be assessed. This can be applied, for example, to assess the risk for mold growth on the interior surface of the external envelope using realistic internal boundary conditions resulting from the zone simulation. A helpful tool to assess the performance and the processes inside the components is the visualization of the temperature and humidity distribution across the building layers in the form of a dynamic visualization. Figure 5.11 shows an example of the temperature and humidity in the different layers of the exterior wall assembly at a certain point in the dynamic time sequence.

5.6 Discussion and conclusions

The combination of both steady state and dynamic models in a single tool with a user-friendly interface has the potential to transform the passive building design process by making very complex processes accessible to more design professionals. Improvements start from a simple workflow perspective since WUFI® Passive organizes the input process along a clearly guided path using a tree

5.11
Temperature and humidity visualization of a component under dynamic hygrothermal simulation

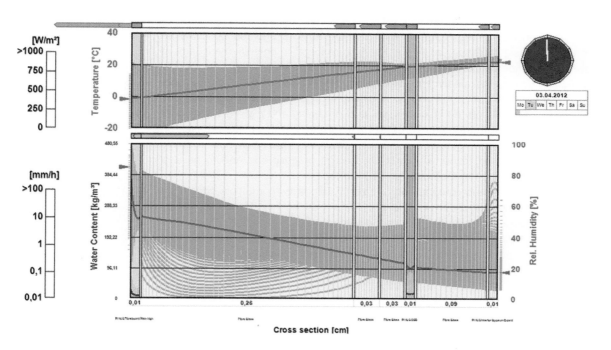

structure while providing constant feedback on missing data entries. The design optimization process is assisted in passive verification mode by allowing the modeler to store (side by side) an essentially infinite number of different cases. WUFI® Passive organizes all of the required project and systems data for certification into one file and has the potential to simplify the certification process by eliminating opportunities for mistakes, thus improving quality assurance during the planning process. The steady state calculation is fast and efficient and outputs include both numerical and illustrative graphical representations of the results, which are very helpful in discussions with clients.

Even more significant are the improvements with respect to the design process. Previously, the designer lacked sufficient information to readily prescribe the correct window value combinations for greatly varying climates. The recommended low window U-values and g-values (solar heat gain coefficients) greater than 50 per cent might contribute to overheating, and in some cases produce the need for heating and cooling during the same day during shoulder seasons. Previously, the designer lacked the resolution of information that would help to identify the most effective climate specific combination of those values while assuring hourly thermal comfort (as demonstrated in the example above where the designer was forced to come up with a best guess).

Hitherto, many designers have been forced to master and use separate hygrothermal tools and secondary dynamic energy models to assess their designs and specifications. All additional tools necessitate some form of double entry of material properties, geometry and mechanical specifications. During the design process, many of those pieces of information are still in flux and therefore require the continual updating of three models whenever a single design change is made. The use of non-integrated models is not only labor intensive but also increases the likelihood of human error.

In conclusion, the most significant improvements attained by using an integrated design tool such as WUFI® Passive are the all-in-one risk management and optimization capability. The next generation of passive modeling for varying climates needs to include dynamic simulation to improve the model with respect to cooling and dehumidification load accuracy as well as to improve the ability to predict thermal comfort issues, such as overheating and high relative indoor humidity. The few optimization conclusions highlighted in this chapter based on the dynamic model outputs of the Urbana, Illinois example show how dynamic results can be used to better inform the design process and ensure passive building designs are more efficient and comfortable.

As refurbishment projects and larger buildings with multiple zones are being increasingly modeled to meet the advance energy standards, it will become imperative to model and verify comfort and performance in multiple zones and components. WUFI® Passive provides an integrated design tool that can help facilitate the delivery of more complex design challenges.

References

Antretter, F., Sauer, F., Schöpfer, T. and Holm, A. 2011. Validation of a hygrothermal whole building simulation software. *Proceedings of Building Simulation 2011: 12th Conference of International Building Performance Simulation Association*, Sydney, Australia, 14–16 November.

ASHRAE (2007) Standard 140: *Building Thermal Envelope and Fabric Load Tests*. Atlanta, GA: ASHRAE.

ASHRAE (2010) Standard 55: *Thermal Environmental Conditions for Human Occupancy*. Atlanta, GA: ASHRAE.

EN ISO 13790:2008. *Energy Performance of Buildings— Calculation of Energy Use for Space Heating and Cooling*; German version EN ISO 13790:2008 Energieeffizienz von Gebäuden – Berechnung des Energiebedarfs für Heizung und Kühlung. s.l.: ISO.

EN ISO 15251:2007-08. *Indoor Environmental Input Parameters for Design and Assessment of Energy Performance of Buildings Addressing Indoor Air Quality, Thermal Environment, Lighting and Acoustics*. s.l.: ISO.

Fanger, P. O. 1982. *Thermal Comfort*. Malabar, FL: Robert E. Krieger Publishing Company.

Feist, W., Pfluger, R., Schnieders, J., Kah, O., Kaufmann, B., Krick, B. and Bastian, Z. 2007. *PHPP Handbook. 2007*. Darmstadt: PHI.

Künzel, H. M. 1994. *Simultaneous Heat and Moisture Transport in Building Components*. Dissertation, University of Stuttgart.

Künzel, H. M., Holm, A., Zirkelbach, D., Karagiozis, A. N., Simulation of indoor temperature and humidity conditions including hygrothermal interactions with the building envelope, *Solar Energy*, Volume 78, Issue 4, April 2005, Pages 554–561, ISSN 0038-092X.

Notes

1   Residential, standard 2.1W/m^2; Residential, elderly/students 4.1W/m^2; Non-residential, school 2.8W/m^2; Non-residential, office/admin 3.5W/m^2.

2   Note: At the time of writing WUFI Passive is not recognised by the PHI as a certification tool, however some national organisations such as PHIUS recognise its use for both design and certification purposes.

6

Heat and hot water generation for domestic buildings

MAREK MIARA

6.1 Introduction

In all residential buildings, a heating system has to cover two types of energy demand: the space heating (SH) demand and the demand for domestic hot water (DHW). In a Passivhaus, the space heating demand is reduced by approximately 70–80 per cent in comparison with a conventional (new) building (Feist *et al.*, 2005; Schiano-Phan *et al.*, 2008), with the DHW demand remaining typically the same for all types of houses. Thus, whereas in a conventional building, the space heating demand dominates, in a Passivhaus, both energy demands are at approximately the same level, or the space heating demand may be even lower. These considerations have a large impact on the choice, design and operation of a heating system in a Passivhaus.

One of the major features of the Passivhaus concept is the reduction of heat losses. The transmission losses are reduced by improving the thermal performance of the building envelope, characterized by very low U-values of walls (<0.15 W/(m²K)) and windows (0.8 W/(m²K)) and the avoidance of thermal bridges. Ventilation losses are reduced by a very low air leakage and the use of a mechanical ventilation system with a highly efficient heat recovery system. All these measures combine to achieve a maximum space heating load (in most cases) of less than 10 W/m². Figuratively, this means that a single 100 W light bulb would be almost enough to heat a 10 m² room in a Passivhaus. The design power output of a heat generator for a single-family Passivhaus dwelling is typically about 1–2 kW. For the Central European climate, the aforementioned load corresponds to a yearly space heating demand below 15 kWh/(m²a). This value is often used as a definition of a Passivhaus. Only around one-third of the total heat losses are covered by the heating system. The remaining two-thirds are covered by useful solar gains and useful internal gains. All three types of gains are of the same order of magnitude.

Since the space heating load of a Passivhaus is so low, it may be covered by an air heating system alone, with a maximum supply air temperature of about 50°C. There is no longer a need to place radiators on the outer walls to counter-balance the downdraughts from windows thanks to a negligible difference

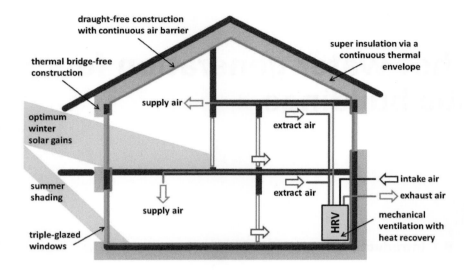

draught-free construction
with continuous air barrier

thermal bridge-free
construction

super insulation via a
continuous thermal
envelope

supply air

extract air

optimum
winter
solar gains

summer
shading

extract air

intake air

exhaust air

triple-glazed
windows

supply air

HRV

mechanical
ventilation with
heat recovery

6.1
The principles for Passivhaus
with a heat recovery system
and an air-based heat
distribution system (heat
generator is not shown)

between the surface temperature of the outer walls and windows and the room air temperature. The air-based heat distribution system is thus sufficient for a Passivhaus, although the use of conventional water-based heating systems is not excluded.

In addition to the low heating load of a Passivhaus, the heating season for such a building is also shortened. The need for space heating is reduced to four to six months in Northern and Central Europe, compared with up to nine months for conventional buildings. This is attributable to a strong reduction of heat losses combined with a much-improved utilization of solar and internal gains. These aspects underline the unique character of heating systems in a Passivhaus and underline the considerable share of heating energy required for DHW.

The following are consequences arising from the aforementioned features whilst taking into account the economic implications:

- The significant share of DHW in the energy demand is an important factor in the choice of the heating system for a Passivhaus. In some cases, the production of DHW by an independent system could be considered a more reasonable option. For example, a wood stove for heating can be supplemented by a solar thermal system for DHW.
- The low space heating load makes it possible to distribute the heat effectively with the air, and not through a water-based system, without compromising the thermal comfort for the occupants. This allows a reduction of heating system costs.
- Since the costs of heat generators are not directly proportional to their heating power, the specific costs of the heating are higher than for conventional buildings. The investment and operation costs are accompanied by a low heat demand. Accordingly, the payback period of systems with high investment costs and low heat demand is much longer than in the case of buildings with high heat demand. As a consequence, systems with very low investment

Heat and hot water generation for domestic buildings

costs, even with high operation costs, can be better from a purely economic perspective. For example, operation costs of heating and DHW supplied by direct electric heating for a 150 m² family dwelling are approximately £600 (for electricity price of 15 pence/kWh). Taking into account the very low investment costs of direct electric heating (compared to other generators), the payback period of systems with lower operational costs is very long. There are not many heat generators on the market with a heat power low enough (in the range of 1–3 kW) for a single-family house. Oversized appliances cause unnecessary investment costs, risk of overheating the rooms and finally, in many cases, less efficient operation of the appliances (due to poorly matched power factors).

- The low space heating load makes it possible to distribute the heat (through water-based systems) with low temperatures. This fact is beneficial if the heating system is based on a heat pump, as it contributes to its higher efficiency.

- In case of systems with house service connection, such as district heating or natural gas, the cost for the connection stands in adverse relation to short heating periods and low heat demand (Humm, 1998). According to that, systems not requiring any connection (e.g. wood stoves) or using connections available anyway (e.g. electrically driven heat pumps) may be beneficial from an economic point of view. However, when assessing the economic aspects many factors are to be considered: the initial investment costs, operating costs and maintenance/service costs. All these may vary depending on the local/national market characteristics.

6.2 Various possibilities

6.2.1 Direct electric (DE) approach

This method is characterized by the lowest investment and easiest installation. Unfortunately, compared to other solutions, a direct electrical heating system is the least ecologically friendly and results in the highest primary energy consumption and the highest operational costs. This perspective changes though if the electricity comes partly or fully from renewable sources. Due to their low costs and versatility, electric heating elements are very often combined with systems described below or serve as back-up solutions for non-electric approaches.

6.2.2 Heat pumps

There are two different approaches for heat pumps in a Passivhaus. In both of them, a heat pump (Figure 6.2) can provide the heat required for space heating and domestic hot water.

The first approach is based on a standard heat pump, using outside air or the ground as a heat source. Ground source heat pumps use horizontal

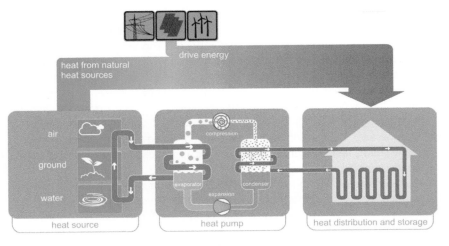

6.2
Scheme of the engine-driven
compression heat pump

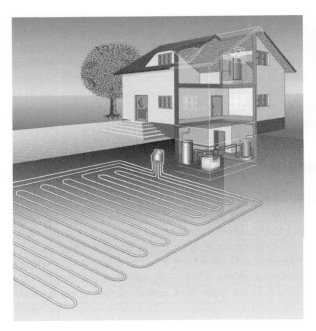
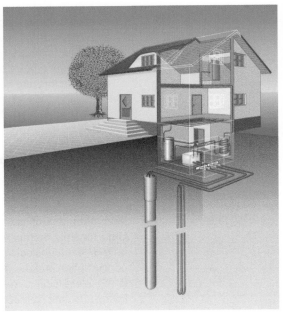

6.3
Scheme of horizontal and
vertical (boreholes) collectors
for ground source heat pumps

(ground collectors) or vertical (boreholes) pipes to extract heat from the ground (Figure 6.3). In this approach, the heat produced is delivered to rooms using a water-based heat distribution system (radiators or underfloor). The advantage of ground source heat pumps (GSHP) is high efficiency of the system and the possibility of passive cooling in summer months.

The capital costs of air source heat pumps (ASHP) are significantly lower than for ground source; unfortunately, their efficiency is also lower. From an economic point of view, the difference in the investment costs has to be compared with the difference in the running costs. Since the heat demand in a Passivhaus is very low, the running costs are generally very small as well. Thus, a higher investment for a ground heat pump is usually difficult to offset via its higher efficiency and lower net running costs within the typical calculation period of 20 years. From the ecological and energetic point of view, however, given that electrical heat pumps use electricity, obviously the higher their efficiency the better.

The second approach is based on heat pumps developed specifically for a Passivhaus. So-called compact ventilation units or compact service units (CSUs) combine ventilation with heat recovery and a small heat pump using the exhaust air as a heat source (Figure 6.4). The heat pump extracts heat even further after the heat recovery from the ventilation, which is then used to further post-heat the preheated supply air exiting the heat recovery unit. The system includes an integrated DHW tank and also produces domestic hot water. The heat for the space heating is distributed through the supply air of the ventilation system. To avoid odour emissions from dust carbonization on heated surfaces, the maximum temperature of the supply air in the air heater is restricted to 55°C. Considering the recommended air flow rates, the total heat deliverable to the rooms with the aforementioned temperature is approximately 10 W/m² (Feist et al., 2005). This value correlates very well with the target space heating load for Passivhaus. Compared with other heat pumps (e.g. ground coupled heat pumps), the compact service units achieve lower efficiency (usually SPF values less than 3.0). Other disadvantages of CSUs are the comparatively small DHW tanks and the low DHW reheat power (in some cases, this could lead to an increased use of a direct electric back-up heater). Some CSUs are equipped with bigger buffer tanks and solar thermal collectors (Figure 6.4). This solution improves the ecological balance of the system but makes the already-high investment costs of the unit even higher.

6.4
Scheme of compact ventilation unit in combination with solar collector

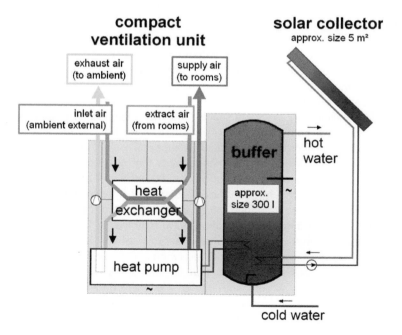

6.2.3 Natural gas

In countries with well-developed natural gas grids, it may be a practical solution to use a natural gas boiler in a Passivhaus. A possible disadvantage may be the cost for the home service connection, making the specific heating costs higher. To avoid the connection costs, liquid petroleum gas (LPG) could be an alternative. It must be taken into account that the costs of liquid gas are higher than those of natural gas, and there is the need to store large bottles externally.

One more problematic aspect for a heating system based on natural gas is the power of the gas boiler. The majority of gas boilers available on the market are oversized for the heat requirements of a single-family Passivhaus dwelling. Even using the modulation, the delivered power is usually still too high (Georges *et al.*, 2012). Installation of a heat buffer proves necessary in order to avoid frequent start/stop cycles of the boiler; such a buffer is required anyway if the heating system also includes a solar thermal collector. The combination of natural gas and solar energy is advantageous from the ecological point of view because gas has lower carbon intensity than electricity. Unfortunately, as a result of the very low heat demand in a Passivhaus and the high investment costs, this solution is usually not favorable from an economic point of view.

6.2.4 Wood-based approaches

Another type of heating solution appropriate for a Passivhaus are wood-based approaches. Only the highly efficient devices should be taken into account, so that a proper environmental performance can be ensured. Good examples are pellet stoves. Due to their semi-automatic operation combined with the short heating period and low energy demand in a Passivhaus, the additional work usually associated with cleaning and feeding wood stoves occurs very rarely.

Small wooden (pellet) stoves without any water-based heat distribution system radiate their power directly to the spaces where they are located. In a Passivhaus, they usually pose a danger of localized overheating (Feist *et al.*, 2005) as their heating power is too high for the demand. Without good air circulation in the whole dwelling (e.g. in closed spaces and with a large number of separated rooms), there is a contiguous risk of undersupplying heat to other rooms. A separate subsystem for DHW generation is necessary when using room stoves.

There are also wood and biomass stoves that connect to a water-based heat distribution system with a buffer tank and a hot water storage vessel. The volume of the buffer should be sufficient to store the heat produced with the nominal power of the stove during the minimal combustion cycle. For the wood pellets, this time amounts to approximately 30 minutes. In the case of a stove with the thermal power of 3 kW, a buffer of approximately 200 liters is needed.

Safety issues shouldn't be neglected when using wood-based approaches in a Passivhaus. It is very important that no flue gases can infiltrate into the house. Because of the airtight envelope of the building, wooden stoves have to be equipped with an independent air supply and flue gas removal. The safety strategy should be elaborated separately for each project when planning a wood-based approach in a Passivhaus. It is important that a safety interlock exists that will cut off the air supply to the wood stove if a pressure imbalance occurs (i.e. the room containing the combustion device becomes depressurized or the combustion becomes overpressurized). Where wood-based stoves are installed in rooms with a ventilation system typical for Passivhauses, only approved products are to be used. The stove must be operated in room-air-independent mode.

6.2.5 Solar thermal collectors

Solar collectors can be combined with all of the aforementioned solutions. Without using big (inter-seasonal) buffer storage and significantly oversizing the area of the collectors, they cannot provide sufficient energy to cover the annual energy demand for both space heating and DHW. However, solar thermal collectors can provide the majority of the yearly energy for DHW (Schnieders and Hermelink, 2006) if they are well designed. The greatest environmental benefit is obtained if the solar thermal collectors substitute the use of direct electricity. (In other words, using solar to offset biomass results in a far less substantial carbon saving.)

6.3 Best practice using heat pump solutions

6.3.1 Single-family dwelling in Styria region (Austria)

6.5
South façade of a single-family Passivhaus in the Styria region (Austria)
Source: Zottl *et al.* (2010)

The first example is a detached single-family house with four inhabitants, located in Austria. The house was built in 2008 to a low energy performance standard in lightweight construction and with a heated area of 210 m². The designed heat load (according to BS EN 12831:2003) was 3.5 kW or 17 W/m². The efficiency of the heating and cooling system in the house was investigated by the Austrian Institute of Technology (AIT) in the framework of the International Energy Agency (IEA) Heat Pump Programme (HPP) Annex 32.

6.3.1.1 Technical concept

The building is equipped with an integrated groundwater heat pump and CSU with ventilation heat recovery. This single CSU covers all the building functions: space heating (SH), domestic hot water (DHW), space cooling (SC) and ventilation. Contrary to common compact unit designs for a Passivhaus where the heat emission is provided by the ventilation system (i.e. the system is equipped with air heating and uses only the exhaust air as heat source), this system uses a ground source and a water-based heat distribution system that enables higher capacities and lower supply temperatures. The design temperatures of the underfloor heating (UFH) are 35°C/30°C (flow/return). The source system consists of a 200 m horizontal ground collector, which also provides passive space cooling in summertime. For the emission of cooling power to rooms, the system does not use the underfloor pipes (as for space heating mode) but, rather, makes additional use of the ceiling with 200 m of pipes embedded in the concrete. Thereby, the passive cooling can be operated with even higher supply temperatures near the indoor temperature, since the ceiling yields a better heat transfer in cooling mode than the floor.

Moreover, a 300 l domestic hot water storage tank charged by a desuperheater (secondary heat exchanger) is integrated in the casing.

6.3.1.2 Results of field monitoring

The monitoring period covers year-round monitoring data from October 2008 to October 2009. The total energy produced by the heat pump and source system in the monitored period was 9,37 kWh. Sixty-two per cent or 5,82 kWh corresponding to 27.7 kWh/(m²a) was consumed for space heating which is consistent with the low energy building but higher than the intended SH demand of a Passivhaus. The annual DHW consumption with 1,54 kWh was quite low and comprised 21 per cent of the total consumption of space heating and DHW. The typical range of Passivhaus is 30–50 per cent.

The seasonal performance factor (SPF) of the generator system including source auxiliary energy was split up into the SPF for heating and the SPF for domestic hot water. The whole system reached an SPF value of 4.1. The space heating reached a value of 4.3 and the domestic hot water production, 3.7. The high seasonal performance factor for DHW was due to the high heat source temperature during summer, which was increased by the passive cooling operation. By considering all auxiliary drives, the SPF value reached a value of 3.4. The relatively high fraction of auxiliary energy consumption of 45 per cent of the total electricity consumption was also due to the passive cooling operation since, heat pump electricity was used solely for the DHW operation in the summer, while only the pumps were running in passive cooling operation.

6.3.2 Single-family Passivhaus located in southern Germany

The second example shows a Passivhaus with 133 m² heated area, which was built in 2002 in southern Germany. The calculated heat energy demand amounts to 14.8 kWh/(m²a). The measurement of that house was a part of project '100 Passivhaus' led by Fraunhofer Institute for Solar Energy Systems ISE.

6.3.2.1 Technical concept

The main part of the heating and ventilation system is a compact ventilation unit with an integrated heat pump using exhaust air as a heat source. The system also includes a 320 l domestic hot water tank and solar thermal collectors with 4.6 m² absorber area. The heat for space heating is distributed through a ventilation system. For the SH, as well as for the DHW, additional direct electric heating elements have been installed as a back-up solution. An additional ground heat exchanger has been installed to preheat the outside air entering the heat recovery unit in winter and to precool it in summer.

6.6
East façade of prefabricated single-family Passivhaus in southern Germany

6.3.2.2 Results of field monitoring

The monitoring period covers three years monitoring data from July 2002 to June 2005. The yearly average value of total electric energy consumption for ventilation, space heating and DHW was 2,55 kWh respectively 19.1 kWh/(m²a). The share of the direct electric heating amounted to approximately 20 per cent.

The average yearly value of space heating energy consumption amounted to 21 kWh/(m²a) respectively 2,79 kWh, which comes close to the calculated demand of 14.8 kWh/(m²a). The rule of thumb says that an increase of the room temperature by 1°C causes the increase of SH energy consumption in a Passivhaus in the range of 20 per cent. Considering the average room temperature during the measurement period of approximately 22°C, it could be said that the investigated building functioned very well as a Passivhaus and the predicted values have been confirmed. The annual DHW consumption amounted to 1,52 kWh and comprised 35 per cent of the total consumption of space heating and DHW. The solar thermal collector covered 67 per cent of the delivered energy needed for the actual DHW consumption and the heat losses of the DHW buffer tank.

The seasonal performance factor (SPF) of the heat pump (not including the direct electrical back-up heater) for space heating and domestic hot water reached the average value of 2.5. Compared with the first example of the Passivhaus from Austria, the value is rather low. It must be noted, however, that there are big differences between heat source and heat sink temperatures of both systems. Taking into account the high supply temperature of 45°C for the air heat distribution system and the less advantageous heat source (exhaust air compared to ground) in the second building, the SPF value is at an acceptable level and is within the typical range of SPF values for heat pumps combined in ventilation systems (compact ventilation units).

References

BS EN 12831:2003. *Heating Systems in Buildings. Method for Calculation of the Design Heat Load.* Brussels: European Committee For Standardization.

Feist, W., Schnieders, J., Dorer, V. and Haas, A. 2005. Re-inventing air heating: convenient and comfortable within the frame of the Passive House concept. *Energy and Buildings*, 37 (11): 1186–203.

Georges, L., Massart, C., Van Moeseke, G. and De Herde, A. 2012. Environmental and economic performance of heating systems for energy-efficient dwellings: case of passive and low-energy single-family houses. *Energy Policy*, 40: 452–64.

Humm, O. 1998. *NiedrigEnergieHäuser und PassivHäuser*. Staufen: Ökobuch Verlag.

Schiano-Phan, R., Ford, B., Gillott, M. and Rodrigues, L. T. 2008. The Passivhaus standard in the UK: Is it desirable? Is it achievable? *25th Conference on Passive and Low Energy Architecture*, Dublin, 22–24 October.

Schnieders, J. and Hermelink, A. 2006. CEPHEUS results: measurements and occupants' satisfaction provide evidence for Passive Houses being an option for sustainable building. *Energy Policy*, 34 (2): 151–71.

Zottl, A., Huber, H. and Köfinger, C. 2010. *Best Practice, Passive House with Ground-Coupled Heat Pump Compact Unit and Ventilation Heat Recovery*. s.l.:IEA.

7

Heating and cooling of nonresidential Passivhaus buildings using passive and environmental energy strategies

DOREEN E. KALZ

7.1 Introduction

Today, energy-optimized nonresidential buildings with a comparatively low heating and cooling demand can be realized (see Chapter 1). In these buildings, it is possible to establish a pleasant interior climate largely by passive measures without costly building services equipment. This is made possible primarily by a combination of carefully coordinated measures with the following basic elements: very good thermal insulation and solar protection, sufficient thermal storage capacity in the building, and an airtight building envelope in conjunction with basic ventilation as well as heat recovery (see Chapters 3 and 8). Avoiding mechanical cooling and air conditioning in summer in favour of low energy cooling is possible if the buildings are planned carefully so that architecture, structural design, occupants' requirements, and building services equipment are carefully synthesized in an integrated overall concept.

Efficient and sustainable building and energy concepts need to respect the occupants' requirements for thermal, visual, and acoustic comfort (see Chapters 2 and 8), but also foster building concepts that feature highly energy-efficient systems for heating and cooling with significantly reduced energy consumption. Under this premise, a holistic approach to the evaluation of heating and cooling systems seeks to achieve a global optimum of interior thermal comfort, useful cooling and heating energy use, and the primary energy use of the entire building services systems.

In Germany, buildings contribute 35 percent to the total final (delivered) energy consumption. This corresponds to an output of 342 million tonnes of CO_2 for space heating, air conditioning, cooling, and lighting (Wietschel *et al.*, 2010). Reducing the emissions from buildings is an essential component for achieving the climate change objectives of the federal government and ensuring sustainable energy supply. In 2008, the final (delivered) energy consumption in Germany amounted to 2,500TWh (AGEB, 2013). About one-third was attributable to the heat consumption for space heating (29 percent, 720TWh) and hot water (5 percent, 125TWh). Seventy per cent of this heat demand is accounted for by households, 20 percent by trade, commerce, and services, and about 7 percent by industrial buildings.

In terms of cooling, about half the office and administration buildings in Germany are equipped with cooling or air conditioning devices (BMVBS/BBR, 2008). The typical useful energy demand for cooling of nonresidential buildings ranges between 10 and 35 $kWh_{therm}/(m^2_{net}a)$ (VDMA, 2011; Bettgenhäuser *et al.*, 2011). Many studies predict an increase in energy demand for cooling of nonresidential buildings in Germany and in Europe. The authors of a joint study by Prognos and Öko-Institut (Kirchner and Matthes, 2009) assumed that all newly constructed nonresidential buildings will be equipped with cooling devices from 2015 onwards. In the case of refurbishments, it is probable that considerable upgrades with cooling systems will be made.

In order to pave the way for energy savings in nonresidential buildings, the German Federal Ministry of Economics and Energy (BMWi) has launched an intensive research program (Energy-Optimised Building: EnOB, 2014) for the planning and evaluation of demonstration projects. The EnOB Program was established on the premise that appropriate monitoring and evaluation of building and HVAC performance contribute significantly to the design of energy-efficient building concepts. Following a stringent load-reduction strategy, a limited primary energy use of 100 $kWh_{prim}/(m^2_{net}a)$ and a final energy use of 60 $kWh_{final}/(m^2_{net}a)$, comprising 40 $kWh_{final}/(m^2_{net}a)$ heating energy and 20 $kWh_{final}/(m^2_{net}a)$ electrical energy, were proposed as goals for the complete building services technology (HVAC and lighting) for all newly constructed nonresidential buildings.

The final energy use for new nonresidential buildings monitored within the EnOB program lies between 30 and 65 $kWh_{final}/(m^2_{net}a)$. This value is five to ten times lower than the amount typically used by air-conditioned buildings (Wagner and Wambsganß, 2004).

7.2 Use of environmental energy for heating and cooling

Cooling concepts utilizing natural or mechanical night ventilation have been successfully implemented in office and commercial buildings in recent years. Experience gained in low energy office buildings in Mid-European climates cooled via night ventilation shows that pleasant room temperatures can be achieved during summer even without air conditioning systems. However, when high temperatures persist for longer periods (e.g. in the summers of 2003 and 2006), relatively high outdoor overnight temperatures prevent sufficient cooling of the building's thermal mass. In such cases, structural measures and mechanically supported night ventilation are often insufficient to guarantee a comfortable interior climate during the daytime (Pfafferott, 2004; Santamouris, 2007).

Water-based thermo-active building systems (TABS) are considerably more effective. These systems cool the building structure using tube heat exchangers, which are integrated into the ceiling and floor in order to condition the office, either completely or as support system. If TABS are supplied with cold from the ground, or from the outdoor air via a cooling tower, electrical energy is only needed for distribution, and not generation, of the cooling energy. Buildings with low heating requirements can also be heated using TABS (Kalz and Pfafferott 2007; Kalz 2011).

7.2.1 Ground as heat source and heat sink

The almost constant temperatures in the ground (from a depth of 25 m to 100 m) can be utilized very economically in terms of energy and operating processes for (direct) geothermal heating/cooling. The geothermal heating and cooling performance depends on the thermal conductivity of the geological formation, the heat capacity of the soil, the material and type of the heat exchanger and the filling of the borehole (borehole thermal resistance), the existence of groundwater flows, and the distance between the heat exchanger, the operation (heat source and/ or sink, continuous or intermittent operation) and the building's heating/cooling demand. To a smaller extent, the specific heat (per volume) also plays a role; for example, when storing and/or extracting heat from the ground. The borehole heat exchangers consist of two to three double pipes, with a diameter of 32 mm, which are lowered into a borehole 30 m to 100 m deep (Koenigsdorff 2011).

Fluid temperatures in boreholes are subjected to fluctuations due to seasonal weather and operational influences. Averaged supply temperatures in summer range between 10°C and 17°C, given a sufficiently dimensioned geothermal system. Maximum supply temperatures can reach 17°C to 20°C (Figure 7.1). If the heat storage capacity of the ground is depleted due to inadequate sizing of the borehole heat exchangers (BHEXs), supply temperatures can rise up to 22°C. In this case, effective cooling of the building is not guaranteed.

7.1
Measured temperature [°C] of the undisturbed ground (sensor placed 8 m from the next three thermally activated borehole heat exchangers). Portrayed are supply and return water, the ambient air and the ground temperatures in 1 m, 3 m, and 50 m depths over the course of one operation year

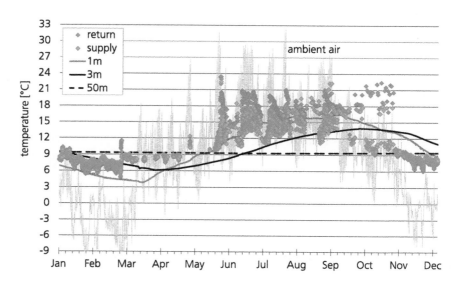

During winter months, supply temperatures range between 6°C and 14°C and differ typically about 2K to 4K from the return temperatures. Values for supply/return temperatures and their differences vary over a much wider range in summer than in winter. This can be explained by the cooling demand that fluctuates more than the heating demand of the building and by the temperature difference between the ground and the fluid in the BHEXs. In winter, return water temperatures lie between 8°C and 10°C and the mean ground temperatures, between 8.2°C and 10.8°C.

7.2.2 Groundwater as heat source and heat sink

Near-surface ground layers often contain aquifers, which, if certain prerequisites are met (small amounts of dissolved iron and manganese, no water protection area), allow for an easy and quite inexpensive extraction of groundwater to deliver heating or cooling to a building via a heat exchanger. In an open loop system, groundwater can be extracted by a production well and injected into a second well within a distance of at least 8m in order to prevent thermal short-circuits. A second approach extracts water by means of a production well and disposes it into a water surface such as a river. In Mid-European climates, groundwater exhibits nearly constant temperatures between 8°C and 12°C over the course of a year, and there is no obvious dependency on the ambient air (Figure 7.2). Therefore, groundwater offers excellent conditions for use as a heat source/ sink. The performance is primarily dependent on geological circumstances and the volume of the available groundwater. There is no distinct dependency of the water supply temperature on the water return temperature. Temperature differences between supply and return water are in the range of 2K to 5K in the heating mode and 4K to 8K in the cooling mode.

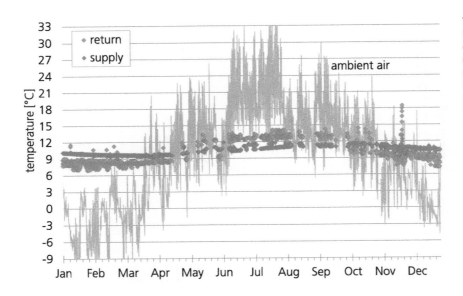

7.2
Measured temperature [°C] of groundwater used as heat source for a heat pump and as a heat sink for direct cooling. Portrayed are supply and return water, and the ambient air temperature for one year of operation

7.2.3 Ambient air as heat source and heat sink

The cool night air can be used as a further heat sink via a cooling tower. Here, a distinction between wet and dry cooling towers is drawn. With dry towers, recooling of the carrier fluid in the thermo-active building system (TABS) is only possible if the outdoor temperature is below the required water temperature. Thus, during warm seasons, the recooling period is restricted to the night and the early hours of the morning. Wet cooling towers make use of the evaporation cooling effect since the heat exchanger on the air side is sprayed by means of a secondary water circuit. In this case, the wet bulb temperature (which is significantly lower than the outdoor air temperature, especially if the outdoor air is dry) can be taken into account. This enables an extended duration of the recooling period. It also has a positive effect on the energy efficiency and the maximum cooling capacity. But unlike the ground or groundwater, outdoor air can scarcely be considered a viable option as a heat source for operation in winter. Water supply temperatures delivered by the cooling tower are strongly dependent on the ambient air and the wet bulb temperature. The higher the nocturnal outdoor air temperature, the higher are the supply water temperatures.

7.2.4 Energy efficiency

The performance characteristic and final energy use of the primary pump have a large impact on the efficiency of the environmental heat sources/sinks. The primary pump circulates the heat carrier fluid through the borehole heat exchangers or to the cooling tower within a closed loop. Furthermore, it pumps the water from the well in an open loop. As a matter of fact, the installed power demand for the primary pump is higher in open loop (well systems) than in closed loop systems. It is important to decrease the duration of operation and to reduce the flow with decreasing temperature difference between the supply and

7.3

Use of near-surface geothermal systems as direct environmental heat sink: supplied cooling energy [kWh$_{therm}$/(m²$_{net}$a)], required electrical auxiliary energy for primary pump [kWh$_{el}$/(m²$_{net}$a)], and energy efficiency expressed as seasonal performance factor (SPF) [kWh$_{therm}$/kWh$_{el}$]. Target value for efficiency is SPF 20. Values are derived from long-term monitoring campaigns in nonresidential demonstration buildings in Germany Source: EnOB (2014) Notes: Buildings are labeled by letters; numbers indicate the year of monitoring. Environmental heat sink is based on: use of groundwater (buildings A, B, and C) and ground (D to N).

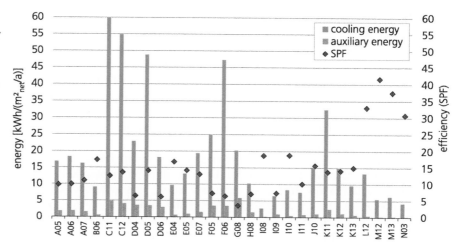

the return. It is favourable to install variable and highly energy-efficient pumps in order to decrease the electrical energy use. Considering groundwater wells, the delivery height is essential. Therefore, the heat exchanger should be located close to the head of the well in order to reduce the geodetic height.

7.2.5 Benefits:

- TABS operate with low water supply temperatures in heating mode (24°C to 32°C) and high water supply temperatures (16°C to 20°C) in cooling mode. Therefore, TABS allow for the efficient use of environmental heat sources and heat sinks at the building site. In winter, the temperature level of environmental heat sources can be utilized economically by means of a heat pump system. In summer, environmental heat sinks can be utilized directly by means of a heat exchanger so that auxiliary energy is only required for the distribution (not for generation) of cooling energy.
- The direct cooling by means of near-surface geothermal energy enables cooling of the built environment with high energy efficiency – provided there is a proper design, installation, and operation of geothermal systems. For the operation mode 'direct cooling' (without the use of a reversible heat pump or refrigerating machine), annual values of energy efficiency of 10–20 kWh_{therm}/kWh_{el} were measured. Some systems perform exceptionally well, achieving SPFs about 30 kWh_{therm}/kWh_{el} (Figure 7.3).
- Like any thermal storage, TABS (e.g. the thermally activated concrete ceiling) bridge the time difference between energy supply and energy demand and partially shift the thermal loads in the nighttime hours. The separation of air conditioning during the time of occupancy (heating or cooling of the supply air) and operation of TABS in the night-time hours thus allows a reduction in power of the geothermal system and the heat and cold generator and saves investment costs.

7.2.6 Requirements:

- The energy efficiency of environmental heat sources and sinks is determined by the auxiliary energy; i.e. it depends on the electrical power consumption of the primary pump (groundwater or brine pump). The installed electric pump capacity in the projects studied varies between 20 and even 230W_{el} per kilowatt heating/cooling capacity of the heat source/sink. Consequently, target values for the energy efficiency of geothermal systems should be determined during the design phase of the building.
- It is expected that the energy efficiency of the demonstration systems studied will increase by 30 to 50 percent through application of the following optimization measures: optimally sized pipe network with low pressure losses (less than 300 Pa/m), correctly sized primary pump (less than 40W_{el}/kW_{therm}), controls for the primary pump according to the temperature difference between supply and return (3 to 5 Kelvin), and optimal

operation strategies (annual electrical energy consumption of primary pumps less than $2\,kWh_{el}/(m^2a)$). These evaluations show that efficiency values of $20\,kWh_{therm}/kWh_{final}$ can be achieved by the geothermal system for the operation mode 'direct cooling' (Figure 7.3).

- The operation of highly efficient geothermal systems requires good and careful planning, both of the hydraulic circuits and the thermal design of the borehole heat exchangers and groundwater wells. Incorrect assumptions in the design and planning process (e.g. undisturbed soil temperature, extraction capacity for geothermal borehole heat exchangers, available flow rates for groundwater) result in insufficient heating/cooling performance and low energy efficiencies, which can hardly be compensated for or corrected during system operation. Then, the upgrading of an additional heat/cold generator is necessary.

7.3 Heat pump systems

Concepts for low energy office buildings often employ heat pumps in order to heat the buildings via thermo-active building systems and to preheat supply air during occupancy. The energy analysis of the heat pump system considers the generation of heating energy from the environmental heat source, and the increase of the given temperature level by a heat pump system. In case of a higher cooling energy demand in the summer season, the heat pump can be used in a reversible mode to provide active cooling. In the nonresidential buildings, the heat pump typically does not produce domestic hot water.

The performance of the heat pumps is characterized by the electricity consumption relative to the net floor area, which varies from 0.9 to $6.9\,W_{el}/m^2_{net}$ in the buildings that were investigated. Usually, the plant systems use water storage tanks with a capacity of between 750 and 8,000 liters (i.e. 4 to $36\,l/kW_{therm}$), which hydraulically decouple the generation of energy and its distribution. Water storage units foster energy-efficient performance by reducing the number and amplitude of operation cycles and bridging the period when the heat pump cannot operate. In the buildings investigated, the annual thermal energy provided by the heat pumps ranges between 15 and $65\,kWh_{therm}/(m^2_{net}a)$. Evidently, the heating demand of the buildings varies noticeably during the years of operation. Electricity to operate the heat pumps ranges from 4 to even $17\,kWh_{el}/(m^2_{net}a)$. In addition, the brine and submerged pumps of the primary hydraulic circuit use 1 to $3.3\,kWh_{el}/(m^2_{net}a)$ (Figure 7.4).

The seasonal performance factor of the heat pump system (SPF-HP) over the heating period is the ratio of supplied thermal energy to electrical energy needed for the compressor of the heat pump. All investigated heat pump systems yield good SPF-HP between 3.1 and $6.6\,kWh_{therm}/kWh_{el}$, resulting from advantageous temperature levels of the environmental heat sources (6°C to 14°C) and low water supply temperatures of the heat pump (30°C to 40°C).

The efficiency of the entire heating system considers the auxiliary energy use of the heat pump and the primary pump over the operation period. There is an obvious decrease of the energy efficiency caused by the auxiliary energy use needed for the heat pump system. Measured annual seasonal performance factors are in the range of 3.0 to 6.1 kWh$_{therm}$/kWh$_{el}$ (Figure 7.4).

The use of ground-coupled chillers and reversible heat pumps is an efficient and sustainable approach to cool buildings. Relatively high supply water temperature of 16°C to 20°C for cooling results in high values for energy efficiency. Heat pumps and chillers must be carefully selected for the specific application and dimension. Oversized systems result in a frequent cycling of the machines, which negatively affects the efficiency and the lifetime of the aggregates. When choosing the systems, attention needs to be paid to the efficiency in the intended range of operating temperatures. Further, electrical stand-by losses are not negligible.

7.4 Thermo-active building systems

Hydronic radiant heating and cooling systems encompass both thermo-active building systems (TABS) integrated into the building structure and additive systems such as radiators or cooling panels that are suspended from the ceiling. Due to a suitable construction method, TABS actively incorporate the building structure (ceiling, wall, floor) and its thermal storage into the energy management of the building (Figures 7.5 and 7.6). The wide range of TABS differs in dimension and spacing of the pipes, layer of thermal activation (near-surface or core), activated building component (ceiling, floor, wall), and implementation (dry or wet construction). In general, TABS are classified according to the thermally activated layer of the building component: (i) concrete core conditioning (CCC) (activation of concrete ceiling slabs), (ii) grid conditioning (GC) (capillary tubes embedded in plaster or gypsum board and mounted on the ceiling or walls), and (iii) radiant floor conditioning (RFC) (activation of floor screed), (iv) near-surface and (v) two-layer conditioning (Figures 7.5 and 7.6).

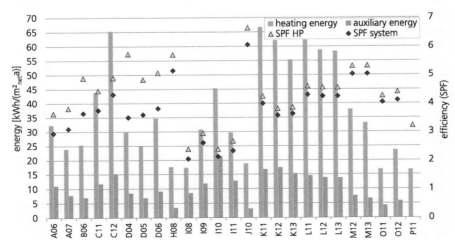

7.4
Performance of heat pump systems coupled to the groundwater or ground: supplied heating energy [kWh$_{therm}$/(m²$_{net}$a)], required electrical auxiliary energy for primary pump and compressor [kWh$_{el}$/(m²$_{net}$a)], and energy efficiency expressed as seasonal performance factor (SPF-HP) for heat pump only (grey) and for the entire system (SPF system) (black) [kWh$_{therm}$/kWh$_{el}$]. Target value for efficiency of the heat pump system is SPF 3.5. Values are derived from long-term monitoring campaigns in nonresidential demonstration buildings in Germany
Source: EnOB (2014)
Notes: Buildings are labeled by letters, numbers indicate the year of monitoring. Environmental heat sink is based on: use of groundwater (buildings A, B and C) and ground (D to N).

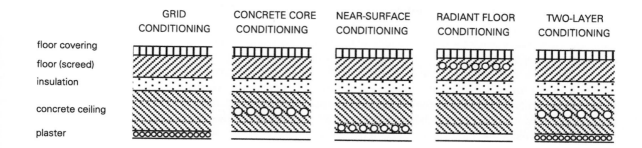

| GRID CONDITIONING | CONCRETE CORE CONDITIONING | NEAR-SURFACE CONDITIONING | RADIANT FLOOR CONDITIONING | TWO-LAYER CONDITIONING |

floor covering

floor (screed)

insulation

concrete ceiling

plaster

7.5

Construction element sections for common thermo-active building systems. Additionally, TABS also can be integrated into wall constructions.

The specific volume flow for the concrete core conditioning systems varies between 5.5 and 12 kg/(m²$_{TABS}$h). Near-surface TABS systems (grid conditioning) and the ceiling suspended cooling panels usually use higher volume flow rates between 20 and 35 kg/(m²$_{TABS}$h).

In heating mode, the water supply temperatures range between 22°C and 28°C for concrete core conditioning systems and between 22°C and 38°C for near-surface and floor conditioning systems. Heating energy is usually provided by a heat pump system whose energy efficiency performance benefits from the low water supply temperatures. However, there are energy concepts that combine high-temperature heat sources, such as biomass, waste heat, or district heat, with TABS. In cooling mode, TABS operate with water supply temperatures between 17°C and 23°C for concrete core conditioning systems and 14°C to 22°C for the near-surface and grid conditioning systems. If a dew point controller is not installed, the water supply temperature is usually limited to 18°C in order to prevent condensation.

7.6

Thermo-active building systems: (left) pipe circuit between upper and lower reinforcement, (right) floor area with pipe circuits, and connection at ceiling for TABS
Source: Fraunhofer ISE

The temperature difference between supply and return water is typically low, ranging from 0.5 to 3 Kelvin in heating mode and 0.5 to 4.0 Kelvin in cooling mode. However, hourly measurements demonstrate that the TABS system is sometimes operated with temperature differences below 1.0 Kelvin between supply and return water. The water supply temperatures are then close to the building component and to the surface temperature. Consequently, only a small

amount of heating and cooling energy is delivered while the circulation pump operates continuously. This requires an improved operation strategy in order to minimize the auxiliary electrical energy for operating the pumps without violating occupant thermal comfort.

The heating and cooling power of thermo-active building systems strongly depends on the following six parameters: operative room temperature, volume flow, supply water temperature, temperature difference of supply and return water, surface temperature of the building component, and the convective and radiative heat transfer (heat transfer coefficient depends on horizontal and vertical surfaces as well as air movement). Thereby, the cooling power represents the heating load that is discharged from the thermally activated building component.

A maximum cooling power is achieved at an increased volume flow and at high operative room temperatures (and therewith elevated surface temperatures of the building component). Evidently, the cooling power diminishes with increasing water supply temperatures. Measured cooling power of the concrete core conditioning system ranges between 20 and 40W/m^2_{TABS}. Ceiling suspended panels and near-surface grid conditioning systems reach cooling power values of 20 to 70W/m^2_{TABS}. These measured values correspond well to the theoretically derived power values.

7.4.1 Benefits of TABS:

- In steady state cooling, capacities from 30 to 40W/m^2 can be achieved. Near-surface TABS can achieve a cooling power of up to 70W/m^2. The cooling performance is limited by the dew point of the room temperature as, otherwise condensation on the ceiling can occur. The dew point is around 15°C for a room temperature of 26°C and 50 percent relative humidity. Therefore, heat loads by solar gains need to be reduced by effective solar-shading systems in order to meet comfort requirements. Due to the relatively high supply water temperature of environmental heat sinks, ceiling temperature below the dew point hardly occurs in Mid-European climates. The heating power of TABS is in the range of 25 to 30 W/m^2.
- Utilization of environmental energy: This can be for cooling or heating, e.g. by means of cooling towers, borehole heat exchangers, ground collectors, or groundwater. The environmental energy can be utilized economically, either directly or with slight temperature adjustment via chillers or heat pumps.
- Low primary energy consumption: Storage losses, limited controllability, and heat flow from the ceiling/floor to the room (or vice versa) which cannot be manipulated, cause higher consumption of heat and cold than in ideal room conditioning. The nature of this type of system results in effective energy consumption, which is higher in comparison to that of easily controllable systems that achieve room temperatures that deviate only slightly from the target temperatures. However, due to the use of environmental energy for heating and cooling, the primary energy consumption of concrete core conditioning systems is significantly reduced. The auxiliary energy used for distribution of heat and cold is less in water-driven systems than in air-driven systems.

- Reduction of peak loads: A sufficiently dimensioned concrete core conditioning system leads to a reduction of peak loads, and a partial shift of this load to outside the occupancy. Overnight operation allows energy consumption to be reduced due to greater efficiency (coefficient of performance, COP) and may also allow profit from lower overnight electricity tariffs.
- Reduction of the ventilation system: TABS uncouples thermal room conditioning (heating/cooling) from ventilation requirements. Reduction of the air volume flow to the hygienically required level results in downsizing of the ventilation network by up to 70 percent and reduction of operating costs and energy consumption.
- Comfort: The system temperatures and surface temperatures which are close to the indoor air temperature, as well as the high proportion of radiation in the heat transfer, the absence of high air exchange rates and (depending on the system) high air velocities, all improve thermal comfort.
- Architecture: As the tube heat exchangers are integrated in the building element, the interior design is barely affected – although suspended ceilings are to be avoided.

7.4.2 Requirements of TABS:

- New buildings: Concrete core condition systems cannot be implemented in building refurbishments, and are restricted to new buildings. Retrofitted buildings can be activated with grid conditioning or ceiling-suspended systems.
- Building envelope: An integrally planned building concept (optimal coordination of architecture, construction physics, and building services equipment) with consistent limitation of the heating/cooling loads is a prerequisite for the implementation of TABS.
- Building mass: As the storage capacity is "actively" incorporated into the building's load management, a good thermal storage capacity is required. To guarantee heat exchange with the room, the concrete slabs should not be covered by cladding or hangings.
- Indoor acoustics: Installations of uninterrupted suspended ceilings with insulating elements to influence the indoor acoustics (reverberation time, sound distribution) in rooms with concrete core conditioning is not possible, or very limited in terms of surface and layout. Rooms with strict acoustic requirements call for appropriate indoor acoustic concepts.
- Controllability: Due to the large thermal mass and inertia of concrete core conditioning systems, precise control to achieve a target room temperature is not possible. If specific room temperatures are to be guaranteed, an additional controllable and quick-reacting heating/cooling system is required.
- Zoning: In projects carried out to date, tube heat exchangers have been installed in the slab surface mostly without consideration of the subsequent room layout. For this reason, there has been no individual, room-specific control. Today, heat exchangers for concrete core conditioning systems are often divided into zones on a room-by-room basis, which allows the temperatures of individual rooms to be controlled independently of one another.

7.5 Achieved thermal interior comfort

The European comfort standard DIN EN 15251:2007-08 differentiates buildings according to the HVAC systems installed: (i) "mechanically cooled buildings" which must guarantee the very stringent comfort conditions specified by DIN EN ISO 7730:2005-06, and (ii) "non-mechanically conditioned buildings", which allow the application of the adaptive comfort model. The term "mechanically cooled" encompasses all concepts that employ a mechanical device to condition the space, such as supply and/or exhaust air systems, thermo-active building systems, and convectors. Only buildings that employ natural ventilation through open windows fall into the category of "non-mechanical" concepts. This method may be applied when certain requirements are met. Thermal conditions are primarily regulated by the occupants through operating windows that open to the outdoors. Further, occupants are engaged in near sedentary activities and are supposed to feel free to adapt their clothing to thermal conditions.

Previous investigations (Kalz and Pfafferott, 2014) reveal that the variety of heating and cooling concepts of the building stock and new constructions cannot be covered by just two categories in the current standard DIN EN 15251:2007-08, i.e. mechanically cooled and non-mechanically cooled buildings. Consequently, it is proposed to define six buildings standards:

1 buildings with air conditioning;
2 buildings with mixed-mode cooling (combination of air conditioning and air-based or water-based mechanical cooling);
3 low energy buildings with water-based mechanical cooling;
4 low energy buildings with air-based mechanical cooling;
5 low energy buildings with passive cooling; and
6 buildings without cooling.

7.5.1 Low energy building with passive cooling

A passive cooling concept covers all natural techniques of heat dissipation, overheat protection and related building design techniques, providing thermal comfort without the use of mechanical equipment and therefore auxiliary energy use. Passive cooling refers to preventing and modulating heat gains, including the use of natural heat sinks. Techniques are, for example, high-quality building envelope, solar control, internal gain control, microclimate and building site, and free night ventilation. "Free night ventilation" is simply a non-mechanical or passive means of providing ventilation through naturally occurring effects such as wind pressure on a building façade or stack effects within a building. Most of the buildings show an exceedance of comfort class II during 2 to 10 percent of the time of occupancy. The buildings employ free night ventilation by means of open windows and ventilation slats, which do not allow for manual control of room temperature. During daytime, heat is stored in the structural elements of the building and then is ejected to the outdoor environment. However, only a certain amount of heat can be dissipated by night ventilation due to the available nocturnal temperature level, the limited time for night ventilation, the feasable air change rate, and the usable heat storage capacity of the building. Thermal comfort in the buildings with passive cooling differs a lot, achieving the comfort classes I to II or even failing the classes.

7.5.2 Low energy building with air-based mechanical cooling

Besides the use of passive cooling techniques, night ventilation is realized by a mechanical ventilation system. If an exhaust air ventilation system is employed, indoor air is continuously exhausted to the outdoor environment. Fresh air is supplied over open windows or ventilation slats. Often the buildings employ a supply-and-exhaust air system in order to make use of heat recovery in winter. Then indoor air is centrally exhausted to the outdoors and supply air is centrally sucked in and distributed to the individual rooms.

The demonstration buildings monitored with air-based mechanical cooling comply with comfort class II during 80 to 95 percent of the occupancy when considering the adaptive approach. Buildings that employ mechanical night ventilation by means of an exhaust or supply-and-exhaust system allow for a fixed air change rate between 2 and 4 ACH. Therefore, cooling capacity is higher and less dependent on prevailing wind situation and difference between indoor and outdoor temperatures. Evidently, air-based systems are not as effective as water-based thermo-active building systems, in particular during prolonged periods with high ambient air temperatures. Taking the extreme summer conditions of 2003 in Europe as indicative of a global warming scenario, thermal comfort in compliance with DIN EN 15251:2007-08 cannot be ensured in buildings that employ night ventilation only. Rising ambient air temperatures decrease the cooling potential of night ventilation and demand elevated air change rates for a mechanical ventilation system. Besides, longer hot periods exhaust the building's thermal storage capacity. TABS are essentially unaffected by these disadvantages and thus present an effective concept for conditioning buildings in Central European climates, even in very hot summers, given a building with a high-quality envelope, solar shading devices, and reduced internal loads. Some naturally ventilated buildings provided good thermal comfort during the hot summer of 2003. This reduced cooling demand is attributed to the high quality of the building envelope and the stringent load-reduction strategy (day lighting concept, solar shading system, energy-efficient office equipment).

7.5.3 Low energy building with water-based mechanical cooling

Due to the large area for heat transfer, cooling is realized with a relatively high supply water temperature of between 16°C and 22°C. This favors the use of environmental heat sinks in the close proximity of the building site such as near-surface geothermal energy of the ground and groundwater, and ambient air. Water-based mechanical cooling by means of thermo-active building systems and environmental energy provides good thermal comfort during summer. Applying the PMV comfort approach, most buildings meet the upper comfort requirements of class II. The restricted cooling capacity of concrete-core conditioning systems requires a consequent reduction of interior and solar-heat gains through a holistic design process considering the building physics, architecture, HVAC systems, and the use of the buildings. The combination of concrete-core conditioning with a controllable and thermally fast-responding auxiliary cooling system (TABS near-surface or suspended systems) is reasonable – in case of a higher cooling demand – for office spaces with changing conditions of use or in areas with higher comfort requirements, e.g. meeting rooms. The additional cooling system should also be operated at the same temperature level as the concrete-core conditioning system. This allows for the use of the same distribution system and therefore for saving investment costs.

In Northern European climates, water-based cooling by means of environmental heat sinks or even active cooling with compression chillers is only required for buildings with very high comfort requirements (class I) or limited user influence (dress codes, sealed windows). In contrast, in Southern European summer climates, a relatively high cooling capacity must be provided to dissipate strongly fluctuating cooling loads. Since the temperature difference between the ambient air and the indoor comfort temperature is low, an active cooling system is often required to meet the comfort requirements. Water-based cooling concepts are generally suitable in all climate zones of Europe. However, thermally slow-responding systems such as concrete-core conditioning systems reach cooling capacity limits during periods of high and fluctuating head loads under Southern European climate conditions.

In winter, the investigated buildings employ an environmental heat source (ground, groundwater and rainwater) in combination with a heat pump for heating the built environment. Both the DIN EN 15251:2007-08 and the DIN EN ISO 7730:2005-06 require the same set points for lower limits of occupant thermal comfort in winter, i.e. 21°C (class I), 20°C (class II), and 19°C (class III). The analyses show that the comfort limits are seldom violated. Deviation from the lower comfort limits in winter might be caused mainly by missing internal (unoccupied rooms) and solar (closed solar shading due to glare) loads, or even an opened window. Insufficient heating energy from the heat source in combination with the heat pump or an improper heat delivery by the TABS can be excluded, since there is no decisive difference in the comfort ratings between a conventional heat source employing radiators compared with an environmental heat source using TABS.

7.6 Holistic approach for the design and operation of low energy buildings

Ambitious planning concepts stand at the crossroads of political conditions, rising energy costs, the shortage of primary energy sources, and the demand for high comfort use. At the same time, the new or renovation project should be economically sustainable. The flood of information and a wide range of planning concepts and available technical building solutions, as well as personal preferences of stakeholders and varied expectations on the particular project, make it difficult to choose an optimal combination.

In Article 9 of Directive 2010/31/EU on the energy performance of buildings, the European Union calls on its member states to "ensure that by 31 December 2020, all new buildings are nearly zero-energy buildings" (The European Parliament and the Council of the European Union, 2010). Following this requirement on new buildings, retrofit buildings are also becoming increasingly energy-efficient. This

Table 7.1 Categorization of building types for the evaluation of thermal comfort. PMV and adaptive comfort models in accordance with DIN EN 15251:2007-08

Building	Heating/cooling concept	Ventilation concept	Occupant	Comfort approach
I: AIR-CONDITIONED (AC) BUILDING				
(Usually) sealed building envelope	Heating and cooling by air only	De-/humidifying air	No influence (closed windows, no solar shading), no adjustment of temperature set point for heating/cooling, dress code	PMV comfort model
II: MIXED-MODE (AC) BUILDING[2]				
Standard quality building envelope, use of few passive heating and cooling technologies[1]	Heating and cooling by air only	De-/humidifying air and additionally natural ventilation through open windows	Operation of windows and solar shading, no adjustment of temperature set point for heating/cooling, dress code	PMV comfort model, during periods with natural ventilation more frequent exceedance of comfort boundaries is allowed
III: LOW ENERGY BUILDING WITH WATER-BASED MECHANICAL COOLING[3]				
High-quality building envelope, use of passive heating and cooling technologies[1]	Heating: fossil fuels, environmental energy sources, biomass, cogeneration, heat pump and TABS Cooling: environmental heat sinks and TABS	Hybrid ventilation[2] for hygienic fresh air (30–40 m³/h and person) if necessary, de-/humidifying of air	High user influence (operation of windows, doors, solar shading system), no or minor influence of occupant to adjust temperature set point for heating/cooling, no dress code	PMV comfort model

Building	Heating/cooling concept	Ventilation concept	Occupant	Comfort approach
IV: LOW ENERGY BUILDING WITH AIR-BASED MECHANICAL COOLING[3]				
High-quality building envelope, use of passive heating and cooling technologies	Heating: fossil fuels, environmental energy sources, biomass, cogeneration, heat pump and TABS Cooling: mechanical night ventilation	Hybrid ventilation	High user influence (operation on windows, doors, solar shading system), no adjustment of temperature set point for heating/ cooling, no dress code	Adaptive comfort model
V: LOW ENERGY BUILDING WITH PASSIVE COOLING[1]				
High-quality building envelope, use of passive heating and cooling technologies	Heating: fossil fuels, environmental energy sources, biomass, cogeneration, heat pump and TABS Cooling: passive night ventilation through inlet vents, windows	Natural ventilation	High user influence (operation on windows, doors, solar shading system), no adjustment of temperature set point for heating/ cooling, no dress code	Adaptive comfort model
VI: BUILDING WITHOUT COOLING				

Notes:

1 passive heating/cooling technologies: high-quality building envelope, passive use of solar heating gains, day-lighting concept, sun-protection glazing, static solar shading devices, heavyweight building construction, moderate ratio of glass-to-façade.

2 hybrid ventilation: natural ventilation through windows and inlet vents and mechanical ventilation (supply and exhaust air system).

3 The term *mechanical cooling* does not encompass full air conditioning (heating, cooling, de-/humidifying of air).

development is accompanied by low energy heating and cooling systems, which have been developed for more than 20 years.

Sustainable and environmentally responsible non-residential building concepts are:

- Guarantee enhanced visual, acoustic and thermal comfort and therefore provide a high-quality workplace environment, which improves the occupant's productivity and reduces the impact of the built environment on the occupant's health.

Passive Cooling: Free Night Ventilation

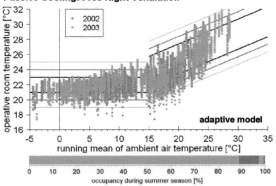 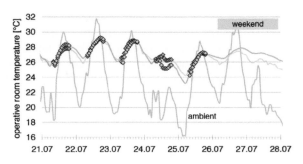

Air-based Cooling: Mechanical Night Ventilation

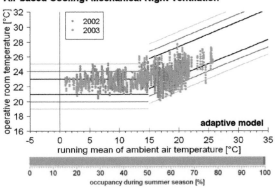 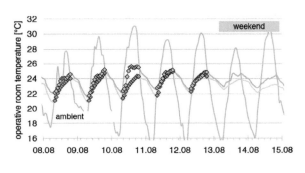

Water-based Cooling: Thermo-active building systems and ground as heat sink

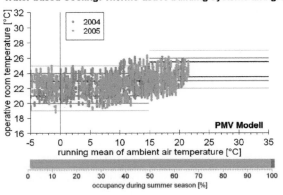 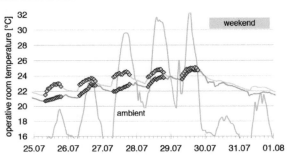

7.7

Evaluation of thermal room comfort during the occupancy of the use according to the European comfort guideline
DIN EN 15251:2007-08; adaptive and PMV comfort model. (Left) hourly measured room temperature (average of all rooms) during
occupancy is plotted versus the running mean ambient air temperature. Grey lines indicate the comfort boundaries for the classes
I, II and III (from I lightest to III darkest). (Right) hourly room temperatures for two reference rooms and the prevailing ambient air
temperature are given for one hot summer week. Time of daily occupancy is indicated by markers
Note: Winter period: running mean ambient air temperature is smaller than 15°C; summer period: running mean ambient air
temperature is greater than 15°C.

- Harness the building's architecture and physics in order to considerably reduce the annual heating and cooling demand (building envelope, day lighting concept, natural ventilation, passive heating and cooling technologies).
- Put emphasis on a highly energy-efficient heating and cooling plant with a significantly reduced auxiliary energy use for the generation, distribution, and delivery of heating and cooling energy. The applied components and technologies are soundly orchestrated by optimized operation and control strategies.
- Use less valuable primary energy; e.g. renewable energy from environmental heat sources and sinks, solar power, biomass, etc.

A holistic approach to the evaluation of heating and cooling concepts is proposed that seeks to achieve a global optimum of interior thermal comfort, energy efficiency, and primary energy use for both newly constructed and refurbished buildings (see Section 7.7).

Under this premise, a holistic approach is proposed for the evaluation of heating and cooling concepts, seeking to achieve a global optimum of (1) interior thermal comfort, (2) interior humidity comfort, (3) useful cooling-energy use, and (4) the building's total primary energy use for heating, cooling, ventilation, and lighting.

Figure 7.8 illustrates an individual building signature that shows results from a monitoring campaign and its evaluation in accordance with the guidelines given. The thermal indoor environment meets the requirements of class II. The useful cooling energy meets the building physical requirements on summer-heat protection. Only the primary energy demand of the building is higher than the target value and does not meet the requirements.

7.7 Building examples

The selected demonstration buildings, shown in Figures 7.9–7.14, allow for both natural ventilation and mechanical air conditioning and are well instrumented for both comfort and energy performance evaluation.

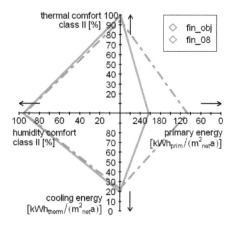

7.8
Building signature correlating cooling-energy use [kWh$_{therm}$/(m$^2_{net}$a)], the building's total primary energy use for heating, cooling, ventilation, and lighting [kWh$_{prim}$/m^{2}a], and thermal and humidity comfort classifications in accordance with EN 15251:2007-08. The green rectangle represents the target objective for these four parameters and the arrows indicate the direction of the optimum

The buildings are supposed to demonstrate the rational use of energy by means of innovative and soundly integrated technologies for the technical building services. The type of environmental and primary energy use for heating, cooling, and ventilation is given in the following:

Ventilation system: During occupancy, the ventilation strategy uses hybrid ventilation in the buildings depending on operation time and user behavior. The ventilation concepts include heat recovery in winter (efficiency between 65 and 85 percent) from the exhaust air, which is essential to reduce the annual heating demand.

Cooling system: In the summer, environmental heat sinks are used directly to cool the buildings via nighttime ventilation or thermo-active building systems. Borehole heat exchangers provide water supply temperatures between 10°C and 22°C. Some buildings use groundwater to cool the building and/or additional free cooling by hybrid cooling towers.

Heating systems: In winter, the heat supply is realized by a heat pump, which is coupled to the ground or groundwater. Some buildings make use of the waste heat from central server rooms and printers, supplying it to the TABS. Additionally, district heat is available at some demonstration buildings.

The buildings are described using:

- Schematics of energy concept for heating, cooling, and ventilation (Figures 7.9 and 7.12).
- Thermal comfort evaluations: mean operative room temperature of the building [°C] during the time of occupancy plotted against the running mean ambient air temperature [°C] according to the comfort guideline DIN EN 15251:2007-08 (Figures 7.10 and 7.13). Grey and black lines indicate the upper and lower comfort boundaries I, II, and III (from I lightest to III darkest).
- Building signatures correlating useful cooling energy use [$kWh_{therm}/(m^2_{net}a)$], energy efficiency related to the final energy use (here, electrical energy) of the entire building taking into consideration heating, cooling, ventilation, and lighting [kWh_{therm}/kWh_{el}] as well as thermal and/or humidity comfort classification according to DIN EN 15251:2007-08, class II (Figures 7.11 and 7.14). The green rectangles represent the target objective for these parameters and the arrows indicate the direction of the optimum. The orange rectangles present the performance of the building and the HVAC systems derived by measurements. The scales are chosen individually for each criterion.

EGU Ulm | Germany

BUILDING AND USE

use	office
completion	2002
refurbishment	-
number of floors	5
total floor area [m²]	6,911
total volume [m³]	32,223
area-to-volume ratio [m⁻¹]	0.22

BUILDING ENVELOPE

solar shading	exterior venetian blinds
U-value exterior wall [W/(m²K)]	0.13
U-value window [W/(m²K)]	0.84
g-value window [–]	0.5
window-façade ratio [%]	30-48%

COOLING CONCEPT

environmental heat sink	ground
energy carrier	electricity
cooling system	direct cooling by 40 BHEX, length 99 m
power of system [kW$_{therm}$]	108
distribution system	CCC[e], CP[d]

VENTILATION CONCEPT

operable windows	yes
night ventilation	no
mechanical ventilation	yes, heat recovery 61%
dehumidification	no
precooling of supply air	yes, by BHEX

HEATING CONCEPT

environmental heat source	ground, waste heat
energy carrier	district heat (DH)
heating system	DH, BHEX
power of system [kW$_{therm}$]	185 (DH)
distribution system	CCC

PERFORMANCE

useful heating energy [kWh$_{therm}$/m²a]	38.8
useful cooling energy [kWh$_{therm}$/m²a]	13.2
efficiency heat generation	- (district heat)
efficiency cool generation[a]	16.2
total final energy [kWh$_{therm}$/m²a][b]	46.8
comfort winter, class II [%][c]	95
Comfort summer, class II [%][c]	94

Notes

a efficiency direct cooling by BHEX expressed as SPF [kWh$_{therm}$/kWh$_{el}$];
b total final energy for heating, cooling, ventilation and lighting, no plug loads;
c PMV comfort model;
d cooling panels in meeting rooms;
e concrete core conditioning.

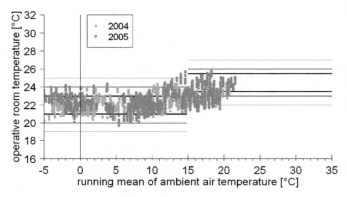

7.9
Schematic for heating, cooling, and ventilation (borehole heat exchangers (BHEX), district heat (DH), mechanical ventilation (MV))

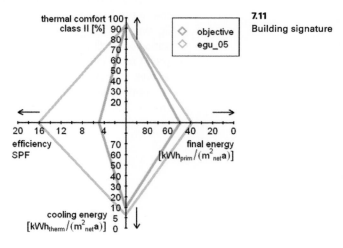

7.10
Evaluation of thermal comfort

7.11
Building signature

SIC Freiburg | Germany

BUILDING AND USE

use	office
completion	2003
refurbishment	-
number of floors	6
total floor area [m²]	13,833
total volume [m³]	53,629
area-to-volume ratio [m⁻¹]	0.29

BUILDING ENVELOPE

solar shading	exterior venetian blinds
U-value exterior wall [W/(m²K)]	0.19
U-value window [W/(m²K)]	1.30
g-value window [-]	0.6
window-façade ratio [%]	33-49 %

COOLING CONCEPT

environmental heat sink	ambient air
energy carrier	electricity
cooling system	mechanical ventilation
power of system [kW$_{therm}$]	-
distribution system	supply air

VENTILATION CONCEPT

operable windows	yes
night ventilation	yes
mechanical ventilation	no, exhaust ventilation system
dehumidification	no
precooling of supply air	no

HEATING CONCEPT

environmental heat source	-
energy carrier	district heat (DH)
heating system	district heat
power of system [kW$_{therm}$]	-
distribution system	radiator

PERFORMANCE

useful heating energy [kWh$_{therm}$/m²a]	28.8
useful cooling energy [kWh$_{therm}$/m²a]	5.0
efficiency heat generation	- (district heat)
efficiency cool generation[a]	1.7
total final energy [kWh$_{therm}$/m²a][b]	47.7
comfort winter, class II [%][c]	-
comfort summer, class II [%][c]	99.6

Notes

a   efficiency of mechanical night ventilation SPF [kWh$_{therm}$/kWh$_{el}$];
b   total final energy for heating, cooling, ventilation and lighting, no plug loads;
c   adaptive comfort model.

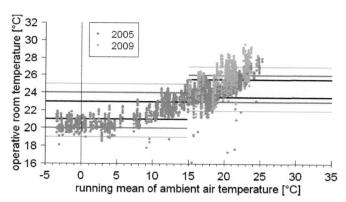

7.12
Schematic for heating, cooling, and ventilation (mechanical ventilation (MV) mechanical night ventilation (NV))

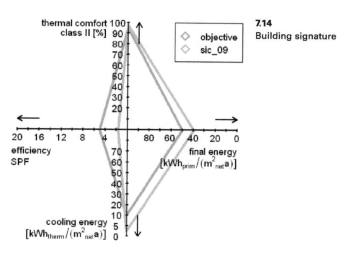

7.13
Evaluation of thermal comfort

7.14
Building signature

References

AGEB. 2013. *Anwendungsbilanzen für die Endenergiesektoren in Deutschland in den Jahren 2010 und 2011. Studie beauftragt vom Bundesministerium für Wirtschaft und Technologie Projektnummer: 23/11*. Berlin: AGEB. Available at: www.ag-energiebilanzen.de/

Bettgenhäuser, K., Boermans, T., Offermann, M., Krechting, A., Becker, D., Kahles, M., Pause, F. and Müller, T. 2011. *Klimaschutz durch Reduzierung des Energiebedarfs für Gebäudekühlung*. Dessau-Roßlau: Umweltbundesamte. Available at: www.uba.de/uba-info-medien/3979.html (accessed June 2011).

BMVBS/BBR (Hrsg.). 2008. *Folgen des Klimawandels: Gebäude und Baupraxis in Deutschland, BBR-Online-Publikation 10/2008*. [Online]. Available at: http://d-nb.info/988933985/34.

DIN EN ISO 7730:2005-06. *Ergonomics of the Thermal Environment – Analytical Determination and Interpretation of Thermal Comfort Using Calculation of the PMV And PPD Indices and Local Thermal Comfort Criteria*. Berlin: Beuth Verlag GmbH.

DIN EN 15251:2007-08. *Indoor Environmental Input Parameters for Design and Assessment of Energy Performance of Buildings Addressing Indoor Air Quality, Thermal Environment, Lighting and Acoustics*. Berlin: Beuth Verlag GmbH.

EnOB. 2014. *EnOB: Research for energy-optimised building*. [Online]. Available at: www.enob.info (accessed March 2015).

The European Parliament and the Council of the European Union. 2010. Directive 2010/31/EU of the European Parliament and of the Council of 19 May 2010 on the energy performance of buildings. *Official Journal of the European Union*, 53 (L 153): 13–35.

Kalz, D. (2011) *Heating and Cooling Concepts Employing Environmental Energy and Thermo-Active Building Systems: System Analysis and Optimization*. Stuttgart: Fraunhofer Verlag.

Kalz, D. and Pfafferott, J. (2007) *BINE Themeninfo: Thermoaktive Bauteilsysteme (TABS)*. Bonn: BINE Themeninfo FIZ Informationsdienst Karlsruhe.

Kalz, D. and Pfafferott, J. (2014) *Thermal Comfort and Energy-efficient Cooling of Nonresidential Buildings*. Cham, Heidelberg, New York, Dordrecht, London: Springer.

Kirchner, A. and Matthes, F. (2009) *Modell Deutschland Klimaschutz bis 2050: Vom Ziel her denken*. Berlin/Basel: WWF Deutschland, Prognos, Öko-Institut.

Koenigsdorff, R. (2011) *Oberflächennahe Geothermie für Gebäude, Grundlagen und Anwendungen zukunftsfähiger Heizung und Kühlung*. Stuttgart: Fraunhofer IRB Verlag.

Pfafferott, J. (2004) *Enhancing the Design and Operation of Passive Cooling Concepts: Monitoring and Data Analysis in Four Low-Energy Office Buildings with Night Ventilation*. Stuttgart: Fraunhofer IRB Verlag.

Santamouris, M. (2007) *Advances in Passive Cooling: Buildings, Energy, Solar Technology*. Abingdon: Earthscan.

VDMA (Hrsg.) (2011) *Energiebedarf für Kältetechnik in Deutschland: Eine Abschätzung des Energiebedarfs von Kältetechnik in Deutschland nach Einsatzgebieten*. VDMA: Frankfurt am Main.

Wagner, A. and Wambsganß, M. (2004) *Energiekennwerte und Gebäudeanalysen für die neuen Verwaltungsgebäude der Deutschen Bahn AG, Geschäftsbereich Netz. Final Report*. Karlsruhe: Universität Karlsruhe. Available at: www.fbta.uni.karlsruhe.de/enerkenn

Wietschel, M., Arens, M., Dötsch, C., Herkel, S., Krewitt, W., Markewitz, P., Möst, D. and Scheufen, M. 2010. *Energietechnologien 2050; Schwerpunkte für Forschung und Entwicklung: Technologienbericht*. Stuttgart: Fraunhofer Verlag. Available at: www.gbv.de/dms/zbw/619023767.pdf

8

Ventilation concepts
Planning and implementation

MICHAEL SWAINSON

8.1 Why ventilate?

The fabric of a building provides the occupants with very effective separation from the outdoor environment. However, with the requirement to achieve ever-higher levels of energy efficiency (by reducing unwanted heat losses and gains), building envelopes are becoming increasingly airtight. As a result, odours, pollutants, moisture and heat are trapped inside the building. It is essential therefore to incorporate an effective means of ventilation that will introduce outside air and remove 'stale' internal air.

The design of ventilation for non-domestic buildings has for a long time been viewed as a key part of the overall building services concept. This has not traditionally been the case for dwellings, where typically ventilation has been achieved through a mix of infiltration, *ad hoc* window opening and local inter-mittent extract fans in kitchens and bathrooms.

In some locations, the outside air is highly polluted with both gaseous and particulate pollutants. However, it is often the case that the concentration of pollutants recognised by the World Health Organisation (WHO) is actually higher within a house than outside (WHO, 2010). The reasons for this are that many of the particulate pollutants brought into a house from outside are deposited as the air speed and level of turbulence falls, but at the same time, the rate of pollutant generation internally creates an additional load. This can result in inside air exceeding exposure guidelines for pollutants in locations where the outside air is 'clean'.

Breaking down the reasons for undertaking ventilation provides an under-standing of the ventilation rates required to achieve good indoor air quality. The key reasons for ventilating are:

- To provide oxygen for the occupants. The actual flow rate of fresh air required to provide sufficient oxygen for a human to live is very small: less than 0.1 l/s (California Environmental Protection Agency, 1994).
- To remove moisture generated internally. Elevated levels of moisture in a building lead to dampness and mould growth. ASHRAE (2010) and CIBSE

(2006) suggest relative humidity (RH) levels in the range of 30 to 60 per cent and 40 to 70 per cent, respectively, to provide a comfortable and healthy domestic environment. In the USA, it has been estimated that exposure to dampness and mould in houses raises the risk of various adverse respiratory outcomes, such as asthma and other respiratory allergies, by 30 to 50 per cent (Mudarri and Fisk, 2007). House dust mites can be controlled if their immediate microclimate is maintained at a relative humidity of less than 73 per cent (Arlian, 1975), and most moulds require surface RH values of 80 per cent or greater to grow. Using ventilation to control moisture is dependent on both the rate of moisture generation and the outside air conditions. Ventilation with cold, dry air will remove a significantly greater moisture load than ventilation with cool or warm wet air. Control of moisture may therefore be more difficult in temperate climates than in cold climates.

- To remove odours generated by human activity and provide a 'fresh' feel. Very high levels of ventilation are required in order to dilute odours to acceptable levels for everyone. Guidance is provided on ventilation rates that achieve an adequate control of odours in standards such as EN 15251:2007. It is, however, noted that an air flow rate of 10 l/s/person would result in 15 per cent of occupants being dissatisfied with the indoor air quality. This value increases to 20 per cent at an air flow rate of 7 l/s/person, and is greater than 30 per cent as the air flow rate falls below 4 l/s/person.

- To dilute and remove pollutants generated internally. The generation of pollutants within a building may not have any direct relationship to occupancy. Consequently, determining ventilation rate based on CO_2, an indicator of occupancy, may fail to address other important pollutants. The major types of pollutants and their sources within buildings are detailed in Table 8.1. However, unless it is considered that a very significant source of pollutant must be controlled, basing ventilation on removal of odours will generally supply sufficient fresh air to provide good indoor air quality (IAQ) in relation to other pollutants.

Based on an understanding of the relationship between the need for fresh air, good indoor air quality and the likely rates of pollutant emissions from normal sources, the Passivhaus approach to ventilation is to prescribe a fresh air ventilation rate for each occupant of 20–30 m³ per hour (5.6–8.3 l/s). This supply air is delivered to the main 'living' rooms within the dwelling. The living rooms are defined as the spaces the occupants spend extended periods of time in (i.e. bedroom, living room, etc.). As a means of ensuring that moisture, as well as odours from human activities, are controlled, the extract is taken from the wet rooms. Wet rooms are defined as the rooms where activities are undertaken that may produce increased levels of moisture, or odours (i.e. kitchens, bathrooms, utility rooms, etc.). The recommended extract air flow rates for different wet rooms are set out in Table 8.2.

In recognition that some houses may have low occupancy and a relatively small number of wet rooms, Passivhaus also sets a minimum whole-house air exchange rate per hour (ac/h) of 0.3. This means that every hour a minimum of 30 per cent of the volume of air within a house is replaced with fresh air. For the

Table 8.1 Sources and types of indoor air pollution

Source of pollutant	Main pollutants
Outdoor air	SO_2, NO_x, ozone, particulates, biological particulates, benzene
Combustion of fuel	CO, NO_x, VOCs, H_2O, particulates
Tobacco smoke	CO, VOCs, arsenic, formaldehyde, particulates
People	CO_2, H_2O, organic compounds
Building materials	VOCs, formaldehyde, radon, fibres, other particulates, ammonia, thoron
Consumer products	VOCs, formaldehyde, fire retardants, pesticides
Furnishings	VOCs, fire retardants, formaldehyde
Office equipment	VOCs, ozone, toner dust, particulates
Bacteria and fungi	VOCs, biological particulates
Contaminated land	Methane, VOCs, hydrofluorocarbons, contaminated dusts, e.g. metals
Ground	Radon, H_2O, thoron
Animals	Allergens, methane, H_2O

Source: Crump *et al.* (2009)

Table 8.2 Guideline extract air flow rates from wet rooms

Room	Extract air flow rate (m³/hour)
Kitchen	60
Bathroom	40
WC, store room, etc.	20

purpose of calculating the ventilation air volume (V_v) of a Passivhaus, the floor to ceiling height should be assumed to be a maximum of 2.5 m (or the actual ceiling height if this is lower).

Example 1: Apartment for three people, 85 m² TFA floor space: three 'living' rooms, kitchen and bathroom

- Fresh air demand: 3 P × 30 m³/(h.P) = 90 m³/h
- Recommended minimum extract rate from wet rooms – kitchen and bathroom: 60 m³/h + 40 m³/h = 100 m³/h
- Minimum air change rate: 0.30/h × 85 m² × 2.5 m = 64 m³/h

This is a relatively small apartment and a ventilation rate of 90 m³/h should be used for the standard ventilation rate. The minimum ventilation rate should not be less than 64 m³/h.

Example 2: Detached house with only two residents, 150 m² TFA floor space: three 'living' rooms, kitchen and bathroom

- Fresh air demand: 2 P × 30 m³/(h.P) = 60 m³/h
- Recommended minimum extract rate from wet rooms – kitchen and bathroom: 60 m³/h + 40 m³/h = 100 m³/h
- Minimum air change rate: 0.30/h × 150 m² × 2.5 m = 112.5 m³/h

This is a low occupancy property with a relatively large floor area; therefore the limiting factor for ventilation is the overall air exchange rate. It is recommended that the minimum background ventilation rate should be set to 113 m³/h.

8.2 Means of ventilating

8.2.1 Natural ventilation

Natural ventilation of buildings is achieved when air exchange is driven by wind and thermal buoyancy. However, there are significant disadvantages in using a ventilation strategy that relies solely upon these natural driving forces.

For example, in winter when winds tend to be stronger and the temperature difference between inside and outside is at its greatest, the desire is to minimise the entry of air in order to reduce heating loads and minimise draughts. For this reason, ventilation openings need to be small and easy to control. By contrast, the winds during the summer months tend to be lighter and the temperature difference between inside and outside, smaller. The need for ventilation to maintain good indoor air quality remains the same, but the need to remove excessive heat build-up requires that very large volumes of air are used to ventilate the building. The purging of excess heat requires large openings as the natural driving forces are minimal.

Control of natural ventilation has traditionally relied on the occupants of a building to operate vents or to open and close windows. Inevitably, this leads to crude and highly irregular control and offers no potential to recover heat from the exhaust air.

The inability to continuously control natural ventilation results in the haphazard removal of internal pollutants such as water vapour or CO_2. A Passivhaus does not solely rely on natural ventilation; instead some form of continuous mechanical ventilation system is utilised for at least part of the year. In this way, heat loss is minimised and indoor air quality is maintained through a controlled ventilation rate.

8.2.2. Mechanical ventilation

There are two basic means of undertaking controlled mechanical ventilation: 'extract only' or 'balanced' ventilation (with or without heat recovery).

Central or local extract-only ventilation offers the opportunity to closely control the overall ventilation rate of a building and to remove the key pollutants – such as odours and water vapour from the wet rooms. Fresh air is introduced into the living rooms through vents in the building fabric. This means that little conditioning of the air, either thermally (e.g. heating very cold winter air) or by filtering can be undertaken before it enters the occupied spaces. Thermal comfort and air quality are therefore potentially reduced. In addition to this, there is no potential to recover heat in winter. For these reasons, extract only ventilation systems are not used in Passivhauses.

Local or central balanced ventilation systems overcome the limitations of extract only ventilation systems by allowing air to be treated thermally and filtered before it is delivered to occupied rooms. The rate of ventilation can be controlled along with the way the air is introduced into rooms, thus minimising the potential for draughts. This method also offers the potential to recover heat from the exhaust air. However, if no heat is recovered in winter, this system, like an extract only ventilation system, places the entire ventilation heating load on the heating system.

Very energy-efficient buildings are best ventilated using a balanced ventilation system. Such a system offers high levels of local ventilation control: temperature control of the supply air, the potential to filter outside air before it enters the occupied spaces, and the means of reducing the ventilation heating loads by a very significant percentage through recovery of heat from the exhaust air. In hot climates, or periods of hot weather in temperate climates, a heat recovery ventilation system can help to keep the heat out and retain 'coolth'.

The building envelope of a Passivhaus is very airtight in order to minimise infiltration-related thermal load. The ventilation system controls all the air movement within these buildings. The aim is to create cross ventilation; i.e. the air moves from one area of the building to another. For this reason, the location of the supply and extract points of the ventilation air and the air flow path through the building are a critical part of the design.

The supply air, warmed by the heat recovered from the outgoing exhaust air, is delivered to the 'living' rooms. Sources of pollution in these rooms tend to be odours and CO_2 generated by the occupants, as well as off-gassing from the building fabric, furnishing materials and cleaning products. Supplying air to the 'living' rooms holds them at a positive pressure relative to other rooms in the building.

The air is extracted from the wet rooms (i.e. the bathrooms and kitchens) where the major pollutants such as odours and water vapour are generated. These rooms are therefore held at a relatively low pressure and the pollutants are removed, at source, thus minimising their potential to spread and reduce the air quality in the living rooms.

As air is being delivered to the 'living' rooms and extracted from the wet rooms, there is a pressure differential between the spaces and air will tend to move from one zone to the other. To ensure that this occurs most effectively, an air transfer path must be provided. This is achieved with undercuts under doors or purposely provided vents in doors or walls. The ventilation air then moves freely between spaces, via circulation spaces such as halls or stairways.

8.2.3 Mixed-mode ventilation

Most Passivhaus buildings are designed to be naturally ventilated during the milder months of the year. This is largely achieved through opening windows. This is known as a mixed-mode ventilation strategy, changing seasonally to

8.1
Air movement between spaces within a house, from 'living' to 'wet' rooms

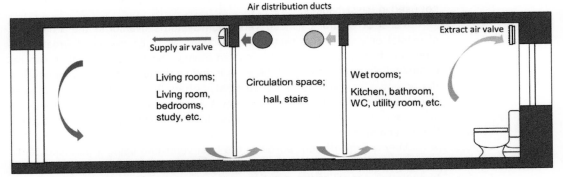

Air distribution ducts

Supply air valve

Extract air valve

Living rooms;

Living room, bedrooms, study, etc.

Circulation space; hall, stairs

Wet rooms;

Kitchen, bathroom, WC, utility room, etc.

Air transfer openings

8.2
Schematic of typical MVHR system components

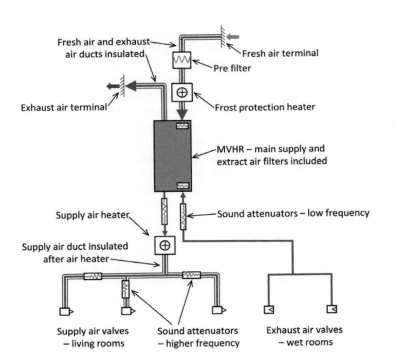

Fresh air and exhaust air ducts insulated

Fresh air terminal

Pre filter

Exhaust air terminal

Frost protection heater

MVHR – main supply and extract air filters included

Supply air heater

Sound attenuators – low frequency

Supply air duct insulated after air heater

Supply air valves – living rooms

Sound attenuators – higher frequency

Exhaust air valves – wet rooms

minimise energy use while maintaining good indoor air quality. If this mixed-mode approach is used for ventilation, then the design of the building must ensure all wet rooms have openable windows. If, as is the case in many modern houses and non-domestic buildings, the bathrooms and shower rooms are placed in the core of the building, then the ventilation system should be capable of running in extract only mode and windows or vents opened in the living rooms to provide the make-up air.

In urban and deep urban areas, this approach may be undesirable or unacceptable to some residents. In such cases, a mechanical ventilation system which can maintain good indoor air quality and thermal conditions within the building throughout the year is necessary.

Currently, there is no mechanical ventilation system designed and sized to undertake the normal background ventilation function of a dwelling which can also accommodate the greatly increased air flow rates required to remove the excessive heat gains that occur in summer. Therefore most Passivhaus designs require purge ventilation to be achieved through the use of opening windows.

8.2.4 Demand controlled ventilation (DCV)

One approach to controlling ventilation is to control it on demand. This approach ventilates each space, or the whole building, based on the need for ventilation rather than a fixed air flow rate. This is achieved through the use of sensors which vary the air flow rate based on occupancy and/or indoor air quality. This control approach is known as demand controlled ventilation (DCV).

The advantage of this approach to ventilation is that when a space is not being occupied, the ventilation rate can be reduced and therefore the fan power reduced. Additional savings in heating energy resulting from the adoption of DCV will be modest due to the use of highly efficient heat recovery devices minimising the ventilation heating load.

In non-domestic buildings, DCV is used to provide very closely controlled heating and cooling to individual zones by varying both supply air flow rate and temperature. However, this approach may not be appropriate for dwellings where ventilation is undertaken to provide good indoor air quality as well as a proportion of the space cooling and/or heating but at a fixed ventilation rate.

For houses, the most common approaches are to sense occupancy and/or relative humidity (RH). Although occupancy can be determined using PIR (passive infrared) sensors, CO_2 sensors are more commonly used as an indication of occupancy levels. It is clear that if only one sensor type is used, say for occupancy, then the RH in a space may remain totally uncontrolled. On the other hand, if only RH is used as the control variable then the indoor air quality may vary significantly with little or no change in air flow rate. This highlights the potential problem of DCV; if the pollutant is not monitored then it cannot be used to control the ventilation rate and may be high or low with an associated impact on indoor air quality. It is therefore suggested that if DCV is used as a ventilation control strategy, the background ventilation rate must be sufficiently high to remove all sources of pollution that are not being monitored, i.e. volatile organic

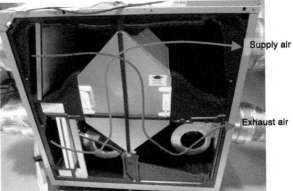

compounds (VOCs), formaldehyde, etc. Without detailed knowledge of emission rates, the Passivhaus recommended supply and extract ventilation rates detailed in Section 1 should be used.

8.3 Components of a MVHR unit

There are many mechanical ventilation heat recovery (MVHR) units currently on the market that claim impressive levels of performance, and choosing a product can be daunting. However, limiting choice to products only detailed in the Passivhaus list of certified products (PHI, 2012) makes the decision easier and has clear advantages. All products on the list are tested to the PHI test method, which is very thorough and includes a range of functional tests of the controls. In comparison, the UK-based testing for the Standard Assessment Procedure (SAP) is based solely on the thermal and fan power performance, with no regard for the operational characteristics of the unit.

A MVHR product is made up of the following components:

CASING

The materials of the casing have a significant bearing on the acoustic and thermal performance of the unit. There is a move away from the traditional metal double-skinned insulated panel construction to extensive use of rigid foam materials, making products lighter, better insulated and offering better internal aerodynamics. There are, however, some regional requirements that products made of flammable foams are clad in a fire-resistant casing. This has led to some products retaining an outer metal casing. This is not required in all EU countries and many products have no outer casing.

Due to the relatively low levels of casing insulation, some of the metal panel products may need additional insulation to prevent condensation forming on areas of the panel when the outside air temperature is low. This is particularly

8.3
Different fan locations – both fans pulling air through the heat exchanger, or exhaust fan pulling and supply fan pushing. The latter has the acoustic advantage of the fans being on the outside of the heat exchanger, reducing fan noise entering the supply duct, but at a potential loss of thermal performance

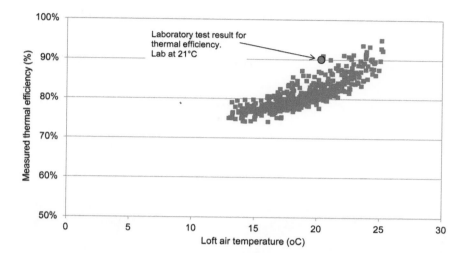

8.4

Monitored thermal efficiency of MVHR located outside the thermal envelope, showing clear reduction in thermal efficiency as loft air temperature falls

the case with metal cases where thermal bridges link the outer surface of the product to the fresh and exhaust air streams.

If the MVHR unit is to be located outside the building thermal envelope then all products currently on the market will require additional casing insulation to minimise heat losses. Very few manufacturers offer effective additional insulation jackets for MVHR products. Placing a unit in a totally unheated space is, therefore, not recommended as the performance of the MVHR system can be significantly reduced with the additional risk of condensation and icing.

FILTERS

It is common for almost all models on the list of certified MVHR products to include filters within the casing. Many products also include a pre-filter before the main F7 filter in the fresh air stream. Filters need to be easily accessible so that they can be changed at regular intervals. To make access to the fresh air filters easier, filter boxes containing both the pre- and main filters may be installed before the MVHR unit.

Filters installed within the MVHR unit will be sized specifically for that product and, therefore, replacements may only be available directly from the manufacturer.

Filters appropriate for use in MVHR systems are discussed in Section 7.

FANS

The change of fan motors from AC to DC is almost complete across all the products listed as certified. This move has lowered the fan energy use over the past few years and led to the widespread adoption of electronic controls for MVHR units.

Forward curved centrifugal fan

Backward curved centrifugal fan

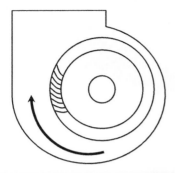

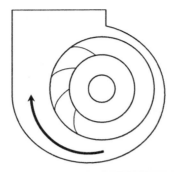

Large number of forward curved blades.

Low pressure development and relatively low efficiency. Shape of casing is important to achieving efficiency. Relatively low rotational speed resulting in lower mechanical noise.

Blades tilt away from direction of rotation.

High efficiencies, high pressure development with low air noise development.

8.5
MVHR fan characteristics

An EC or Electronically Commutated fan motor is similar to a BLDC (brushless direct current) motor, being a permanent magnet design but having on board electronics for both mains voltage rectification (conversion to DC) and the motor drive electronics. An EC motor can operate directly from an AC power source and provides similar performance from either 50 Hz or 60 Hz supplies. As the power is converted to DC via onboard drive circuits, accurate speed control is possible from either a 0 V–10 V or PWM (pulse width modulated) signal. EC motors offer significant advantages for fans used in heat recovery systems, including:

- high efficiency is maintained at reduced speed settings;
- cooler motor temperatures compared to AC motors;
- simple speed control interface and fan fault monitoring;
- low noise levels;
- reliability, as the electronics are protected inside the motor.

The type of fan impeller used is still split between forward and backward curved with manufacturers opting for one or the other based on considerations of air flow/pressure development characteristics, acoustics and air flow control functions.

HEAT EXCHANGER

There are currently two main heat exchanger types used in domestic and small commercial MVHR units. These are:

Flat plate heat exchangers – where supply and exhaust air streams pass each other separated by thin sheets of metal or plastic.

The advantage of this type of heat exchanger is that it is passive, with most designs achieving a high level of counterflow, which increases the overall efficiency of the best products to above 90 per cent. The air flows are totally separated and there is no chance of cross-contamination or recirculation.

The disadvantage of flat plate heat exchangers is that they need frost protection to ensure that the condensation occurring on the exhaust air side of the plates does not freeze and restrict the air flow path. This requires active or passive heating of cold outside air up to a temperature of approximately –3°C to ensure that the condensate in the exhaust air remains above freezing.

Many of the heat exchangers in MVHR units currently on the market are small, with plastic plates and very small air flow channels maximising the heat exchange area. These developments have increased the efficiency of the

8.6
MVHR heat exchanger types and typical thermal efficiencies

Plastic counter flow heat exchanger. Thermal efficiency up to 85~94%

Metal rotating regenerative heat exchanger. Thermal efficiency up to 75~85%

exchangers, but have made the need for filtration and frost protection more critical.

Rotating heat exchangers – where air passes through a matrix of material as it rotates, alternating between the supply and exhaust air streams. These heat exchangers are known as regenerative heat exchangers. The matrix is heated by the exhaust air and liberates that heat to the supply air stream. Due to the nature of these heat exchangers, there will always be a small level of recirculation, although good design of the wheel will ensure that this is minimised.

The advantage of this type of heat exchanger is that it requires no frost protection as the wheel is continually moving through both air streams. These heat exchangers also offer the potential to recover some of the moisture from the exhaust air, which may reduce or eliminate the need for humidification in dry, cold climates.

The significant disadvantage to having an active heat exchange element is that the motor driving the wheel requires electricity to rotate it and currently the motors used for this function are not efficient. However, at times when heat recovery is not required, the wheel stops without any change in the air flow rate. In this way, summer ventilation is achieved with no change of air flow paths, and during this period when the wheel motor is not being used, overall energy use is much lower.

CONTROLS

At first glance, the control of the operation of a MVHR unit appears to be a simple task; however, the functionality of modern MVHR unit controls is becoming increasingly sophisticated. At the simplest level, the controls required are fan speed control and a means of controlling the summer bypass. Most products now come equipped with a mimic screen that provides a wide range of operational feedback. This level of sophistication is not just a gimmick. The ability to control a MVHR unit across a range of typical usage patterns (from empty to high-occupancy mode), and the feedback of such an interface, allows useful information about the operation of the unit and the need for maintenance.

Ideally, the control interface should not be located solely on the MVHR unit. It is vital that both the control and the feedback are located in a position that is both convenient and obvious.

From a commissioning engineer's point of view, the ability to control each fan and set each fan speed separately using digital control removes the hit-and-miss approach which results when fans are controlled using potentiometers with no definitive feedback on fan speed. This tends to result in quicker and more accurate matching of fan speed to the required air flow rate, minimising fan power at all fan speeds.

The minimum level of controls that should be sought include:

- fan control for three set speeds (trickle, normal and boost) as required for Passivhaus-approved products;
- individual fan control for commissioning at 1 per cent steps or similar levels of resolution;

- indication of the need for a filter change; at the simplest, level this should be based on time, but ideally, on pressure differential across the filter itself;
- indication of a fan failure;
- indication of frost protection mode;
- indication of summer bypass mode.

SUMMER BYPASS

A summer bypass is a means of passing the air directly from outside into the building without it recovering any heat from the extract air. This is required in the spring, summer and autumn seasons when heat recovery is not required.

8.7
Bypass flaps close off heat exchanger and fresh air is diverted around heat exchange

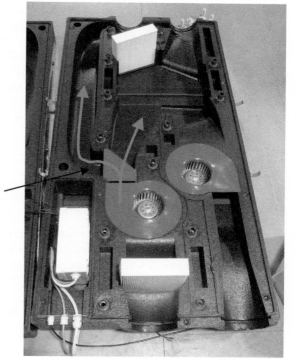

Bypass flap diverts air around heat exchanger

The inclusion of an automatic summer bypass is highly recommended in a MVHR system installed in a Passivhaus. With the heating degree base temperature of a Passivhaus being very low, there is a significant period of the year when little or no heat recovery is actually required. During these periods, the only reason to raise the supply air temperature is to minimise the potential risk of cold draughts if the supply air is delivered to the living rooms too cold.

When assessing the summer bypass design of a MVHR unit, it should be checked to ensure that the air flow path is fully diverted around the heat exchanger. The summer bypass cooling capacity of a mechanical ventilation system is limited due to the small volumes of air used for ventilation, but delivery of cool night air into bedrooms may be sufficient to minimise the risk of high night-time temperatures affecting sleep and potentially the health of occupants.

ACCESSIBILITY

The location of the installed MVHR unit should ensure that access is sufficiently easy to undertake basic maintenance. Installation in a utility room is hugely preferable to a roof space with poor access. The MVHR unit itself should allow simple access for maintenance and replacement of key components. Tools should not be required to change the filters.

Noise is a very critical consideration when assessing a MVHR product. The manufacturer will have a full set of acoustic data. This should be obtained so that the need for effective attenuation can be determined and the suitability of a particular installation location within the building assessed. The quietest domestic products may be installed within the living space with little additional treatment, while others may need to be installed in an acoustically insulated 'plant room'. Acoustic attenuation requirements are discussed in Section 9.

The actual thermal and electrical performance of a MVHR unit is given on the Passivhaus Certificate, which includes details of the minimum limits and the actual tested performance, for thermal efficiency $\eta_{HR,eff} \geq 75\%$, where

$$\eta_{HR,eff} = \frac{(\theta_{Extract} - \theta_{Exhaust}) + \dfrac{P_{el}}{v.C_p \rho}}{\theta_{Extract} - \theta_{Intake}} \qquad [1]$$

and:

$\theta_{Extract}$ is the temperature of air extracted from wet rooms (°C),
$\theta_{Exhaust}$ is the temperature of air exhausted from the MVHR unit to outside (°C),
θ_{Intake} is the temperature of fresh air entering the MVHR unit from outside (°C),
P_{el} is the total electrical power of the MVHR unit – including controls and sensors (W),
v (or v_{ave}) is the average volumetric flow rate of air through the MVHR unit (m³/h), and
$C_p \rho$ is the volumetric specific heat capacity of air (Wh/m³.K).

8.8

Typical variations of thermal
performance and fan power
(W) with air flow rate

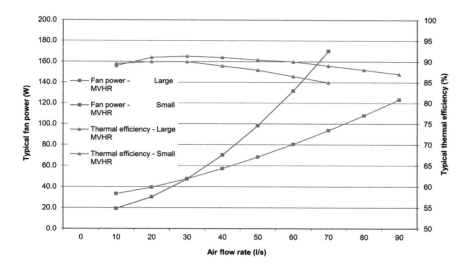

8.9

Example of Passivhaus-
certified component certificate
for a MVHR

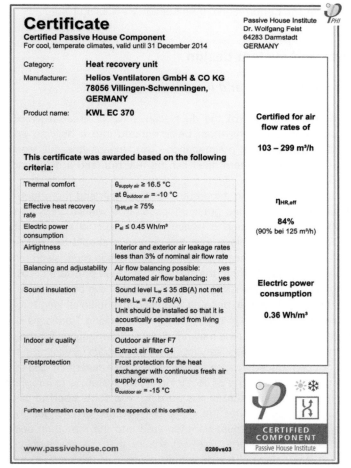

Great care should be taken if performance data from a source other than a Passivhaus Certificate is used because measurement techniques, test points and calculation procedures differ between countries. The calculation detailed in EN 308:1997, used by many manufacturers when quoting thermal efficiency, is acknowledged to result in higher thermal efficiency values; however, it provides a useful comparative measure of performance between different products.

Thermal efficiency varies with air flow rate. The thermal performance of the heat exchanger is optimal at very low flow rates and falls as the flow rate increases. The rate of reduction in efficiency is a function of the size of the heat exchanger. Larger heat exchangers of a given design have lower reductions in efficiency as the air flow rate increases. It is therefore vital that actual performance at a given operating condition is used, rather than an optimum efficiency figure.

Both the PHI test methodology and the European test standard EN 308:1997 assume that test laboratory temperatures are at 'normal' building temperatures. For EN 308:1997, this is 17°C to 27°C with most test laboratories limiting the temperature to approximately 20°C. However, if the MVHR unit is to be installed within an unheated loft, the thermal performance of the casing is critical to the *in situ* performance. (See section 3 – Casing.)

8.4 Ducts and system design

8.4.1 Ductwork design and installation

The design and installation of the ducts can make or break a MVHR system. Carefully designed duct runs must be integrated into a building and be well sealed and accessible for maintenance. This means the full energy-saving potential of the MVHR system itself can be realised, and a quiet and effective ventilation system achieved.

The friction of air being forced through ductwork and the effects of bends, valves, filters, etc. all generate pressure losses in a ventilation system. The aim of good MVHR system design is to achieve the required air distribution at the minimum fan power. To achieve this, the duct runs should be kept as short as practical. The number of bends and changes of direction must also be minimised, and all other components within the system that cause pressure drops should be evaluated to ensure that the most efficient products have been chosen. On some occasions there are, however, benefits to adding an additional length to ducting at the beginning of a system to provide a degree of balancing. Caution is also needed where extremely short duct runs may not allow sufficient space for the installation of sound attenuators. Branches (serving supply and extract valves) from the primary leg should not be reduced to such an extent that they cannot include attenuators.

One of the hardest parts of designing a duct system is to integrate it effectively with the overall structure of the building. The ducts need to pass through voids and access rooms with the minimum number of changes in direction. To achieve this, the ducts must be integrated into the structural design of the dwelling at a very early stage. This will ensure that the space they require is considered at every stage of the design. If this level of design integration can be achieved, then one of the key problems with ductwork installation can be largely overcome; i.e. the need to re-route the duct at the installation stage in order to avoid some other structure or service (e.g. water or waste pipes).

Many of the MVHR system suppliers offer design services. If this approach to design is to be used effectively, it is vital that the suppliers provide their input at the earliest stages. It may therefore be necessary for the supplier/system designer to become part of the design team. Suppliers/designers have considerable experience and will often use three-dimensional drawing packages to allow the route of the duct to be truly integrated with all other components of the house.

Sharing a common Building Information Modelling (BIM) platform is a significant advantage in integrated design development. Once a design is complete, the operating pressures in the ducts at each air flow rate must be determined. This information is critical to assessing if an installation is achieving its design intent in terms of fan energy use. The limiting electrical power use of the system for a Passivhaus-compliant MVHR unit is 0.45 Wh/m³.

8.4.2 Duct layout

The first stage of any building services design is to consider the layout of the rooms and how each room will be served by the ventilation system. Once the layout has been fixed, the most appropriate type of duct system can be determined. There are two distinct duct layout approaches which can be used: single leg (trunk and branch) and radial.

SINGLE LEG

As the name implies, a single leg duct system has a primary duct off which other ducts are tee'd. The primary duct will reduce in size as the air flow through it falls, reducing down to a minimum as it serves the furthest room. The ducts are rigid and can be metal or plastic.

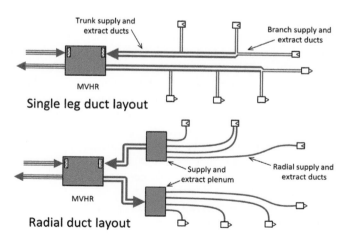

8.10
Schematic of different MVHR duct layout options

8.11
Proprietary duct joint sealing
systems, removing the need
for on-site sealing

This duct layout is easy to understand and is familiar to installers. The disadvantage of this duct system is that it is made up of a significant number of components. Each component has to be joined and the joint sealed. Proprietary duct systems do exist that have rubber seals at each joint fitting. These joints are very effective and will not leak over time. However, if these are not used then each duct section needs to be mechanically joined (riveted) and sealed.

Additionally, the ducts need supporting and access must be provided to allow for cleaning of the extract system. The supply ducts should remain clean because they are protected by the supply air filters before the MVHR unit. Cleaning of single leg systems can be difficult as the Tee junctions make pushing brushes through the duct very difficult.

RADIAL

The radial system uses a single duct from the MVHR unit to a plenum. It then breaks out into smaller-diameter single ducts radiating out to each valve. The duct used between the plenum and each valve is normally a semi-rigid duct. Using this duct design allows the duct from the plenum to the room valve to be one continuous length.

The key disadvantage of this system is that the plenums require considerable space, and as the ducts leave the plenum, there are many ducts that need to access the void space. At higher air flow rates, the pressure loss along single small-diameter duct runs can be high; therefore overall fan power may be higher under these operating conditions. For this reason, many kitchen valves are served by two or three semi-rigid ducts, ensuring that higher air flow rates can be achieved in these locations. The advantages of this system are considerable; with no joints from valve to plenum box, the semi-rigid plastic duct can be threaded through structural elements and bent around obstacles. Cleaning this type of duct is very straightforward as each duct can be brushed back to the plenum where dust can be easily removed. However, this concept requires that the plenum boxes are easily accessible.

The joints between the ductwork and other components are mechanical and, therefore, will not leak or deteriorate over time.

8.12
Examples of radial duct
systems and a typical
mechanical seal used in these
systems

Rigid and semi-rigid duct used to achieve air distribution.

Mechanical seals used with most semi-rigid duct systems provide a long term
seal that can be dismounted quickly if required.

8.4.3 Access and cleaning

Possibly one of the most overlooked aspects of domestic ventilation system design and installation is the need to access the ducts for cleaning. Larger non-domestic systems have to be accessible for inspection and cleaning as this is a legal requirement (The Health and Safety Commission, 1992), ensuring places of work are healthy and safe. In addition to this, many non-domestic systems are replaced on a relatively regular basis as building use changes. However, a domestic system should be considered to be there for the life of the major structural components of the house, i.e. at least 50 years. When considered in this light, it is clear that access must be provided to clean the extract ducts and intake duct prior to filtration, even though it may only be required once every five or even ten years. If access points are to be provided, then the choice of duct material is, in practice, limited to metal, as such fittings can be readily accommodated in metal ducting. If a radial system is adopted using semi-rigid ducts, the need for access points is removed as each radial leg can be swept back to the plenum.

One way of minimising the rate at which ducts will become dirty is to place the filters at the beginning of each duct section. This is normally the case with the supply air ductwork as the filter will be located before or within the MVHR unit. The extract ducts, however, are often left unfiltered from the extract valve to the filter at the MVHR unit. This results in these ducts becoming very dirty over time. One very effective means of slowing the accumulation of dirt and grease is to place the filters within, or as part of, the extract valves. In this way, the filters are easily accessible (see Section 7).

8.4.4 Ductwork and system insulation

The choice of location of the MVHR unit will dictate which of the ducts require insulating.

- If the MVHR unit is to be placed outside the heated envelope then the warm extract duct and the supply duct must be very heavily insulated. The level of insulation should mimic that of the building fabric as these ducts can be considered as part of the internal space.
- If the MVHR unit is to be placed within the building envelope then the exhaust air duct and the fresh air intake duct must both be insulated. As noted above, the level of insulation would ideally be equal to that of the envelope on the exhaust air duct as any heat gains to this duct are a heat loss direct to outside. This, however is generally impractical and the recommendations are that insulation levels should be a minimum depth of 50 mm for ducts that are less than 2.0 m in length; above this, the insulation depth must be increased to 100 mm.

It is vital that these duct lengths are minimised to reduce the heat loss. It is also essential that both of these ducts have a very effective vapour barrier applied. This vapour barrier needs to be 'perfect', as any gaps allowing warm inside air to

Ventilation concepts

come into contact with the cold inlet and exhaust ducts will result in considerable condensation occurring. If the insulation is a mineral fibre type then this will become wet and the actual insulation value will reduce significantly. To minimise the potential for condensation becoming a problem, it is recommended that the ducts are insulated with closed cell foam insulation and very effectively sealed to the warmer components at each end. The depth of the insulation can be increased using less expensive mineral fibre-based material where there is no chance of condensation occurring.

Where the exhaust duct is taken out of the heated envelope and rises (e.g. through the roof), the duct should incorporate a condensate trap. The air being discharged from the MVHR unit will (across a significant period of the year) be saturated. Therefore, any further cooling will cause condensation to occur within the duct. If this is not removed, it will pool and may run back into the MVHR unit and onto the fan.

If a post heater is to be used to provide space heating, it is vital that all the heat from the heater is delivered into the rooms that require the heat and is not lost to the ceiling voids and other unoccupied spaces. To ensure that this is achieved, it is important that the ducts between the post heater and all the supply valves are insulated with 20–25 mm foil-backed mineral wool or a vapour-tight closed cell foam. The same applies where a cooling coil is used to provide summer cooling to the supply air; in this case, it is particularly important that the vapour-tight seal is maintained on the insulated supply ductwork.

Table 8.3 Summary of insulation requirements

Ducts	Insulation thickness required
Warm ducts outside the building thermal envelope	**Minimum 100 mm**, recommended equal to the thickness of the thermal envelope insulation For heated supply air, 150 mm
Cold ducts inside the thermal building envelope	**Minimum 50 mm, diffusion-impermeable** If longer than 2 m, minimum 100 mm
Heated (or cooled) supply air ducts inside the building thermal envelope	**20–25 mm**

8.13
Insulation applied to ducts before installation. All joints are over-taped to ensure a vapour-tight seal is achieved

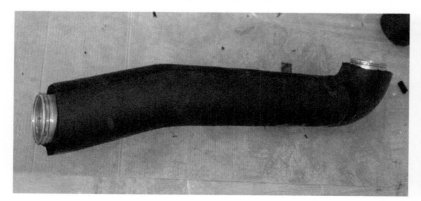

Although not required in single dwellings, it is highly recommended that a simple pressure test is carried out to determine if there are any significant sources of leaks before ducts are finally built in. Testing the duct at a relatively low test pressure would allow any significant breaks in the duct seals to be identified and rectified. If this is not undertaken then final balancing of the system will always be difficult to achieve. Furthermore, if the leak is significant, it may necessitate opening up finished surfaces to allow access. In multi-occupancy residences and non-domestic buildings, pressure testing of the ducts should be routinely undertaken and the results of the test recorded as part of the commissioning process.

Ducts are available in a range of materials, the most common being plastic and metal. One of the advantages of metal ducts in the past has been that they are available with very effective seals that make installation quicker and guarantee a near airtight connection. Mechanical push fit connections are now becoming available for some of the most common plastic ducts. Another advantage of metal ducts is that bends are swept and not tight, thus reducing the pressure loss at each bend. As a rule of thumb, the inner radius of a bend should be at least the same as the diameter of the duct. Most duct manufacturers provide pressure loss data for all components and these can be used to calculate the overall pressure loss of the system.

There are a range of duct sizes that are standard; typical sizes available in Europe are given in Table 8.4.

8.14
90° bends. Plastic duct bends are typically sharp, resulting in increased pressure losses and potentially noise generation. Metal duct bends are typically swept, resulting in less air flow disturbance

Table 8.4 Typical European duct sizes

Material and shape	Size (mm) (Ø nominal)
Plastic, circular (diameter)	100, 125 and 150.
Plastic, rectangular	110 × 54, 150 × 70, 204 × 60 and 220 × 90.
Metal, circular (diameter)	80, 100, 125, 150, 160, 180 and 200. Larger sizes (up to 1,600) are available and sizes other than those listed can be made to order.
Metal, rectangular	Generally not available off the shelf, but 150 × 50 and 200 × 50 can be ordered and other sizes manufactured.

8.15

Typical pressure losses in rectangular ducts

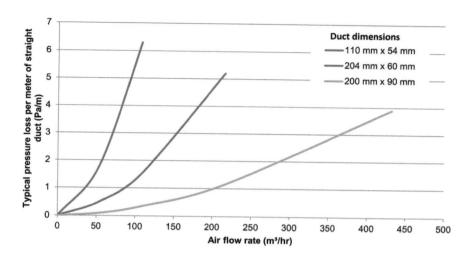

8.16

EPP duct used for outside terminal to MVHR duct runs, reducing the risk of condensation forming on these ducts in cold weather compared to metal or plastic ducts

Flexible duct has been traditionally used for many ventilation applications in the UK and North America. Due to the very high pressure losses in this type of duct, the risk that it may be crushed and the fact that it is hard to join and clean, it should not be used in a Passivhaus installation.

Recently, a range of ducts manufactured directly from insulation materials (expanded polyethylene: EPE; expanded polypropylene: EPP; and expanded polystyrene: EPS) have become available. The manufacturer of this expanded polypropylene (EPP) duct recommends it is used as the intake and exhaust ducts. It is claimed that this eliminates the need to further insulate these ducts in order to prevent any risk of condensation.

The air speed in a duct should be minimised to reduce both noise generation and pressure losses. However, there is a practical balance to be made, and the size of the duct should not be so large as to require excessive amounts of space. It is, therefore, recommended that the limiting air speeds set out in Table 8.5 are not exceeded.

Table 8.5 Limiting air speeds in different ducts

Location of duct	Limiting air speed (m/s)
Vertical risers. Risers are not typically used in a single house; they are found in multi-occupancy residencies and non-domestic buildings distributing air between take-off ducts serving each residence.	3
Distribution ducts. These are the primary ducts which connect directly to the MVHR unit in a small system, and all the ducts that connect either the primary ducts or the risers to the final duct runs.	2
Final ducts. These ducts connect the distribution ducts to the air valves.	1

As a check to see what diameter a duct should be, the following simple equation can be used:

$$D \geq \sqrt{\dot{v}/(V_{max} \times 2872)} \qquad [2]$$

where:

$\dot{v}$ is the air flow rate through duct (m³/hour),
V_{max} is the limiting air speed in duct (m/s) (see Table 8.5),
2,872 is $\pi/4 \times 3{,}600$ (s/h), and
D is the duct diameter (m).

8.5 Outside terminations

The external terminations of the intake and exhaust air ducts can have a very significant effect on the overall effectiveness of the ventilation system.

The level of pollution in the vicinity of the intake is possibly the most critical issue that has to be addressed when deciding where to locate the intake air grille. It is often recommended that intakes should be at a minimum of 3m above ground level. This height is suggested as it is well above the exhaust level of any fumes emitted from cars adjacent to a building (i.e. on a driveway). If the intake is located away from such sources of pollution then the height recommendation can be reduced. However, it is advised that the intake is never placed at ground level as this will tend to draw in debris. A draft version of EN 13779 in 1999 (CEN, 1999) noted that there should be a minimum distance of 2m or 1.5 times the maximum thickness of snow between the ground and an air intake (and, where possible, a minimum of 3m). This guidance was revised in the current version of this Standard (CEN, 2007b) to reference only the depth of snow and advise that the intake should not be 'just above the ground'.

It is important that if roof cowls are to be used, the intake cowl properly protects the intake against driving rain and snow ingress. For roof cowls to provide weather protection, they need to turn the air flow direction through more than 90 degrees, which results in very high pressure losses compared to wall terminals. This fact needs to be considered in the specification as it has knock-on effects on MVHR fan speed requirements and overall fan energy.

In the recent past, external termination grilles have been supplied with relatively fine insect screens. However, a recent monitoring exercise revealed the inappropriateness of fitting such coarse pre-filters in locations that are not directly accessible as part of a routine maintenance schedule (Dengle and Swainson, 2013). The filters shown in Figure 8.17 had been checked four months prior to the air flow rates being noted to have dropped very significantly. It was revealed that the blocked fly screen had reduced the supply air flow into some houses by over 95 per cent, leaving the occupants with little effective fresh air supply to the living rooms. Investigation of the material on the filters showed that it consisted of a very high percentage of leaf and other plant organic material. The speed of the depositing of this material reinforces the argument that all filters (including external grilles) must be checked regularly if automatic sensors are not installed to report pressure loss.

Fly screen installed on supply air terminal totally blocked with fibrous material.

8.17
Result of inappropriate fly screen used in a fresh air terminal

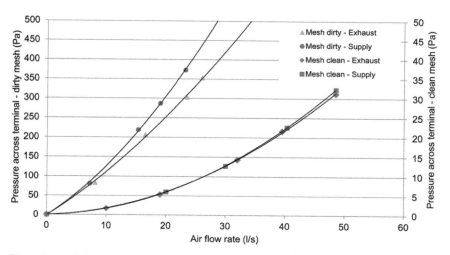

The effect of the blockage increased the pressure drop across the screen from approximately 5 Pa at 20 l/s to between 250 and 300 Pa.

In many installations, the MVHR unit may be located on an external wall in which case the intake and exhaust air terminations may be located relatively close to each other.

There is little definitive guidance on the separation of supply and exhausts from domestic MVHRs. EN 13779:2007 which provides guidance for non-residential buildings states that an intake should be placed at least 2.0 m from an exhaust and, if possible, the intake should be below the exhaust.

ASHRAE Standard 62-2-2010 Section 6.8 (ASHRAE, 2010) states that intakes should be located at a minimum of 3.0 m from known sources of contaminants.

However, in 2012 the US Government Accounting Office (US Government Accountability Office, 2012) undertook modelling using the ASHRAE dilution equations and found that a horizontal separation of 1.0 m and a vertical separation of 1.0 m was equivalent to a horizontal separation of 3.0 m.

Overall compliance with the relevant national Building Regulations (HM Government, 2010) requirements for separation of intakes from boiler flues must always be followed. It is recommended that separation of the supply and exhaust terminals should either follow the guidance in EN 13779:2007 or have a minimum separation of 1.0 m horizontally and 1.0 m vertically. Anecdotal evidence in the UK has suggested that locating the exhaust below the supply does not result in any recirculation. This is due to the fact that exhaust air is jetted out and down by the weather louvres in the terminal, whilst air flow tends to be across a vertical façade and therefore recirculation is unlikely.

If the location of the fresh air intake is flexible, then the opportunity may exist to source warm solar-heated air from the south side of the building in winter, and cool air from the shaded north side in summer. If this opportunity does not exist, or installation of additional dampers to control the air source is considered a potential maintenance problem, then locating the fresh air intake on the north side (i.e. away from areas that will be heated by the summer sun) is recommended. The potential for intake air to be preheated from occasional winter solar gains is relatively small compared to the potential for summer solar gains to a façade (i.e. wall or roof) to result in very warm air being drawn into a building. This may contribute to overheating of the building across much of the sunnier and warmer months of the year.

When commissioning a MVHR system, it is a requirement that the air flow rates through each room terminal are measured, recorded and compared to the design, and the total air flow rate into and out of the house is measured. This information should be recorded on the Ventilation Protocol commissioning log-sheet (Figure 8.34). Access to the outside terminals must be possible if access to 'in-duct' measurements is not made. Logically, the terminals should therefore be placed in a location that is easy and safe to access.

Air discharging from an exhaust air termination will be at, or very close to, its dew point temperature. Therefore the exhaust air should not be discharged onto part of the building fabric that would be affected by condensate forming on it over the winter months.

In very cold climates, there is a risk that condensate within the exhaust air will freeze on the terminal. Terminals that minimise the potential of this occurring are available and should be used in such locations.

8.6 Frost protection

An efficient heat exchanger will cool the outgoing air down to within a few degrees centigrade of the incoming fresh air. If the fresh air is significantly below freezing then the outgoing air will be cooled below zero centigrade and condensation forming on the plates of the heat exchanger will freeze.

If this is not addressed very quickly, the air flow paths on the exhaust air side of the heat exchanger will become restricted and this will further reduce the exhaust air flow rate. Reducing the exhaust flow rate will result in the air being cooled further and it will approach the temperature of the incoming fresh air. This situation will cause the freezing to spread throughout the entire heat exchanger very quickly. The overall effect of this is that the exhaust air channels will become blocked and the exhaust air flow will stop.

There are two basic approaches to frost protection: either reduce the intake air flow rate or preheat the intake air. Reducing the intake/supply air fan speed based on a control algorithm has the effect of raising the heat exchanger temperature, preventing freezing. This approach, while relatively effective, requires the air flow rates to be imbalanced, with the balance of the air being drawn into the building through infiltration. In cold climates, this may occur over an extended period which could have implications for indoor air quality and peak heating loads. The Passivhaus approach is, therefore, to prevent the heat exchanger freezing whilst maintaining continually balanced supply and extract air flow rates.

To prevent the heat exchanger freezing, the intake air must be maintained at a temperature that will not freeze the condensate on the exhaust air side. If a heat exchanger could be 100 per cent efficient, this would clearly require the intake air to be maintained above 0°C. For most heat exchangers, the efficiency will approach 95 per cent at best; thus even in very cold conditions the exhaust air will tend to have a dew point temperature above 0°C. Therefore, the reduction in exhaust air temperature will be less than the temperature gain to the supply air as the latent heat of condensation is transferred to the incoming supply air. The overall result of this is that an intake air temperature of approximately –3°C onto the heat exchanger should not result in any freezing on the exhaust air side. The exact temperature below which frost protection is required will be given by the MVHR manufacturer and should be followed closely.

In many countries, the air temperature falls below –3°C in winter, and in many locations, it remains below this temperature for a significant period of time. A Passivhaus ventilation system therefore needs to include a means of increasing the outside air temperature to –2°C or –3°C throughout this period. There are many options available to achieve the required level of preheating, but the key is to achieve it with minimal energy impact.

All MVHR units listed on the PHI website have been tested for operation at –15°C over a 12-hour period to ensure that they do not freeze, and also tested by slowly lowering the intake air temperature from 0°C to –10°C to check when the frost protection becomes operational. During the MVHR commissioning process, it is important to verify the correct operation of the frost protection sensor setting.

Methods of providing frost protection preheating suitable for Passivhaus MVHR units are summarised below.

1 *Electric heater* – Direct electric heating of the fresh supply air before it enters the MVHR unit is a very simple and controllable means of providing frost protection. Provided the control of the heater element is proportional to the heat required (i.e. the heater is not simply on/off), its output can be controlled to maintain a constant air temperature at the MVHR inlet spigot and the electricity use can be minimised. However, the correct setting of the control set point is critical, as is the calibration of the temperature sensor. Drift of the temperature sensor may result in the heater either running for too long and wasting electricity or, conversely, cutting in too late with the risk of freezing the heat exchanger.
2 *Water/glycol-based heating coil drawing heat from a water-based space heating system installed in the duct before the MVHR heat exchanger* – An electric or glycol heater battery can be sized easily to provide a controlled level of preheating, ensuring that air does not enter the heat exchanger at a temperature low enough to cause freezing. One of the key issues with both of these systems is that the controls must ensure that the heat supplied to the cold air stream is the minimum required to achieve frost protection. Any heating of the air above this temperature is reducing the potential to recover heat from the exhaust air stream and will be exhausted to outside. The heaters must therefore be closely controlled by a temperature sensor located at the MVHR inlet spigot, or within the MVHR unit if the MVHR controller is controlling the heater battery. To prevent dirt build-up on the coil, the intake air pre-filter should be placed upstream of the coil.
3 *Air-based ground-air heat exchanger (GAHE) (earth tubes)* – Although accepted as a means of preheating and pre-cooling ventilation air, and potentially very efficient as a means of defrost protection, earth tubes are no longer promoted by PHI as they are considered too expensive (EDU, 2008). Questions have also been raised about potential mould growth due to condensation within the ducts. Although the reasons for problems of mould growth have not been fully determined, many closed loop brine/glycol coil ground heat exchangers

8.18
Ceramic and resistance element frost protection heaters

Ventilation concepts

are now being installed to achieve the same functions as earth tubes at a fraction of the installation cost. In temperate/warm climates, a more appropriate use of GAHEs may be the potential to reduce peak day summer supply air temperatures and therefore minimise the heat gains to a building.

4   *Closed loop brine/glycol coil ground heat exchanger* – A closed loop laid beneath the slab insulation, or within the surrounding grounds of a building, can be used to provide frost protection. A brine or glycol fluid is pumped through a small bore polyethylene (PE) pipe located at a depth of 1.5 m to 2.0 m using a very small circulation pump. The fluid is then passed through a coil placed in the supply air path before the MVHR unit.

Control of the brine loop circulation pump should be based on the temperature of the supply air at the inlet spigot to the MVHR unit. The pump should operate to ensure that the supply air does not fall below approximately –3°C, as discussed previously. The pump may also be used to pre-cool the supply air during the summer months. However, care must be taken to avoid excessively high humidity levels in the supply air and a condensate drain should be installed at the location of the coil.

8.19
Schematic of components in a ground heat exchanger frost protection system (Helios)

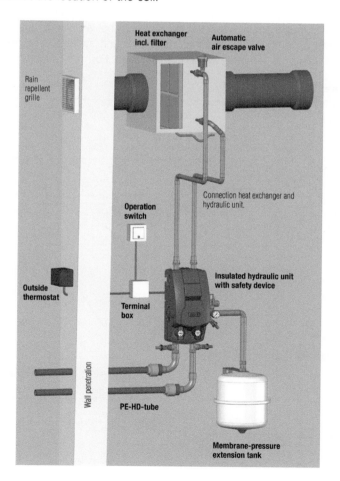

8.7 Filters

One of the key ideas behind the Passivhaus concept is that the internal air should be clean and healthy. To achieve this, filtration is required in all mechanical ventilation systems installed in Passivhaus buildings.

There are two key reasons for undertaking filtration of air:

- removal of pollutants from the fresh air drawn into the house and supplied to the occupants;
- removal of debris from the air that may over time clog the heat exchanger, ducts and fans, reducing the efficiency of these components.

The pollutants in air that can be captured in a filter can be broken down according to their size, as detailed in Figure 8.20.

The classes of filters are detailed in Table 8.6.

The requirements for filters in ventilation systems for non-domestic buildings in the UK are backed up by the HSE requirements at work Code of Practice 1992, Regulation 6 (The Health and Safety Commission, 1992). This requirement stipulates that where spaces are to be ventilated, the ventilation air shall not cause ill health, and that the ventilation system shall be regularly checked to ensure it remains clean and effective. For non-domestic buildings,

Table 8.6 Filter classes (EN 779:2012)

Filter group	Coarse				Medium		Fine		
Filter class	G1	G2	G3	G4	M5	M6	F7	F8	F9

Source: CEN (2012)

8.20
Efficiency of different filter classes compared to a range of typical airborne particles

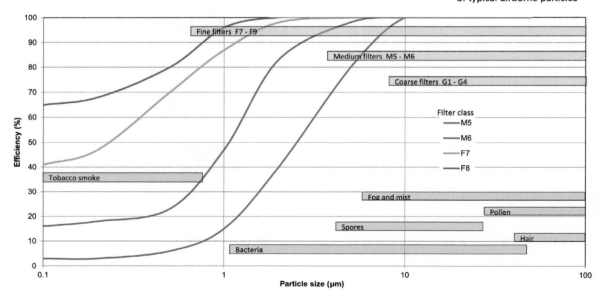

Table 8.7 Recommended minimum filter classes for a range of inside and outdoor air quality classes given in EN 13779:2007

Outside air class	Typical location	Air quality	Indoor air class			
			1 – High	2 – Medium	3 – Moderate	4 – Low
1	Rural	Pure	F9	F8	F7	M5
2	Small town	Dusty	F7 + F9	M6 + F8	M5 + F7	M5 + M6
3	City centre	Very high concentrations of dust or gases	F7 + GF + F9	M6 + GF + F9	M5 + F7	M5 + M6

Note: GF is a gas or carbon filter.

EN 13779:2007 states that M5 is considered the lowest-grade filter that is appropriate for the filtration of the supply air. As the level of pollutants in the outside air increases, the grade of filtration required increases.

For a Passivhaus, the fresh air filter should be a minimum of F7 and the exhaust air filter should be G4.

Many MVHR units now come with filters fitted as standard. All products listed on the PHI website must carry an F7 class filter for the fresh air supply and a G4 class filter for the exhaust air. However, if filtration is to be undertaken outside the MVHR unit then the following points need to be taken into account.

The pressure drop across a filter is directly related to the class of filter and the area of filter material open to the air stream. To cut costs, many MVHR units are provided with filters which have relatively small effective areas. The effect of this is that as the filter picks up dirt, the pressure drop across it increases. The smaller the area of the filter for a given filter material, the faster the pressure drop will increase.

The difference in total pressure across a filter is calculated using Bernoulli's equation:

$$\Delta P = K \tfrac{1}{2} \rho V^2$$

[3]

where:

K is the pressure loss coefficient for filter (–),
ρ is the density of air (kg/m^3), and
V is the face velocity of air passing through filter (m/s).

It is clear from equation 3 that the surface area of a filter is critical to both the initial pressure drop and the rate of change of the pressure drop as the filter becomes dirty. A small flat filter will have a relatively high initial pressure drop and this will increase quickly as dirt accumulates. A larger bag-type filter will have a lower initial pressure drop due to the increased area and thus lower air face velocity, and after a given time, the change in filter pressure drop will be significantly smaller. Therefore, it is necessary to inspect the type and style of the

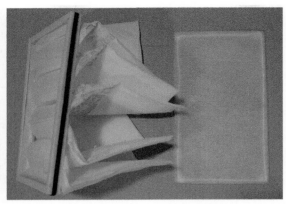

F7 bag filter with a very large surface are compared to the face cross sectional area.

Two G3 filters installed in similar maximum air flow rate MVHRs. The bag filter has a filter area in excess of six times that of the plain filter increasing the time interval between changes significantly.

filters installed in a MVHR unit before procurement to make sure that they are good quality and generously sized.

8.21
Different filter types – bag filters offering lower pressure drop and longer service life

To minimise the need to replace an expensive F7 filter frequently, it is normal practice to install a coarse G4 filter or similar as a pre-filter. These lower-grade filters are much cheaper and can be replaced more frequently, and in some cases, can be washed several times before requiring replacement.

Most manufacturers recommend that filters are replaced annually. However, this makes a significant assumption about the rate of soiling. In practice, it is recommended that the filters be inspected on a two- to three-month basis for the first year of operation. In this way, any seasonal build-up can be identified and appropriate replacement intervals can be determined. For example in a rural setting, it may be assumed that air quality is very high and filters could quite reasonably be changed annually. However, haymaking, for example, releases very significant levels of dust into the air and this may clog the supply air filter over a matter of days. After becoming dirty, if automatic filter soiling is not indicated by the MVHR control panel, air flow rates will remain reduced until the filters are changed. Similarly, if the MVHR unit has constant volume fan control, the fan power will increase significantly in order to maintain air flow rates.

Life cycle cost analysis has been undertaken on the cost of filters (Eurovent, 2009). Generally, findings indicate that if the air flow rate is maintained at a constant level then the cost of purchasing and maintaining filters is around 20 per cent of the total cost, with 80 per cent being the energy cost of the fans overcoming the pressure loss of the filters over their life.

8.7.1 Extract air filtration

Filtering of the extract air is vital to keep the ducts and MVHR unit clean. Extract air from the kitchen carries very significant levels of dust and grease, deposits

8.22
Filtered extract valve and a
metal grease filter used in
kitchen extract valves

of which can build up over time and can be very hard to remove effectively from the ducts (see Section 4.3).

The extract duct from the kitchen should be placed away from the cooker. A recirculating extract hood should be used above the cooker, but not connected to the MVHR system. In this way, the room is ventilated but the extract air is not laden with grease. To minimise dirt build-up in the duct from the kitchen, it is recommended that the valve has a washable (or disposable) grease filter installed and that the first couple of meters of duct are easily accessible to allow for regular removal and high-pressure cleaning, or replacement. The bathroom valve should also contain a disposable or washable filter.

8.8 Post heater

One of the key features of a Passivhaus is that the design heating load is very small. In addition to this, to minimise the overall heating demand, the system must be able to respond very quickly to internal or external heat gains to ensure that the operative temperature does not overshoot. All forms of water-based heating system have an inherent thermal mass that has to liberate its heat once it has been warmed by the heat generator. Therefore, the responsiveness of any water-based system can vary from very slow (underfloor heating) systems to relatively slow (radiators and skirting heaters). The alternative often used in Passivhauses is to heat the supply air. In this way the heat to a building can be regulated back almost instantly as heat gains occur, maximising the fraction of overall heating provided by passive gains.

If an air-based heating system is to be installed then care must be taken to assess if the heating load at design condition can be met, or largely met, by this means. The heating capacity of the ventilation air is relatively small due to the low air flow rates required for ventilation of buildings and the maximum off-coil air temperature being limited to 52°C.

The heating capacity of the ventilation air is

$$P_v = \dot{v} \, C_p \, \rho \, dT \qquad\qquad [4]$$

where:

P_v is the ventilation heating power (kW),
$\dot{v}$ is the volumetric flow rate (m³/h),
$C_p\rho$ is the volumetric specific heat capacity (Wh/m³K) (typically 0.33Wh/m³K), and
dT is the temperature difference (K).

Therefore, if the ventilation rate is 125 m³/h and the internal air temperature is 20°C then the maximum heating capacity of the ventilation air is:

$$P_v = 125 \times 0.33 \times (52 - 20)$$
$$\approx 1.3\,\text{kW}$$

There are two main types of post heater: water and electric.

8.8.1 Water-based heaters

Linking of a heater battery to a hydraulic heating system, or the domestic hot water (DHW) cylinder, allows heat to be supplied to the supply air in a very controlled manner. The heat output must be controlled by a valve or variable speed pump. This is linked to the room air sensor, a duct air sensor and a controller. As the space calls for heat, the controller will control the valve or pump to achieve a given supply air temperature. If the room air sensor does not detect an increase in temperature, the supply air temperature in the duct is increased to a maximum of 52°C.

One potential problem with a water-based heating coil used as the post heater is that if the extract fan were to fail or if the heat exchanger were to freeze due to condensate freezing on the exhaust air side, the supply air would not be warmed and may be supplied at significantly below freezing. Under such conditions, there is potential for the post heater to freeze and burst the coil pipes. To ensure that this will not occur, one of the functional tests of the controls of a MVHR unit listed by PHI (Passivhaus Institut, 2009) is that the supply air must not be allowed to fall below 5°C. If this occurs then the supply fan must stop and the control interface must indicate a fault has occurred.

8.8.2 Electric heaters

Electric heaters recommended for installation in ducts are known as PTC (Positive Temperature Coefficient) heaters. The ceramic heating element of a PTC heater exhibits a very unusual feature in that its resistance increases very sharply as the temperature of the element rises. This makes these heaters self-limiting to a predefined temperature and, therefore, very safe. The control of such heaters can be very simple, running off a room thermostat. However, the disadvantage with this approach is that the supply air temperature will always be the same when the heating is on. Controlling the heater proportionally to the heat demand requires a more complex controller which adjusts the electrical power to the heater based on the heat load.

One of the disadvantages of using a post heater to supply most of the heat to a building is that it results in very little potential for individual control of the temperature within each of the zones or rooms within a building. Because the supply air is delivered at a uniform temperature, one possible source of dissatisfaction is that all the rooms will tend to be at the same temperature. Maintaining bedrooms and living rooms at the same temperature may not be desirable. One potential solution to this is to zone the heating and have local post heaters and controllers covering different zones of the building. This will add to the complexity and cost, but may be desirable from a thermal comfort perspective.

One other point to note is that heating a dwelling with a single duct mounted post heater may tend to make bathrooms feel cool when the occupants are bathing. It is therefore common for local heaters (such as heated towel rails) to be installed in the bathrooms to allow the temperature to be raised when necessary. When additional zone heaters are used, it is important that time controls are installed such that the heat emitter is not left on when the room is not in use.

8.9 Acoustics

The concept of hygiene with respect to a Passivhaus includes the acoustic environment, and the ventilation system plays a very significant part in this. To ensure that noise generated by the ventilation system is not a nuisance in a Passivhaus, very strict recommended limits are set for different rooms as given in Table 8.8.

There are three sources of noise that have to be considered when looking at the installation of a MVHR unit in a dwelling:

- Noise ingress into the dwelling from a noisy external environment.
- Noise generated by the MVHR unit and within the distribution ducts. The MVHR unit has two fans which generate both mechanical noise and vibration. In addition to this, noise is generated by the air within the fans and within the distribution ductwork.
- Noise generated within one space travelling through the ducts to other spaces within the dwelling; this is sometimes referred to as 'telephony' or 'cross-talk'.

Table 8.8 Recommended limiting sound levels in rooms in a Passivhaus

Rooms	Sound
Room or space containing a MVHR unit	35 dB(A)
Rooms other than living areas – wet rooms, circulation spaces, etc.	30 dB(A)
Living areas – living room, bedrooms, etc.	25 dB(A)

8.9.1 Externally generated noise

The fabric of a Passivhaus is by its very nature very effective at minimising the transmission of noise from outside the building. However, a weak point in the fabric is found where the ventilation ducts penetrate the fabric. If it is very noisy outside a building and the air terminals cannot be located on a quiet elevation then it is vital that noise entering both the intake and exhaust air ducts is effectively attenuated at the point where the ducts enter the building. If this is not undertaken, a low level of noise will break out of the ducts and may cause acoustic discomfort.

If the outside environment is not very noisy, the installation of sound attenuators between the MVHR unit and the outside terminals is not required to protect against internal nuisance. Conversely, in some very quiet locations, attenuation may be required on these ducts to minimise the noise of the fans causing a nuisance in the external environment.

8.9.2 Noise generated by the MVHR unit

Noise generated within a MVHR unit could enter the occupied zones of a building via a range of paths, and it is vital that each of these is identified and, as far as is practical, minimised.

The fan impellers within the MVHR unit spin very quickly and, although the impellers are balanced, inevitably there will be a small level of vibration that is transmitted from the fan to the casing of the unit. This vibration, if transmitted directly to the structure of the building, will be transferred through the structure of the house and manifest itself as noise. To minimise this, the MVHR unit must be mechanically isolated from the structure of the building. This can be achieved through special mounting fittings that contain a rubber spacer between the sections that attach to the MVHR unit and the building structure. An alternative for reducing transmission is to place the MVHR unit on an anti-vibration mat. This material is used for mounting mechanical plant and designed to provide an effective mechanical break.

The other mechanical connection of the MVHR unit with the building structure is through the ducts. Anti-vibration gaiters should be used to effectively isolate the MVHR unit from the distribution ducts. An alternative to the use of gaiters is to use a very short length of flexible duct between the MVHR spigots and the duct. Although this will provide a high level of mechanical isolation, ensuring the airtightness and the thermal performance of the duct will be hard to achieve. Noise breakout must be minimised by heavily insulating this section of duct.

Air will be travelling very fast as it passes through the various components of the MVHR unit and this will create noise. This noise may either be transferred through the casing of the MVHR unit or it may travel through the air into the ducts. Since noise transfer through the casing to the space cannot be treated, careful consideration of the product in relation to the proposed installation location within the building is required. If the unit is to be located in a basement or other isolated non-living space then the noise radiated from the casing may not be an issue. However, if the unit is, for example, to be installed in a small apartment, any noise generated must be minimal and attenuated locally. Locating a MVHR unit in a loft is rarely a good solution as the roof fabric tends to transmit sound through the whole dwelling.

Airborne noise that travels along the ducts from the MVHR unit must be attenuated as close as is practical to the unit to minimise breakout noise from the ducts. The attenuators installed in this location should be capable of removing low frequency noise, i.e. the noise of the fans and air within the MVHR unit.

The 35 dB(A) limit on noise within the space containing the MVHR unit may require the space to be acoustically lined. The need for this will be evident when reviewing the manufacturers' data for a particular product.

8.9.3 Noise generated in the distribution ducts

Noise may be generated as air moves through ducts and changes direction, or is forced around objects within the duct, such as fire dampers. To minimise this noise, the air speed in the various ducts in a distribution system is limited to practical maximum.

For a **vertical riser** the maximum air speed should be limited to 3 m/s. Vertical risers are not used in a typical system installed in a single house. They are more typically found in multi-occupancy residencies and non-domestic buildings, distributing air between horizontal take-off ducts serving each residence. Risers are normally located in a dedicated service shaft and so the potential for noise generated within the duct causing a nuisance is minimal.

For **distribution ducts**, the maximum air speed should be limited to 2 m/s. The distribution ducts are defined as the primary ducts which connect directly to the MVHR unit in a small system, and all the ducts that connect either the primary ducts or the risers to the final duct runs (which connect directly to the supply and exhaust valves).

For **final ducts before air valves**, the maximum air speed should be limited to 1 m/s. These ducts connect the distribution ducts to the individual room valves. In some systems, these could be very short; however, there may be a need to include 'cross-talk' sound attenuation within the final duct, which will dictate its minimum length.

The ducts themselves must be securely fixed to solid structures. Mechanical separation of larger ducts from the building structure in non-domestic and multi-occupancy residencies may be desirable; however, in a single-occupancy residence, it is generally not required.

8.9.4 Noise generated at the supply and exhaust valves

There is potential for noise to be generated at the supply or extract valves if the air flow rate is high in relation to the opening area. Valve manufacturers publish data on the noise generated at valves as a function of the pressure difference across them and the air flow rate through the valve.

A duct layout that contains a single leg that is much longer than the others will often require the valves close to the MVHR unit to be set with only a small opening. This will ensure that pressure is maintained within the longer distribution ducts and the required air flow rate achieved at the furthest valve. However, the effect of closing in a valve to limit the air flow through it is that the air speed will increase and this may generate excessive noise. This should be prevented through proper design of the duct layout or the inclusion of regulating dampers within the distribution ducts. The latter approach is only recommended if the design cannot be more effectively balanced through careful attention to duct sizing and routing.

To ensure that the noise requirements in each room are met, acoustic attenuators must be installed within the supply and extract ducts. A single attenuator in each of the primary ducts may be sufficient to meet these requirements. However, it is usually found that additional attenuators are required in the final duct lengths before the supply valves in order to prevent noise generated in the distribution ducts entering living areas.

8.9.5 Transfer of noise between rooms within a dwelling (cross-talk)

With the transmission of external noise significantly reduced and the noise generated by the MVHR unit attenuated, the internal spaces will be very quiet. This raises the potential for noise, particularly conversations or sound from the TV/radio, transferring through the ducts between rooms. This 'cross-talk' may be less of a problem in the extract rooms but for living areas (such as the living room, dining room and bedrooms), this may be highly undesirable. It is, therefore, a Passivhaus requirement that attenuators are installed between each living room as a minimum. This ensures that the rooms are acoustically isolated from each other even though the length of duct between them may be relatively short.

8.9.6 Duct attenuators

Typical attenuator lengths are given in Table 8.9.

8.10 Supply valves (diffusers)

Supply valves (also known as diffusers) are the components through which the supply air is delivered to the occupied rooms of a building from the final distribution ducts.

8.23
Acoustic attenuators, available
in a range of shapes and sizes,
and rigid or semi-flexible

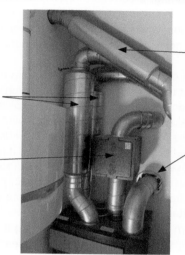

Final branch
attenuator prior to
supply valve

Primary supply and
extract attenuators

Attenuator on exhaust
to outside located
within wall structure

Frost protection
heater in supply air
inlet

Table 8.9 Typical sound attenuator lengths

Duct	Typical attenuator length (mm)
Supply duct, immediately after the MVHR unit	900
Extract duct, immediately before the MVHR unit	600
Final branch before the supply valve	5–600
Intake duct and exhaust duct between the MVHR unit and outside terminals	600

The traditional approach in dwellings is for the supply air to be delivered to
a midpoint in the ceiling of the living areas. The valves are positioned to minimise
the risk of short-circuiting, where the fresh air is drawn out of the room before it
mixes fully with the room air. Mixing of the air within the room is not driven by
the fresh air supply but by the convection currents which result from the different
temperatures of the surfaces in the room, radiators, windows, etc. In addition to

this, typical existing dwellings have a relatively high level of infiltration which will tend to increase the ventilation of a given space.

By contrast, a Passivhaus is designed with very high levels of fabric insulation and high-performance glazing which results in very small temperature differences between the room air and the building fabric. If the supply air was introduced in the traditional way, during periods when the supply air temperature is below that of the room air, the fresh air will tend to fall to the floor and then be drawn out of the room. Overall the level of ventilation effectiveness, a measure of the quality of the air at a given location relative to that at the point of supply, could be very low, indicating that the air quality may not be very good due to the lack of effective mixing.

To prevent this occurring, a common Passivhaus approach is to use the delivered fresh air to drive air movement within the living rooms, achieving a high level of mixing and very good ventilation effectiveness. One of the key considerations with this approach, however, is to avoid creating draughts that affect the comfort of the occupants.

To achieve the required mixing, the air is jetted from the supply valves into the room at up to 1 m/s. At this speed, the noise generation at the supply valve is likely to be minimal. It is recommended that the valve is placed on a wall at up to a maximum of 200 mm below the ceiling. The jet of air will then tend to 'stick' to the ceiling, caused by a phenomenon known as the 'Coanda effect'. The result of this is that the air will travel deeper into the room than if it has been jetted away from the ceiling. Alternatively, supply air valves can be located in ceilings with either directional valves (used to jet air across a room), or non-directional valves (used to jet air outwards from a valve located towards the middle of the room). In all cases, the air is jetted into the room at a relatively high speed. This has the effect of creating room air movement, thus ensuring that the supply air has fully mixed with the room air whilst ensuring the air speed has reduced below 0.15 m/s before it enters the occupied zone of the space (i.e. floor to 1.8 m). An air speed of 0.15 m/s is the lowest that can be detected as air movement or a draught.

To ensure the thermal comfort of the occupants is never compromised, compliance with the Passivhaus requirement that the supply air has a minimum delivery temperature of 16.5°C is critical. Furthermore, the temperature difference between the supply air and the room air should be less than 4°C so that negative buoyancy does not overcome the Coanda effect, which would result in the supply air being dumped down into the occupied zone of the room.

The data available from some valve manufacturers allows the characteristics of the jet of air from the supply valve to be defined. The data is usually in terms of the 'throw', with the figures given for the point at which the velocity of the jet of air falls to 0.2 m/s. See Figure 8.24.

Jetting the supply air into a room and locating the supply valve on, or close to, a wall reduces the need to run ducts through ceiling voids to the centre of a room. As well as minimising the duct runs, this allows most ducts to be located in bulkhead ceiling voids above circulation spaces where lowered ceilings and access hatches may be more aesthetically acceptable.

8.24
Throw of air from a ceiling mounted supply valve indicating distance from the centre of the valve to the point where velocity reduces to 0.2 m/s

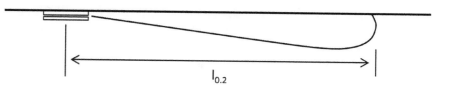

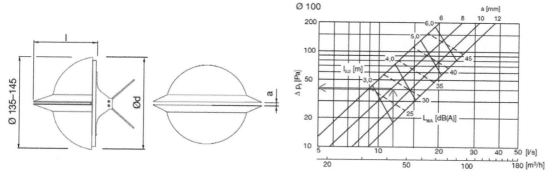

Required; 12 l/s and a jet throw of 3.5 m
Result; valve opening of 8 mm and pressure drop of 40 Pa

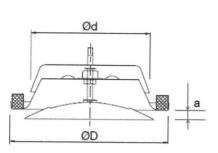

8.25
Examples of data available for supply valves showing use to determine throw, pressure drop and opening setting (Lindab)

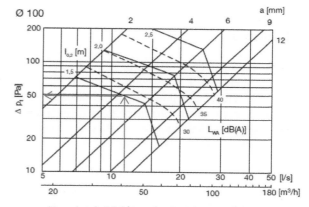

Required; 12 l/s and a jet throw of 1.5 m
Result; valve opening of 4.5 mm and pressure drop of 50 Pa

8.11 Extract valves

Extract valves are the components through which the air is drawn from the wet rooms into the extract air distribution ducts.

The valves are non-directional and must be placed at, or close to, ceiling level to remove moisture and odours generated in the wet rooms.

Many of the extract valves available from manufacturers have similar levels of design and performance data to supply valves (Figure 8.26). However, as the air does not need to pass through extract valves at a high speed, the main criteria are balancing of the system and minimising noise generation by the valve. As most MVHR units have individual fan controls, the exhaust fan can typically run at a lower speed, thereby reducing the potential for noise transfer through the ducts or noise generated at the extract valves.

As noted in Section 7, in kitchens, the cooker hood should never be connected to the MVHR ductwork directly. The extract valves in kitchens should be placed at a distance of at least 1 m from the cooker as this will minimise the grease carried into the duct.

It is general practice that all other valves are simple volume control valves. However, significant levels of lint and dust can be generated within a house so it is suggested that all extract valves should have filters at the valve. This may not be aesthetically the most desirable option but if it can be achieved, it provides protection of the distribution ductwork and reduces the need for cleaning.

Placing the filters at the valves increases the maintenance requirement by having a larger number of small filters. There is also the potential that if the filters become dirty and this is not noticed, the overall performance of the ventilation system will fall and this may not be picked up by sensors located within the MVHR unit that are designed to detect filter cleanliness. A very clear maintenance schedule must be set up to ensure that these filters are all regularly inspected and cleaned or replaced as required.

8.12 Controls

Appropriate controls for a MVHR unit are discussed in Section 3. There is, however, the question of what controls should be available to the user on an everyday basis and where they should be placed. For example, a MVHR unit maintains a constant ventilation rate at a given fan speed, but boosting the ventilation rate may be desirable while the shower is being used or during cooking. Therefore, local switches should be provided to allow occupants easy selection

8.26
Example of data available for extract valves (Lindab)

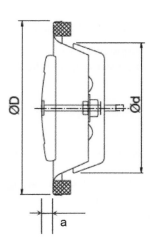

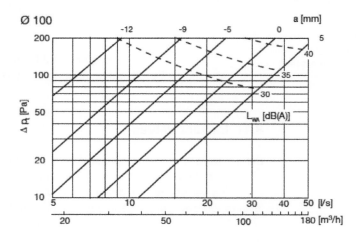

of boost flows. In bathrooms it is appropriate to have the boost on a time control to ensure that the system is not accidentally left in boost mode for extended periods. In the kitchen it is suggested that an indicator should be used to clearly show that the system is running at boost speed.

The controls available on many of the MVHR units currently on the market are relatively complex with options for a very wide range of functions. However, it is vital that the display interface should allow simple control of the basic functions such as normal or boost fan speed. Access to higher levels of control should be clearly explained in the user manual but everyday use must be intuitive.

The central controller of the MVHR unit should be located in a prominent position so that any error messages can be immediately picked up and acted upon.

8.13 MVHR systems layouts/configurations

There are several different possible MVHR system configurations that can be used to ventilate a Passivhaus. The classification of different types of system can be broken down based on the spaces served by the unit, e.g. centralised multi-occupancy, local single dwelling, etc.

The different options for the location of the MVHR unit and the spaces served by it are often determined by the size and nature of the space as described:

8.27
MVHR system layouts for single- and multi-occupancy dwellings

Central single dwelling
This is a MVHR unit located in a single dwelling serving the needs of that dwelling only. The dwelling could be a single house or part of a multi-occupancy residence. The advantage of this type of approach to ventilation provision is that every occupant is responsible for their own unit. Personal preferences can be fully catered for, i.e. summer/winter differences in operation. The disadvantage is that if the unit is installed in a multi-occupancy residence, maintenance is decentralised and access to each dwelling will be required in order to undertake any works. Furthermore, noise is generated in each dwelling and the fabric of the building is punctured by the fresh and exhaust air ducts in each dwelling. This latter point results in a large number of potential thermal and airtightness weak spots in the overall building fabric.

Central multi-occupancy
This is a single MVHR unit that is located centrally and serves a range of different dwellings in a single building. The air may be delivered to the dwellings from central risers or distributed from the plant room to each dwelling separately. The means of delivery is usually governed by space limitations. The advantage of this approach to ventilating a number of dwellings is that it removes the major noise and maintenance issues to a central plant room where they can be addressed without impacting the living space within the dwelling. Localised post-heating and cooling is possible with this system.

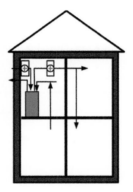

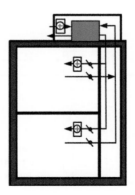

Decentralised single room
The single-room MVHR unit is a recent development. However, the adoption of single-room MVHRs has very limited application in Passivhaus due to the limitations on cross ventilation and air mixing.

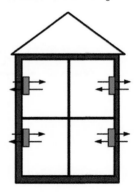

8.14 Types of MVHR units

The different means of recovering heat from the ventilation air and the different uses for the heat are:

- A simple MVHR unit, with a passive plate or thermal wheel, which recovers heat from the exhaust air and transfers it to the incoming fresh air stream.
- MVHR units incorporating an air source heat pump (ASHP) to increase the level of heat removed from the exhaust air which provides additional space heating and/or domestic hot water. Such units are often referred to as compact service units (CSUs) and may also include integral solar thermal connections.

The following diagrams show the potential range of combinations of heat exchangers and heat pumps, as well as heat delivery options that are currently on the market.

When considering the potential of a CSU or heat pump-based MVHR unit, there are several aspects of their operation that must be understood to ensure that they meet the design intent.

1 *Heating capacity as a function of intake air temperature* – The inclusion of a heat pump into a MVHR unit offers the theoretical potential to recover more heat from the exhaust air than is required to heat the supply air to the extract air temperature. As a result of this process, the extract air is cooled to below the temperature of the intake air.
2 *Heating capacity as a function of ventilation air flow rate* – The additional excess heat delivered by the heat pump can be used for space heating.

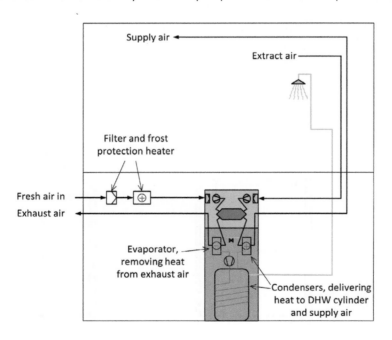

Supply air

Extract air

Filter and frost
protection heater

Fresh air in

Exhaust air

Evaporator,
removing heat
from exhaust air

Condensers, delivering
heat to DHW cylinder
and supply air

8.28
Schematic of MVHR
incorporating a heat pump to
provide heat to both domestic
hot water and the supply air
as required
Source: adapted from JPW,
Drexel and Weiss, Aerostat

1.

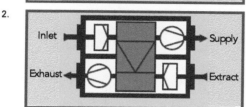

The basic MVHR unit with a heat exchanger recovering heat from the exhaust air stream and delivering it to the supply air stream

2.

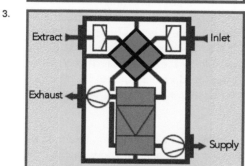

Replacing the heat exchanger (plate or wheel) with a heat pump, extracting air from the exhaust air stream and delivering it to the supply air stream. The potential to extract additional heat from the exhaust air makes the efficiency of this type of system greater than 100%. To counter this, however, the fan power will be at least equal to that of the basic MVHR unit and the electricity used by the compressor has to be offset against any heat recovered.

3.

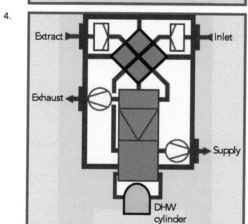

To overcome the limitations of the heat pump-only based MVHR, there are several products on the market that offer both a passive flat plate and heat pump combination. Introducing two heat exchangers results in higher fan powers than system types 1 or 2. The advantage of this is that the heat pump is now only recovering the heat that cannot be recovered by the heat exchanger. This configuration is limited to recovering heat to provide space heating.

4.

This combination of heat exchanger and heat pump allows heat to be recovered throughout the year and any excess not required for space heating can be used to heat domestic hot water.
The refrigeration circuit contains twin condenser coils, one in the supply air stream and one in a DHW cylinder allowing the recovered heat to be delivered to either. This configuration of MVHR unit and heat recovery heat pump forms the basis of many of the CSUs on the market.

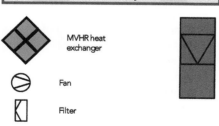

8.29
Types of MVHR unit and heat pumps
Source: adapted from EN 13141-7:2010

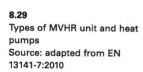

However, it is more often the case that ASHP/CSU systems deliver the heat to a domestic hot water cylinder. This results in a small but continuous heat input to the cylinder throughout most of the year, reaching a maximum in summer when the intake air temperature is at its highest.

The amount of excess heat generated is a function of the air flow rate. If, for example, the exhaust air is 20°C, the heat pump cools the air to 0°C and the volumetric air flow rate is 30 l/s. The potential heat recovery is 720W based on sensible heat recovery only. The heat delivered by the heat pump includes the heat of the compressor. Assuming a CoP (Coefficient of Performance) of 2.5, this would bring the heat delivered to approximately 1.2 kW where:

$$Heat\ delivered = \frac{CoP}{CoP-1} \cdot Heat\ recovered$$

If the air flow rate were lowered to around 20 l/s then the heat delivered would be around 800W. Raising a cylinder of water to a usable temperature following a large draw-off would take several hours with a heat input of only 800 W. Depending on the control strategy prioritisation, during this period there would be no recovered heat available to the supply air. This situation would mean that all of the ventilation heat load would need to be met by a back-up heater and, if hot water were required again quickly, an immersion heater would also need to be used.

Overall the capacity and usage pattern of an exhaust air heat pump needs to be very clearly understood before assumptions are made regarding how much of the overall heating and/or DHW load will be met. The desire to have hot water on tap immediately may significantly limit the DHW heating capability in reality, whilst on paper the annual demand sizing matches very well.

8.15 Fire and ventilation systems

8.15.1 Air transfer grilles and fire door undercuts

Fire doors must maintain compartmentation and cannot be undercut as a means of air transfer. The appropriate fire-rated transfer grille is the recommended method to incorporate air transfer through fire compartments (BS 8214:2008).

Air transfer grilles have until recently been non-fire-rated devices providing an aperture through which air is passed as part of a ventilation system (IFSA, 2012). Fire-only, and fire and cold smoke transfer grilles are now available:

- Fire containment air transfer grille. These permit the free passage of air, but when activated by a rise in air temperature, intumescent materials close off the air stream providing containment of fire and hot gases.
- Fire and cold smoke containment air transfer grille. These close off the air stream providing containment of fire and hot gases through the use of intumescent materials. They also contain electromechanically activated physical barriers designed to contain ambient temperature smoke.

8.15.2 Ducts

When the ventilation duct layout is being designed, routes must be planned such that, where possible, they avoid protected escape routes such as hallways and stairs. Where crossing these areas is unavoidable, fire protection of ductwork is needed as an integral part of compartmentation and to ensure that all means of escape from the building are maintained.

Two solutions are available:

- The use of fire-resistant ducts. Fire-resistant ducts are constructed of rigid steel and must be adequately fire-stopped to the surrounding structure. Where non-fire-resistant ductwork is used, fire resistance can be created by insulating the duct with a mineral duct wrap or suitably supported fire-resisting boarding. The fire resistance of the ductwork should not be less than the fire resistance required for the elements of construction in the area through which it passes (ASFP, 2010).
- The use of fire dampers. Fire dampers are installed where the duct passes through a fire compartment wall. The damper should have a fire resistance rating equal to that of the barrier it penetrates (HVCA, 2000a; ASFP, 2011).
- There are a variety of different types of heat-activated dampers. Where ducts pass through compartment walls of protected escape routes, dampers providing cold smoke protection are required.

It is very important that all dampers and sleeves should be installed in accordance with the manufacturers' instructions to ensure their correct operation in case of fire.

Access must be provided to all dampers for maintenance and testing purposes. To ensure this is possible, access to both sides of dampers is recommended (ASFP, 2011).

8.15.3 Ventilation systems fans

MVHR systems installed in Passivhauses do not recirculate air within the dwelling and must not supply or extract air directly from protected stairs. There is no requirement in the UK Building Regulations to shut down the MVHR system in the event of a fire; however, clarification of local requirements should be sought as this may differ in other countries.

8.15.4 Valves

Existing fire test data for timber floors confirms that installation of multiple recessed lights does not have a significant effect on the fire resistance of floors requiring up to 30 minutes fire resistance. It is therefore concluded that isolated penetrations of the ceiling lining by extract ductwork may be considered acceptable in terms of the effect on the fire integrity of the floor construction.

Therefore, the penetration of the ceiling lining and installation of extract ductwork within the floor void can be accepted without additional fire protection (i.e. a fire damper or intumescent collar). The extract ductwork may be of any suitable material, i.e. flexible or rigid PVC or metal (NHBC, 2010).

8.16 System design

The objectives of effective ventilation system design are to:

- Achieve the required ventilation rate in the intended rooms. This is a function of the MVHR unit and the system pressure loss. The MVHR model must be chosen to achieve the required duty point (i.e. pressure/air flow rate).
- Minimise any noise nuisance. This is vital and has been covered in Section 9. If noise is a nuisance, especially in the bedrooms where it is interrupting sleep, residents will turn MVHR units off. In a very airtight house, this will have a detrimental impact on indoor air quality very quickly.
- Install a mechanical system in a building which is easy to maintain. If this is not the case then the routine maintenance is likely to be missed and the system will gradually fail to fulfil its purpose.
- Achieve the required ventilation in the most energy-efficient manner possible.

It is the last of the points above that raises the most significant challenge since it requires more than a good MVHR unit and efficient duct layout. The system must actually fit inside the building (i.e. there must be sufficient space for the MVHR unit and for the ducts to run). Furthermore, the design of the system must be integrated with every other element of the building design (i.e. not clash with other services). Finally, the installation must be correctly sequenced with all other aspects of the construction. In order to achieve this, the ventilation system must not be an afterthought. On the contrary, the ventilation system must be considered at the very outset of the design and its integration into the building fabric thought out at every stage of the process to ensure that duct runs are not compromised by apparently minor changes to other elements.

When self-building, allocation of space within the building for the MVHR unit is not a problem. The gains in overall thermal efficiency make it an obvious component to accommodate. However, the commercial drive to squeeze as many houses as possible into the smallest possible area leaves space allocation for ventilation low on most architects' and developers' list of priorities. Possibly one of the most important roles of MVHR system designers is to re-educate other professionals to understand that ventilation must be an integral part of building design, in the same way that windows are for light and water is for washing.

Wherever the MVHR unit is located, sufficient space must be provided to undertake routine maintenance. This may mean changing the filter every few months or annually, or could involve changing the fan motors after ten years. If the MVHR unit is located in an unheated loft then access ladders, a safe work area and light should be provided.

Sometimes the need to drain condensate from a MVHR unit is overlooked at the design stage. If the MVHR unit has a thermal wheel then this may not be necessary, but the manufacturer's instructions should always be reviewed. The condensate will be cold and so the drain will need insulation if it is inside the building thermal envelope, and may need to have insulating and trace heating tape applied if it is located outside the thermal envelope. In all cases, the condensate drain must be connected to the waste drain via a dry seal (or anti-siphon) trap.

The initial design concept should be sketched out onto a copy of the floor plans and sections. In order to balance the supply and extract air flow rates across the dwelling, the volumetric flow rate entering and leaving each room should be specified at this stage and recorded on the PHPP 'Ventilation Protocol' worksheet. An example is given in Figure 8.30.

The final design of the duct system is best undertaken using a software tool. BIM-compatible CAD or dedicated duct design packages may be used. It is critical that the integration of all elements of the fabric and other services can be undertaken easily to minimise the occurrence of clashes which require ducts to be rerouted, as this usually results in the installation of additional bends. This may have a knock-on effect throughout the system with fan speeds needing to be increased, any noise generated requiring additional attenuators, etc.

Transfer zone air flow paths from the living rooms through the circulation spaces and into the wet rooms must not present any appreciable pressure drop. The preferred method of allowing the air to pass between spaces is via door undercuts. It is vital that these are detailed explicitly on drawings to ensure that they are not missed. It is recommended that an undercut of 20 mm will be sufficient to ensure that air speeds remain below 1 m/s and pressure differences across doors remain at or below 1 Pa. See Section 8.15 for details regarding undercutting of fire doors.

8.17 Use of MVHR units in different climate regions and across seasons

The choice of ventilation system and how it is used is, to a large extent, governed by the climate.

In both cold and hot climates, a MVHR unit can be used to recover heat or 'coolth' for most of the year. However in a mild climate, the need for recovery may be limited to the peak seasons only. The different requirements are given below.

8.17.1 Hot environments

In hot environments (assuming active cooling is used) a MVHR unit will recover 'coolth' or transfer heat from the incoming hot air stream to the cooler exhaust air stream. This will reduce the cooling load and, therefore, offer a significant energy benefit over a ventilation system that does not include any heat recovery capability.

FINAL PROTOCOL WORKSHEET for Ventilation Systems: DESIGN
Supply- / Extract-Air Ventilation System with Heat Recovery

Project

Object:	Model House Type
Location Street, No.:	
Location Postcode, Town	
Building Owner Name:	
Building Owner Phone No.:	
Year of Construction	

Ventilation Planning

Company:	BRE
Person in Charge:	
Street, No.:	
Postcode, City:	
Phone No.:	
Date:	
Signature:	

Standard use or special requirements:

Dimensioning of the ventilation system according to standard use conditions

2. Criteria for dimensioning the airflow volumes

	reference values		number			resulting starting values	
fresh air demand:							
per person:	30	m³/h x	4	=	120.0 m³/h	120.0	m³/h
extract air demand:							
kitchens:	40	m³/h x	1	=	40.0 m³/h		
bathrooms, utility rooms etc.:	30	m³/h x	2	=	60.0 m³/h		
WC, storage, etc.:	20	m³/h x	1	=	20.0 m³/h		
				sum:	m³/h	120.0	m³/h

starting value nominal airflow (standard operation): 120.0 m³/h

3. Distribution of the airflow volume flow rate

Nr.	Room (each valve individually)	Area A m²	Clear Height h m	Room Volume A x h m³	V$_{SU}$ m³/h	V$_{EX}$ m³/h	V$_{THROUGH}$ m³/h	Air Change Rate n 1/h	Type of Flow-Off Vent (door gap, grid in door leaf door frame, valve ...)
1	Ground: Hall 1	5.55	2.40	13.3			30	2.25	
2	Ground: Living Room	18.85	2.40	45.2	30			0.66	Door gap
3	Ground: Dining room	8.96	2.40	21.5	30			1.40	Door gap
4	Ground: Kitchen room	11.06	2.40	26.5		40		1.51	Door gap
5	Ground: Cloakroom/Downstairs WC	1.63	2.40	3.9		20		5.12	Door gap
6	First: Hall 2	5.11	2.36	12.1			30	2.49	
7	First: Bedroom 1	15.04	2.36	35.5	30			0.85	Door gap
8	First: Ensuite	3.60	2.36	8.5		30		3.53	Door gap
9	First: Bedroom 2	16.60	2.36	39.2	30			0.77	Door gap
10	First: Bathroom	4.78	2.36	11.3		30		2.66	Door gap
11									
12									
13									
14									
15									
16									
17									
18									
19									
20									
	sum:	91.17	--	217.00	120.0	120.0	--	0.55	

4. Adjusted airflow volumes, control range

base ventilation:	92.3	m³/h	at least 30% below nominal airflow volume
nominal airflow volume:	120.0	m³/h	fresh air demand, at least 0.3-fold air change rate
peak ventilation:	156.0	m³/h	at least 30% above nominal airflow volume
ventilated area:	91.2	m²	
ventilated volume:	217.0	m³	
nominal airflow volume, sum:	0.6	1/h	

5. Efficiency requirements

ventilation unit (manufacturer, product):	Paul Multi 150 DC		
efficiency of heat recovery:	79	%	(according to PHI testing method for the PHPP)
max. power consumption in nominal operating mode:	0.36	W	(for fans and control)

6. Requirements for noise protection

A-weighted noise pressure level of the unit in the living space:	25	dB(A)
A-weighted noise pressure level of the unit in the installation room:	35	dB(A)

7. Hygienic requirements

fresh air filter:	F7	first link in the chain, if applicable before subsoil heat exchanger
extract air filter:	G4	at least bathroom and laundry rooms; recommendation: all extract air rooms

8.30
PHPP 'Ventilation Protocol' worksheet – Design

8.31
Detailed system and duct
layout design is best achieved
using design packages. Full
component specifications
can be developed ensuring a
smooth installation process
Source: Andrew Farr, Green
Building Store

8.17.2 Hot dry – recover coolth

In regions where the air is hot and dry, the MVHR unit will cool the incoming air towards the temperature of the outgoing exhaust air. If the air is very dry, little or no condensation will occur and so the thermal efficiency of the heat exchanger will be similar to recovering heat in a cold environment.

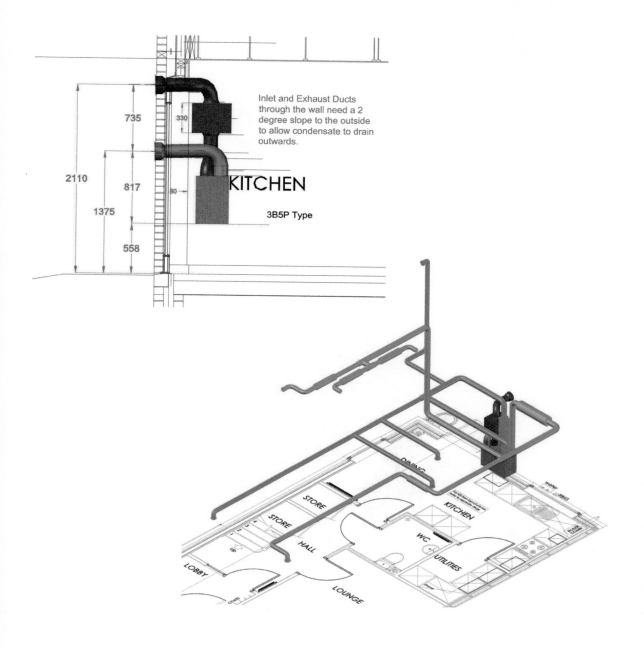

Inlet and Exhaust Ducts through the wall need a 2 degree slope to the outside to allow condensate to drain outwards.

KITCHEN

3B5P Type

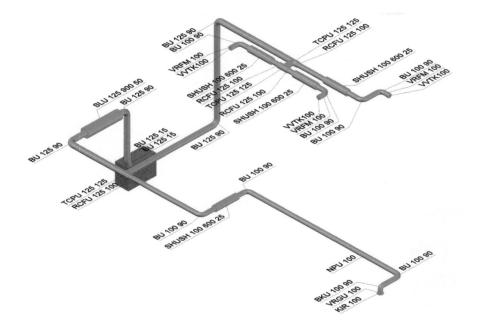

BU 125 90
BU 100 90
VRFM 100
VVTK100
SHUSH 100 600 25
RCFU 125 100
TCPU 125 125
RCFU 125 100
TCPU 125 125
RCFU 125 100
SHUSH 100 600 25
VVTK100
VRFM 100
BU 100 90
BU 100 90
BU 100 90
VRFM 100
VVTK100
SLU 125 900 50
BU 125 90
BU 125 90
BU 125 15
BU 125 15
BU 125 90
BU 125 90
TCPU 125 125
RCFU 125 100
BU 100 90
SHUSH 100 600 25
NPU 100
BU 100 90
BKU 100 90
VRGU 100
KIR 100

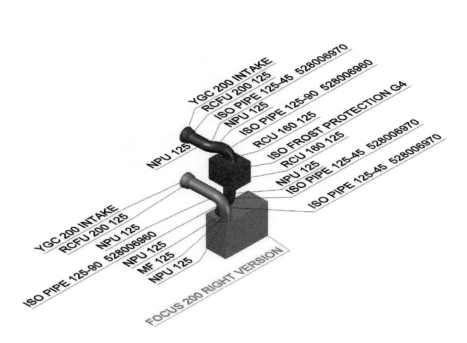

YGC 200 INTAKE
RCFU 200 125
ISO PIPE 125-45 528006970
NPU 125
ISO PIPE 125-90 528006960
RCU 160 125
ISO FROST PROTECTION G4
RCU 160 125
NPU 125
ISO PIPE 125-45 528006970
ISO PIPE 125-45 528006970
NPU 125
YGC 200 INTAKE
RCFU 200 125
NPU 125
ISO PIPE 125-90 528006960
NPU 125
MF 125
NPU 125
FOCUS 200 RIGHT VERSION

8.17.3 Hot and humid – recover coolth and dehumidify the incoming air

In regions where the air is hot but the moisture content (of the air) is relatively high, cooling the incoming air will result in condensation occurring on the fresh air side of the heat exchanger as the incoming air is cooled to its dew point. For many MVHR units, this situation is not considered and a condensate drain is located only on the exhaust side of the heat exchanger. Condensation on the fresh air side of the heat exchanger would result in such products flooding, potentially damaging the MVHR unit and possibly causing damage to the dwelling when the water eventually finds its way out of the casing. The potential of this occurring must be predicted and an appropriate MVHR unit installed.

Cooling air below its dew point releases latent heat and, therefore, the thermal efficiency of a MVHR unit will not be as high as when cooling hot, dry air. The air being delivered into the building will be both warmer than the internal air and saturated. Consequently, there is potential for condensation to occur throughout the supply distribution ducts. In such situations, an air conditioning/dehumidification system should be integrated to further cool and dehumidify the supply air. This will cool the supply air below the internal air dew point temperature, and as the supply air warms up, the RH will fall and condensation will not be a risk. Proprietary MVHR systems are available which incorporate an exhaust air/supply air heat pump with all of the components necessary for cooling and dehumidification.

8.17.4 Cold environments

In very cold areas, the need for effective frost protection is of paramount importance and could be a significant area of energy use. In these locations, passive means of tempering the outside air (such as brine loops or GAHEs) are very beneficial. An alternative, often used in Scandinavia, is thermal heat wheels, which do not suffer freezing and therefore can potentially achieve substantial energy savings during this part of the year.

8.17.5 Cold dry – recover heat – need for humidification

In cold climates, the introduction of very dry air into a building will tend to draw the internal relative humidity down to levels that have health impacts. There are several options available to minimise the effect of this:

- Use of a humidifier. These are very energy intensive and should be avoided.
- Reducing the ventilation rate. For a given moisture generation rate within a building, reducing the ventilation rate will allow the relative humidity within the building to rise. This action must not reduce the ventilation to such an extent that it may reduce the indoor air quality.

- The use of a heat recovery unit that offers moisture recovery. Thermal wheels offer this capability as the condensation occurring on the exhaust section of the wheel rotates to the dry supply air stream where it evaporates and is returned to the building. This capability is increased if the wheel is treated with a desiccant coating (enthalpy heat exchanger). There are plate heat exchangers that offer a similar potential for moisture recovery. One approach is to run the heat exchanger as a recuperator heat exchanger, similar to the wheel, where exhaust air passes through one part of the heat exchanger and condensation builds up on the plates. The air flow is then reversed and as the supply air passes through this area of the heat exchanger, the condensation evaporates and is carried back into the building in the supply air (see Figure 8.30). The other approach currently available is for the plates of the heat exchanger to be made of a permeable membrane that allows water vapour to pass through from the extract air to the supply air.

8.17.6 Cold wet – recover heat – no need for moisture recovery – use latent heat to maximise heat recovery.

In cool/wet climates, the moisture content of the outside air is relatively high during the winter. Therefore, the moisture content of the air within the house is generally not unhealthily low and moisture recovery is not required. In colder weather, the external air temperature will be below the dew point of the exhaust air and condensation will occur on the extract side of the heat exchanger. The liberation of this latent heat will tend to increase the thermal efficiency of the MVHR unit.

8.32
Counter flow heat exchanger configured as a recuperating heat exchanger with air flow direction reversing, allowing moisture recovery (Recair)

8.17.7 Mild – this could be summer in a cold climate, winter in a hot environment, or a significant part of the year in a mild maritime climate (e.g. the UK).

During such periods, the only requirement is that the supply air does not fall below 16.5°C when delivered to the habitable rooms. Outside the heating season, an alternative ventilation strategy may be appropriate; many Passivhaus buildings adopt a natural ventilation strategy or extract-only strategy during these periods. There are, however, practical issues with the operation of a changeover type mixed-mode design. Purpose-built vents, for example in window frames, are very rarely included in a Passivhaus design as the additional heat loss and potential for air leakage around any such vent are extremely difficult to minimise. This leads to the assumption that windows will be left open in summer to provide make-up fresh air. In rural and suburban areas, this may be an option; but in urban and deep urban areas this may not be practical, or desirable, and the MVHR unit will need to operate all year round.

If it is not possible to leave windows open all night then the sizing of the ventilation system components needs to be appropriate to meet all the ventilation requirements. In such cases, the MVHR unit, ductwork and diffusers may need to be significantly oversized in order to achieve the substantially greater air changes required to remove excess heat from the building. (Overheating is discussed in Section 8.18.)

8.18 Overheating

Overheating has not traditionally been considered a problem in Central and Northern European dwellings. However, there is an ever-increasing list of cases where temperatures are remaining elevated throughout much of the year, resulting in health problems and discomfort for the occupants of those dwellings. The main problems are in deep urban locations where the urban heat island effect and local environmental issues exacerbate the situation (McLeod *et al.*, 2013).

It is vital when considering overheating as a potential problem of low energy buildings that the issue is separated from the problems caused by summer heat waves. Heat waves have a serious effect on the health of vulnerable groups (e.g. the old and very young), but they are transitory. Their frequency may increase as weather extremes become more common but any incident will end as the weather returns to its normal pattern.

Overheating is the result of the link between the internal and outside air temperatures being almost totally broken, such that the diurnal variation in temperatures outside is almost totally missing within a dwelling. This link has been broken as the fabric insulation has become so good that heat losses are minimal and at night the increased temperature difference between inside and outside results in almost no fall in the internal air temperature. Additionally, the ventilation rates of new buildings are relatively low compared to those of older buildings, where the level of infiltration alone would have exceeded typical current ventilation rates. Therefore, the only means of rejecting excess heat from a dwelling is through opening the windows.

The evidence from a range of cases of overheating (BRE, 2007) is that in deep urban locations, the outside air quality is poor, the noise levels are often high, and (due to security issues) occupants are unwilling to leave windows open at night. This scenario leaves the occupants with no acceptable means of rejecting heat, and in some cases, vulnerable occupants suffer serious health issues as a result of dwellings permanently remaining at temperatures significantly above 25°C (Dengle and Swainson, 2012).

One of the problems for designers is that there is no clear guidance on what constitutes overheating and, therefore, what is acceptable. Almost all guidance for designers is based on thermal comfort, which does not really address the issue resulting from cumulative impacts on health of extended periods at moderately high temperatures.

Evaluating where excess heat is coming from is vital to understanding how to minimise it. Solar gains through windows can be minimised by effective shading or reducing glazed areas. Internal heat gains have been identified as a cause of overheating in a lot of multi-occupancy residences (Dengle and Swainson, 2012). The main source of internal gains is often the communal heat exchanger and its associated pipework. A heat meter is usually installed within the heat exchanger casing to allow billing of the heat consumed by an individual dwelling. However, the electronics of such units must remain cool and so the casing is rarely insulated. This results in significant areas of pipe and fittings being exposed with relatively high water temperatures passing through them 24 hours a day. The heat liberated can be significant and, combined with solar and occupancy gains, can exacerbate the level of overheating.

One source of unwanted heat that is rarely assessed is the heat drawn in through the ventilation system itself. Placing the fresh air intake on a west or south-west elevation will tend to mean that the air drawn into the building at the end of the day is significantly warmer than the free air due to the heating of the air in the boundary layer adjacent to the structure of the building. Wall surface temperatures in excess of 40°C have been recorded on south and west elevations of buildings in London late in the afternoon (Dengle and Swainson, 2012). This heat is then liberated very slowly from the fabric of the building, resulting in air drawn into the ventilation system being significantly above free air temperature almost all night. The location of the fresh air intakes is important on all buildings, but in deep urban locations, it can make the difference between a building that follows the diurnal variation of the free air and a building that remains hot all night.

Once the source of any excess heat has been identified and minimised, the means of rejecting heat must be addressed. Removal of heat using ventilation requires very high levels of air exchange. It is noted by CIBSE (2006) that heat removal from buildings overnight can require upwards of 4 ac/h. If it is considered that the normal ventilation rate of a building is up to approximately 0.3–0.6 ac/h then night purging requires upwards of eight times that air flow rate. Even if the MVHR fans were capable of delivering such a high air flow rate, the ductwork, supply and extract valves, etc. could not, and the pressure loss and noise of a system attempting to achieve anything close to this would be prohibitive.

It is, therefore, suggested that if a dwelling is located in an area that may result in the occupants being unwilling or unable to open the windows and leave them open overnight, very serious consideration must be given to providing a means of removing heat from the bedrooms so that sleep disturbance is minimised. One approach may be to consider the bedrooms as a separate ventilation zone and to look to achieve the high air change rate in just these areas of a house. This may require the system to run at a high fan speed with dampers to divert most of the air through the bedrooms. If this is to be undertaken then the sizing of all components of the ventilation system needs to be carefully considered to ensure that it remains draught-free at all times and there is no noise nuisance.

The alternative to rejecting the excess heat through the ventilation system is the use of active comfort cooling, which in some locations and climates, may be necessary to ensure that health and comfort are maintained. Active cooling may be incorporated using a number of low energy methods, such as Thermally Active Building Systems (TABs) (see Chapter 7).

8.19 Installations and site practice

One of the key aims of the Passivhaus design philosophy is that houses should be healthy places for people to live in. For the ventilation system, this means that site practices are very tightly controlled to ensure that all components are kept clean from delivery through to final handover.

When materials are received on-site they must be treated appropriately. Ducts are often viewed as simply another building material, rather than part of a 'clean' system. Each component of the ventilation system should be treated as a final-fix item that has a direct impact on the quality of the overall building. This requires that ducts are kept capped at all times and valves are only installed at final-fix. It is interesting to note that whilst this is common practice in large non-domestic buildings, good installation practice needs to occur in the domestic sector as well.

The installation of every part of the ventilation system needs to be scheduled into the build programme to ensure that activities that generate dust or other contaminants do not occur when parts of the ventilation system are open. Upon completion of installation, all ducts must be capped. This will not only prevent dust getting into components, but also moisture and fauna.

The MVHR unit itself should not be installed as part of the first-fix. If required, a template of the MVHR unit and spigots should be made to ensure that the ducts are run and terminated correctly. This will save the MVHR unit from becoming damaged and dirty as other trades work in the same area.

Once installed, the fans of the MVHR unit must not be run until the whole building has been decorated and thoroughly cleaned and is ready to handover. Only then should the caps be removed from the ducts, the valves installed and the MVHR fans started. This makes commissioning of the ventilation system one of the very last tasks to be undertaken prior to handover.

Throughout the build process, it is vital that detailed photographic records are kept of each component of the ventilation system as they are installed. This is particularly important as the distribution ducts are usually hidden within floor and ceiling voids and cannot be easily investigated if questions arise at a later stage. Photographic evidence of installation of acoustic attenuators in particular will allow any questions about noise to be addressed, and will provide an accurate log of exact installation locations so that access can be made easily if required for any reason.

In a single dwelling, ducts are not normally pressure tested; however, this is a requirement in larger multi-residential buildings and in non-domestic buildings. When pressure testing is undertaken, the source of the air used to pressurise the system must be clean and filtered. It is recommended that a F7 filter is used to minimise any dirt ingress.

8.20 Commissioning

The act of commissioning is required to ensure that the system is operating as intended in the design. It is vital that every aspect of the system is checked and its installation, setting, and performance recorded. This not only demonstrates that the design intent has been met but also provides a starting point for a log of how the system performs. This log will allow changes to be identified and the cause of variations investigated.

8.20.1 Commissioning procedure

When commissioning a MVHR system, the commissioning engineer should start by checking that the system has been installed in keeping with the design. The following checks should be carried out:

- The MVHR unit has been ducted correctly; i.e. the correct duct is connected to the appropriate spigot.
- The condensation outlet has been connected to the waste outlet, preferably through a dry seal trap. If outside the thermal envelope, the condensate pipe must be properly insulated.
- All ducts are appropriately insulated, and if inside the thermal envelope, the intake and exhaust have non-air permeable insulation or a well-fitted vapour barrier.
- All air valves are the right type for the location and the mountings are properly fixed.
- Visual inspection of the duct connection to the air valves, as far as possible. The air valves must be locked after the commissioning process is complete. All air valves should be set fully open prior to commissioning.
- Door undercuts or air transfer grilles must be provided to allow the air to travel freely from the living rooms to the wet rooms. The correct provision of these undercuts or grilles should be checked throughout the building.

Every aspect of this inspection should be recorded and photographs taken where appropriate to back up written notes.

Prior to starting the fans, the filters should be checked to ensure they are the correct class, clean and in position. The fans should never be used to 'flush' the system of dust. If, for any reason, the dust covers on ducts and valves have been dislodged during the construction phase then it is recommended that the ducts are cleaned. This can be undertaken using a rodding cleaning brush. The dust should be vacuumed at an appropriate access point. It is vital that this is undertaken because any cement or plaster dust that is within the ducts (or gets into the heat exchanger) and becomes damp will be almost impossible to remove at a later date.

It will be necessary to know how to make adjustments to the MVHR unit so a copy of the installation and commissioning manual should be to hand. The commissioning engineer must have a copy of the ducting system plans so that installation of all the valves can be checked. They must be fully conversant with the controls of the MVHR unit as access will be required to the set-up levels of the controller. Most manufacturers provide detailed manuals covering most levels of operation of the controller, but if commissioning is to be undertaken effectively, prior understanding of the operation of the system is vital as some control logic is not intuitive. Design air flow rates at each user fan speed setting should be fully detailed on the system plans for each valve and the combined flow at the external terminations.

Under current UK Building Regulations (HM Government, 2010), there is only a requirement to measure the air flow rates at the supply and extract valves in the rooms. The Passivhaus commissioning method also requires that the total air flow rate in and out of the thermal envelope is measured. This is easiest to achieve if the intake and exhaust terminals are in an accessible position on an external wall.

8.20.2 Balancing air flow rate at each valve

The MVHR unit should be left to run at normal speed for a minimum of 30 minutes to allow the fans to attain normal running temperature. After this time, an initial set of air flow rates at each of the valves should be taken and compared with the design values. Summing all the supply and exhaust values will give the overall ventilation rate. As a means of checking that there are no major leaks and that the MVHR unit itself is not short-circuiting, the air flow rates at the external terminals should also be taken at this point. Due to the instruments used to measure these air flow rates, a perfect balance will rarely be achieved; but any major differences should be investigated. Logically working through any significant differences between the total flows outside and the combined flows at the room valves will identify any major leaks or the source of short-circuiting. If a very significant leak is suspected then it is recommended that a pressure test is undertaken on the ductwork. Based on the result of this test, remedial works should be undertaken as appropriate.

Balancing air flows is an iterative process. The valve furthest away from the MVHR unit usually has the greatest duct pressure loss, and so the fan must be running with sufficient speed to generate the correct pressure at this valve. There is a balance to be achieved here. Running the fan too fast will require all the valves to be closed slightly to reduce the air flow through them, increasing the MVHR fan power. However, opening the valves to reduce the system pressure may result in the air not jetting into the room with sufficient speed to ensure adequate mixing before it enters the occupied zone of the room (i.e. the lower 1.80 m).

Measurement of air flow at the valves must be undertaken using appropriate instruments. Rotating vane anemometers will give a reading, but they impose a small additional pressure on the air flow through the valve and thus have an influence on the reading. The balanced flow balometer (see Figure 8.33) is a more appropriate type of instrument for undertaking these measurements. These air flow instruments balance the air flow through the instrument via a balancing fan without restricting the air flow through the valve.

Once the system has been commissioned at normal air flow rates, its operation at low and maximum flow should be checked. Both of these air flows should ensure that thermal comfort is achieved and that the valves do not make any noise. If noise is found to be an issue at the maximum air flow rate then the system must be rebalanced to run at a lower pressure; i.e. the supply valves should be opened slightly to reduce the pressure across them. Noise generated from an extract valve is rarely a problem. Should this be the case then the extract fan must be slowed and the valves recommissioned to achieve the required air flow rate at a lower system pressure.

The measured air flow rates should be entered onto the PHPP 'Ventilation Commissioning' worksheet (see Figure 8.34) and the imbalance between the supply and exhaust noted. The requirement for balancing is that the difference between the total inlet air supply and exhaust air flow is below 10 per cent, measured at the outside terminals or in the intake and exhaust ducts.

8.33
A balometer used to measure air flow rate at valves and terminals. Balancing fan ensures no flow resistance is placed on the valve or terminal, ensuring good levels of accuracy

Ventilation concepts

FINAL PROTOCOL WORKSHEET for Ventilation Systems: Initial Start-up
Supply- / Extract-Air Ventilation System with Heat Recovery

Project

Object:	Model House Type
Location Street, No.:	
Location Postcode, Town	
Building Owner Name:	
Building Owner Phone No.:	
Year of Construction	

Initial Start-up

Company:	BRE
Person in Charge:	
Street, No..:	
Postcode, City:	
Phone No.:	
Date:	

Ventilation System

Manufacturer:	
Product Name:	
Unit No.:	
Control No.:	

1. Record of the air flow volumes, supply and extract air

Nr.	Room	Design V_SU m³/h	Design V_EX m³/h	Design V_THROUGH m³/h	Meas. 1 V_SU m³/h	Meas. 1 V_EX m³/h	Meas. 2 V_SU m³/h	Meas. 2 V_EX m³/h	Meas. 3 V_SU m³/h	Meas. 3 V_EX m³/h	Type of Valve	Adjustment	Flow-Through V_THROUGH m/s	Noise dB(A)	Filter Grade	Filter Clean?
1	Ground: Hall 1			30										<25		yes / no
2	Ground: Living Room	30			28		31						Door gap	<25		yes / no
3	Ground: Dining room	30			25		28						Door gap	<25		yes / no
4	Ground: Kitchen room		40			42		39					Door gap	<25		yes / no
5	Ground: Cloakroom/Downstairs		20			22		21					Door gap	<25		yes / no
6	First: Hall 2			30										<25		yes / no
7	First: Bedroom 1	30			28		29						Door gap	<25		yes / no
8	First: Ensuite		30			28		29					Door gap	<25		yes / no
9	First: Bedroom 2	30			31		31						Door gap	<25		yes / no
10	First: Bathroom		30			24		29					Door gap	<25		yes / no
11																yes / no
12																yes / no
13																yes / no
14																yes / no
15																yes / no
16																yes / no
17																yes / no
18																yes / no
19																yes / no
20																yes / no
	sum:	120.00	120.00	—	112.00	116.00	119.00	118.00	—	—			—	—	—	—

2. Balance of airflow volume

	Meas. 1 V_AUL m³/h	Meas. 1 V_FOL m³/h	Meas. 2 V_AUL m³/h	Meas. 2 V_FOL m³/h	Meas. 3 V_AUL m³/h	Meas. 3 V_FOL m³/h	Adjustment	Disbalance	Type of Control	Noise dB(A)	Filter Grade	Filter Clean?
1 fresh air inlet	108	—	116	—	—			5 %		32	F7	yes
2 exhaust air outlet	—	125	—	122		—				34	G4	yes

8.34
PHPP 'Ventilation Protocol' worksheet – System commissioning

8.20.3 System and control checks

The following should be checked:

- All the control functions.
- The boost function and all of the control locations for activating it.
- The delay timer on the boost returns the fans to normal speed after the set time interval.
- The frost protection control settings. If set too high then the frost protection system will be running before it is required, thereby reducing the heat recovery of the MVHR unit. A set point temperature of −3.0°C is recommended generally, but the manufacturer's recommendations should be followed. The choice of this temperature can be influenced by many things, including the efficiency of the heat exchanger, the position and accuracy of the air temperature sensors, etc.

For communal systems, or systems in commercial buildings, pressure testing of the ducts should always be undertaken as part of the installation process. It is recommended that this is undertaken before the ducts are finally enclosed and not at the commissioning stage so that, if remedial works are required, finished surfaces will not have to be opened up. When pressure testing ducts, care should be taken to ensure that the suction of the pressurising fan is located in free clean air and the inlet is filtered using a F7 filter as a minimum. The equipment for pressure testing ducts can be hired and details of how to undertake the tests can be found in HVCA DW/143 (HVCA, 2000b).

One of the protections against any potential problems is the requirement to take continuous photographic records of all aspects of the installation of these systems throughout the building. If a problem is suspected then reference to these photographs may help identify the potential problem area.

References

Arlian, L. G. 1975. Dehydration and survival of the European house dust mite, Dermatophagoides pteronyssinus. *Journal of Medical Entomology*, 12 (4): 437–42.

ASFP. 2010. *Blue Book, Fire Resisting Ductwork: Classified According to BS EN 13501 Parts 3 and 4, European Version*. 1st edition. Bordon: ASFP.

ASFP, 2011. *Grey Book, EN Fire Dampers (European standards)*. 2nd edition. Bordon: ASFP.

ASHRAE. 2010. *Standard 62.2-2010: Ventilation and Acceptable Indoor Air Quality in Low Rise Residential Buildings*. Atlanta, GA: ASHRAE.

BRE. 2007. *Overheating in Urban Flats (Client Report 234742)*. Watford: BRE.

BS 8214:2008. *Code of Practice for Fire Door Assemblies*. s.l.: BSI.

California Environmental Protection Agency. 1994. *How Much Air Do We Breathe? (Research Note 94-11)*. [Online]. Available at: www.arb.ca.gov/research/resnotes/notes/94-11.htm

CIBSE. 2006. *CIBSE Guide A: Environmental Design*. 7th edition. London: CIBSE.

Crump, D., Dengel, A. and Swainson, M. 2009. *Indoor Air Quality in Highly Energy Efficient Homes – A Review*. Watford: IHS, BRE Press on behalf of NHBC Foundation.

Dengle, A. and Swainson, M. 2012. *Overheating in New Homes – A Review of the Evidence*. Watford: IHS, BRE Press on behalf of the NHBC Foundation.

Dengle, A. and Swainson, M. 2013. *Assessment of MVHR Systems and Air Quality in Zero Carbon Homes.* Watford: IHS, BRE Press on behalf of the NHBC Foundation.

EDU. 2008. An interview with Wolfgang Feist. *Energy Design Update,* 28 (1): 1–6.

EN 308:1997. *Heat Exchangers – Test Procedures for Establishing the Performance of Air to Air and Flue Gas Heat Recovery Devices.* Brussels: CEN.

EN 13779:1999. *Ventilation for Buildings – Performance Requirements for Ventilation and Air Conditioning Systems.* Brussels: CEN.

EN 15251:2007. *Indoor Environmental Input Parameters for Design and Assessment of Energy Performance of Buildings Addressing Indoor Air Quality, Thermal Environment, Lighting and Acoustics.* Brussels: CEN.

EN 13779:2007. *Ventilation for Non-residential Buildings – Performance Requirements for Ventilation and Room-conditioning Systems.* Brussels: CEN.

EN 13141-7:2010. *Ventilation For Buildings — Performance Testing of Components/Products for Residential Ventilation Part 7: Performance Testing of a Mechanical Supply and Exhaust Ventilation Units (Including Heat Recovery) for Mechanical Ventilation Systems Intended for Single Family Dwelling.* Brussels: CEN.

EN 779:2012. *Particulate Air Filters for General Ventilation – Determination of the Filtration Performance.* Brussels: CEN.

Eurovent. 2009. *Air Filters for Better Indoor Air Quality (Recommendation 06).* Paris: Eurovent.

The Health and Safety Commission. 1992. *Workplace Health, Safety and Welfare: The Workplace (Health, Safety and Welfare) Regulations 1992, Approved Code of Practice and Guidance.* London: HMSO.

HM Government. 2010. *Approved Document F: Means of Ventilation (2010 Edition). The Building Regulation 2010.* London: NBS.

HVCA. 2000a. *Specification for Plastic Ductwork.* 1st edition. Penrith: HVCA.

HVCA. 2000b. *DW/143 Ductwork Leakage Testing: A Practical Guide.* 5th edition. Penrith: HVCA.

IFSA. 2012. *Air Transfer Grilles in Non-Ducted Building Ventilation Systems (Information Sheet No. 7).* IFSA: Princes Risborough.

McLeod, R. S., Hopfe, C. J. and Kwan, A. 2013. An investigation into future performance and overheating risks in Passivhaus dwellings. *Building and Environment,* 70: 189–209.

Mudarri, D. and Fisk, W. 2007. *Public health and economic impact of dampness and mold. Indoor Air,* 17 (3): 226–35.

NHBC. 2010. Ductwork Passing through Protected Entrance Halls in Dwellings, Building Regulations Guidance Note. Milton Keynes: NHBC Building Control.

Passivhaus Institut. 2009. *Requirements and Testing Procedures for Energetic and Acoustical Assessment of Passive House Ventilation Systems for Certification as 'Passive House Suitable Components'.* Darmstadt: Passivhaus Institut.

PHI. 2012. *Database of Certified Passive House Components.* [Online]. Available at: www.passiv.de/komponentendatenbank/en-EN (accessed 11 November 2014).

US Government Accountability Office. 2012. *Manufactured Housing Standards, Testing and Performance Evaluation Could Ensure Safe Indoor Air Quality (Report to Congressional Requesters).* Washington DC: US Government Accountability Office.

WHO. 2010. *WHO Guidelines for Indoor Air Quality: Selected Pollutants.* Copenhagen: WHO.

9

Renewable power technologies

ANDREW PEEL

9.1 Introduction

Passivhaus is a standard that primarily focuses on reducing the energy demand of a building's key services: HVAC, lighting, appliances, and auxiliary energy demands. However, in designing a Passivhaus, there are often opportunities to incorporate one or more renewable power technologies (RPTs). And they are often integral to projects with wider sustainability targets, such as BREEAM, LEED, or Living Building Challenge. Under the right conditions, it is even possible to design a zero carbon or energy plus building by incorporating RPTs.[1]

This chapter explores suitable RPTs that can be incorporated into the design of Passivhaus buildings, both domestic and non-domestic.[2] As the technologies are numerous and new developments are announced frequently, it is not possible to provide a complete picture of the entire renewable technology landscape. Additionally, this chapter is not meant as a guide to designing and installing RPTs. There are plenty of excellent resources available for this purpose, and specialist subcontractors are generally employed for such purposes. Rather, its aim is to present a broad overview of the most relevant power technologies and their characteristics, along with the key aspects that a Passivhaus designer should consider in the selection and integration of RPTs in Passivhaus developments.

RPTs can be categorized by the source of the energy. For buildings, the relevant sources are solar, wind, and water. In the context of this chapter, a technology is considered renewable if it generates electricity solely from a renewable resource. This definition ignores small auxiliary demands (such as circulation pumps). Thus, air- and ground-source heat pumps are excluded from this discussion as they consume a considerable amount of electricity from the building. Micro-CHP (micro combined heat and power) has also been excluded, as these units usually consume natural gas in their operation. Some of these low and zero carbon technologies (LZCTs) are covered in Chapters 7 and 8.

The discussion in this chapter is restricted to the following small-scale power technologies: solar PV and wind. Micro hydro turbines have been omitted as they have little bearing on the design of a Passivhaus building. However, they may be suitable for a building site provided the resource is available.

Various other renewable energy technologies exist, including wave, tidal, geothermal, anaerobic digestion, and biomass combined heat and power. However, these are large-scale technologies that provide power for a large number of buildings or entire districts, or feed energy directly to the grid. Since the discussion in this chapter is focused on single buildings and small developments, they have been excluded.

9.2 Renewable power systems

A renewable power system comprises a renewable generation unit, a mounting system, one or more inverters, an electricity meter, and some supporting electrical equipment (cables, etc.). It may optionally have an array of storage batteries, a charge controller, and a monitoring system.

The amount of the solar or wind resource at a site naturally fluctuates throughout the day, causing a variation in the amount of electricity generated. When the system produces more electricity than the building requires, the inverter exports the excess to the mains grid. Conversely, when there is a shortfall, it imports electricity to make up the difference. The inverter also helps regulate the power quality, to ensure that the power being fed to the appliances or the grid is compatible. The meter keeps track of the imports and exports to help determine any payments required. The monitoring system watches the system to ensure correct operation and notifies the owner or system operator when it detects a problem.

9.1
Main components of a grid-tied domestic solar PV renewable power system
Source: © Andrew Peel

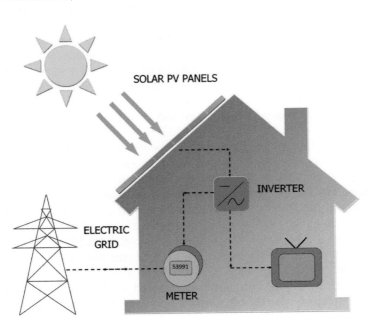

SOLAR PV PANELS

INVERTER

ELECTRIC GRID

53991

METER

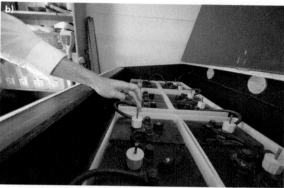

9.2
a) Stand-alone (off-grid) solar
PV renewable power system
in Waratha Bay/Australia; and
b) off-grid solar batteries: the
blue stick is an electrolyte
level indicator
Source: © C. Hopfe

This type of system is known as grid-tied, since it is connected to the mains grid. In a sense, the system uses the grid as a storage medium, freely storing and taking energy as it needs. An alternative system is a stand-alone (off-grid) system, which is not connected to the mains grid. Instead, an array of storage batteries (or other storage medium) is used to store excess energy and release it under shortfall. A charge controller determines how and when the batteries are charged and discharged. A diesel-powered generator may also be included to provide power when the renewable energy system is not producing energy (e.g. during scheduled maintenance). Stand-alone systems are uncommon in buildings and are usually installed in rural or remote areas that do not have access to the grid. They are also more expensive and require more maintenance due to the batteries.

9.3 General considerations

Numerous factors come into play when determining whether a renewable energy system is suitable for integration in a Passivhaus building or development. The following are general considerations for all technologies.

9.3.1 Resource availability

The most important factor to consider is the availability of or access to the renewable resource at the site. Solar and wind will always be present, but not necessarily in sufficient quantities. A proper assessment of the availability of the resource(s) is crucial to determine the feasibility of incorporating a RPT. Methods for resource estimation are discussed within each technology subsection.

9.3.2 Costs

Capital costs vary considerably between technologies, contractors, and countries. Product developments, market conditions, grid connection, grants, incentives, and planning requirements also heavily influence prices. Therefore, specific costs have not been provided as they would be out of date soon after publication. In order to obtain up-to-date information, it is best to consult the local or national energy advice organization (e.g. Energy Saving Trust in the UK, National Renewable Energy Lab (NREL) in the US) or market reports. Operating costs, on the other hand, are more stable and tend to decrease as technology develops. This is due to increased reliability, better designs, and a reduced number of components, which decrease maintenance requirements and replacement costs.

Installed correctly, and with appropriate incentives, RPTs can be financially viable investments over their lifetime. However, Passivhaus buildings generally require a higher capital investment than standard buildings. Since a primary goal of Passivhaus dwellings is to minimize energy demand, investment should be focused on demand reduction measures first. Sacrificing such measures in favour of RPTs is counter to this philosophy. It also generally results in higher capital costs, as RPTs are more expensive than energy efficiency measures on essentially every cost measure ($/kW, lifecycle costs, etc.). Furthermore, maintenance costs will be higher with RPTs since there is more active equipment to look after. On a tight budget, RPTs may have to be excluded from the project.

If capital costs are a restriction, there are alternative financing arrangements. Some contractors offer rental agreements, whereby the building owner or landowner is paid an annual rental fee in exchange for the use of the building or land to install the renewable energy system. Alternatively, the owner may receive electricity generated by the system for free. The company bears the capital costs of the system but maintains ownership of the system and collects the income it generates, either from the sale of electricity or from payments from the applicable incentive. In such arrangements, the contract must clearly state who is responsible for maintenance, repair, and replacement of property (e.g. roof) in case of damage or end-of-life replacement.

9.3.3 Planning permission

The procedures and requirements to obtain planning permission differ enormously between technologies, countries and even municipalities. Obtaining planning permission may be a relatively painless process, or may be very difficult, time-consuming, and costly. For systems that will require a detailed planning application, it is recommended that a planning consultant be employed to develop and submit this. In all cases, discussing the plans with the local planning office early in the design phase is advised in order to understand the requirements and any conditions, and to ensure the design is adapted in response to these to avoid difficulties later on.

Permitted development:

In the UK, certain solar PV and wind installations are deemed permitted development. This means that their installation does not require planning permission. Permitted development is subject to significant restrictions, including size, location, and noise levels. Currently PV systems (domestic and non-domestic) and domestic wind turbines are the only eligible RPTs covered under permitted development. However, the scope could in future be expanded to include non-domestic wind.

9.3.4 Design integration

As with energy efficiency measures, it is important that RPTs are considered early in the design stage of the project. There are great opportunities to identify and realize functional and aesthetic synergies between the building and the RPTs. Early consideration also helps mitigate conflicting requirements and potential issues with integration.

It can also be beneficial to engage an independent renewable energy consultant as part of the design team, particularly for larger systems. This will help ensure the design reflects the requirements and inherent restrictions of the RPT. The consultant should be product-independent to ensure they provide impartial advice. They may also help with planning and grid connection applications.

9.3.5 Grid connection

Grid connection procedures vary considerably by country and region. Early discussions with the local utility company are essential to understand connection requirements, permits, time frames, and costs. In order to obtain general advice, the local or national energy advice organization should be consulted.

Load shifting is a technique being introduced by some jurisdictions to manage peak demand. It works by having customers agree to preferentially turn on loads when a renewable power system is actually generating electricity. For instance, a dishwasher may be programmed to run when the PV system is at peak output. Standard residential PV systems typically cover around 25 percent of the annual household demand. With load shifting, coverage up to 50 percent is possible.

The introduction of smart meters in some countries is also changing how consumers and utilities interact. Smart meters communicate energy consumption and generation to utility companies in real time, allowing them to better manage the grid. They also provide live consumption information to consumers. In the UK, there is a timetable to have smart meters deployed in all homes and businesses by the end of 2019 (Department of Energy and Climate Change, 2012). The situation is similar in North America, with many states or provinces adopting regulations that require or encourage the installation of smart meters (US Energy Information Administration, 2011).

Unfortunately, not all smart meters are bidirectional, which means they can't be used to export locally generated power. This necessitates an additional meter to separately track PV system production.

9.3.6 Financial incentives

One of the driving forces behind the large global uptake of RPTs in the last decade has been the numerous financial incentives offered in different countries. Without incentives, RPTs are not competitive with grid electricity in most countries. Incentives have enabled investors to reap favourable returns on investments in RPTs, which would otherwise not be possible. This has spurred huge investment in the industry. In 2011, wind and solar power accounted for more than 30 percent of newly installed electric capacity globally (Sawin, 2012: 29).

The most common types of incentives are grants, Feed-in-Tariffs (FITs), tax credits, and net metering. Grants provide a one-time payment to the owner to help offset the capital costs of the system. FITs provide an ongoing payment per kWh electricity generated and/or exported to the grid over a fixed time period. With tax credits, a percentage of the capital costs are provided as a tax credit that can be used to reduce the owner's tax liability.

Net metering tracks household consumption and generation, including exports, over the entire year. Owners benefit either from a reduced demand for electricity or by receiving a credit towards electricity costs. Unlike FITs, no additional payment per kWh beyond the retail price is provided for either generation or export. Indeed the per kWh credit is often less than the per kWh price. Where both FITS and net metering are available, FITS are the more financially attractive option

One significant advantage of FITs compared to the other incentive types is that they encourage owners to maintain the system since receiving income relies on the continued generation of energy. FITs availability and eligibility should definitely be explored when considering RPTs.

The types of incentives, levels of compensation, and eligibility criteria vary considerably between countries and regions. For instance, Germany has operated a FIT program for many years. In the US, tax credits and net metering have been the main subsidies.

Due to both political and economic forces, the financial incentives landscape is continually evolving. Changes to a scheme can alter the eligibility and economic viability of a RPT drastically and rapidly. It is, therefore, impractical to provide an overview of incentives in different countries. It is advised to inquire with their local or national energy advice organization about available incentives.

9.3.7 Contractors

Choosing the right contractor is critical to ensuring a RPT achieves a high level of performance and is reliable and cost effective. The introduction of financial incentives encourages many new companies into the market. These new entrants naturally have less experience and unfortunately some are unscrupulous. Employing an inexperienced contractor generally leads to higher long-term costs, poorer performing systems, and more frequent equipment replacement. In some cases, systems may not operate correctly.

To mitigate these issues, the appointed contractor should be properly qualified and have a proven track record of installations. Where one exists, the contractor should be certified under a regional or national renewable energy certification scheme (e.g. MCS Installer scheme). They should also have a good relationship with established suppliers and specify equipment that has been independently certified to international standards, or national ones where these are more demanding. Some incentive schemes require that both the installer and equipment be certified to a particular scheme. Ideally, the supplier would also be part of a code of conduct, such as the REAL consumer code (Renewable Energy Assurance Ltd, 2012) in the UK. Such codes stipulate the level of information (e.g. system performance guarantees, maintenance requirements, etc.) a supplier should provide to potential consumers and also provides a mechanism for complaints.

UK Microgeneration Certification Scheme (MCS)

The MCS certifies both installers and products of renewable energy technologies (both power and heat) in the UK. It covers a variety of technologies, including solar PV, solar thermal, wind turbines, and biomass. In order to qualify for the UK FITs program, both the installer and equipment must be MCS certified. The **Small Wind Certification Council (SWCC)** runs a similar scheme in North America for small wind turbines. However, it certifies the turbines only, not the installers.

Independent contractors are preferable as they are less likely to push a particular product. Evidence of long-term performance of previously installed systems based on monitored data (e.g. participation in field trials) provides further reassurance of the contractor's competence, although this is unlikely to be generally available. More information on certification schemes and products can be obtained from local or national energy advice organizations.

9.4 Solar photovoltaics (PV)

A solar PV system converts solar radiation into Direct Current (DC) electricity. A single PV panel (known as a PV module) contains many individual semiconductor cells that generate the actual electricity. Since a single panel has a small capacity (~100W), panels are grouped together into an array. The combined electrical output of the array is sent to the inverter, which converts it from DC to Alternating Current (AC). This conversion is required because most major home electrical appliances, as well as the grid, operate on AC power. DC appliances are available, however, they are more expensive and are generally only sold by specialty retailers. And if the system will connect to the grid, an inverter will be required, regardless of the appliance type.

Array sizes in the built environment can vary from 1 kW on houses to 1 MW plus on large industrial buildings (e.g. warehouses). Typical system sizes for residential buildings are 2–5 kW, with some large homes installing up to 10W.

9.4.1 Resource estimation

The output of a PV panel is directly proportional to the solar radiation it receives. Since radiation hits all regions of the Earth, PV panels will produce electricity in any location. Naturally, the amount of radiation varies by location. Annual radiation (measured in kWh/m^2) can be estimated from radiation maps (Figure 9.3). Many national maps are based on measured data from many weather stations recorded over many years and are, therefore, very reliable. However, there may be local microclimatic weather patterns that affect annual radiation levels, particularly in coastal and mountainous areas. If you are using a local climate data file in PHPP, you can obtain the annual global horizontal radiation by summing the monthly global radiation in cells G95–R95 (PHPPv8.5) on the 'Climate' worksheet.

9.3
Solar radiation map of the UK at 30° tilt
Source: © GeoModel Solar

Radiation maps generally show global horizontal radiation (i.e. the total radiation hitting a horizontal surface). However, since PV panels produce far more electricity under direct radiation than diffuse radiation, it is important to maximize the amount of direct incident radiation. Unless the site is near the equator, maximum direct incident radiation (and therefore electricity generation) will not occur on the horizontal, but rather at a particular inclination angle (optimum tilt angle). Since the sun's average angle from the horizon decreases with increasing latitude, the array should be tilted higher the further north the location is (or further south in the southern hemisphere). The general rule of thumb is to set the tilt angle equal to the latitude. The optimum tilt angle for energy generation is generally less than the latitude. The further north the location, the greater the discrepancy between the latitude and the optimum tilt (Table 9.1). Discrepancies of a few percent may appear insignificant, but can affect the return on investment. For ground-mounted systems and roofs that are flat or only slightly inclined, the PV system can be installed at any tilt angle using an inclined mounting structure. For steep pitched roofs, the roof pitch will determine the tilt angle of the array. Where possible, the roof pitch should be chosen to match the optimum tilt angle.

The above analysis does not take into account self-shading, which affects the optimum tilt angle (see Section 9.4.2).

There are situations where using a non-optimal tilt angle is preferred. For instance, the objective may be to reduce summer peak demand. In this case, a lower tilt should be used, as this favours energy production in the summer. Conversely, if greater production in winter is desired, a higher tilt angle is best.

When an array is tilted, its orientation also affects electricity generation. The steeper the tilt, the greater the impact orientation has on generation. For optimally tilted arrays, this means output at higher latitudes will be more sensitive to the orientation. As with windows, the array should ideally be oriented due south (or north in the Southern Hemisphere) in order to optimize output. In the UK, deviations of up to 45° from south do not lead to a significant reduction in

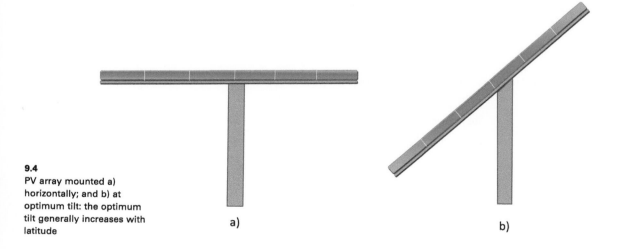

9.4
PV array mounted a) horizontally; and b) at optimum tilt: the optimum tilt generally increases with latitude

a)

b)

output, but beyond this point, the output drops considerably (Table 9.2). In sunnier locations, the impact can be even greater. Thus, pitched roofs that will accommodate a PV system should be orientated between southwest and southeast.

9.4.2 Energy yield

The main factors that affect the amount of electricity generated by a PV system are solar radiation, peak power, shading, and system losses. An explanation of each follows.

9.4.2.1 Solar radiation

Estimation of the solar radiation hitting the PV has been discussed in Section 9.4.1.

Table 9.1 Radiation predicted at optimum tilt angle and tilt angle equal to latitude for four locations

	Latitude	Optimum tilt angle	Radiation at tilt angle = latitude [kWh/m²/yr]	Radiation at optimum tilt angle [kWh/m²/yr]	% difference
Inverness, UK	57.5	40	1,040	1,080	−4
Cornwall, UK	50.5	37	1,260	1,290	−2
Toronto, Canada	43.7	33	1,486	1,503	−1
San Francisco, US	37.8	31	1,951	1,957	0

Table 9.2 Impact of orientation and tilt on radiation incident falling on a PV panel in Cornwall, UK

Orientation	Tilt (degrees)	Annual incident radiation [kWh/kWp]
South	38	1,289
South	0	1,111
Southeast	38	1,216
East	38	1,029

9.4.2.2 Peak power

Peak power (kWp) refers to the power outputted by the panel under standard laboratory conditions (1,000 W/m² radiation at 25°C) and is provided in manufacturers' literature. Since solar radiation fluctuates throughout the day and is often less than 1,000 W/m², PV panels will generally output less than their peak power. The peak power of an entire array is calculated by multiplying the panel's peak power by the number of panels.

9.4.2.3 Shading factor

PV panels are subject to shading from surrounding permanent objects, such as neighbouring buildings, trees, and features of the building's roof (e.g. chimneys).

Even the panels themselves can shade neighbouring panels (Figure 9.5). As previously discussed, flat roof and ground-mounted systems are generally tilted to maximize energy production. This tilt will cause the panels to cast a shadow behind them. If rows of panels are placed too close to each other, each row will shade the row behind it. To minimize self-shading, sufficient space must be allowed between the rows.

However, completely eliminating self-shading is unrealistic as it would require too large a distance between rows, particularly in northern locations. There is balance to be struck between tilt angle and inter-row spacing. It is common for a system at a lower tilt angle (e.g. 20°) to produce nearly as much electricity on a kWh/kWp basis (within 1–2 percent) as one at the optimal tilt

9.5
Self-shading of PV arrays
Source: © solarEdge

angle, but with less inter-row spacing. Closer rows mean more panels can be packed into the same space. This is relevant for systems mounted on roofs that are flat or only slightly inclined as they can be installed at any tilt angle using an inclined mounting structure. For steep pitched roofs, the roof pitch will determine the tilt angle of the array. In this case, the roof pitch should be chosen to match the optimum tilt angle.

Generally, suburban and rural rooftop systems are less prone to shading, as surrounding objects (trees, other buildings) are generally not much higher than the planned buildings and of sufficient distance from them. Urban systems, in contrast, can be subject to significant shading. Regardless of location, if significant shading cannot be avoided, a PV system is unlikely to be financially viable.

The impact of shading on PV systems can be assessed using the PHPP 'Shading' worksheet. This requires a survey of neighbouring objects to determine their height, size, and distance from the planned building(s). This information can be entered in PHPP to estimate shading factors (winter and summer) for the PV system. In fact, the PV system can be treated as one or more large roof lights. There are also specialist tools (such as Solar Pathfinder(™)) that can undertake more detailed calculations of shading objects. These tools generally require experience to be used correctly.

9.4.2.4 System losses

A PV system is subject to numerous losses, including:

- **Panel mismatch:** The power output characteristics of each PV panel vary due to manufacturing tolerances. Leading manufacturers will sort the panels by their power characteristics. However, panels cannot be matched perfectly, so some panels in an array will perform worse than others. Unfortunately, PV panels connected in series will perform only as well as the poorest-performing panel.
- **Inverter losses**: the inverter consumes energy in the DC-AC conversion and for its other functions.
- **Imperfect Maximum Power Point Tracking (MPPT)**: The power output of a panel is directly proportional to the current and voltage. There is a certain combination of voltage and current at which a panel produces maximum power. Since the amount of radiation hitting the panels continually changes, the maximum power point does as well. A well-designed inverter continuously checks the array to ensure the maximum power point is being maintained; however, it does not achieve this 100 percent of the time.
- **Temperature effects**: panel performance reduces as its temperature increases (see Section 9.4.5 for further information).
- **System losses**: losses from power cables and other electrical components.
- **Soiling**: accumulation of dirt, snow, etc. reduces the radiation hitting the PV cells.
  - Areas with high airborne pollution and low rain are more prone to dirt accumulation.

- Snow accumulation depends on the amount of snow received and how long it remains on the PV panels. It accumulates more if the PV array is closely integrated into the roof and surrounding structures encourage snowdrift. Snow remains longer under sub-freezing temperatures and on systems with low tilt angles, which prevents snow from sliding off.

The cumulative effect of these losses is captured in a system losses factor, which is typically between 15–25 percent.

Another factor that affects performance, but is not generally included in the system losses, is localized shading. This occurs when an object shades only a portion of one panel. This can include fallen leaves, branches, and bird droppings. Areas with large bird populations or surrounding foliage are more prone to this. As mentioned above, a series of panels will only perform as well as its weakest panel. Therefore, a drop of 50 percent in one panel results in the same drop for all panels connected to it serially.

9.4.3 Energy yield estimation tool

The European Commission has developed a free tool called PV GIS (European Commission Joint Research Centre, 2012) to estimate annual electricity production from PV systems at any geographical location in Europe or Africa. The user can enter a variety of parameters, including array power, orientation, tilt angle, system losses, etc. Note that the electricity estimate does not include the shading factor (SF). This can be applied to the output of PV GIS using the following formula:

$$E_{system} = E_{PVGIS\ output} \cdot (1 - SF) \tag{1}$$

Alternatively, the system losses parameter can be modified to include the shading factor as follows:

$$L_{system\ (new)} = 1 - [1 - L_{system\ (old)}] \cdot [1 - SF] \tag{2}$$

The tool can also be used to produce maps, tables, or graphs of daily or monthly radiation at a given location.

9.4.4 PV technologies

There are three main commercially available PV technologies: monocrystalline, polycrystalline, and thin-film. The main differences between the technologies are cost and how efficiently they convert radiation into electricity. This directly affects the amount of space required by the array. The more efficient the panel, the less space is required for a given capacity. Table 9.3 provides typical efficiencies and space requirements of the three main technologies.

Although less efficient, thin-film technologies offer one distinct advantage: they can be applied to flexible substrates. This increases their application range,

Table 9.3 PV Panel efficiencies and space requirements for different PV technologies typically used in building projects

Technology	Conversion efficiency	Space requirement [m²/kWp] (pitched roof)
Monocrystalline	16–21%	7–9
Polycrystalline	15–17%	8–9
Thin-film	CIS: 12–14% CdTe: 13–14% Amorphous: 7–10%	9–20

which includes PV tiles and flexible laminates (see Section 9.4.6). Thin-film technologies also benefit from a higher shading tolerance and better performance in hot climates. Efficiency drops by only 0.3%/°C versus 0.5%/°C for crystalline panels (see Section 9.4.5).

Another technology is concentrated PV (CPV), which uses lenses or curved mirrors to concentrate solar radiation onto the cells. This increases the efficiency dramatically, up to 30 percent. However, the high efficiency is only achieved under direct sunlight. To maximize direct sunlight, the array must be installed on a tracker that follows the position of the sun in the sky. Unfortunately, the high concentration levels raise the temperature of the cells, often necessitating active cooling. CPV is best suited to very sunny areas and installation on buildings is uncommon.

The most common technologies are mono- and poly-crystalline, comprising far greater than 80 percent of the world market. Thin-film products had been gradually gaining market share, but this has regressed more recently. Many amorphous companies have gone out of business. Research is ongoing to increase PV cell conversion efficiencies, but these gains are incremental and are not leading to substantial improvements. Efforts in other areas, such as improving manufacturing techniques and reducing system losses, are having a greater impact on system performance and cost. New technologies are being developed, such as organic PV cells, but these are either still at the research stage or in the early commercialization phase.

One very interesting development for PV systems is the micro-inverter. A micro-inverter functions the same as a standard inverter but is connected directly to each PV panel. The micro-inverter optimizes the power production of each panel and converts it to AC. This reduces losses due to panel mismatch, imperfect maximum power point tracking, and localized shading. The presence of multiple inverters means there is no single point of failure and allows each panel to be monitored individually.

This increases system reliability and availability. However, micro-inverters have lower conversion efficiency, which can offset the gains from the above-mentioned losses. In general, the technology is best suited to installations with substantial localized shading.

Another developing technology is the hybrid PV/thermal solar system (PVT). This typically comprises metal pipes or plates attached to the back of a PV panel. A working fluid (e.g. glycol) collects heat from the panel through the pipes and exchanges it with a thermal storage tank. This can improve panel efficiency (due to reduced operating temperature) while providing hot water for use in the building. The performance of a hybrid system does not match the performance of each system individually. However, they make more efficient use of roof space and may be more cost effective. No separate test standard exists for evaluating the combined performance of PVTs. However PVTs can be MCS certified separately to both the PV and solar thermal standards, providing reassurance in terms of their expected performance.

9.4.5 Mounting systems

A standard PV array can be installed on a roof or the ground.

9.4.5.1 Roof-mounted systems

The PV array is mounted on a frame that is installed directly on the roof. For flat roofs, the frame can be ballasted or anchored to the roof. For pitched roofs, the array is anchored to the roof. Different mounting techniques exist, with choice of the most appropriate based on the type of roof covering. The PV manufacturer can advise on the best roof-covering mounting system combinations for their products.

The roof must be designed to accommodate the additional weight and wind loading of the PV system, which is typically 15–25 kg/m². The roofing contractor should be provided with details of the PV system so that he can incorporate these into his structural calculations.

If an external air barrier is used on the roof, care must be taken that the panel screws/fixings do not penetrate the barrier. Where this cannot be avoided, additional measures, such as a butyl rubber tape, should be used at the penetrations.

The performance of panels decreases significantly at high temperatures. At peak power production, panel efficiency can drop by 0.5%/°C. A panel operating at 50°C above standard conditions (20°C) may see an efficiency drop of 25 percent. The panel operating temperature is most influenced by the amount of radiation and the heat dissipation capability of the panel. Unvented panels may operate at temperatures 15°C higher than vented panels. In locations with higher irradiation, PV panels should be installed a certain distance above the roof. This distance will vary with climate (e.g. radiation, wind speed, and direction, etc.) and the panel casing materials. Active cooling strategies (e.g. water spraying) have been proposed, but the additional energy and water requirements for these should be evaluated before such strategies are employed.

For retrofit projects, the structural condition of the roof should be checked to ensure it can accommodate a PV system. If the roof is going to be replaced, a PV system can be incorporated into the roof design to help reduce costs and improve aesthetic quality.

9.6
A roof-mounted PV system
Source: © solarcentury

9.4.5.2 Ground-mounted systems

The PV array is mounted on a frame that sits directly on the ground. These are usually sited in open fields, such as fallow land, which accommodate large systems that can be ideally sited for maximum energy production. However, if there is sufficient land on the property with good solar access, ground-mounted arrays can be incorporated into the project.

9.7
A ground-mounted PV system
Source: Wikipedia

9.4.5.3 Adjacent features

PV arrays can also be integrated into features surrounding the building, for instance canopies above parking lots. This makes more efficient use of the features and can be used to visually emphasize the sustainability credentials of the building. It may also be the only option where restrictions prevent the installation on the roof.

9.4.5.4 Tracking systems

To further improve energy yield, some developers mount PV arrays on trackers that continually follow the sun's position in the sky. As mentioned, this is essential for CPV systems. Trackers are generally used for large-scale PV systems to optimize performance. Their additional installation and maintenance requirements and cost make them impractical for most building-scale systems.

9.4.6 Building integrated PV systems

PV technologies can be integrated into the fabric of the building, replacing traditional building components. Used in this way, they perform more than one function (e.g. weather protection) and can potentially reduce PV system costs. The most common types are discussed here.

9.4.6.1 Solar roof tiles and shingles

These replace the outer roofing material and act as a weather barrier. Products exist that can replace all sorts of roofing materials, including asphalt shingles,

9.8
Solar Tree® array by Envision Solar

9.9
Solar PV tiles
Source: © solarcentury

fiber cement shingles, slates, single and double camber tiles, and interlocking tiles. Some of the key benefits are:

- *Reduced load:* The roof does not need to be adapted to accommodate the additional weight of a frame and PV panels. Neither is the wind load on the roof increased.
- *Reduced installation time:* The solar tiles can be installed like regular tiles and do not require a specialist contractor.
- *Easier planning:* Due to their low aesthetic impact, there are less likely to be issues in obtaining planning consent.
- *Efficient roof space utilization:* Tiles can be incorporated into sections of the roof where traditional panels will not fit.

One main disadvantage with integrated systems is that air movement is reduced behind the tiles since the tiles do not stand proud of the roof. This air movement is important for cooling the panels. Reduced cooling may decrease performance, particularly on hot days. Another issue is that these products tend to be specialty products, which could make replacement problematic down the road.

9.4.6.2 Flexible laminates

These thin, lightweight laminates can be adhered directly to building components. Examples of compatible components include waterproofing roof membrane, metal roofing sheets, and polystyrene insulation laid on waterproof membranes. Laminates share the same benefits as roof tiles. Additionally, their flexibility enables curved installations. Unfortunately, their performance is lower than standard panels as they are a thin-film technology and are more likely to be installed at suboptimal tilt angles (e.g. horizontally on flat roofs).

9.10
Flexible PV laminates
Source: © Kalzip

9.4.6.3 PV shades

PV panels can be incorporated into awnings and brise-soleils to provide shading to windows. This is an elegant means of incorporating a PV system into the building, particularly where rooftop installation is impractical. Proper design should ensure that the panels are tilted optimally for electricity generation while providing sufficient shading. In dense urban areas, awnings installed on lower building levels may experience significant shading from neighbouring structures. As with other external shading devices, care must be taken to minimize thermal bridging and air barrier penetrations of the awning's connections to the building structure.

9.11
PV awning
Source: © Michael Tavel
Architects

9.4.6.4 Façade- and window-integrated

PV panels can act as an outer skin and weather barrier, replacing façade elements such as curtain walls. Unfortunately, the vertical tilt has a significant negative impact on performance. PV material can also be incorporated directly into windows, either as cells applied directly to the glass or as a thin-film deposit. These windows are used in various applications (e.g. skylights, spandrel panels) to control daylighting, provide visual effect, and produce electricity. However, their thermal performance does not meet the Passivhaus requirements for cool temperate climates and cold climates. This is because the PV layer replaces the low-e coating on layer 2 of the glass. Indeed, no Passivhaus window manufacturer currently produces such a window. Also, the PV material blocks incoming solar radiation, thereby reducing solar gain. This helps reduce summer overheating but will increase heat load in the winter. These disadvantages make façade- and window-integrated PV systems currently unsuitable for Passivhaus buildings. Advances in both PV and glazing technology (e.g. external coatings) may eventually make these feasible.

9.4.7 Performance

The three main PV technologies are well established and have strong track records of good long-term performance. Provided they are sited well and installed correctly, they should perform as predicted. Well-sited PV arrays can output from 750 kWh/kWp in northern climates to 2,000 kWh/kWp in desert climates. Typical outputs in the UK are between 750 kWh/kWp in northern Scotland and 950 kWh/kWp in the southwest. The output does gradually decrease over time, generally by about 1 percent per year. This should be accounted for in any financial calculations.

9.4.8 Maintenance

PV panels have a long lifespan, generally assumed to be 20–25 years. However, this is a conservative estimate as some panels have lasted in excess of 35 years. Product warranties, which cover manufacturing defects, etc., are generally provided for 15–20 years. Manufacturers also provide performance warranties, which guarantee a certain output level after a set number of years. This is typically 80 percent over 25 years, meaning the panels will still produce 80 percent of their initial output after 25 years. Inverters, on the other hand, typically only have warranties for 10 years and last 10–15 years.

In contrast, micro-inverters are claimed to last much longer, with some having warranties for up to 25 years. However, as they are a newer technology, they have not been field-tested for long enough to validate this. Since they are installed next to the panels, they are more difficult to access for service or replacement. If the greater longevity and reliability are validated, the maintenance and replacement costs will be lower compared to regular inverters. This will help offset their additional capital costs.

To mitigate system losses and equipment failure, a monitoring system can be installed to track the PV system's performance and alert the building owner of issues. This includes online access to monitor performance in real time, identify and address issues, and optimize performance. Traditionally, only larger systems had monitoring systems. However, installation companies are now routinely providing such systems in homes as well.

Surrounding trees may need periodic trimming to prevent their growth from shading the panels. Biannual cleaning of the panels by either the building owner or an external maintenance company is recommended, as rainwater alone does not always suffice in cleaning accumulated dirt and debris. In addition to reducing performance, debris may cause panels to overheat and fail.

Access to both the array and inverters should be considered during the design of the building to avoid troublesome maintenance. Cleaning can be problematic for pitched roof systems on tall buildings. If scaffolding is the only means of accessing the array for cleaning, the system may be financially infeasible. An alternative to scaffolding is to incorporate anchor points on the wall to allow roped access.

9.5 Wind

A wind turbine converts the kinetic energy of the wind into electricity. Turbines range in size from around 50W generators powering batteries on sailboats to 5 MW offshore turbines. This section focuses mainly on small wind turbines (SWTs) up to 50 kW. This is the upper limit used by the International Electrotechnical Commission (IEC) and the MCS. Larger turbines can be integrated into the plans of a single building or development. However, capital costs and planning considerations often restrict the size. Also, the variety and availability of medium-sized turbines (50–500 kW) is limited due to manufacturers focusing on multi-MW machines.

A wind turbine can be installed at almost any type of building site. Applications include single or multi-residential developments, community centers, commercial premises, car parks, industrial sites, and farms. Where sufficient space and capital is available, multiple turbines can be installed.

9.5.1 Resource estimation

The performance of wind energy systems is much more sensitive to the local resource than solar PV. This is because the power output increases eightfold for every doubling of the wind speed. It is, therefore, crucial to obtain an accurate estimate of the local annual average wind speed (AAWS). An initial estimate can be obtained from a national database, such as NOABL in the UK (RenSMART, 2012). NOABL provides the AAWS at heights of 10m, 25m, and 45m for all postcodes in the UK. Linear interpolation can be used to estimate the wind speed at different hub (i.e. rotor) heights. Unfortunately, NOABL and other databases tend to overestimate wind speeds for small wind turbines, as they generally do not take local topography and obstructions (e.g. trees, neighbouring buildings) into account. This is particularly evident for urban and suburban locations, which contain more obstructions. Field trials have shown that NOABL can overestimate wind speeds by more than 50 percent (Encraft, 2009).

To improve on these estimates, adjustment factors have been incorporated in the MCS installer standard for SWTs MIS 3003 (Department for Business, Enterprise, and Regulatory Reform, 2008) to account for the impact of local obstructions. Adjustment factors have also been developed as part of the Warwick Wind Trials (Encraft, 2009). The revised AAWS is calculated by multiplying the NOABL wind speed by the appropriate factor. While this is a simplified method with many caveats for its use, it does provide an estimate that helps determine whether a turbine should be considered further. If the adjusted AAWS is at least 5 m/s then the site can be considered as potentially viable.

Estimates can also be obtained from local weather stations and nearby turbine installations or feasibility studies, where available. These sources may provide the following additional information:

1 *Wind speed distribution* – this indicates the frequency of each wind speed (i.e. the number of hours per year at each wind speed), and is usually displayed graphically in bins of 1 m/s (Figure 9.12). A Weibull distribution is fitted to the measured data to determine a shape factor (k-value). The k-value is used in the calculation of annual energy yield. If no measured data is available, a standard k-value of 2 is typically assumed.
2 *Prevailing wind direction* – this can help improve turbine siting, both to avoid surrounding obstacles and to assess whether future developments may act as obstacles to the turbine.
3 *Turbulence intensity (TI)* – this indicates how quickly and greatly the wind speed fluctuates. Higher turbulence decreases the energy that can be extracted from the wind and increases the wear on the turbine. It can also influence the choice of turbine as some are built to withstand greater levels of turbulence. Typical figures have yet to be established for SWT sites as not enough field measurements have been undertaken. The limited measurements to date have shown that TI can range from 15 percent at coastal sites (Sustainability Victoria, 2010) to over 35 percent at poorly chosen urban sites (Carpman, 2011).
4 *Annual temperature and altitude* – these are used to calculate the air density, which impacts the energy yield.

Naturally, the relevance of nearby sources will depend on their proximity and how similar the terrain and local obstructions are.

To provide a more accurate prediction, it is best to measure the wind speed at the proposed location and hub height using a met mast. Measuring at the proposed hub height is important since wind speeds vary with height, especially in the urban environment. Measurements should be recorded for at least one but ideally two years. Naturally, this is a long waiting period and measurement

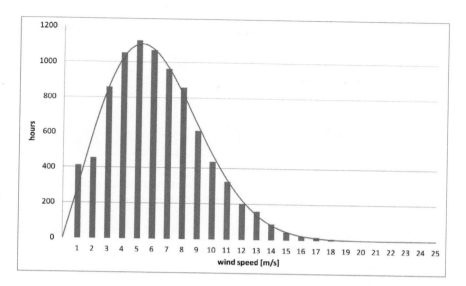

9.12
Wind speed distribution. Each vertical column represents the total number of hours of the year at the respective wind speed. A Weibull distribution (curve) is fitted to the data
Source: © Andrew Peel

isn't even possible on proposed buildings that have yet to be built. Also, planning permission may be needed to erect a met mast. Furthermore, care must be taken with met mast placement to ensure accurate readings. Collected data should be compared to long-term data from local weather stations to improve confidence.

Urban Wind Energy (Stankovic, 2009) is a good source for further information on wind speed monitoring, as well as national wind energy associations.

9.5.2 Turbine siting

The ideal location for a turbine is on a smooth hilltop (of less than 18° inclination) without obstruction in the prevailing wind direction. The wind will speed up along the hill and be relatively free from excessive turbulence. For small wind turbines installed on building sites, this is generally not achievable. The urban environment is particularly unsuited to turbines due to local obstructions. As the wind passes over and around the obstructions, it loses speed and becomes more turbulent. As mentioned, this leads to poorer performance and greater wear on the turbine. However, there are general turbine siting rules that can be followed to improve the quantity and quality of the wind resource:

1 Maximize hub height. For every doubling of the hub height, the wind speed increases by roughly 10 percent. This translates to a 30 percent increase in power, since power is proportional to the cube of the wind speed.
2 Choose an open, exposed location free from obstructions, especially in the prevailing wind direction.
3 If obstructions cannot be avoided, site the turbine away from the biggest obstruction at a distance of ten times the obstruction's height. Alternatively, choose a hub height at least two times the height of the biggest local obstruction.

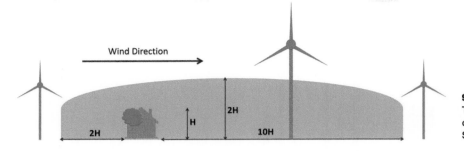

9.13
Turbine siting rules near obstacles
Source: © Andrew Peel

4 For building-mounted turbines, site the turbine at the most upwind side of the building. The turbine should be at least 5 m above roofline.

Additionally, the turbine should be sited at a distance of at least the hub height +10 percent from the property line, public right of ways, and power lines. This is to protect neighbouring assets in the (extremely) rare event that the turbine falls over.

Naturally, site constraints may prevent one or more of these rules from being followed. For instance, planning restrictions may limit the height of the turbine. Ultimately, the most important criterion for a viable site is the AAWS at hub height. General siting rules can help determine where the best wind speeds may be located on the site, but they cannot supplant the value of actual measured data.

9.5.3 Turbine performance

There are several measures used to determine and compare the performance of turbines:

1 *Swept area* – this is the area the blades sweep as they rotate. The larger this area, the greater the theoretical power the turbine can generate. On its own, it is not a very useful measure since many other factors influence power generation. But it is helpful in assessing the visual impact of the turbine.
2 *Rated power* – this is the actual power output of the turbine at a reference wind speed. The rated power is not the maximum power, which is likely to be higher. The Small Wind Turbine Performance and Safety Standard (SWTPSS) uses a reference wind speed of 11 m/s.

Small Wind Turbine Performance and Safety Standard (SWTPSS): Both the American (AWEA) and British Wind Energy Associations (BWEA) have developed respective Small Wind Turbine Performance and Safety Standards, based on the IEC 61400:2013 standard. These standards provide a method for evaluating wind turbines for power performance, reliability, safety, and acoustic characteristics. All MCS-certified and SWCC-certified turbines conform to the respective standard.

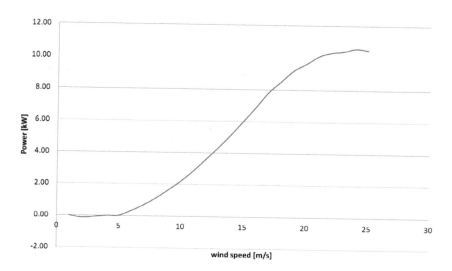

9.14
Wind power curve
Source: © Andrew Peel

3 *Power curve* – this shows the measured output of a turbine at different wind speeds. This is not very useful on its own, but it is used in combination with the site's wind speed distribution and other parameters to calculate the predicted annual energy generation. Power curves should be independently certified, for instance, under the MCS.

4 *Wind class* – this defines the wind conditions under which the turbine is designed to operate. There are four classes, each with a defined annual average wind speed, extreme 50-year gust, and turbulence intensity. The wind class determines whether a turbine is suitable for the typical wind conditions of a particular site.

5 *Peak Efficiency (also Power Coefficient)* – this shows the maximum efficiency that the turbine can achieve. It will only achieve this at a particular wind speed or narrow range of wind speeds. The maximum theoretical peak efficiency is 59 percent (known as the Betz limit). SWTs typically have peak efficiencies between 20 percent and 35 percent. However, most achieve these at wind speeds greater than 10 m/s, which they will see infrequently while in operation. Some MCS-certified units do achieve efficiencies around 30 percent at wind speeds of 5–7 m/s. Claims of efficiencies above 25 percent should, unless certified, be treated with suspicion, especially at wind speeds below 10 m/s. A method for checking the plausibility of a manufacturer's theoretical performance claims is described by PelaFlow Consulting (2008).

6 **Annual Energy Production (AEP)** – this is the expected annual output of a turbine at a reference AAWS and hub height. The SWTPSS uses 5 m/s as the reference speed. This is somewhat helpful for comparing the performance of different turbines. However, turbine performance varies with wind speed, so the AEP is less relevant for sites with different AAWS.

7 **Cut-in Wind Speed** – this is the wind speed at which the turbine begins to produce power, when starting from a standstill. A high cut-in speed translates to lowered energy production in low wind conditions.

Some small wind energy manufacturers make overoptimistic claims about the performance of their turbines. Ideally, manufacturers should provide performance results from actual installations. However, this is unlikely to be available. It is, therefore, crucially important that only turbines independently certified to a recognized standard are specified. As noted, the MCS currently only covers turbines up to 50 kW. However, an international group is currently developing a MCS scheme for medium turbines.

Another aspect to consider is overspeed protection. A turbine should incorporate measures to protect itself in high wind speeds, which otherwise can cause significant wear on the blades and bearings. All turbines are designed with a maximum (cut-off) wind speed beyond which they will shut off. Overspeed protection is covered under the SWTPSS.

9.5.4 Turbine technologies

There are two main turbine technologies: horizontal axis and vertical axis. A horizontal axis wind turbine (HAWT) has a rotor that sits horizontally and changes direction with the wind. They have streamlined blades that capture energy via the lift force, similar to airplanes. They are the more efficient technology, with really good designs typically achieving peak efficiencies above 35 percent. Three-bladed HAWTs are the dominant technology, having proven themselves very reliable over years of operation in many different conditions. Single- and two-bladed HAWTs are rare and generally do not perform as well as their three-bladed counterparts.

A vertical axis wind turbine (VAWT) has a rotor that stands vertically. There are two variants: Savonius and Darrieus. Savonius turbines have scoops instead of blades that capture energy via the drag force. They have very low peak efficiencies, typically 5–10 percent, and are generally regarded as unsuitable for

9.15
Horizontal axis wind turbine
Source: © Kingspan
Renewables Ltd

Renewable power technologies

9.16
Darrieus type vertical axis
wind turbine
Source: © quietrevolution

energy generation. Darrieus turbines have streamlined blades like HAWTs and can achieve peak efficiencies above 25 percent. There are many interesting VAWT designs, with differing numbers of blades. However, the vast majority have no proven track record.

VAWTs generally experience greater wear than HAWTs. They are also heavier and can be more costly. Manufacturers often claim that VAWTs are advantageous because they operate better in more turbulent winds and at lower wind speeds. However, significantly less energy is produced under either condition.

Despite differences between HAWTs and VAWTs, small-scale designs of either type have historically not achieved the same performance as large wind turbines (LWTs). One reason is because LWTs have undergone decades of research, development, and real-life performance monitoring that have led to significant performance improvements. Another reason is that SWTs are typically installed at sites with lower average annual wind speeds, where they are less efficient. However, the renewed interest in urban wind has sparked increasing investment in SWTs, both HAWTs and VAWTs. The emergence of new designs, technological developments, and standards is leading to better-performing SWTs. Indeed, some MCS-certified turbines achieve efficiencies around 30 percent at 5–7 m/s. But ultimately, further *in situ* monitoring of well-sited SWTs is required to confirm that they can consistently achieve a high performance, particularly in the urban environment.

9.5.5 Mounting systems

A wind turbine can either be mounted on a stand-alone tower or on a building. A stand-alone tower can be a steel monopole, a steel lattice, or cable (guy) supported steel tower. A crane is usually needed to lift the turbine onto the tower, although some towers have winch systems that can be used for erection. In either case, sufficient access to and around the site must be available for the installation. Access to the turbine hub for routine maintenance should also be provided.

Building-mounted turbines are also installed on a supporting structure, such as a mast or lattice. The supporting structure may be secured directly to the side of the building (e.g. gable wall), or installed on top of a flat roof. Securing them to walls or chimneys, however, is not recommended, as they are generally not built strongly enough to withstand the types of prolonged stresses originating from a turbine mast. It is also unlikely that the achievable hub height will be sufficient to attain a good wind speed. Regardless of installation, the building must be assessed to ensure structural integrity under both static and dynamic loads. The turbine manufacturer should be consulted for information on the expected loads. The turbine installation should also not compromise the weather resistance of the building. Building-mounted turbines are available up to 10 kW, although most are below 2 kW.

SWT tower heights typically range from around 10 m to 40 m. Each manufacturer will have one or more tower heights for each of their turbines. The choice of turbines may be restricted to those which have tower heights that match the required hub height.

There has also been recent interest in building-integrated turbines. These turbines are designed into and form part of the actual building. There have been a few examples built, mainly as demonstration projects. They present significant design and engineering challenges and are not relevant to Passivhaus developments.

9.5.6 Energy yield

The annual energy yield of a turbine can be expressed in kWh/yr or as the capacity factor (CF), also known as the load factor. The CF is the percentage of the rated power that a turbine outputs on average. For instance, a 50 kW turbine operating at a CF of 10 percent will generate 50 kW × 8,760 hr/yr × 10% = 44 MWh/yr. The CF has the advantage that sites with different characteristics can be easily compared.

UK field trials have shown that SWT performance varies tremendously between sites. The CF of SWTs can range from less than 1 percent to over 30 percent. The main factor in poor performance is low wind speeds due to poor siting. Building-mounted turbines have been shown to perform particularly poorly, often achieving a CF below 3 percent. Decent performance can be achieved, provided they are well sited. One building-mounted turbine achieved a CF of 14 percent in the Warwick Field Trials (Encraft, 2009). This turbine was installed on a

14-storey building 5 m above the flat roof near the roof edge. The building was in an exposed suburban site with a 6.2 m/s AAWS.

Stand-alone turbines performed noticeably better in field trials. The Energy Saving Trust small wind field trials recorded an average CF of 19 percent, with some turbines achieving above 30 percent (Energy Saving Trust, 2009). Remote rural locations near the coast or on exposed land were found to be the best locations. The largest turbine in the field trials was a 6 kW stand-alone. Turbines larger than 6 kW may perform even better, due to higher wind speeds at higher hub heights. For perspective, the average load factor for all UK turbines above 1 MW between 2003 and 2010 was approximately 28 percent (Renewable Energy Foundation, 2011).

The Frauenhofer Institute for Wind Energy and Energy System (IWES) has published an Excel tool for estimating the yield of a small wind turbine (Frauenhofer IWES, 2010). It allows the user to enter site and turbine characteristics and suggests defaults where information is missing or uncertain. Comparisons with real installations have shown a fairly good match between the tool's predictions and actual performance. Naturally, the results are only as reliable as the information inputted.

9.5.7 Key development considerations

The development process for installing a SWT can be time-consuming and costly. In the UK, non-permitted development is likely to take at least nine months. This increases dramatically if wind speed measurements are undertaken for a whole year. Permitted development is fairly restrictive for wind turbines. Hub heights are restricted to 15 m for roof-mounted and 11 m for stand-alone turbines. Roof-mounted turbines are further restricted to a hub height of no more than 3 m above the top of the roof. At these heights, there is unlikely to be a sufficient wind resource to justify the investment. Also, non-domestic properties are not currently covered under permitted development. It is, therefore, likely that a planning application will be required. In this case, it is advisable to engage an independent consultant to aid with the application.

The key aspects considered by planning authorities are landscape and visual impact, noise, impact on wildlife (bats and birds), aviation, electromagnetic interference (radar, TV transmission), and archaeology and heritage. In the UK, it is unlikely that an Environmental Impact Assessment (EIA) will be required. However, the local authority may still require detailed investigation of sensitive issues. The extent will depend heavily on the location and size (particularly height) of the turbine. The application will likely be subject to public consultation. Even if consultation is not required, having open and frequent dialogue with the local stakeholders is beneficial and can mitigate issues later on, such as noise complaints.

RenewableUK has published a useful planning guide for small wind in the UK entitled *Small Wind: Planning Guidance* (RenewableUK, 2011). For other countries, it is recommended to contact the local or national energy office or planning department.

The maturity of the SWT market varies considerably between countries. It is advisable to approach manufacturers early in the building design stage to understand turbine availability, lead-in times, and certification status. Also, some SWTs require a three-phase connection, so early discussion with your local grid operator is important to ensure this can be accommodated.

9.5.8 Reliability

Documented evidence of the long-term performance, reliability, and lifespan of SWTs, particularly in the built environment, is limited compared to large turbines. Therefore, there is inherently more risk in installing a SWT. Manufacturers often claim a design life of 20 years. However, very few manufacturers offer warranties of this length. Warranty periods vary from manufacturers and are typically between two and ten years. Turbines and towers may have different warranty periods.

9.5.9 Maintenance

Maintenance requirements of SWTs are low, usually only requiring an annual inspection for safety and component wear and soiling (particularly the blades). Guy wire tension, bolts, and lubricants should also be checked. In cold climates, ice can form on blades, inhibiting performance. The blades may also throw off ice into the air, potentially causing damage to local objects. A turbine should also be inspected after very strong winds (above 35 m/s). Access to the turbine is required for these inspections. If access is unavailable, the turbine will need to be brought down for maintenance. If the turbine is not on a winch system, this may be prohibitively expensive.

Some minor components (e.g. seals, brakes, sensors) are likely to need replacing or recalibrating after a few years due to wear or in order to optimize performance. Major components may be difficult to source if they fail, particularly if the turbine design is relatively new. As with PV systems, the inverter may need replacing every seven to ten years. It is advisable to have the maintenance undertaken by a qualified professional. Some warranties may require this.

Some manufacturers claim that no routine maintenance of the turbine is required due to a long design life. However, long-term performance data is needed before such claims can be verified.

9.6 Case study: Centre for Energy Efficient Design (CEED)

The Centre for Energy Efficient Design in Rocky Mount, Virginia is the first public school in the United States built to the Passivhaus standard. The educational building is also LEED-platinum certified and contains numerous renewable energy technologies. It serves as a learning laboratory for local students to explore sustainable technologies and building design. It is also acts

9.17
The Centre for Energy Efficient Design
Source: © James Madison University

as a demonstration platform for builders and homeowners to learn about these technologies.

The center has one Skystream 3.7 HAWT, two Windspire VAWT wind turbines, seven different solar PV systems, and a solar thermal system (all south facing). The number and diversity of turbines and PV systems was chosen in order to compare the performance of each, both against their predicted performance and against each other. Different solar inverter technologies have also been installed for comparison. A summary of each system is shown in Table 9.4. Other technologies at the center include a geothermal heat pump, a CO_2 controlled rotary heat exchanger with moisture recovery (also known as a rotary energy recovery ventilator), rainwater harvesting, and a green roof.

Virginia is a good state for solar PV, with an expected annual solar radiation at the site of 1,700 kWh/m² at a tilt equal to the latitude (37°). The wind resource, on the other hand, is poor. The regional wind map predicts an AAWS of 2.57 m/s at the site at a height of 20 m. This is at a much higher height than the respective hub heights of 10m and 18 m for VAWTs and HAWTs. The prediction also does not account for local obstructions. The turbines are located 10–20 m from the building and only 5–10 m from the nearby treeline. Year-long wind speed monitoring undertaken by James Madison University prior to the building's construction confirmed the poor wind resource. At a height of 20 m, the measured AAWS is 2.1 m/s. This is well below the recommended minimum of 5 m/s as well as the cut-in wind speed of 3.0 m/s for the Skystream and 4.4 m/s for the Windspire.

The low wind speed and local obstructions clearly make this site infeasible for wind energy generation. Energy monitoring has confirmed this to be the case – the turbines are often not producing any electricity. However, the turbines have not been installed as income generators but rather as educational tools. Visiting students can witness up close the turbines in operation and observe and compare their performance in real time. And information about wind energy, along with other sustainability topics, has been built into the center's curriculum. Even routine maintenance is used for educational purposes. For instance, when

Table 9.4 Renewable Energy Systems installed at CEED

Technology	Mounting	Special features
2.8 kW Thin-film PV	Fixed array on roof of building	
1.05 kW c-Si* PV	Fixed array on roof of building	Micro-inverter
1.05 kW c-Si* PV	Single-axis tracker on ground-mounted pole	Micro-inverter
3.0 kW CPV	Fixed array on ground-mounted pole	
3 × 2.9 kW c-Si* PV	Dual-axis tracker on ground-mounted pole	System 1: standard inverter System 2: micro-inverter at each panel System 3: MPPT at each panel with a central inverter
1.8 kW HAWT	Ground-mounted pole	
2 × 1.2 kW VAWT	Ground-mounted pole	

Note: *c-Si = monocrystalline.

the PV panels become soiled, the students can clean one of the panels to observe the impact on energy generation.

Separate monitoring of each PV system only began in October 2012. Thus, insufficient data has yet to be collected for a comparison of performance.

The wind energy systems were designed and installed by the respective turbine manufacturers, while the PV systems, save the CPV system, were designed and installed by a local contractor. Installation was problem-free for all but a couple of the systems. The first issue arose with the Skystream 3.7 HAWT, which is normally installed on a guyed lattice tower. The local school department required that the turbine be installed on a freestanding pole. This prompted the development of a prototype tower made from extruded aluminum. The custom tower and additional foundation work doubled the cost of the system. The second issue arose with the CPV system. Unfortunately, the CPV manufacturer went into receivership and could not complete the installation. In contrast to traditional PV systems, the CPV system's components are proprietary. Finding workable solutions has been difficult and the system is to date (July 2014) yet to be commissioned.

Planning permission was not required for either the turbines or the PV systems, since there was no zoning ordinance in place at the time. The increased interest in wind and solar power in the region has prompted the introduction of a zoning ordinance.

CEED's focus on public education has been a dominant factor in its success. Public acceptance of the center and technologies has been very high, even without public consultation. The center has been hugely successfully in attracting large numbers of visitors. Indeed, many people driving by stop to enquire about the center, drawn in by the wind turbines.

Bibliography

British Wind Energy Association. 2008. *Small Wind Turbine Performance and Safety Standard*. [Online]. Available at: www.renewableuk.com/en/utilities/document-summary. cfm?docid=97D39F8A-0760-45C5-8D9D6B8E7F2302FD (accessed 28 September 2012).

Carpman, N. 2011. *Turbulence Intensity in Complex Environments and its Influence on Small Wind Turbines*. Uppsala: Uppsala University. Available at: http://diva-portal.org/smash/get/ diva2:415655/FULLTEXT01 (24 October 2012).

Department for Business, Enterprise, and Regulatory Reform. 2008. *MIS 3003 Requirements for Contractors Undertaking the Supply, Design, Installation, Set to Work Commissioning and Handover of Micro and Small Wind Turbine Systems. Issue 1.2*. London: DECC. Available at: www.microgenerationcertification.org/mcs-standards/installer-standards (accessed 17 October 2012).

Department of Energy and Climate Change. 2012. Smart Meters. *DECC*. [Online]. Available at: www.decc.gov.uk/en/content/cms/tackling/smart_meters/smart_meters.aspx (accessed 20 September 2012).

Eiffert, P. and Kiss, G. 2000. *Building-Integrated Photovoltaics for Commercial and Institutional Structures: A Sourcebook for Architects and Engineers*. Golden, CO: National Renewable Energy Lab. Available at: www.nrel.gov/docs/fy00osti/25272.pdf (accessed 24 September 2009).

Encraft. 2009. *Warwick Wind Trials Final Report*. [Online]. Available at: www.warwickwindtrials.org. uk/2.html (accessed 20 September 2012).

Endecon Engineering with Regional Economic Research. 2001. *A Guide to Photovoltaic (PV) System Design and Installation*. Sacramento, CA: California Energy Commission. Available at: www.energy.ca.gov/reports/2001-09-04_500-01-020.PDF (accessed June 2014).

Energy Saving Trust. 2009. *Location, Location, Location: Domestic Small-scale Wind Field Trial Report*. London: Energy Saving Trust. Available at: www.energysavingtrust.org.uk/Publications2/ Generating-energy/Location-location-location-domestic-small-scale-wind-field-trial-report (accessed 28 September 2012).

European Commission Joint Research Centre. 2012. *Photovoltaic Geographical Information System – Interactive Maps*. [Online]. Available at: http://re.jrc.ec.europa.eu/pvgis/apps4/pvest.php# (accessed 10 September 2012).

Frauenhofer IWES (2010) *Small Wind Turbine Yield Estimator: Version 2.2010*. [Online]. Available at: http://windmonitor.iwes.fraunhofer.de/windwebdad/www_reisi_page_new.show_page?page_ nr=445&lang=en (accessed 31 October 2012).

IEC 61400:2013. *Wind Turbine Generator Systems*. Geneva: IEC (International Electrotechnical Commission).

Moharram, K. A., Abd-Elhady, M. S., Kandil, H. A. and El-Sherif, H. 2013. Enhancing the performance of photovoltaic panels by water cooling. *Ain Shams Engineering Journal*, 4 (4): 869–77. Available at: www.sciencedirect.com/science/article/pii/S2090447913000403 (accessed 18 July 2014).

National Renewable Energy Lab. 2012. *PVWatts*. [Online]. Available at: www.nrel.gov/rredc/ pvwatts/ (accessed 15 Sept 2012).

PelaFlow Consulting. 2008. *Windpower Program: Basic Concepts*. [Online]. Available at: www. wind-power-program.com/Downloads/basics.pdf (accessed 20 October 2012).

Renewable Energy Assurance Ltd. 2012. *Renewable Energy Consumer Code*. [Online]. Available at: www.realassurance.org.uk/scheme/consumer-code (accessed October 2012).

Renewable Energy Foundation. 2011. *Low Wind Power Output 2010*. [Online]. Available at: www. ref.org.uk/publications/217-low-wind-power-output-2010 (accessed 21 October 2012).

renewableUK. 2011. *Small Wind: Planning Guidance*. London: renewableUK. Available at: www. renewableuk.com/en/publications/guides.cfm/Smallwindplanningguidance (accessed 23 October 2012).

RenSMART. 2012. *NOABL Wind Map*. [Online]. Available at: www.rensmart.com/Weather/BERR (accessed 15 September 2012).

Sawin, J. 2012. Green growth still setting the pace. *Renewable Energy World*, 15(4): 29. Available at: www.renewableenergyworld.com/rea/news/article/2012/10/green-growth-still-setting-the-pace (accessed 18 October 2012).

Stankovic, S., Campbell, N. and Harries, A. 2009. *Urban Wind Energy*. 1st edition. London: Earthscan. Available at: www.scribd.com/doc/87705599/Urban-Wind-Energy-2009-BBS#page=1 (accessed 28 September 2012).

Sustainability Victoria. 2010. *Victorian Urban Wind Resource Assessment*. 2010 Revision. [Online]. Available at: www.sustainability.vic.gov.au/resources/documents/Victorian_Urban_Wind_Resource_Assessment_%282010_Revision%29.pdf (accessed 25 October 2012).

US Energy Information Administration. 2011. *Smart Grid Legislative and Regulatory Policies and Case Studies*. Washington DC: US Energy Information Administration. Available at: www.eia.gov/analysis/studies/electricity/ (accessed 27 June 2014).

Notes

1 Renewable power technologies cannot be used to meet the Passivhaus Primary Energy Target. Only technologies that directly displace fossil fuel consumption on-site (e.g. solar thermal) can contribute to reducing the total primary energy demand. Renewable power technologies only produce electricity, so they do not directly displace fossil fuel use. However, the Passive House Institute has developed new standards that build on the existing standard while recognizing contributions from RPTs. Further details on these standards can be found at www.passipedia.org/certification/passive_house_categories.

2 'Domestic' is a British term that refers to residential buildings.

10

Project and site management, contractual arrangements and quality assurance

JOHN MOREHEAD

10.1 Introduction

The performance of a Passivhaus building is not limited to measurement in PHPP and achieving all the facets of the certification process at desktop level. Where architectural construction projects are concerned, matters such as planning, form, ambience and spatial requirements must also take on board functional, technical, social, environmental and aesthetic considerations.

The application of PHPP (Chapter 1) naturally engenders a design and review discipline which provides a framework upon which the other attributes of a project can also be structured. Indeed the PHPP file (including all the drawings, spreadsheets, supporting calculations and analyses as well as the product literature) creates a useful project backbone.

Though early Passivhaus projects clearly had building physics as their primary focus, recently completed projects have confirmed that other attributes leading to the delivery of architectural excellence are not compromised in any way through the achievement of Passivhaus certification. The demands for Passivhaus quality components and increasing alignment of EU building codes with Passivhaus levels of energy performance have instigated a renaissance in building construction methods and expectations. Improved levels of Passivhaus training of design professionals and trades have begun to inject the knowledge required for all stakeholders to be informed as to what is required for the delivery of these projects. Wider factors to be considered when procuring components are sustainability and embodied energy (Chapter 3), durability, ease of maintenance and fitness for purpose in the local environment.

10.2 Common approaches to delivering Passivhaus in practice

10.2.1 'Passivise' – reconfiguring existing schemes to meet the Passivhaus standard

The term to 'passivise' is a neologism used to describe the situation where a previously designed project is to be modified or re-engineered and where Passivhaus principles are post-applied with the aspiration of achieving Passivhaus certification levels of performance and quality. This can be applied to a new project that has achieved planning permission or indeed an existing property which is to be renovated or extended.

The design would be reviewed by the Passivhaus consultant/designer using PHPP and optimised to endeavour to achieve Passivhaus levels of performance. If the building has not been designed with the core principles of Passivhaus design in mind, the costs incurred as a result of over-specifying the performance of key components to attain Passivhaus levels can be prohibitive or impractical, and have a detrimental effect on the functional and aesthetic features of the building.

The input of a contractor during the review phase can have a significant impact on finding appropriate and cost effective construction methods to achieve the Passivhaus criteria.

10.2.2 Passivhaus principles

The project is designed with Passivhaus principles in mind, but the technical aspects of the project need to be further developed. This method is applicable to new-build projects.

This is not an uncommon practice and gives some level of flexibility in the construction options open to the client at a later stage. It can be ideal for two-stage tendering where the architect's design indicates the intent, and overall performance levels of key elements are determined in the PHPP for preliminary calculation, with default levels for airtightness and thermal bridging assumed. Certain fallback systems are put in place to mitigate the risk of non-performance due to incomplete design analysis of the project.

The requirements are further assessed by a Passivhaus-trained contractor, who takes on the role of designing the components and structure to achieve Passivhaus standards.

10.2.3 Fully certified Passivhaus/EnerPHit

The project has taken on board Passivhaus principles from the outset and a fully populated PHPP is available reflecting the project design. The construction method is determined based on the developed design, Passivhaus components are specified and all thermal bridging and ventilation requirements are fully detailed. The functional and aesthetic characteristics of the building are fully developed throughout the design stage and achieving performance targets will not significantly amend early design decisions. The architect, with the assistance of an experienced Certified Passivhaus designer/consultant (CEPHD/CEPHC), will have integrated the requirements for achieving Passivhaus excellence from the outset. This project is expected to achieve Passivhaus or EnerPHit certification from the outset.

10.3 Contracts and procurement

Once a project charter has been issued, to initiate the project, many facets of the project need to be identified and determined in order for it to be managed effectively. Passivhaus is rapidly being applied to a very broad sector of construction projects which are being implemented by a variety of client bodies. A Passivhaus project charter is usually issued by a project initiator or sponsor who can be any of the following: an individual, an enterprise, a government agency, a company, a developer or a combination of these. The mere fact that the project charter calls for Passivhaus performance levels sets a performance benchmark requirement with respect to energy performance, comfort levels and quality assurance which has not previously been demanded in the construction industry.

10.3.1 Project charter (or strategic brief)

The project charter (or strategic brief) is a document that sets out the project's scope, constraints and objectives. The charter comes about as a result of external stimuli or needs, and developing the charter in simple terms demands that the clients' requirements and, in Passivhaus projects, their performance requirements are clearly stated. This is essentially the high-level document that sets the deliverables and drives the framework for the delivery of the project.

In a Passivhaus project, the charter will typically address:

- project/building functional requirements;
- certification requirements;
- statutory/regulatory requirements;
- design team structure, organisation and responsibilities;
- summary milestone schedule/programme;
- performance-related targets and cost-benefit assumptions;
- project budget constraints.

The charter is a fluid document in that it is reviewed, updated and continually referred to in order to validate project decisions as they arise. As with all structures applied to the management of projects, there are inputs, tools, techniques and outputs.

The initial input will be defined in the contract upon which the architect, the Passivhaus design consultant and/or project manager are initially engaged. The form of agreement/conditions of appointment should be appropriate to the type of consultancy being provided and should address roles, responsibilities, design, liability and insurances, etc.

Traditionally, once the project charter was issued, the design team leader would develop the brief for the project and oversee the engagement of the appropriate design team consultants.

It is critical that due diligence at charter stage will have confirmed the suitability of the site from a Passivhaus perspective, so that these performance levels can be realistically achieved.

10.3.2 Project scope (or project brief)

The project scope statement (or project brief) is fundamentally the 'definition of the project' – defining what the project will deliver.

The preliminary scope statement addresses not only the project objectives, accommodation requirements and performance levels but also the specification requirements for products and materials, project extents, insurance requirements, risks, milestones, budget estimates and the project organisation structure.

The project scope is usually developed once the project team have analysed the charter and the contributing demands and influences set down by the client. Once the project scope is agreed, the deliverables and project objectives are stated.

10.3.3 Contracts and appointments

The procurement method for delivering a Passivhaus project is typically determined at project charter stage. The aspirations of the client will determine which aspects of the project's design will be prioritised and dictate the performance levels anticipated. Some projects may adopt the Passivhaus approach without demanding full compliance or certification. There may be aesthetic, functional or planning requirements that compromise the project's ability to achieve Passivhaus certification, despite Passivhaus principles being followed.

Where the level of individual design that is traditionally provided by an architect may not be required, the option to go direct to a design and build contractor for a standard design package may be appropriate. The project may involve the renovation or extension of an existing building to EnerPHit requirements (Chapter 12), sometimes requiring the input of specialist skill sets, particularly where works to protected or historic structures are an issue.

The appropriate form of building contract will be decided by the architect or contract administrator; however, the precise selection of the appropriate forms of contract documentation are outside the scope of this book. It is imperative that a fully informed selection process is applied when choosing the appropriate contract. Contracts can be limited to drawing and specification or drawing specification and bill of quantities, or they can be simply performance based where the drawing and performance targets are identified. In Passivhaus projects, the PHPP building model is usually identified in the contract.

10.3.4 Traditional approach

Whether the architect for the project is a Passivhaus designer or an external Passivhaus consultant is appointed, the fundamental deliverables required by the Passivhaus approach will influence the delivery methods available to the project at a very early stage.

In this form of procurement, the employer will have the scheme developed to an advanced stage before appointing a contractor. The contractor's responsibilities are limited to the construction of the project and not the design. Being in a position to nominate, the contract administrator has better control of some of the key components and their integration from an early stage.

It is important that those with design responsibilities, such as the MVHR installer, have a collateral warranty with the client. As the PHPP collation will require significant input in relation to the mechanical installations, having the suppliers or installers on board at an early design stage can be beneficial.

The design, specification and either Schedules of Work or Bills of Quantities are issued to a selection of individual contracting firms for tendering. The supply of specific components or services can be controlled and the coordination of the project is the responsibility of the appointed contractor.

This type of tendering is well suited to traditional building methods but not always appropriate for Passivhaus projects. Although nominating the various suppliers and subcontractors for Passivhaus components may facilitate this process, the overall coordination and ability to control quality may be outside the competence of many conventional contractors, who may be unfamiliar with the exemplary levels of thermal bridge control and airtightness that are demanded in Passivhaus projects.

Conversely, upskilling the traditional contractor has benefits as there are many aspects of a project's delivery that Passivhaus detailing may not necessarily address. The input of an experienced traditional contractor is generally invaluable. There is little point in having a Passivhaus project that does not stand up to the ravages of time due to a contractor's construction inexperience. Many traditional methods have been tried and tested and have been proven to withstand the

10.1
Traditional contract structure

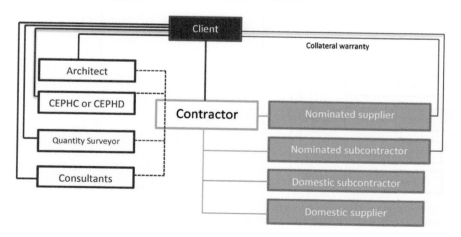

demands of local climate and environments. It is important that these context-specific design issues are not overlooked when detailing and selecting specialist components and materials.

In the traditional contract approach, it is expected that some contributors to the construction of the project may not be familiar with Passivhaus tools or techniques. Passivhaus construction inductions and 'toolbox talks' should be regularly provided by the Passivhaus consultant/designer throughout the project.

10.3.5 Design and build

This is a contractual framework where the contractor is responsible for the complete design and construction of the project based on the project charter.

During the late 1990s, a demand for higher levels of energy efficiency and rapid delivery led many away from the traditional form of project delivery. Variants on the design and build approach were offered. It was not unusual for an architect to secure planning permission for a design following which the client would go direct to a design and build contractor for 'turnkey' delivery.

It is not uncommon for the transition from the outline planning drawings to the construction set, upon which the design and build price is agreed, to lead to significant disappointment and dispute, particularly if the deliverables are not fully or adequately described. The transition from scheme design to detailed design is a critical phase in any project, and it may be compromised where there is a lack of continuity in the design development.

Some disadvantages:

- Limited opportunity for changes in client requirements;
- Limited choice available for components;
- Suppliers and components at contractor's discretion;

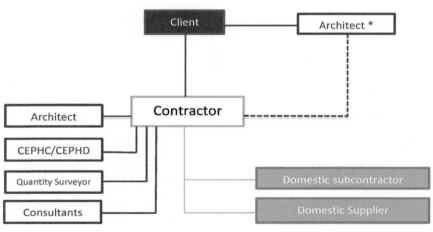

10.2
Design and build contract structure

* an additional architect/architectural advisor who may be retained by the client to protect their interests once the project has been tendered to the main contractor.

- Contract defining scope and quality can be open to interpretation;
- Architect acting for contractor, not client.

The architect will have the contractor's rather than the client's interests in mind when making design decisions.

However, the design and build approach also has advantages:

- Speed of delivery;
- Single point of contact and responsibility for design and construction;
- Reduction in potential for claims;
- Build-ability;
- Cost certainty.

Notably, through the use of modern off-site manufacturing techniques, many design and build projects can deliver significant improvements in quality compared to what can be achieved on-site. Furthermore, contractors may be selected based on their financial standing, design capability, experience with Passivhaus and, finally, their management structure. The client will need to be aware that Passivhaus-certified products are not regionally specific and other performance characteristics and requirements must be identified. Warranties, agrément certificates, product certification and conformity with national and international standard requirements should all be identified. The company may have a defined quality control procedure in place (e.g. ISO 9001:2008 certification) as well as clearly defined procurement, health and safety, and environmental management policies.

10.3.6 Traditional-hybrid

Design and build projects can also be limited to the delivery of key elements such as walls and roofs, where the design and build contractor effectively manufactures the components based on a standardised building process, but to the specific project requirements. The project is started and completed by a general contractor and the specialist components would be supplied by a nominated supplier or subcontractor. This is common in Passivhaus projects where an insulated slab may be constructed by a general contractor, a high-performance building envelope may be manufactured and assembled by a specialised contractor, and the fit-out may be finalised by the general contractor. The traditional form of procurement can be used but with significant emphasis on nominated elements of the contract. At times, the nominated subcontract elements can far outweigh the main contractor elements in monetary value. It is therefore critical that the responsibility for the design of these elements is structured robustly with collateral warranty and insurance provisions in place.

There are pitfalls where responsibilities in the delivery of key elements can be compromised when both design and construction services are provided by subcontractor agreements. For example, the location of all services required at slab level needs to be fully determined and coordinated prior to the ground

10.3
Example traditional-hybrid
divisions of responsibility

floor slab being poured. The responsibility for this coordination will generally rest with the slab designer. However, the information informing the location of the various pop-up waste positions, edge detailing and service duct requirements, etc. may fall under the remit of a nominated subcontractor. It is advisable that each sequential trade is requested to accept the previous work packages as being compliant prior to proceeding if the client is to be protected from complex and protracted disputes.

A Passivhaus project is by its nature front-loaded in respect of the timing of which design and validation stages are considered. Other standards do not necessarily require such rigorous analysis or detailed design in so far as thermal performance and environmental standards are concerned. It is this front-loading and quality assurance that has attracted many professionals to adopt it as a voluntary standard. It is particularly critical in a Passivhaus project, for instance, that the responsibility for maintaining airtightness of the envelope is clearly defined and regularly monitored. The levels of airtightness are over eight times those required under building regulations in Ireland (Department of the Environment, Community and Local Government, 2011: paragraph 1.4.5.2) and five times those presently demanded in the UK Building Regulations Part L (HM Government, 2013). The level of quality demanded in Passivhaus projects must not be underestimated, and key targets and milestones for their achievement should be identified and agreed before works commence.

The scope of the external envelope first fix should facilitate complete testing of the envelope once complete, prior to fit-out works commencing. The competence and certification of the airtightness tester should be agreed and must in any case meet BS EN 13829:2001 and national requirements.

Rigorous checking during the project will maintain quality levels and reduce the risk of compliance failure.

10.3.7 Collateral warranties

Collateral warranties effectively create a direct contractual relationship between parties which may not otherwise exist under the main form of contract. A Passivhaus designer owes a duty of care not only to the original client but also to a subsequent occupier of the building. A subsequent owner or occupier, due to privity of contract rules, may have no recourse for liabilities due to defective design without a collateral warranty being in place. Collateral warranties are regularly provided on design and build projects for both the main contract and any subcontracts where responsibility for design is identified. It is critical that the nature of the collateral warranty requirements is identified in the procurement documentation.

10.3.8 Partnering contracts

Partnering is applied either in a project situation known as project partnering or in a long-term relationship known as strategic partnering. Negotiation rather than competitive tendering is the key to partnering contracts. One of the primary benefits is that integration of the design process with the construction process means that innovative and practical alternatives can be incorporated into the building more easily. This is particularly useful in Passivhaus projects where innovative solutions are often required.
Advantages:

- A reduction in numbers of disputes;
- Benefit of early supply chain involvement;
- Open book and a win/win culture;
- Integration of design and construction process;
- Continuation of partnering over multiple projects yields even more benefits.

Disadvantages:

- The approach can be abused by one of the parties;
- The approach requires more client resource to compensate for less competition;
- To be effective, partnering needs to be practised over a number of projects;
- The initial development costs can be prohibitive for one-off projects;
- The approach requires excellent project management and communication between all parties.

10.4 Programming and working with PHPP

10.4.1 Importance of preparing a work breakdown structure (WBS)

The PMBOK® (PMI, 2004: 379) describes the WBS as 'a deliverable-oriented hierarchical decomposition of the work to be executed by the team'. Under this approach, the top levels in a construction project will define the final deliverable.

In Passivhaus projects, it is particularly useful to be able to identify organisational and resourcing issues and the impact they can have on achieving airtight and vapour control strategies. Unique to Passivhaus, the PHPP would be considered a top-level work item which is consistently modified and updated throughout a project.

10.4
Example of breakdown structure, showing top-level items

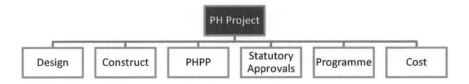

The work breakdown deliverable in, say, the services area will identify how first fix elements cannot be installed until airtight membranes are in place and how work packages can require defined skill sets to complete. The WBS procedure can also be useful in preparing a project risk register.

10.4.2 Using PHPP to validate initial designs

As previously indicated, with any project, a thorough understanding of the site, solar access, topography, context, culture, access and servicing availability will support the key decisions made at concept stage by the designer.

Once initial designs are at scheme design level, meeting the requirements of the project charter and incorporating the defined objectives of the project scope, it is time to put the design through the rigours of PHPP. The objectives of the initial PHPP study are to:

- Rely on default or basic, informed values initially to get a preliminary result.
- Identify the core characteristics of the project model at an early stage. An experienced designer will be able to achieve Passivhaus levels of performance without too much difficulty at scheme design stage, although certain projects may be more problematic in this respect.

Once the principal wall types, floor constructions and roof slabs are determined, they are input in to PHPP as accurately as possible. It is important that the nomenclature used will readily assist in identifying individual entries and their corresponding locations in the drawings. The PHPP file should be filed together with the relevant scheme design drawings and details. It is prudent to add a revision tracking sheet to the PHPP file from an early stage so that the PHPP can be rolled back during the design evolution.

A project output template should be implemented, if not already in place. This template will determine layer and labelling conventions for maintaining simple data extraction from the CAD system for outputting to PHPP later. It is critical, for example, that window and wall references on drawings and in the PHPP correlate. It is also critical that wall areas and levels have an inherent logic for all project stakeholders to understand. Any deviations in construction or window specification can be quickly tracked and updated in PHPP so that the PHPP is always current. Regardless of how small or apparently insignificant a change to the model may be, adjust the PHPP file and, most importantly, review the results of any decisions. The nature of this process lends itself to seamless integration with the various BIM tools employed at this time and which will soon be commonplace in every design office.

As data is confirmed, more refined PHPP results can be relied upon and the defaults revised and adjusted. It is important to start out with the thermal envelope, including an indication of anticipated U-values and window performance specification.

Figure 10.5 indicates the high-level work areas that need to be addressed at the initial stage to establish an indicative performance of the building in PHPP. Each work item is then further expanded upon as the project progresses. Cooling,

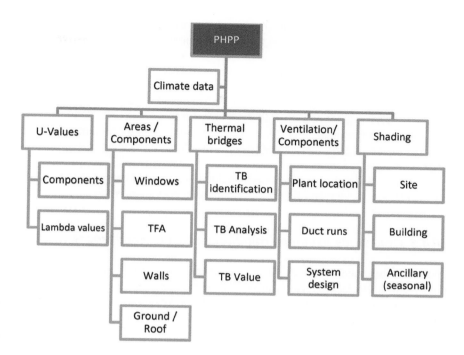

10.5
Hierarchical workflow
mapping of initial PHPP inputs

Heating, Domestic hot water, Electrical use and Heat generation sources are subsequently addressed as the design is developed.

Take an initial high-level approach to the ventilation system specification but make the effort to accurately determine the overall building volume in accordance with BS EN 13829:2001[1] and BRE guidance (McLeod *et al.*, 2014). It is strongly recommended to retain a base airtightness level of $0.6 h^{-1}$ (@ n_{50}) and select a MVHR of reasonable performance. It is not unusual to achieve ≤ 10 W/m² or ≤ 15 kWh/m².yr at first pass. If overheating is significant, adjustments to glazing ratios and solar shading can reduce this, but watch the specific heat demand in particular as it may increase significantly.

Continue to adjust the key elements until the project is performing within reasonable parameters. Ensure that revisions and modifications to the design are monitored and logged and that the influence each parameter change has on the results is considered and understood before proceeding. During this phase, the Passivhaus consultant or designer is applying their knowledge intuitively to fine-tune the PHPP model, assisted by energy balance (for example, Chapter 12) graphs and verification outputs.

Once adjustments to opaque elements, shading and window specifications are complete and the fundamental decisions regarding airtight layers and construction methods and perimeter detailing are finalised, the project can be fully assessed at a detailed performance level.

At this point, it is recommended that a cost appraisal is carried out to accurately reflect the performance specification levels. The client may then be presented with a scheme which will comply with Passivhaus performance levels and the project budget. It may be useful to prepare some cost engineering analysis at this stage showing the cost-benefits of some of the decisions made, or indeed the impacts of various cost savings the client may wish to achieve. As previously discussed, some cost savings can have a detrimental effect on important performance issues other than those directly addressed in the Passivhaus assessment. With the approval of the client, the project can then be lodged for planning permission with confidence at this stage.

A word of caution: there is no point in getting statutory approvals for a project outside budget. Passivhaus projects do not respond well to ad hoc value engineering post design.

By this stage, the client will have decided whether the project is to proceed on a traditional, design and build, or partnering procurement process.

10.4.3 Case study example: traditional procurement process

The approved scheme needs to be developed to a larger scale and level of detail. Critical decisions relating to set-out points, etc. should be determined at this stage to ensure accuracy is retained and the various consultants/designers can work from a standard project template. If not already done, an accurate site survey must be procured at this stage.

The design of wet rooms and the location of all waste services and slab penetrations need to be determined to facilitate the slab design. The upper floor loadings and basic information will also be required for the slab design to be progressed. Ground conditions (including the possibility of contaminants and moisture) will have informed the slab insulation selection.

With the project template and slab details determined, the design of the upper floors may now commence. Thermal bridge analysis is critical. The impact and benefit of a negative thermal bridge detail over a significant length can reduce costs appreciably (Chapter 3).

The location of the MVHR and principles for distribution of ductwork should have been determined in the previous phase. At this point, the detailing of services penetrations, the sizing and insulation requirements of ducting (see Chapter 8) and the specification of any supplementary heating system is required. The specification and detailing of any renewable systems (see Chapter 9) and the integration of their components together with all service routes through the building complete the analysis. It is prudent to design in some spare pop-ups which can be effectively plugged and thermally isolated if found to be unnecessary.

The final specification and details must all be included in the procurement documents to avoid project delays, cost increases and the risk of failing to achieve Passivhaus certification.

10.4.4 Heading to site

Before a foot is set on-site, it is incumbent on the Passivhaus designer/consultant to fully brief the contractor in respect of the holistic approach that has been taken to achieve the Passivhaus performance criteria. For instance, the deciduous trees on the site may have had a significant effect on solar shading assumptions, etc. The contractor must understand that any loss or damage to a particular tree or shading device could have a significant impact on the project's built performance and ability to achieve certification.

10.4.5 Pitfalls for the inexperienced contractor and specifier

The level of coordination, expectations and demands on the delivery of quality and documentation control may be outside the comfort zone of many conventional contractors. The integration of Passivhaus air-handling and distribution systems can catch out the unsuspecting contractor. The size and weight of triple-glazed window systems and/or fully insulated front doors require careful handling and installation. The avoidance of thermal bridges and the level of design detailing too can overwhelm. It is important, therefore, that the appropriate construction team is put in place from the outset. There are many training options open to the trades involved in the delivery of Passivhaus envelopes and services, providing not only technical advice but hands-on opportunities to improve the skills of a contractor.

The selection of products and components must not be based purely on manufacturers' performance claims. Check the fine print and demand to see the Conformité Européenne (CE) test certification in accordance with the relevant norm and Passivhaus guidelines. If in any doubt, avoid the product, regardless of the manufacturer's claims. The durability in use of certain components is not necessarily tested. Components must also meet all the relevant building codes and ISO/EN standards and design-specific performances relevant to the context and location; for example, salt-resistant ironmongery should be specified in coastal locations.

Passivhaus certification is no guarantee that the component will achieve all levels of performance the project or location may demand. It is not uncommon to find window systems which claim to have exemplary thermal performance, yet leak air at critical positions such as hinges or indeed locking escutcheons to such an extent that they can compromise the overall airtightness of the thermal envelope (Chapter 3). Others may meet all of these criteria yet their long-term durability in use may be compromised by an overemphasis placed on achieving thermal excellence. A distressed or deformed component will not provide the requisite performance over time.

The construction of sample key details demonstrating the integration of components should always be brought forward or front-loaded in a Passivhaus project. The designer and contractor should agree the principles, source the products, subcontractors, etc. in order to assess the build-ability of the detail. Once a successful sample mock-up has been fabricated, the project can proceed efficiently. It is not unusual, where exemplary standards are expected, to ensure that full-size mock-ups of key details are signed off before the project is fully rolled out. This approach also facilitates the induction of follow-on trades to the peculiarities of building these types of structures and, more importantly, to the peculiarities of this building!

10.4.6 Slab-level services

Where a ground-bearing slab is used, any components that require servicing and waste connections need to be identified prior to the slab being poured. Insulating at slab penetrations is a relatively new concept to those new to Passivhaus levels of construction, and it needs to be articulated effectively during the detailed design and certainly well before the construction phases. Practical issues such as site suitability can have a significant impact on the ease with which Passivhaus can be delivered. The lambda value (λ) of the ground can have a significant impact on the detailed design of the load-bearing slab and its thermal performance. A slab construction on clay or silt will have far better thermal performance than that on rock. Site investigation is critical at the early design stage.

MVHR, plant rooms, wet rooms, kitchens, etc. all need to be designed to at least layout stage to ensure the appropriate levels of services are installed. Opening up a slab to provide a service at a later stage is rarely successful and is extremely costly. For this reason, it is worthwhile considering tile layouts before the pop-up drawing is completed! A common mistake is to combine service risers and have difficulty in sealing them, or to position service risers too close to walls, thereby preventing airtight or radon protection strategies from being efficiently implemented.

A control mechanism must be put in place to ensure that all parties involved in the project sign off the slab service layout/pop-up drawing before the works commence. It is the discipline set down at the start of the project that will ensure it is successful. It can be useful to include a couple of spare pop-ups near key service areas for pulling unforeseen services later – if not used, they can be plugged and will not compromise the insulation/moisture control of the building.

The location of the principle services and components, such as MVHR units, distribution ductwork and any solar thermal cylinders or boiler systems, should be fully agreed to ensure that all condensation drains and other service component connections are facilitated. To enable the comprehensive design review necessary to ensure that these matters are identified in time, it is advised that all subcontractors are appointed prior to sign-off of the slab service layout drawings.

10.4.7 Supply of site services

The location of primary supplies and wastes from the building must be determined and agreed. The placement of utility metering units should be discussed with the providers. In some jurisdictions, the metering cupboards must be located in an external wall, which can compromise thermal envelopes and airtight strategies if not resolved and agreed before production drawings are issued.

10.5 Airtight testing strategy

When the contractor provides a programme, request that the dates for airtight testing are indicated so you can attend. It is prudent to demand a minimum of three tests, carried out in full to meet the BS EN 13829:2001/Passivhaus requirements and to ensure that the integrity of the airtight layer is not compromised. Ensure that both depressurisation and pressurisation tests are also executed at first fix and second fix stages. It is always useful to have additional diagnostic equipment such as thermal anemometers and a certified infrared thermographer available at the time of the tests so that any anomalies can be highlighted, identified and, if necessary, investigated. A careful watch on the weather forecast can decide the most suitable condition for the thermographer to operate in. Always have the V_{n50} air test volume fully calculated before the test day so an anomaly can be identified during and not after the test.[2] Ensure the window subcontractor is on-site during the test and label and record any air leakage ($m^3/m.s$) at the window and door seals.

A pattern usually emerges and common faults can be rectified during the first air test day. As the project proceeds and walls close up, faults become increasingly difficult to identify and rectify.

If an air leak is measured but not readily found, it can be useful to heat up or cool down the building fabric to highlight any anomalies using thermal imaging, particularly in multilayer constructions. Positive and negative test results can yield significantly different results. Inward opening windows and tapes applied to inner linings can yield far better results in a pressurisation test compared to a depressurisation test. Smoke tests are seldom very useful in multilayer components.

The selection of building methods and systems can have a significant impact on the overall programme and the ability to sequence the construction of the project efficiently. Consideration must be given to the fact that traditional wet-build systems have a significant water content during construction which can delay drying out the works and, in extreme conditions, can cause mould growth before the project is commissioned and MVHR systems are activated. A drying out strategy should be agreed with the contractor and integrated into the overall programme.

10.6
Project GANTT chart showing three scheduled air tests

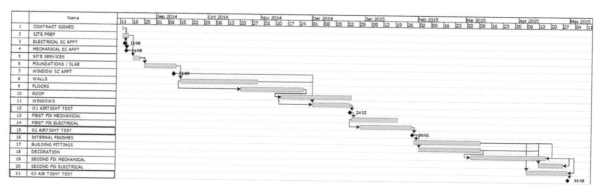

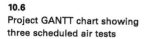

10.6 PHPP review during construction

Always update the PHPP file when finalising or adjusting construction details with the main contractor and subcontractors. Doing so can also mean that some surprises relating to the building's performance can be avoided, and some cost savings may be yielded.

As details are finalised and construction commences, continually update any thermal bridge calculations and moisture and condensation risk studies until that work element is signed off and certified as complete. It is useful to monitor key verification outputs such as the specific annual heat demand and specific heat load as the PHPP file is updated based on both the actual construction and interim air permeability test results.

Any change affecting the defined approach to airtight strategies during construction should be treated with extreme caution. It would not be uncommon for a hasty decision on a busy site to overlook a well-defined strategy adopted within the design. Always carry out transient hygrothermal simulations on any new construction assembly in accordance with BS EN 15026:2007 to ensure that long-term risks of interstitial condensation are mitigated (see Chapter 5).

A flawed strategy will compromise any ability to achieve an airtight building, and a defined target will not protect the client from subsequent claims by a contractor if the target could not be reasonably achieved as designed. The risk of failing to achieve Passivhaus certification and what that could do to the reputation of all concerned must not be underestimated.

10.7 Implications of contractor employment methods

The successful delivery of the Passivhaus standard can be influenced by requiring the tenderer to have fully certified personnel with the relevant Passivhaus Tradesperson training on-site. Although there may be resistance to this requirement with some contractors, the resistance is often due to the contractor not having the conviction that proper training can influence the delivery of excellence on-site.

Always consider the facilitation of project-specific training. This is where project-specific details are used as the basis for training on-site and contractors can use the site to upskill their staff. This can also empower the trainee with an understanding for and enthusiasm towards delivering excellence. Thermography and airtight testing will soon confirm and reward their attention to detail and, on achieving success, be a great source of pride. Airtight construction training on-site by trained personnel can usually be arranged through airtightness product suppliers. It is real-world training, with real detailing challenges that can be fully discussed, with solutions found and knowledge shared.

The demands for exacting standards of construction rely on careful workmanship detailing, and any failure to operate at these standards can lead to difficulties and slippage between the design intent and 'as-built' performance.

Passivhaus projects are performance-driven projects. The key performance criteria that must be met have already been discussed in earlier chapters.

Should these targets be missed due to non-compliance with the project demands, trouble will ensue. What can initially be frustration can soon lead to disappointment, argument and even litigation. It is critical, therefore, that the Passivhaus consultant/designer has mitigated the risks of failure in their design and specification. It is critical that once construction starts, control measures are fully implemented to identify any failure as soon as it may occur. Apart from reducing the likelihood of litigation, a problem caught early can be rectified far more effectively than one caught late.

Regular inspection and sign off at completion of each critical stage is important to ensure this level of quality control can be methodically provided.

Ensure that the appropriate collateral warrants are in place to protect the client from defects in design. Specific indemnification will be required in relation to design defects and copies of the relevant professional indemnifications should be presented.

Where post-occupancy monitoring is required, ensure that the appropriate level of data logging is integrated into the overall design and is provided within the scope of the contract. This can assist with fault-finding and seasonal commissioning during the first year of occupancy.

10.8 Site management

10.8.1 A single point of contact

It is imperative that a site is managed effectively. On domestic projects, the site foreman/contracts manager should take on the role of site management and be the primary point of contact with the Passivhaus designer/consultant. The contracts manager is responsible for coordinating the works and ensuring that the project is executed not only with the quality demands met but also in a timely and safe manner.

The designer who has considered the build-ability of the project from the outset will gain the respect of all those involved. It is the contractor who must ensure that the necessary resources are available and properly coordinated. The use of specialist components such as triple-glazed window systems will require the adoption of appropriate lifting and installation procedures.

10.8.2 Curtailing deviation

From the pre-contract meeting to the appointment of individual subcontractors, the importance of adhering to specified products, components and methods of assembly must be addressed. The preparation of an induction presentation identifying the deliverables and explaining the reasoning behind the performance requirements will empower the contracts manager with an understanding of the project which can be disseminated to others.

The consequences of deviation should be relayed to all operatives. The variation in energy performances of different materials, systems and products and the necessity to have certified test data from a recognised certification body should be conveyed.

The critical nature of the airtight layer already identified graphically on drawings (Chapter 3) must be relayed again and again to all concerned. The necessity of interim testing to verify that this layer is not compromised must be fully understood. Certification of payments should be linked to the independent air test achieving the target performance levels demanded. This link must not be seen as a penalty; it is simply a verification of conformity.

10.8.3 The importance of the airtight envelope

Maintaining the airtight layer integrity throughout the project is critical in Passivhaus. A strict site induction system must be put in place from the outset so that all those involved in the delivery of the project on-site are fully aware of how critical it is not to compromise the airtight layer. An airtightness champion should be nominated as soon as the project is in the build phase. The airtightness champion should be someone who is a member of the contractor's team and will be on-site throughout the build, but not the site foreman/contracts manager as they will be too preoccupied to undertake this role. The airtightness champion is the CEPHD's 'eyes' on the site and must carefully explain the airtightness protocol to all trades and subcontractors working on-site.

Tender documents need to be extremely clear as to the performance levels expected on the project. They also need to identify the nature and extent of airtight membranes, tapes, collars, and gaskets, etc. Typically, a system is specified and the contractor may be facilitated where appropriate to offer an equal or approved variant. The key here is that the building standards and specifications are clearly identified and adhered to.

A numerical n_{50} value of 0.6 ac/h is meaningless to most subcontractors. Physical comparisons between the representative dimension of the equivalent hole area in the first air leakage test to that of a project merely making legislative air permeability requirements can be a useful visualisation tool, readily understood by all. The impact of this figure on the calculation of the PHPP outputs should be identified and marked up on the wall of the room used as the site office.

The effect of liquid water or vapour permeating a multilayer component and the resultant condensation risks should be similarly explained. Protection of materials and components and maintenance of a tidy and dust-free site will help to instil the *modus operandi* necessary for the achievement of the Passivhaus quality standards. When these targets are achieved they are to be celebrated in order to incentivise continued good practice.

10.8.4 Certificates, test records and photographic evidence

At each site meeting, certificates, photographic evidence and test data verifying compliance with the project requirements should be carefully collated and identified. These records should be kept both on-site and in duplicate by the Passivhaus designer in their Passivhaus compliance file. On larger projects, it may be helpful to place a small white board in the field of view of each photograph. Important reference details should be noted on this whiteboard including the building number, the room code and the date of key issues for future reference. Any variations affecting the PHPP or Passivhaus compliance should be recorded and retained separate from the main contract file.

10.8.5 Quality of workmanship

The Passivhaus approach to construction necessitates rigorous standards focused upon the thermal and comfort performance of buildings. These demands require careful assembly and considered construction methods, which soon raise the standard on any construction project.

10.8.6 Cleanliness

A clean site is inherently a safer site. A clean site also reflects a certain approach to quality. An orderly site will also ensure components are properly stored and protected.

Protection of mechanical ventilation ductwork and maintaining hygiene levels throughout the construction process is imperative to the successful installation and commissioning of the MVHR system (see Chapter 8).

Protection of seals and windows and the installation of temporary thresholds or access requirements will help prevent damage and compromise of these airtight components.

The management of dust is critical. No tape, adhesive or seal will perform well in a dusty environment. A dusty environment is also not a safe place to work. Ensure that sufficient cleaning materials, including a reliable industrial vacuum cleaner, are stored on-site.

10.8.7 Air Quality – on-site

Apart from dust, an airtight Passivhaus building under construction must have good air quality maintained within it. The monitoring of humidity levels and maintenance of adequate air changes must be considered at all phases of the project. Drying out requires low humidity levels, and low humidity requires air changes. Make sure that a policy is put in place to address these issues with additional procedures put in place after wet trade procedures such as floor screeding or plastering. Any Mechanical ventilation system must be hygienically protected at all stages of the project (see Chapter 8) and must not be commissioned or utilised until all internal construction work is complete.

10.9 Final handover

Practical completion in contractual terms is generally the point in time when the building project is fit for handover and discharging responsibility to the client. It is critical that the building is functional and safe and that the performance targets and contractual arrangements have been honoured before a client takes over a building. There are practical issues that need addressing, including the formal acceptance of insurance liability for the project by the client. All commissioning certificates, data sheets, maintenance and certification information for all of the plant and components should be retained in the PHPP files.

All collateral agreements relating to the design of the project must be presented and retained since, in most cases, the design data will have been relied upon in the preparation of the PHPP file.

10.9.1 Client induction

Any client who has requested a Passivhaus project is likely to be a well-informed client. However, the client is not always the occupier. An induction meeting should focus on any heat-generating appliances (e.g. heat pumps, geothermal systems, solar systems) with particular emphasis on any safety monitoring issues and maintenance requirements. Given the importance of air quality, the integration of practical humidity adjustment measures (e.g. ventilation rate reduction or plant watering techniques) can lead to a smooth transition and early occupier satisfaction. Whenever possible, the retention of data logging and monitoring units to see out the final commissioning and bedding-in phase is extremely beneficial. Simple matters like maintaining clean windows can be overlooked by the new occupants should the role of the window as the primary heat source not be fully understood.

10.9.2 Regulatory compliance in addition to Passivhaus

The achievement of Passivhaus certification does not obviate the client from the requirement to meet with local building regulatory requirements. Early engagement with the local authority will assist with finding a sensible workaround to any regulatory inconsistencies in so far as energy performance of buildings legislation is concerned.

10.9.3 Drawing updates and as-built documentation

The final product is the construction. The PHPP folder should, therefore, reflect the final built project. It should contain all validations, supporting documentation, as-built drawings, design data and the completed 'as-built' PHPP file.

10.10 Passivhaus certification requirements

To achieve certification, it is critical that a coordinated document control system is applied to the project. The following schedule provides an overview of typical Passivhaus certification evidence required. Since these requirements may vary between countries and certifying bodies, it is strongly recommended that the requirements are agreed with the relevant local Passivhaus certification body.

Complete PHPP file	Current version
Drawings describing project	Site plan 1:200/500 showing orientation and shading features
	Supporting photographs showing environment, horizon, etc.
Design drawings	Annotated drawings 1:100/50 with label references to PHPP inputs
	Identification of thermal envelope 1:100/20
	Identification of airtight layer 1:100/20
	Dimensioned window and door openings 1:100
	Position and linear dimensions of thermal bridges 1:100
Construction details	All junctions of thermal envelope identified on plans and referenced as details at scale 1:5
	All variations in envelope geometries, connections and penetrations
	Material conductivities (BS EN ISO 10456:2007), vapour diffusion values (BS EN 12572-1) and supporting test certificates and by hygrothermal assessments
Ventilation layout	1:50 layout with location of all plant, duct runs and sizes, attenuators, valves/diffusers, transfer grilles and insulation. All duct runs to be clearly identified, labelled and dimensioned with insulation thickness and specifications. Filter placement and grade, MVHR location and controls. External intake and exhaust locations between heat exchanger and thermal envelope, including vapour-tight detailing.
Heating/Cooling and hot water systems	Sketch layouts at 1:50 describing mechanical systems employed for plumbing (including hot water systems), heating, and cooling. Include storage systems and integrated solar hot water systems, circulation pumps and fuel storage and any penetrations of the airtight layer or fire barrier requirements.
Electrical	Layout of electrical services including lighting schedules, controls, thermostats, appliances and any penetrations of the airtight layer.
Supporting documentation	Technical brochures for all insulation products stating thermal conductivities in accordance with regulatory standards (BS EN ISO 10456:2007, lambda 90/90).
	Technical specifications for windows and doors including the following:

Psi glass edge	ISO EN 10077-2:2012
U_f (rounded to 2 decimal places)	ISO EN 10077-2:2012
U_g (rounded to 2 decimal places)	ISO EN 673:2011
g-value/SHGC	ISO EN 410:2011
Psi install	ISO EN 10211:2007
Window and door air leakage test	ISO EN 1026:2000
Window and door permeability classification	ISO EN 12207:2000
Widths of all frames (head, sills and jambs)	

Thermal bridge details	Documentation of the linear and point thermal bridge co-efficients used in PHPP according to ISO EN 10211:2007. Comparable documented thermal bridges from approved Passivhaus sources may be considered (e.g. PHI publications, certified Passivhaus constructions systems and Passivhaus thermal bridge catalogues).
Efficient electricity use	A statement (with EU Energy label documentation where appropriate) indicating how the selection and specification of all electrical appliances, devices, etc. have been made.
Airtight test	Verification of the airtight building envelope in accordance with BS EN 13829:2001. The test is to be carried out for the heated building envelope and a positive and negative pressure test is necessary. The pressure test should be carried out by an independent qualified airtight tester. A drawing or diagram outlining the basis of calculation for the V_{n50} volume calculation on which the test is based is also to be submitted. Further guidance can be found in the BRE airtightness primer (McLeod et al., 2014).
Ventilation flow rate	The ventilation flow rate using the Passivhaus ventilation commissioning sheet fully populated to show the individual room design and achieved flow rates and air changes. There should be no more than 10 per cent imbalance between the total extract and supply rates in the installed system. The name and address of the tester and the date along with the make and model of the ventilation unit and adjusted volumetric flows per valve/diffuser for the system in normal operation mode.
Declaration	A declaration of conformance with the design documentation from the construction supervisor/site manager.
Photographs	Photographic evidence of each façade as well as the building services clearly identifying the project's construction, critical detail execution and principal components, taken at various stages throughout the project.

Further guidance on site management is provided in a number of different BRE Passivhaus primers, such as the Designers guide (McLeod et al., 2012a), the Contractors guide (McLeod et al., 2012b), and the airtightness primer (McLeod et al., 2014).

References

Department of the Environment, Community and Local Government. 2011. *Technical Guidance Document L, Conservation of Fuel and Energy – Dwellings 2011*. Dublin: The Stationery Office. Available at: www.environ.ie/en/Publications/DevelopmentandHousing/BuildingStandards/FileDownLoad,27316,en.pdf

BS EN 13829:2001. *Thermal Performance of Buildings. Determination of Air Permeability of Buildings. Fan Pressurization Method*. s.l.: BSI.

BS EN 12572-1:2007. *Artificial Climbing Structures. Safety Requirements and Test Methods for ACS with Protection Points*. s.l.: BSI.

BS EN 15026:2007. *Hygrothermal Performance of Building Components and Building Elements. Assessment of Moisture Transfer by Numerical Simulation*. s.l.: BSI.

BS EN ISO 10456:2007. *Building Materials and Products. Hygrothermal Properties. Tabulated Design Values and Procedures for Determining Declared and Design Thermal Values*. s.l.: BSI.

HM Government. 2013. *The Building Regulations: Approved Document Part L. Conservation of Fuel and Power*. London: Department for Communities and Local Government.

ISO EN 1026:2000. *Windows and Doors. Air Permeability. Test Method*. s.l.: BSI.

ISO EN 12207:2000. *Windows and Doors. Air Permeability. Classification*.

ISO EN 10211:2007. *Thermal Bridges in Building Construction – Heat Flows and Surface Temperatures – Detailed Calculations*. Geneva: ISO.

ISO 9001:2008. *Quality Management Systems – Requirements*. Geneva: ISO.

ISO EN 410:2011. *Glass in Building. Determination of Luminous and Solar Characteristics of Glazing*. Geneva: ISO.

ISO EN 673:2011. *Glass in Building. Determination of Thermal Transmittance (U Value). Calculation Method*. Geneva: ISO.

ISO EN 10077-2:2012. *Thermal Performance of Windows, Doors and Shutters – Calculation of Thermal Transmittance – Part 2: Numerical Method for Frames*. Geneva: ISO.

McLeod, R., Mead, K. and Standen, M. 2012a. *Passivhaus Primer: Designers Guide: A Guide for the Design Team and Local Authorities*. Watford: Passivhaus, BRE. Available at: www. passivhaus.org.uk

McLeod, R., Tilford, A. and Mead, K. 2012b. *Passivhaus Primer: Contractors Guide: So You Have Been Asked to Build a Passivhaus?* Watford: Passivhaus, BRE. Available at: www.passivhaus. org.uk

McLeod, R., Jaggs, M., Cheeseman, B., Tilford, A. and Mead, K. 2014. *Passivhaus Primer: Airtightness Guide*. Watford: Passivhaus, BRE. Available at: www.passivhaus.org.uk/page. jsp?id=110 (accessed 2 February 2015).

PMI (The Project Management Institute). 2004. *A Guide to the Project Management Body of Knowledge PMBOK Guide* (PMBOK Guides). 3rd edition. Newton Square, PA: PMI.

Notes

1 See also guidance in BRE airtightness primer (McLeod *et al.*, 2014).
2 See BRE Passivhaus airtightness primer (McLeod *et al.*, 2014) for guidance on calculating the V_{n50}.

11

The economics of Passivhaus construction

NICK NEWMAN

Le Corbusier (1887–1965) famously once described the building as a 'machine for living'. If he were alive today and shown a current energy bill for one of his iconic villas, he might agree that we could extend the phrase to read 'a machine for living *irresponsibly*'.

11.1 Modern machines

Those familiar with the work of Le Corbusier, and the modernist movement in which he played an influential role, might consider it inappropriate that work of such iconic importance be criticised for something so trivial as energy usage. Many would point out that the modernist movement had a far greater aspiration and significance for the progression of mankind. Is it not also unfair to pass judgement on a previous generation, made with the benefit of contemporary knowledge? Indeed, the call for energy efficiency in buildings did not come until after Corbusier's death, driven largely by the mid 1970s oil crisis.

It could be suggested that a more reasonable approach to critique should be to evaluate a philosophy or piece of work against the values and ambitions of the society within which it was conceived. From this more even-handed standpoint, one should instead be commending Corbusier and the modernists; not only did they have a profound influence on global architecture, they also made meaningful contributions to the global resource depletion efforts of their society.

Setting aside the motivations of radical architecture for one moment, and reconceptualising a building as a 'machine for providing comfort', it would be difficult to conceive a more imaginatively wasteful machine than one which was covered in steel-framed single-glazed windows, and one which employed a central heating system and/or air conditioning system to balance the heat that poured through them in winter and summer, like a sailor might continuously bail out a leaky boat. That this solution was ever considered normal, let alone acceptable, was likely a result of an apparent abundance of fossil energy reserves, combined with the civic reassurance that there would always be plentiful resources to supply the growing population.[1]

It has only been in recent decades that societies have started to notice the unpleasant side effects of consuming a billion years' worth of fossil energy reserves within a matter of centuries. But now that the effects are becoming harder and harder to ignore, perhaps it is only right that the population start looking for ways to enjoy its energy more responsibly.

If the design brief for the Corbusian building were to be written as 'a machine for living *intelligently*', what would be its key performance indicators? In a resource-constrained world, any prototype would certainly be judged on the energy input it required in order to maintain internal comfort levels. In this context, the best design solution would the one that created the most desirable internal temperatures for the smallest energy input. Some possible options are considered below.

Likening once more the goal of 'maintaining a comfortable indoor environment' to the sailor's goal of 'keeping water out of a boat', one valid design proposal would be to find a leaky boat and buy a pump to bail out the water that poured in. This design might be named 'the conventional building'.

A bolder designer who wanted to challenge convention could buy a much larger pump, cut some extra holes in the hull and then tip the boat on its side for good measure. This second design might be named 'the avant-garde building'.

Valid solutions though they may be, the reason that it is difficult to describe either of these designs as intelligent is that they focus only on the end goal of keeping the boat afloat, with little attention paid to the amount of resources required to make the solution work. The problem here is the brief; the designer was required only to keep the boat from sinking, regardless of the methodology, so it is hard to blame them if their attentions have been absorbed elsewhere.

If one were to write a new brief that required the designer to conserve resources in addition to simply keeping afloat, one might end up with a third boat that was uncannily like a Passivhaus. The methodology prizes energy and comfort in equal measure, and was developed by building physicists during an iterative 20-plus-year cycle of scientific theory, field trials and in-use performance evaluation.

Though it sounds radical, the Passivhaus pioneers realised that if the boat is turned the right way up, and some of the holes in the hull are fixed, only minimal energy is needed to keep it afloat. What is more, as the energy inputs and outputs are much slower, it becomes very easy to maintain a nice bobbing equilibrium.

The difference in performance between the conventional approach and the Passivhaus approach becomes quite apparent if one goes away from the leaky boat analogy and compares the energy inputs and temperature outputs of the two systems using the standard energy consumption unit: the kilo-watt-hour (kWh). To give some context, 1 kWh would allow you to use a 100W incandescent light bulb for ten hours (if you could still find one), a 1 kW rated fan heater for one hour, or a 3 kW rated hairdryer for 20 minutes.

The average home (UK) has a useful floor area of 91 m² (DCLG, 2010) and requires 18,000 kWh of useful heating energy for an average internal temperature of 17.3°C (Palmer and Cooper, 2011). An equivalent 91 m² Passivhaus, with a

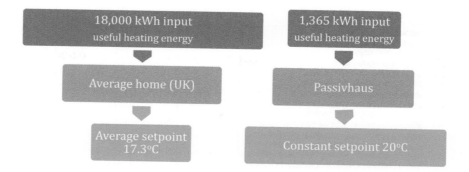

11.1
Diagram comparing heating energy flows between an average house and a Passivhaus

18,000 kWh input useful heating energy	1,365 kWh input useful heating energy
Average home (UK)	Passivhaus
Average setpoint 17.3°C	Constant setpoint 20°C

heating demand of 15 kWh/(m²a), would require approximately 1,365 kWh to achieve a mean internal temperature of 20°C. When viewed in the context of a world with dwindling fossil fuel reserves and rising energy prices, it is perhaps unsurprising that the Passivhaus is winning increasing recognition in the market. Taking gas prices at their current average level of 4.54 pence per kWh and assuming a 90 per cent efficient heating system, the average UK house costs £908.00 to heat (£0.0454 × 18,000 / 0.9), and the Passivhaus costs £68.86 (0.0454 × 1,365 / 0.9). This is a saving of £839.14 a year, or a 92.4 per cent reduction, and certainly one that merits further investigation.

This chapter will be taking a critical look at the 'business as usual approach' of the present. At the same time, it will be evaluating whether it really is economically viable to do business in a more resource-savvy manner. By looking more deeply at the idea of 'cost' and by picking apart a few seams, it is hoped that the reader will be enthused into interrogating their own design decisions more fully. Further, methods for comparing present costs in a transparent fashion will be shown.

As an aside, it may interest the reader to know that the average UK home is around halfway down the league table of EU 27[2] Countries plus Norway and Switzerland when it comes to dwellings' CO_2 emissions whilst at the same time the UK enjoys one of the mildest climates in Europe thanks to the gulf stream (North Atlantic thermohaline circulation). Figure 11.2 compares CO_2 emissions per unit floor area, and is taken from *Europe's Buildings under the Microscope* (BPIE, 2011).

11.2 Definitions and terms

APR – Annual Percentage Rate is the standard industry notation for interest rates, useful for comparing savings accounts, loans and other financial products. The APR is the amount of interest that will be accumulated over the period of one year, whether payments are made in one lump sum at the end of the period or paid on a pro-rata basis each month or quarter.

Capital cost – Used to describe the fixed one-off expenses required to construct or put into operation a building, plant or project.

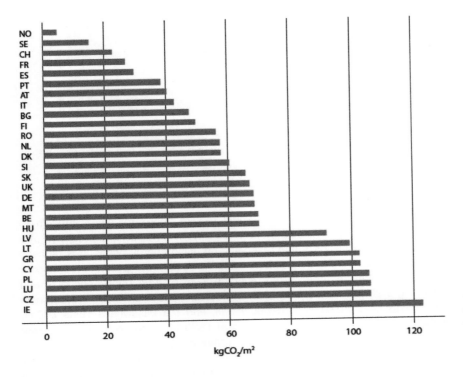

11.2
Chart comparing CO$_2$ emissions per unit floor area in different countries
Source: BPIE (2011)

Contract value – A more specific term to describe the total value of a construction contract, or the amount that will be paid to a contractor on completion of a building project. Note that this is referring to the contract between the (prospective) building owner and the contractor, and so this amount would not include professional fees or VAT.

Cost per m² – An expression of construction cost divided by the unit area of a building. The standard area metric used in the UK is 'Gross Internal Area' (GIA), as below.

Golden Rule – A principle used to test the whole life 'viability' of a retrofit measure. The Golden Rule states that the return on investment for any retrofit measure over its lifetime should be equal to or greater than the original capital cost of the retrofit measure.

Gross internal area (GIA) – The area of a building measured to the internal face of the perimeter walls at each floor level. This is the RICS standard measurement used in building cost estimation, and it is this area that is referred to when using the term 'cost per m²' (RICS Property Measurement Group, 2007). Note that Gross Internal Area is different from 'Treated Floor Area' used in Passivhaus energy calculations most notably as it includes the area of internal walls and staircases.

Life cycle assessment – A methodology used to measure environmental impact of a product or service over its entire useable lifetime, from the point of creation to the end of its life. This assessment period is also referred as 'cradle to grave', although other analysis periods exist.

Net present value NPV – A calculation used to derive the worth of a future series of cash flows in *today's* prices. Each future cash flow is discounted to account for inflation and interest rates, and then totalled to arrive at the NPV. NPVs are described in more detail later in Section 11.4.

Operating cost/running cost – The ongoing expenditure of running a building during its serviceable life. Often expressed on an annual basis. In the context of energy saving calculations, this term is typically used to describe the heating costs or energy costs of a building during a year of operation. In a more general context, this term can also be used to describe other utilities, maintenance and replacement, cleaning and even staff costs, so it is important to be clear about what is being included in any calculation.

Professional fees – The expenditure on consultant services for a construction project, typically charged either as a percentage of the contract value, or as a lump sum. Less commonly, professional fees may be charged on an hourly basis. The main point to note here is that professional fees are *not* included within the contract value.

Residual value – The value of a building or building element at the end of a given costing period, for example, the lifetime of a debt repayment. Residual value describes any inherent value remaining in the building or element after the debt has been paid off; for example, a window with a lifespan of 30 years will have a significant residual value if any loan used to purchase it is paid off after 20 years.

Tax – A chargeable rate on goods or services, such as 'Sales Tax' or 'Value Added Tax' (VAT). Headline figures quoted in building contracts are typically quoted as exclusive of tax. The important point to note is that the level of tax may vary from one form of construction to another, for example, work to listed buildings or new construction. The level will also vary according to country (or state) or even changes in government policy. 'Zero rated' is a term used when tax is charged at 0 per cent.

Whole life costing (WLC) – A calculation methodology used to quantify, in as broad a sense as possible, the incomes and costs associated with a building or project over a prolonged time period. This could include everything from land costs, in-use costs, maintenance costs, end of life and externalities. The duration and inclusions/exclusions of a WLC analysis must be carefully defined.

11.3 The value of cost reporting

In general terms, cost can be defined as 'an amount that has to be paid or spent to buy or obtain something' (Oxford Dictionaries, 2013). This appears on the face of it to be a simple and concise definition, and one might think that no further thought need be paid to it.

When most people ask the question 'how much does something cost?' they are looking to evaluate an object of sale in advance of a purchase. The reported cost, taken alongside other known information such as size or durability, can be used to make an assessment of the object's value when compared to other similar objects.

A basic example of this could be experienced by a hungry consumer, faced with the predicament of choosing a (veggie) burger from one of two competing fast-food kiosks. A 200 g burger at the first kiosk might cost £2.50, and a similar burger at the second might cost £1.99. There is a good chance that the consumer might be confused by these options, so let us use this opportunity to create our first cost report (see Figure 11.3) in order to explain it to them more clearly.

The cost report has given the customer a simple framework within which to evaluate their food purchase, and they can make their decision in the knowledge that they will be 51p richer if they buy Burger 2. But before offering congratulations on a successful first appraisal, it is important to take some time to consider whether this report has really been helpful in providing the consumer with all of the relevant information.

On critical reflection, the customer was actually given a very limited snapshot of what it was that he/she was paying for, and no evaluation as to whether this actually represented a good-value purchase. What's more, by focusing the customer's attention on the headline cost, he/she might even have been distracted from making his/her own appraisal and encouraged to make an impulse purchase.

With a little inside knowledge of the two burger companies, it would be possible to prepare a more detailed cost report (see Figure 11.4) which could separate out the headline cost into subcategories. This could, for example, show the proportion of cost that went into buying raw ingredients, how much went into transportation, storage and general processing, and how much contributed to company overheads and profit.

In the more detailed report, one can see that for the second burger, a significant capital expenditure went toward processing and profit and very little was spent on the raw ingredients. Presented with this additional information, the second burger does not appear to represent such good value for money. It would still be the customer's prerogative to choose the cheaper burger and realise a 51p capital saving, but they would do so from a position of enhanced awareness of the likely inferior quality of the product.

An important observation to draw from the two examples above is that it is very easy to change the entire perception of the offer simply by altering the way the cost report is presented and the information that is included. Certainly one might argue that this places a burden of responsibility on those who prepare cost

11.3
Comparison of two example capital cost reports

11.4
Comparison of two example capital cost detailed reports

The economics of Passivhaus construction

reports to ensure that the information is presented in as clear and transparent a manner as possible.

The construction industry has established methods of cost reporting[3] which attempt to provide such assurances in the form of a common framework for reporting costs.

The above notwithstanding, when the cost of a construction project is reported in the construction press or to the public in general, there is often only occasion for one number and, typically, the contract value is chosen. This figure can be used in conjunction with the reported floor area and other known facts and figures to provide the reader with a measure of the cost of the construction for comparison with other similar buildings. What this figure is less useful for is establishing whether the building has been built effectively for its purpose and whether it therefore represents good value for money. So even when a conventional cost plan is reported to a client, setting out a detailed breakdown of each item and its cost, this is providing only one snapshot of information.

Returning to the fast food example, a customer willing to know the nutritional content of their burger would be able to find out that the burger would provide them with 490 kcal of energy, or approximately 2 MJ. What they would be unable to find on the menu is that it has taken up to 10 MJ of energy to produce this burger. It is even less likely that the customer could be given an estimate of the long-term impact to various ecosystems, social structures and the future climate that the production of this low-cost burger may also have caused.

The cashier would be unlikely to be able to provide such detailed information as the company is unlikely to have any obligation to carry out such an assessment of these life cycle impacts.

In economics, the term 'externality' is used to describe an impact, whether positive or negative, that is not directly accounted for as part of a transaction, and which typically affects parties not involved in the transaction itself. For example, a negative externality of this book might be the pollution caused by its transport from printer to postbox. A positive externality might be that if you store the book against an external wall, you have slightly increased the thermal performance of your building. Neither of these features was directly marketed, but this does not mean that the effect is not there. Obviously, the most complete and most accurate cost assessment is the one that takes into account all of the externalities and the full consequences of any purchase.

11.5
Treemap showing an example breakdown within a conventional capital cost report

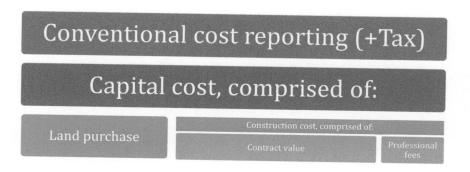

One method that attempts to convey the full impact of a product or service is that of Life cycle assessment (LCA). The term is not so much a fixed definition as one that encompasses a range of different techniques, but what they all share in common is the aim to make a much broader assessment than the capital cost report could provide. One interpretation of LCA can be seen in Figure 11.6, and later in this chapter it will be shown how such an analysis can be used in financial decision-making.

The nice thing about being given the full cost information is that it allows you to make an informed comparison about whether this is the most sensible option. For example, for that same 10 MJ of energy it used to produce the burger, it would be possible to heat a Passivhaus for three hours at the coldest point of the year.[4] Or for the same £1.99, you would instead be able to purchase 44 kWh of town gas, which would heat it for almost two days under the same conditions.[5]

In summary, whenever costs are compared, it is important to be as transparent as possible in the reporting. It is necessary to make absolutely clear what is accounted for and what is omitted, as well as any assumptions or simplifications that have been made along the way.

We should remember that constructing a house, or other building, is typically one of the most expensive things that any individual or business will ever do. Construction professionals therefore have a duty to provide their clients with detailed answers to the question of cost. Whilst capital expenditure forms an essential part of this answer, it is arguable that only when LCA is also considered can a client fully assess the impact of their financial decisions.

11.4 Demonstrating the economics of Passivhaus

If someone was asked to count the number of stars in the sky, the answer he/she would give would differ depending on the point of reference, the chosen time of the study, the clarity of their vision and the accuracy with which it is possible to record the information. Similarly to star counting, it can be seen that there are also many different methods of reporting costs.

The previous section appealed to the reader to be critical in their appraisal of the figures they are presented with, and to be transparent in the figures they are, themselves, presenting. This section will attempt to provide some tools that

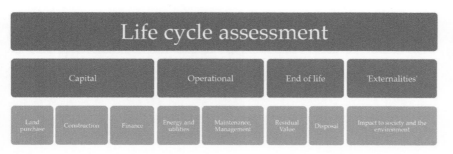

11.6
Treemap showing an example breakdown of a Life Cycle Assessment report

Table 11.1 Excerpt of an example conventional capital cost report

Elemental summary	(1) Passivhaus (mean-climate)	(2) UK Reg. Part L 2010
	One-off cost (£)	One-off cost (£)
1 Substructure	7,392.49	6,710.51
1.1 Foundations	1,159.76	3,501.43
1.2 Basement excavation	0.00	0.00
1.3 Basement retaining walls	0.00	0.00
1.4 Ground floor construction	6,232.73	3,209.08

may be of assistance in doing so. Initial focus will be on preparing an outline capital cost report for a small residential Passivhaus.

In conventional capital cost reporting, the estimated costs of a building are presented in a table, split into categories such as 'substructure' and broken down further into subcategories such as 'foundations', going all the way down to individual unit costs and daily labour rates. The excerpt in Table 11.1 of a cost comparison between a Passivhaus and a conventional house[6] gives an idea of how present costs between the two buildings differ.

Another, less conventional, way of presenting this data is to use a graphical representation. The cost reports that were shown in the earlier fast food analogy were presented using a diagram known as a 'treemap', which uses hierarchy, size and colour to explain relationships. A cost report of all the elements of a Passivhaus using a treemap visualisation is presented in Figure 11.7.

The combined area of the rectangles below the title bar represents the £115,623 capital cost of the two-bedroom social Passivhaus detailed in the case study in Section 11.5. The area and colour of each of the individual rectangles represent the respective capital costs of each of the elements. The higher capital cost items are large and red; the lower capital cost items are small and green.

Treemaps can also be structured into columns, rows or groups to demonstrate hierarchy. In the example in Figure 11.7, the capital costs have been split into the 'Building cost' (materials and labour) and 'On costs' (the contractor's site running costs, overheads and profit). Further subcategorisations could also be made; for example, splitting an item such as 'Windows and External Doors' into 'Supply' and 'Installation'.

Though Figure 11.7 does not include a single number, the relationships shown allow initial conclusions to be drawn about the components that comprise a Passivhaus. It is possible to note the large proportion of the budget that is spent on the superstructure, or the very small amount spent on a heat source. It is conceivable that a similar amount is spent on the ventilation system as the ground floor construction, or to gain an appreciation of the proportion of money designated to the contractor. Beyond this, it quickly becomes apparent that

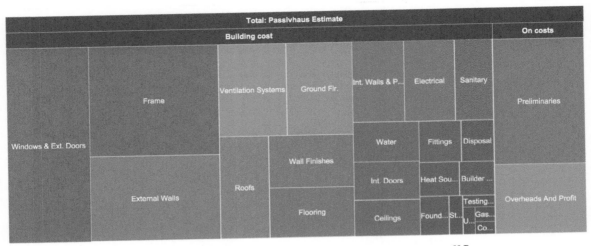

| Total: Passivhaus Estimate | | | | | | | | | | | | | | |
| Building cost | | | | | | | | | | | | | On costs | |

11.7
Treemap showing a visual breakdown of costs within an example capital cost report

in order to gain any appreciation of the value, a comparison is needed with a non-Passivhaus building.

With a quick review of McLeod *et al.* (2013) where the performance of a conventional house complying with the Fabric Energy Efficiency Standard (FEES) was compared to a Passivhaus, the main differences in construction can be summarised as follows.

- extra insulation in walls, ground floor and roof;
- extra excavation for insulation underground;
- increase in superstructure to accommodate insulation;
- airtightness membrane, tapes and grommets;
- triple-glazed windows;
- heat recovery system (MVHR) and ductwork;
- no need for radiators (saving);
- pro-rata increase in overhead/site costs (preliminaries);
- insulation used as formwork for raft foundation (saving over conventional strip foundation).

Using this information, in addition to knowledge about the dimensions of the building, costs can be applied to each of these processes and elements, either through collaboration with a quantity surveyor (as with the case study in Section 11.5) or by making a more approximate estimate using a construction price book such as those published by Spons.

In order to clarify where extra money is spent and where savings are made, a treemap with a slightly different structure is presented in Figure 11.8. Here, one could select only the elements which change between the conventional house and the Passivhaus and split them into the columns 'cost saving' and 'additional cost'. As with the previous example the size and colour of the elements represents the magnitude of the cost, with darker greens representing increasing capital savings, and darker reds additional capital costs. The total to be displayed

The economics of Passivhaus construction

Net Investment £15666

Additional + £22024

Saving - £6358

Ground Floor Construction

Space Heating

Ventilation Systems

Windows And External Doors

External Walls

Preliminaries

Roofs

Frame

Overheads And Profit

Heat Source

Testing A...

Builder...

Foundations

11.8
Treemap showing a visual
breakdown of costs within an
example capital cost report

is still the sum of the two columns, but this time it represents the net capital cost.

In terms of the two-bedroom case study example, an additional expenditure of £22,024 is offset by a saving of £6,358 to arrive at a net additional cost of £15,666, or 15 per cent extra capital cost than the minimum standard house against which it was compared. As this example is anecdotal, it would be incorrect to suggest that 15 per cent should be taken as a 'typical' additional cost for a Passivhaus. There are even instances in non-domestic buildings where the savings on heating/cooling equipment are sufficient to make the improvements cost neutral.

11.4.1 A word of caution

By using a diagram such as the one shown in Figure 11.8, the cost impact of each building element can be compared. If it would be possible to make a digital version (for instance, using google spreadsheets), one could even expand each of the elements and drill down to the next level of detail.

But if one decides to present the cost information in this way, it is advised to consider the fast food example from the beginning and to remember that any form of data visualisation, whether treemap or otherwise, is only as useful as the underlying data that supports it. Whilst this graphic might appear as a useful complement to the traditional cost plan, it cannot substitute the detailed analysis that a quantity surveyor or other cost consultant is trained to do. It is also important to remember that this is just a tool that helps to display differences; learning to interpret what these differences mean is a skill that takes a great deal longer to master.

11.4.2 Life cycle cost assessment (LCCA)

After investigating the capital costs of a Passivhaus, it is necessary to explore what happens when the lifetime operational costs associated with the building are considered as well.

By now, one is contented with the idea that a Passivhaus is able to use a mere fraction of the energy of a conventional building. So how is this accounted for in financial terms?

11.4.3 Energy savings

The first thing that needs to be established is the difference in heating bills that might be expected in a Passivhaus.

An approximate estimate for the heating bills of a typical Passivhaus can be derived by multiplying the specific space heating demand (SHD) of 15 kWh/m^2 by the calculated treated floor area (TFA) (for example, 100 m^2) to arrive at the absolute SHD (1,500 kWh). This can then be multiplied by the unit fuel price to give a rough estimation of the heating costs. Since it is the delivered energy or metered energy that is paid, the inefficiencies of the heating system need to be accounted for (e.g. divide the answer by 0.9 for a 90 per cent efficient boiler system). If these are unknowns, for example at an early design stage, it is advised to always make a conservative estimate.

Another more accurate technique for estimating the annual heating bills of a Passivhaus is to utilise the outputs of the Passivhaus Planning Package (PHPP) (see Chapter 1). This might provide a better indication; however, both of these methods are only predictions, not actual usage data, so unless the actual data is available, the outputs should only be used to provide indicative guidance.

Once the Passivhaus energy bills are established, these can then be compared to those of a conventional house, using the same methodology.

Taking gas prices at their current average level of 4.54 pence per kWh (Energy Saving Trust, 2013) and assuming a 90 per cent efficient heating system, the average UK house costs £908.00 to heat (£0.0454 × 18000 / 0.9), and the Passivhaus costs £68.86 (0.0454 × 1365 / 0.9). This is a saving of £839.14 a year. This will be rounded down to an £800 saving to make the next steps easier to follow (and because it is always better to be conservative).

11.4.4 Cash flow tables and simple payback

If the £800 annual energy saving is considered as a regular ongoing income or 'annuity' then any additional capital build expenditure used to build to the higher energy standard could be treated not as a cost at all but, rather, as an investment.

Investments can be represented graphically using a simple cash flow table, which sorts each of the exchanges of capital into positive and negative cash flows and lists them in chronological order. In the example shown in Figure 11.9, it is assumed that the additional investment for achieving the Passivhaus standard is

£16,000, so this becomes a negative cash flow at the start of the table. The £800 energy saving annuity appears as a positive cash flow in each of the following years, all the way through to year 20 at which point the balance reaches 'break-even point' (of course the cash flow table could be extended forward beyond this point indefinitely into the future).

From the completed cash flow table, it can be established that:

- the investment is profitable;
- the 'payback' period is 20 years;
- from year 21 onward, the building will actually serve as a source of income (relative to the conventional alternative).

The only problem with the simple payback and investment model, and indeed the reason we call it 'simple', is that it does not take any account of the fact that currency depreciates over time due to inflationary rises in the cost of living. In the following section, we will look at why currency depreciates, and what we can do to account for it within our models.

11.4.5 Present value, future value, accumulation and discounting

If someone were to offer a sum of money today, or the option that one could receive the same sum in one year's time, an economist would certainly advise to take the money today. This is because the sooner you receive the money, the sooner it can be put in a bank account to earn interest. As a result of this, future sums of money will always have a lower opportunity for investment, and so we consider them to be worth less than an equivalent sum in today's money. Conversely, money in the present has the opportunity to be invested, and that means that it might be worth more in the future. The terms 'present value (Ko)' and 'future value (Kn)' describe these two moments in time and the difference between them.

If one wants to calculate the future value (Kn) of a sum of money, its present value (Ko) has to be known; that is, the rate at which interest is accrued (i) and the amount of time between the two points (t).

11.9
Cashflow table showing a simple investment and payback projection

Simple investment and payback model		
Year	Cash flow	Closing balance
-	£-16,000	£-16,000
1 ...	+£800	£-15,200
2 ...	+£800	£-14,400
... 20	+£800	£0

An example will evaluate the case: it is assumed that the present value (Ko) is £1,000 pounds and that a savings account is offering an interest rate (i) of 3 per cent APR. From APR or 'Annual Percentage Rate', the interest is accrued on a yearly basis; that means that there will have been one interest period by the end of the first year and that one payment of interest will have been received. If the money is reinvested for a second year, one would receive interest on the full amount of money gathered after the first period, so year-on-year the value will continue to increase. The term used to describe this process is 'Accumulation' and the formula used to calculate it is expressed as follows:

$Future\ value = Present\ Value \times (1 + Interest\ Rate)^{Number\ of\ interest\ periods}$

$$Kn = Ko \times (1 + i)^t \qquad [1]$$

$$Kn = £1,000 \times (1 + 0.03)^2$$

$$Kn = £1,000 \times 1.0609$$

$$Kn = £1,060.90$$

If we go further in time and work out how much the money would be worth in ten years' time, the number of interest periods in the equation needs to be adjusted.

$$Kn = £1,000 \times (1 + 0.03)^{10}$$

$$Kn = £1,343.92$$

The same formula can be used in reverse to calculate the present value (Ko) of any future sum of money. This process is called 'Discounting', and it is the exact opposite of Accumulation.

If one wants to calculate how much £1,000 received in one year's time was worth in today's money, the equation simply needs to be rearranged to make present value (Ko) the subject;

$$Present\ value = \frac{Future\ value}{(1 + Interest\ Rate)^{Number\ of\ interest\ periods}}$$

$$Ko = \frac{Kn}{(1 + i)^t} \qquad [2]$$

$$Ko = \frac{£1,000}{(1 + 0.03)^1}$$

$$Ko = \frac{£1,000}{1.03}$$

$$Ko = £970.87$$

It is worth clarifying here that even though it is about the present and the future, it is not the time that is relevant, so much as the number of times the interest is calculated: an interest period could equally be a day, a month or a quarter, so this should always be checked before making any assumptions. The reason for the focus here on an 'annual' interest period is partly because APR is the standard industry term but mainly because this will allow discounts to be applied directly to the 'annuities' within the cash flow table. This will be discussed soon after the concept of inflation.

11.4.6 Accounting for inflation – nominal and real interest rate

One final phenomenon affecting the value of money over time is that of inflation (r). Unlike discounting, where future sums of money are considered to be worth less simply as a result of lost opportunity, inflation (r) actually decreases the face value of the money over time. The cause of inflation (r) is a complex business but the end result is that shops slowly put up their prices, which is why the chocolate bar of your youth will always seem unfairly expensive at current prices even though it is most probably worth the same.

Like interest rates, inflation (r) is also generally expressed on an annual basis, so when inflation is at 3 per cent, that is how much one should hope salaries rise every year, to obtain the same amount of chocolate.

To account for inflation when using the accumulation/discounting equations, the interest rate simply needs to be changed. Instead of using the standard or 'nominal interest rate' ($i_{nominal}$), it has to be adjusted for inflation, which is referred to as the 'real interest rate' (i_{real}). Published figures for real interest rates can be found from various sources, for example, the website of the World Bank. It can also be calculated. To give an example, for a nominal interest rate ($i_{nominal}$) of 5 per cent with an inflation rate (r) of 3.5 per cent, the real interest rate is as follows:

$$1 + \text{real interest rate} = \frac{1 + nominal\ rate}{1 + inflation} - 1$$

$$i_{real} = \frac{1 + i_{nominal}}{1 + r} - 1 \qquad\qquad [3]$$

$$i_{real} = \frac{1 + 0.05}{1 + 0.035} - 1$$

$$i_{real} = 0.015$$

When the inflation is low (e.g. around 2–3 per cent), a simplification can be used, as below. When inflation gets much higher than this (e.g. 10 per cent), it will produce inaccurate results. In case there is any doubt, it is best to always use the equation above.

$$\text{real interest rate} = nominal\ interest\ rate - inflation$$

$$i_{real} = i_{nominal} - r \qquad\qquad [4]$$

i_{real} = 0.05 – 0.035

i_{real} = 0.015

i_{real} = 1.5%

As inflation has a negative effect on real interest rates, it is important to account for it in financial projections. As an aside, in a hypothetical case where the inflation rate is higher than the real interest rate, money in a savings account would actually decrease in value over time, whilst a fixed rate loan would actually become easier to pay off.

11.4.7 Discounting cash flows and net present values (NPVs)

So far in this section, it has been discussed how to calculate energy bill annuities, how to make cash flow tables, and how to tackle interest rates and inflation. In this section, this will be put together into a cash flow forecast that can be used to establish the full potential of our investment into 'a machine for living intelligently'.

Using a similar cash flow table to the example already used, this time the discounting method will be applied to each of the future annuities to account for the fact that each one of the future cash flows will have a different present value (Ko). To find each present value, the discounting formula should be used, with the same parameters as have been used in previous examples:

Capital investment (K) = £16,000

Real interest rate (i_{real}) = 1.5%

Annuity from energy savings (A) = £800

Number of interest periods (t) = 25

$$\text{Present value} = \frac{Future\ value}{(1 + Interest\ Rate)^{Number\ of\ interest\ periods}}$$

$$Ko = \frac{Kn}{(1 + i)^t}$$

Below, a number of calculations for years 2–23 are skipped; however, with the aid of a spreadsheet, it becomes very simple to continue the cash flow forecast into the future.

$$\text{Year 1 cash flow} = \frac{£800}{(1 + 0.015)^1} = £788.18$$

$$\text{Year 24 cash flow} = \frac{£800}{(1 + 0.015)^{24}} = £559.64$$

$$\text{... Year 25 cash flow} = \frac{£800}{(1 + 0.015)^{25}} = £551.36$$

Discounting method		
Year	Cashflow	Balance
-	£-16,000.00	-£16,000.00
1	£788.18	-£15,211.82
24	£559.64	£24.32
25	£551.36	£575.69

11.10
Cashflow table showing investment and payback using the discounting method

By using the cash flow table and accounting for inflation (r) and interest rates (i), our actual payback period is 24 years, and not 20 as found from the 'simple' method. As discounting provides a more accurate reflection of the worth of currency, it should always be used in preference over the 'simple' method. Though we have focused only on the annuity (A) from energy bills here, exactly the same table can be used to account for other expenditures, such as maintenance bills, debt repayments and income from on-site renewables.

Nonetheless, there is an even simpler way to condense all of the above information into one single number, which can then be used to benchmark one investment option against another. This is called the 'net present value' (NPV), and quite simply it means the sum of all of the present values, which in this scenario, are the cash flows in Figure 11.10. The cash flows for each year in the cash flow table for a given number of years have to be added up, including the initial investment. There are also NPV formulae built in to most spreadsheet packages that will allow one to skip this step.

$$Net\ present\ value = \sum_{i=1}^{n} \frac{Future\ value}{(1+interest\ rate)^{number\ of\ investment\ years}} - Capital\ investment$$

$$NPV = \sum_{i=1}^{n} \frac{K_n}{(1+i)^t} - K \qquad [5]$$

Note that in this example the annuity is used in place of the future value (i.e. $K_n = A$) in order to derive the net present value of the investment in the additional insulation as a function of the energy saved.

That means that with a real interest rate of 1.5 per cent APR and for a time period of 25 years, the NPV of the investment in this example is calculated as follows (with years 2–23 now included).

NPV = −£16,000.00 + £788.18 + £776.53 + £765.05 + £753.75 + £742.61 + £731.63 + £720.82 + £710.17 + £699.67 + £689.33 + £679.15 + £669.11 + £659.22 + £649.48 + £639.88 + £630.42 + £621.11 + £611.93 + £602.89 + £593.98 + £585.20 + £576.55 + £568.03 + £559.64 + £551.36

Net present value = £575.69

A positive NPV, as has been found in the above example, demonstrates that the investment has been profitable and indeed that under the parameters given in the equation, the Passivhaus measures would be a worthwhile investment.

Even if it was unknown how much additional investment is necessary to build to the Passivhaus standard, the NPV calculation could still be of use. By simply omitting the −£16,000 cash flow from the equation, one arrives at a net present value as follows:

NPV = £788.18 + £776.53 + £765.05 + £753.75 + £742.61 + £731.63 + £720.82 + £710.17 + £699.67 + £689.33 + £679.15 + £669.11 + £659.22 + £649.48 + £639.88 + £630.42 + £621.11 + £611.93 + £602.89 + £593.98 + £585.20 + £576.55 + £568.03 + £559.64 + £551.36

Net present value = £16,575.689

This figure is the maximum amount that could be spent on Passivhaus improvements for it to still remain economically viable under the given conditions, and for it to follow the 'Golden Rule' principle. Calculating an NPV can prove very useful at an early planning stage, when budgets are being discussed and when outline cost plans are being put together.

One further life cycle cost example will now be discussed in order to give a sense of how the equations can be applied in a real-world context. The final section (11.5) of this chapter is a case study costing analysis of one of the first Passivhaus dwellings to be built in the UK, and has been referred to on a number of occasions within the text. It was presented at the 16th International Passivhaus Conference in Hannover.

This simplified summary of economics will allow sufficient knowledge to be able to experiment with life cycle cost analysis and to develop one's own lines of critical enquiry. Further information on costs as they relate to the Passivhaus standard can be found on the Passipedia online resource pages, found at www. passipedia.org.

11.5 Case study: costing Larch and Lime houses, bere: architects

Authors: Nick Newman and Richard Whidborne

11.5.1 Introduction

The Larch and Lime houses in Ebbw Vale, Wales were bere:architects' first attempt at producing low-cost social housing for the UK, and also one of their first attempts at achieving Passivhaus certification. Now fully certified, the performance of each house has been monitored with UK government funding from the Technology Strategy Board's 'Building Performance Evaluation' programme (TSB, 2012). Co-heating and tracer gas tests carried out as part of the evaluation process have given early indications that the houses are performing closely in line

with – and in the case of the Larch house, slightly better than – the PHPP design predictions (WSA, 2011).

These initial results can be seen to provide encouragement for UK housing providers wishing to consider Passivhaus construction for their future low energy buildings. However, for Passivhaus to be taken up by housing providers and others, it must be seen to be commercially viable. This study therefore aims to provide some elemental line-by-line cost data to compare one of these houses (the smaller two bedroom Lime house) with an equivalent house designed according to the then current minimum standard in the UK building energy performance regulations (HM Government, 2010).

11.5.2 Method

The case study building is the Passivhaus-certified Lime House, which is the smaller of the two dwellings at Ebbw Vale. The building fabric was designed to meet a 10 W/m² heating load in an exposed Heads-of-Valley microclimate, 300 m above sea level. The building was designed to meet this load using one in ten year weather data, as a precautionary client condition in order to address perceived risks associated with its extreme UK climate, and new technology. It was suggested by Bere (2011) and subsequently in comments by PHI that such an approach was 'far too pessimistic', which led to insulation levels and other component properties of much higher quality than necessary. Recent findings and monitoring undertaken by the TSB follow-up studies suggest that this may not be the case however. Results showed that a cautionary approach in meeting the peak loads via post air heating was indeed prudent, with the Lime House significantly exceeding its design targets in operation despite the cautionary approach.

1 The Passivhaus model specification was adjusted to the 'GB Manchester' standard weather data set, thought to be suitably representative of the UK average climate for the purposes of the research. The specification of the model house was reduced to meet the Passivhaus 'optimum' heat load of 10W/m². This became the 'Lime House mean-climate' test model (see Table 11.2).

2 A second test model was subjected to further reductions in fabric performance to create a building which 'just' met the fabric criteria of Part L 2010 UK building regulations. Junctions were also adjusted to reflect typical UK construction practice using 'accredited construction details' from government guidance (HM Government, 2010) (see Table 11.2).

3 The two building models were then subject to independent cost analysis by e-Griffin Consulting using the standard RICS elemental cost protocol. The summary of this line-by-line analysis is presented in the results table (Table 11.3).

Table 11.2 PHPP model specifications of (1) Passivhaus fabric (2) UK 2010 Building Regulation fabric

	Lime house – as PHI certified	(1) Passivhaus test model (mean-climate optimised)	(2) Regulation test model (UK Part L1A 2010)
Climate data	Ebbw Vale – 10-year extreme	GB Manchester	East Pennines
Treated Floor Area (TFA)		69.1 m² TFA, gross internal area 78 m² (used in RICS elemental cost summary)	69.1 m² TFA, gross internal area 78 m² (used in RICS elemental cost summary)
U-Values	Floor 0.076 W/(m²K) Walls 0.095 W/(m²K) Roof 0.068 W/(m²K)	Floor 0.103 W/(m²K) Walls 0.154 W/(m²K) Roof 0.089 W/(m²K)	Floor 0.246 W/(m²K) Walls 0.285 W/(m²K) Roof 0.200 W/(m²K)
Heating load		10 W/m²	57 W/m²
Ventilation		Balanced PH Ventilation, 0.4 h⁻¹ @ 50 Pa	Pure extract air 15 h⁻¹ @ 50 Pa (9.88 m³/(hm²)eq)
Cold bridges		Ψ 0.019–0.060 W/(mK)	Accredited details used
External wall construction		Lime rendered fibreboard Timber frame with mineral wool Airtightness membrane Sheep's wool in service void Fermacell and skim	Ventilated brick cavity Timber frame with mineral wool Polythene vapour check Uninsulated service void Plasterboard and skim
Final energy – gas		3,489.92 kWh/a	13,438.94 kWh/a
Final energy – electricity		1,212.47 kWh/a	989 kWh/a

11.5.3 Results

Table 11.3 RICS elemental costs of a one-off detached, two-bedroom Passivhaus and an equivalent-sized house (same internal volume and TFA) to meet UK Part L1A 2010 standard

Elemental summary	(1) Passivhaus (mean-climate)		(2) UK Reg Part L 2010	
	One-off cost (£)	% of cost	One-off cost (£)	% of cost
1 Substructure	**7,392.49**	**6.4**	**6,710.51**	**6.7**
1.1 Foundations	1,159.76	1.0	3,501.43	3.5
1.2 Basement excavation	0.00	0.0	0.00	0.0
1.3 Basement retaining walls	0.00	0.0	0.00	0.0
1.4 Ground floor construction	6,232.73	5.4	3,209.08	3.2
2 Superstructure	**55,342.53**	**47.7**	**45,055.33**	**45.1**
2.1 Frame	14,601.60	12.6	13,863.58	13.9
2.2 Upper floors	341.45	0.3	341.45	0.3
2.3 Roofs	5,211.82	4.5	4,424.28	4.4
2.4 Stairs	546.00	0.5	546.00	0.5
2.5 External walls	11,336.03	9.8	7,784.61	7.8
2.6 Windows and external doors	16,451.46	14.2	11,241.24	11.2
2.7 Internal walls and partitions	4,274.64	3.7	4,274.64	4.3
2.8 Internal doors	2,579.54	2.2	2,579.54	2.6
3 Internal finishes	**11,401.24**	**9.8**	**11,401.24**	**11.4**
3.1 Wall finishes	4,569.72	3.9	4,569.72	4.6
3.2 Floor finishes	4,376.12	3.8	4,376.12	4.4
3.3 Ceiling finishes	2,455.39	2.1	2,455.39	2.5
4 Fittings and furnishings	**1,787.05**	**1.5**	**1,787.05**	**1.8**
4.1 General fittings, furnishings, equipment	1,787.05	1.5	1,787.05	1.8
5 M&E installation	**21,300.00**	**18.4**	**19,243.17**	**19.2**
5.1 Sanitary appliances	3,141.50	2.7	3,141.50	3.1
5.2 Services equipment	0.00	0.0	0.00	0.0
5.3 Disposal installations	1,390.50	1.2	1,390.50	1.4

Elemental summary	(1) Passivhaus (mean-climate)		(2) UK Reg Part L 2010	
	One-off cost (£)	% of cost	One-off cost (£)	% of cost
5.4 Water installations	2,678.00	2.3	2,678.00	2.7
5.5 Heat source	1,375.25	1.2	772.50	0.8
5.6 Space heating and air conditioning	0.00	0.0	4,017.00	4.0
5.7 Ventilation systems	6,397.06	5.5	1,081.50	1.1
5.8 Electrical installations	4,140.60	3.6	4,140.60	4.1
5.9 Gas and other fuel installations	309.00	0.3	309.00	0.3
5.10 Lift and conveyor installations	0.00	0.0	0.00	0.0
5.11 Fire and lightning protection	0.00	0.0	0.00	0.0
5.12 Communication, security, control sys.	257.50	0.2	257.50	0.3
5.13 Specialist installations	0.00	0.0	0.00	0.0
5.14 Builder work in connection w/ services	1,216.81	1.0	1,099.30	1.1
5.15 Testing and commissioning of services	393.79	0.3	355.76	0.4
Total house type building cost	**£97,223.00**	**83.8**	**£84,197.00**	**84.2**
10 On costs	**18,200.00**	**15.7**	**15,760.00**	**15.8**
10.1 Preliminaries @ 12%	11,670.00	10.1	10,100.00	10.1
10.2 Overheads and profit @ 6%	6,530.00	5.6	5,660.00	5.7
Total: building works estimate	**£115,623.00**	**100.0%**	**£99,957.00**	**100.0%**

11.5.4 Analysis

11.5.4.1 Capital investment

The UK Part L (2010) house-type building cost is £84,197. The total build cost, including preliminaries, overheads and profit margin is £99,957. The equivalent Passivhaus house-type building costs are £97,223 and £115,623 respectively. It should be noted that these figures are based on one-off house prices, and it follows that equivalent houses on a larger development would be significantly cheaper.

The additional capital investment to build the Passivhaus house type is £13,026, rising to £15,665 with prelims, etc. This equates to an extra 15 per cent investment for the Passivhaus. The difference in capital expenditure is expected to be lower on a larger development, where economies of scale (including communal heating systems) and more efficient design typologies can be exploited (e.g. terrace or low-rise apartment).

11.5.4.2 Mortgage and energy cost analysis

The Passivhaus specification requires an additional 15 per cent capital investment in a mortgage but delivers a building with lower running costs. The hypothesis is that the lower running costs will make the additional investment advantageous over a typical mortgage term.

To test this hypothesis, two scenarios were investigated:

1 A potential Passivhaus homeowner applies for a 25-year 3.9 per cent APR repayment mortgage of £115,623 and pays a 15 per cent deposit (£17,343).
2 A potential Part L 2010 homeowner applies for a 25-year 3.9 per cent APR repayment mortgage of £99,957 and pays a 15 per cent deposit (£14,994).

The UK Part L 2010 house purchaser would save £2,350 on the deposit, which would be invested in a bank (at a compound real interest rate of 3 per cent) for the duration of the mortgage.

The energy bills for each homeowner were predicted using the PHPP. The annual space heating demand and auxiliary electricity figures were multiplied by current market energy prices (7 p/kWh[7] gas and 15 p/kWh electricity kept stable) to arrive at an approximate annual running cost for each house. The sum of the energy bills, mortgage payments and bank account interest was calculated for each year in the 25-year period and for each homeowner. The net present value (NPV) of each investment was derived by discounting the resulting cash flows and subtracting the capital sum.

The NPV for the houses was −£28,518 for the UK Part L 2010 house and −£27,225 for the Passivhaus. The negative NPVs show clearly that neither of the returns were sufficient to outweigh the expenditure on mortgage interest (based on an 8.5 per cent mortgage); however, what is of significance is that the prospective homebuyer would be £1,293 richer by investing in a deposit for a Passivhaus instead of investing that same money into a bank account.

11.5.5 Conclusion

This study has compared a small detached Passivhaus on a single plot with an equivalent house built to UK 2010 Building Regulation standards. It has been shown that even without taking into account economies of scale, optimised form, potential rising fuel prices, improved thermal comfort or the inherent residual value of the house after a 25-year period, under a low interest rate scenario, the Passivhaus investment in the study presented a more economically viable solution for a prospective homeowner than an equivalent house built to current UK building regulations.

A key restriction of this finding is the sensitivity of the calculation to fluctuations in interest rates. The current typical mortgage rates sourced for this analysis can be considered quite low in comparison to historic rates. In recent years, the Bank of England base rates have been at a record low of 0.5 per cent for 36 consecutive months (MPC, 2012) and there are competitive fixed deals on the market for current prospective housebuyers with a reasonably sized cash deposit, which it may not be possible to source in a different economic climate. Low mortgage interest rates clearly favour the additional borrowing required to purchase a more energy-efficient house.

It may be that to provide an incentive for increasing numbers of prospective home buyers to invest wisely in Passivhaus fabric performance, nothing more complicated than a government-backed low interest loan is required. This is in line with the UK's current 'Green Deal' thinking, whereby housing energy retrofit measures are financed 100 per cent up front through low interest loans from industry, providing that they meet the 'golden' condition of creating a positive return on the initial investment during the loan period.

Such a solution would encourage longer-term sustainable growth in low energy housing in a manner that is simple, economically robust and market driven. For precedent, it is necessary to look no further than the German Federal State Bank's 'ESH40/Passivhaus credit', which provided a €50,000 loan, a 100 per cent disbursement and 2.1 per cent interest (correct as of April 2006) for each unit built to the Passivhaus standard (Feist, 2007).

11.5.6 Further study

One only needs to look at Figure 11.12, comparing European build costs over the past ten years, to note how volatile the UK construction markets appear when shown alongside the other European nations.

Since the recent financial crisis began in 2007, it is difficult to comprehend the dramatic fall in residential and non-domestic prices in the UK during a period where the building codes have toughened and when other European prices are rising steadily.

A question for further study would be to explore whether such drastic fluctuations in the UK housing market can be stabilised through longer-term investments in high-quality, affordable low energy housing such as those provided by the Passivhaus methodology.

Acknowledgement

Thanks to Dr. Berthold Kaufmann of the PHI for sharing his detailed expertise in response to an earlier version of this cost study, presented at the 2011 UK Passivhaus conference. His explanation as to why Passivhaus designers are

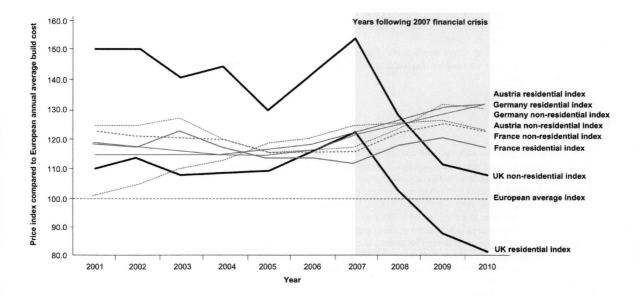

11.12
Ten-year fluctuation of
European build costs
Source: data from Eurostat

prudent to always use stable energy prices and interest rates was a key inspiration for the further expansion of the study.

References

Bere, J. 2011. Cost effective solutions to social housing. *15th International Passive House Conference Proceedings*, Innsbruck, Austria, 27–28 May, pp. 305–10.

BPIE (Building Performance Institute Europe). 2011. *Europe's Buildings under the Microscope*. Brussels: BPIE. Available at: www.institutebe.com/InstituteBE/media/Library/Resources/Existing%20Building%20Retrofits/Europes-Buildings-Under-the-Microscope-BPIE.pdf (accessed 23 Feb 2013).

DCLG (Department for Communities and Local Government). 2010. *English Housing Survey: Housing Stock Report 2008*. London: DCLG. Available at: https://www.gov.uk/government/uploads/system/uploads/attachment_data/file/6703/1750754.pdf (accessed 23 Feb 2013).

Energy Saving Trust. 2013. *Our Calculations*. [Online]. Available at: www.energysavingtrust.org.uk/Energy-Saving-Trust/Our-calculations#general (accessed 23 Feb 2013).

Feist, W. 2007. *Is it Profitable to Build a Passive House?* [Online]. Available at: www.Passivhaustagung.de/Passive_House_E/economy_passivehouse

HM Government. 2010. *The Building Regulations 2010, Conservation of Fuel and Power in New Dwellings. Approved Document L1A*. London: Department for Communities and Local Government. Available at: www.planningportal.gov.uk/buildingregulations/approveddocuments/

Jenkins, H., Jiang, S., Guerra-Santin, O. and Tweed, C. 2011 *Coheating Test, Future Works, Ebbw Vale v. 0.1*. Cardiff: Welsh School of Architecture, Cardiff University. Available at: www.bere.co.uk/sites/default/files/research/387wm%20110516dh%20Coheating%20and%20tracer%20gas%20decay_WSA.pdf

McLeod, R. S., Hopfe, C. J. and Kwan, A. 2013. An investigation into future performance and overheating risks in Passivhaus dwellings. *Building and Environment*, 70: 189–209.

MPC (Monetary Policy Committee). 2012. *Monetary Policy Committee Decisions (2012)*. [Online]. Available at: www.bankofengland.co.uk/monetarypolicy/Pages/decisions.aspx

Oxford Dictionaries. 2013. *Cost*. [Online]. Available at: http://oxforddictionaries.com/definition/english/cost?q=cost (accessed 23 Feb 2013).

Palmer, J. and Cooper, I. 2011. *Great Britain's Housing Energy Fact File*. s.l.: DECC.

RICS Property Measurement Group. 2007. *Code of Measuring Practice*. 6th edition. Coventry: Royal Institution of Chartered Surveyors.

Technology Strategy Board. 2012. *Future Works (Welsh Passive Houses, Ebbw Vale)*. [Online]. Available at: https://vouchers.innovateuk.org/web/building-performance-evaluation/welsh-passive-houses

Notes

1   The more cynical consumer deduced long ago that this was not scientifically possible, and that resources would be bound to run out eventually. Fortunately, they were also able to conclude that they would probably be dead before that point anyway.

2   There were 27 EU countries in 2011 when the data was gathered.

3   One of the most commonly used in the UK is the RICS Elemental summary, an example of which is shown in the case study at the end of this chapter (Section 11.5).

4   A Passivhaus typically requires only 10W/m² of heat input to maintain a 20 degrees Celsius temperature during the peak requirement for heating during the year. A Passivhaus with a TFA of 100 m² (equivalent to a three-bedroom house) could therefore be maintained at a constant temperature by a 1 kW-rated heater. Maintaining the temperature for three hours would therefore consume 3 kWh (approximately 10 MJ) of energy.

5   Using a gas price of 4.54 pence/kWh, £1.99 buys 43.8 kWh of gas or, by the above calculation, 43.8 hours of heating.

6   The extended version is included in the case study in Section 11.5.

7   These prices were based on the utility provider's tariff – rates will fluctuate according to region and time.

12

Passivhaus EnerPHit and EnerPHit[+i] – case studies

LUDWIG RONGEN

12.1 Introduction

The EnerPHit standard was developed for challenging refurbishment projects and, therefore, has slightly relaxed certification criteria compared to the full Passivhaus standard, as indicated in Table 12.1.

This means that if a refurbished building falls within the limits of the Passivhaus criteria (second column), it can be certified as 'full' Passivhaus. As this is not always straightforward to achieve and difficulties may arise in the refurbishment of buildings that are under heritage listing or have other planning constraints (e.g. external façade should not be changed in the refurbishment process), the criteria for retrofitted buildings are slightly less onerous (see Table 12.1).

Another way of obtaining the Passivhaus Certificate in the refurbishment of buildings is by using Passivhaus-certified components, such as MVHR units (see Chapter 8), an upgrade of the building envelope or new window components (see Chapter 3). This will not mandatorily lead to a Passivhaus-compliant building, but it will demonstrate a considerable improvement in terms of energy efficiency, thermal comfort, life cycle costing, and potentially structural stability. That means that certification for the EnerPHit label is either via the specific heat demand criterion (Table 12.1) or elementally via the use of Passivhaus-quality building components (i.e. the elemental U-values achieved). A building that has

Table 12.1 Comparison criteria: Passivhaus versus EnerPHit

Criteria	Passivhaus	EnerPHit
Specific heat demand (SHD)	$\leq 15\,kWh/m^2.yr$	$\leq 25\,kWh/m^2.yr$
Specific primary energy demand (SPED)	$\leq 120\,kWh/m^2.yr$	$\leq 120\,kWh/m^2.yr + [(SHD - 15\,kWh/m^2.yr) \times 1.2]$
Limiting value	$n_{50} \leq 0.6^{-1}$	$n_{50} \leq 1.0^{-1}$

Note: for certification purposes, the current criteria should be verified at www.passiv.de

been refurbished in this way, using Passivhaus components, and that has internal insulation on more than 25 per cent of the opaque external wall surfaces receives the label EnerPhit[+i].

The following case studies present examples of the refurbishment of buildings to the EnerPHit standard. In Example 1, certification is based on the requirements for individual building components (EnerPhit[+i]). In Example 2, the building complies with the original targets of the Passivhaus standard after the refurbishment.

12.2 Case studies

12.2.1 Example 1: church in Heinsberg, Germany

The first example shows the energetic refurbishment of the Protestant Church (Christuskirche) and its parsonage in Heinsberg, Germany. It is a brick building and its date of initial construction dates back to 1950–3.

Previously, the church was heated using gas. Each of the six gas boilers had their own exhaust flue that was located in the roof of the church. The parsonage is heated by a low-temperature heating boiler, and six fluted radiators made out of steel were assembled in the rooms.

The project aim was to achieve a low energy refurbishment of the building in accordance with the EnerPHit certification label from the Passivhaus Institute (PHI) in Germany. Therefore, the buildings' energy balance had to be established using the Passivhaus Planning Package (PHPP) (see Chapter 1).

It was a requirement that the outward appearance of the church remained identical after the refurbishment. That meant that internal insulation was necessary. It is not always possible to aim to achieve the full Passivhaus standard with the refurbishment of old buildings. Sometimes the costs and labour involved are out of budgetary scope, particularly when it involves retrofitting an entire building to be free of thermal bridging and yet still retaining its original appearance. It is very important that thermal bridges are eliminated and thermal components are upgraded as far as possible but without destroying the economic viability of the project.

The Christuskirche refurbishment took place in 2012, and the following Passivhaus components were used:

- additional internal insulation (cellulose fibre) was used on the external walls;
- additional roof insulation (gypsum plasterboard and mineral wool);
- additional cellar ceiling/floor insulation (polyurethane foam: PUR);
- new Passivhaus windows and doors;
- proposed components to be added in the future – solar accumulator tank combined with a ground source heat pump.

In terms of the quality of the renovation work, visitors to the Church in Heinsberg have provided positive feedback regarding the high quality of indoor air despite closed windows and doors. In addition, the excellent acoustics have been repeatedly praised – especially at readings and concerts.

Table 12.2 Summary information and data of the EnerPHit project in Heinsberg

Name of the building and location	Protestant Church in Heinsberg		
Purpose (school, office, domestic)	Church		
Client	Evangelical congregation of Heinsberg		
Architect	Prof Dipl-Ing Ludwig Rongen, RONGEN ARCHITEKTEN GmbH		
Construction manager	Markus Kandziora		
Passivhaus consultant	Passivhaus Institut Prof Dr Feist Darmstadt		
Annual space heating requirement before refurbishment [kWh/m²a]	183		
Annual space heating requirement after refurbishment [kWh/m²a]	30		
Annual primary energy demand [kWh/m²a]	67		
Heating load after refurbishment [W/m²]	19		
Pressure test n [1/h]	0.8		
CO_2 emission/year			
Treated floor area [m²]	394		
U-values of structural components	**after**		**after**
External wall [W/m²K]	0.195	Ceiling [W/m²K]	0.148
Cellar ceiling [W/m²K]	0.350	Glazing [W/m²K]	0.830
U total window [W/m²K]	0.850	Certified? [Y/N]	Y

12.1
Church (Christuskirche) in Heinsberg, Germany before the refurbishment took place

12.2
View (front) of the church after the refurbishment

12.3
Framework for internal insulation of the external walls of the church

12.4
Energy balance (showing gains and losses) of the church after the refurbishment

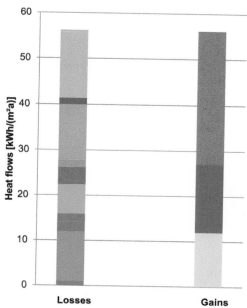

Energy balance

Heat flows [kWh/(m²a)]

- Losses: not usable heat recovery
- Losses: ventilation
- Losses: external door
- Losses: windows
- Losses: external walls non heated rooms
- Losses: ceilings non heated rooms
- Losses: floor slab/ ceiling
- Losses: roof to outside air
- Losses: external wall to ground
- Losses: external wall outside air
- Losses: thermal bridge losses
- Gains: Heating gains
- Gains: Internal heat gains
- Gains: Passive solar gains

Losses   Gains

12.5
Inside the church (left: during the refurbishment and right: after the refurbishment)

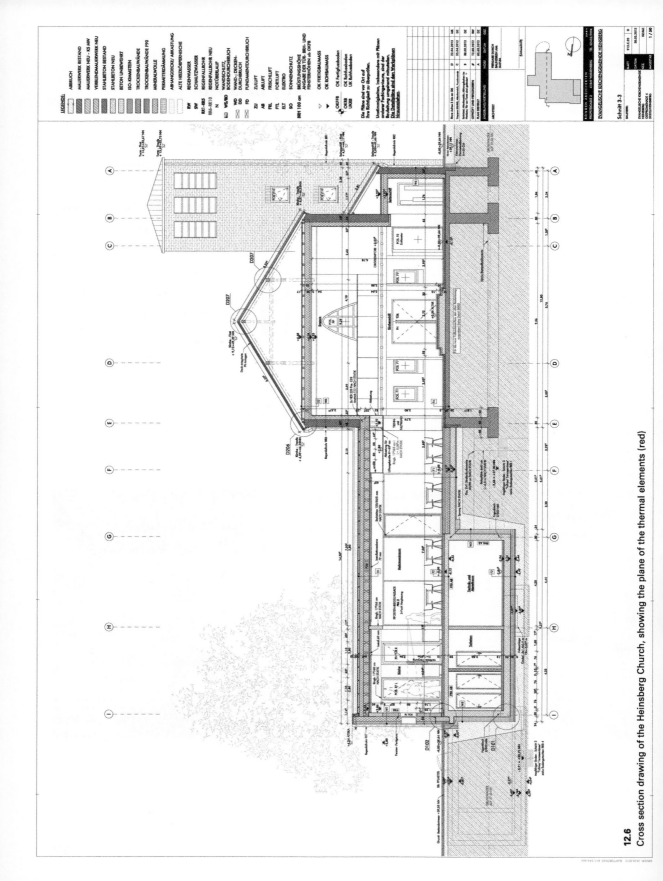

12.6
Cross section drawing of the Heinsberg Church, showing the plane of the thermal elements (red)

12.2.2 Example 2: school in Baesweiler, Germany

The second example is a school building (German: 'Gymnasium'; equivalent to a secondary school or high school) in Baesweiler, Germany. The date of the original construction was in 1917.

Originally, the school had a steel frame construction with curtain wall cladding made out of cement sandwich elements. It was nearly impossible to secure airtightness from the inside. The simplest way was to insulate the building from the outside.

The refurbishment to the Passivhaus Standard took place between 2008 and 2013.

Eventually, as can be seen in Table 12.3, the annual space heating requirement was reduced from the original 220 kWh/(m².a) to only 15 kWh/(m².a)

Table 12.3 Summary information and data of the EnerPHit project in Baesweiler

Name of the building and location	Secondary School (gymnasium) in Baesweiler		
Purpose (school, office, domestic)	School		
Client	City of Baesweiler		
Architect	Prof Dipl-Ing Ludwig Rongen, RONGEN ARCHITEKTEN GmbH		
Building services	VIKA engineers		
Passivhaus consultant	Passivhaus Institut Prof Dr Feist Darmstadt		
Annual space heating requirement before refurbishment [kWh/m²a]	220		
Annual space heating requirement after refurbishment [kWh/m²a]	15		
Annual primary energy demand [kWh/m²a]	108		
Heating load after refurbishment [W/m²]	12		
Pressure test n [1/h]	0.5		
CO_2 emission/year			
Treated floor area [m²]	1,017		
U-values of structural components	**after**		**after**
External wall [W/m²K]	0.126–0.143	Ceiling [W/m²K]	0.079
Cellar ceiling [W/m²K]	0.162	Glazing [W/m²K]	0.6
U total window [W/m²K]	0.9	Certified? [Y/N]	Y

after the refurbishment had taken place. This represents a reduction of the annual heat demand by approximately 93 per cent. The building therefore complies not only to the EnerPHit standard but also to the Passivhaus standard criteria.

Post-occupancy investigations have taken place. Both the teachers and the pupils of the secondary school stated repeatedly that they do not get tired as quickly during class as they did previously. In particular, they have praised the very good air quality in all areas of the school.

These first-hand testimonies demonstrate that the Passivhaus standard not only achieves the highest worldwide standard of energy efficiency, it also provides its users with very high levels of occupant comfort.

12.7
Part of the school building (canteen) – front elevation before the refurbishment

12.8
Part of the school building (canteen) – front elevation after the refurbishment

12.9
Part of the school building
– side elevation after the
refurbishment

12.10
Part of the school building
(top: before the refurbishment;
bottom: after the
refurbishment)

Index